I0188687

L V S H T

L U S H T

The English Qabalah

8TH HOUSE PUBLISHING ‧ MONTREAL, CANADA

8th House Publishing
Montreal, Canada

Second Edition

Published in Canada by 8th House Publishing.

Designed by 8th House Publishing.
www.8thHousePublishing.com

Set in Adobe Garamond Pro, Adobe Caslon Pro, Segoe UI Symbol, MS Gothic and Cambria Math.

Library and Archives Canada Cataloguing in Publication

More, Emery, 1972-, author
The English Qabalah / Emery More. -- 2nd edition.

Includes index.

ISBN 978-1-926716-27-5 (bound).--ISBN 978-1-926716-28-2 (pbk.)

1. Cabala. 2. Gematria. 3. English language. I. Vincent, Samuel K., 1972- . English Qabalah. II. Title.

BM525.V56 2014 296.1'6 C2014-904346-5

Divide, add, multiply, and understand.
-Liber vel Legis I, 25

Do thou study most constantly, my Child, in the Art of the Holy Qabalah. Know that herein the Relations between Numbers, though they be mighty in Power and prodigal of Knowledge, are but lesser Things. For the Work is to reduce all other conceptions to these of Number, because thus thou wilt lay bare the very Structure of thy Mind, whose rule is Necessity rather than Prejudice. Not until the Universe is thus laid naked before thee canst thou truly anatomize it. The Tendencies of thy Mind lie deeper far than any Thought, for they are the Conditions and the Laws of Thought; and it is these that thou must bring to Nought.

This Way is most sure; most sacred; and the Enemies thereof most awful, most sublime. It is for the Great Souls to enter on this Rigour and Austerity. To them the Gods themselves do Homage; for it is the Way of Utmost Purity.

Liber Aleph vel CXI - *The Book of Wisdom or Folly*
DE ARTE KABBALISTICA

Contents

The WORLD Tree xii
The KEY to the ENGLISH QABALAH xiii

Introduction 1

What is the Qabalah? 5
History of the Qabalah 9
The Literal Qabalah 15
- Notariquon 15
- Temurah 17
- Gematria 18

Synchronicity & Coincidence 27
Qabalah & Syncreticism 34
Synchronicity and Syncreticism in a Time-Series 37

The Letters 45

The Roman Script 46
Compound Glyphs 75
H Glyphs 75
The Grand Equivalences 76
The Great Divides 76
Astrological Attributions 77
Liber Trigrammaton 81

The Trees 90

The TREE of LIFE 95
The World TREE 97

The Numbers 99

What is a Number? 101
The Decimal System 104
The *Tetractys* 106

Interpretations of the Arabic Numeral Glyphs 111
Other Interpretations 112
Mystical: 112
Hermeneutical: 113
Psychological: 113
Mathematical: 114
Integer Properties 115
Prime Numbers 115
Perfect Numbers 117
Mystical Numbers of the Planets 117
Summation of the Integers 117

Elemental Gematria Theory 119
Elemental Sets and Operations on Elemental Sets 120
The Algebra of Sets 120
Relations and Functions on Sets 123

The Tables 127
The KEYS 129
The KEY to the ENGLISH QABALAH 128
The English Key 131
The Hebrew Key 132
The Greek Key 133
The Arabic Key 134
The Coptic Key 135
Tarot & ROTA Key Attributions 136
PanTheonic Attributions 138
Flora & Fauna Attributions 140
Formulae & Utilities 142
Hebraic Glyph Set 144
TRIGRAMMATON and the AETHYRS 147

The Cube of Space 157
The Cube of Space - The Hexahedron 159
The Octahedron 160

The Sun on the Cross 161
The 81 Tetragrams of T'ai Hsüan Ching 164
The Magic Square of 9 (The Moon) 169
Liber Trigrammaton, The Cube of Space & Attributions 170
Suggestive Observations for Attributions 178
The Link Between the Eastern and Western Elements 183
On The 81 Tetragrams of the Elemental Changes 186

The Practice of Qabalah 195
The Living Key 200
Active/Passive Values 205
Final Values 207
Averse/Upright Values 207
Pre- and Post- 418 209
The Tree of Life & The Harmony of the Spheres 213
Orders of Magnitude 216
The Three Wheels 217
- Magick & *Qabalah* 217
The Word Made Flesh 222

Gematria 225
Demonstration (Gematria) 226
Analysis of Liber Al Vel Legis 234

Genesis of the English Key 247
Glyph Analysis: Liber al Vel Legis, II, 76 251
Methodology 254

Appendices
A Note on Astrology 263
On the Procession of the Aeons 272
Correspondence 283

LEX I KON 318

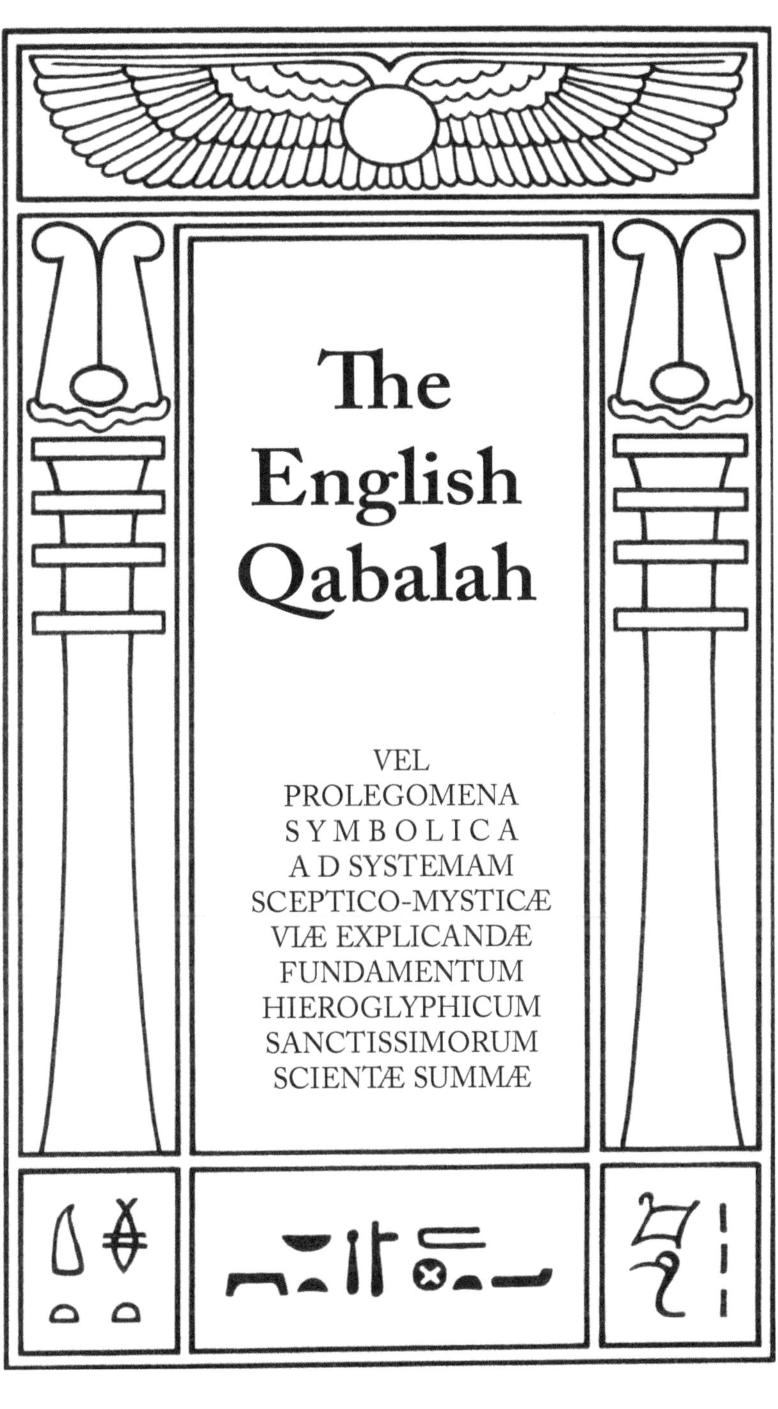
The English Qabalah
VEL
PROLEGOMENA
SYMBOLICA
AD SYSTEMAM
SCEPTICO-MYSTICÆ
VIÆ EXPLICANDÆ
FUNDAMENTUM
HIEROGLYPHICUM
SANCTISSIMORUM
SCIENTÆ SUMMÆ

The WORLD Tree

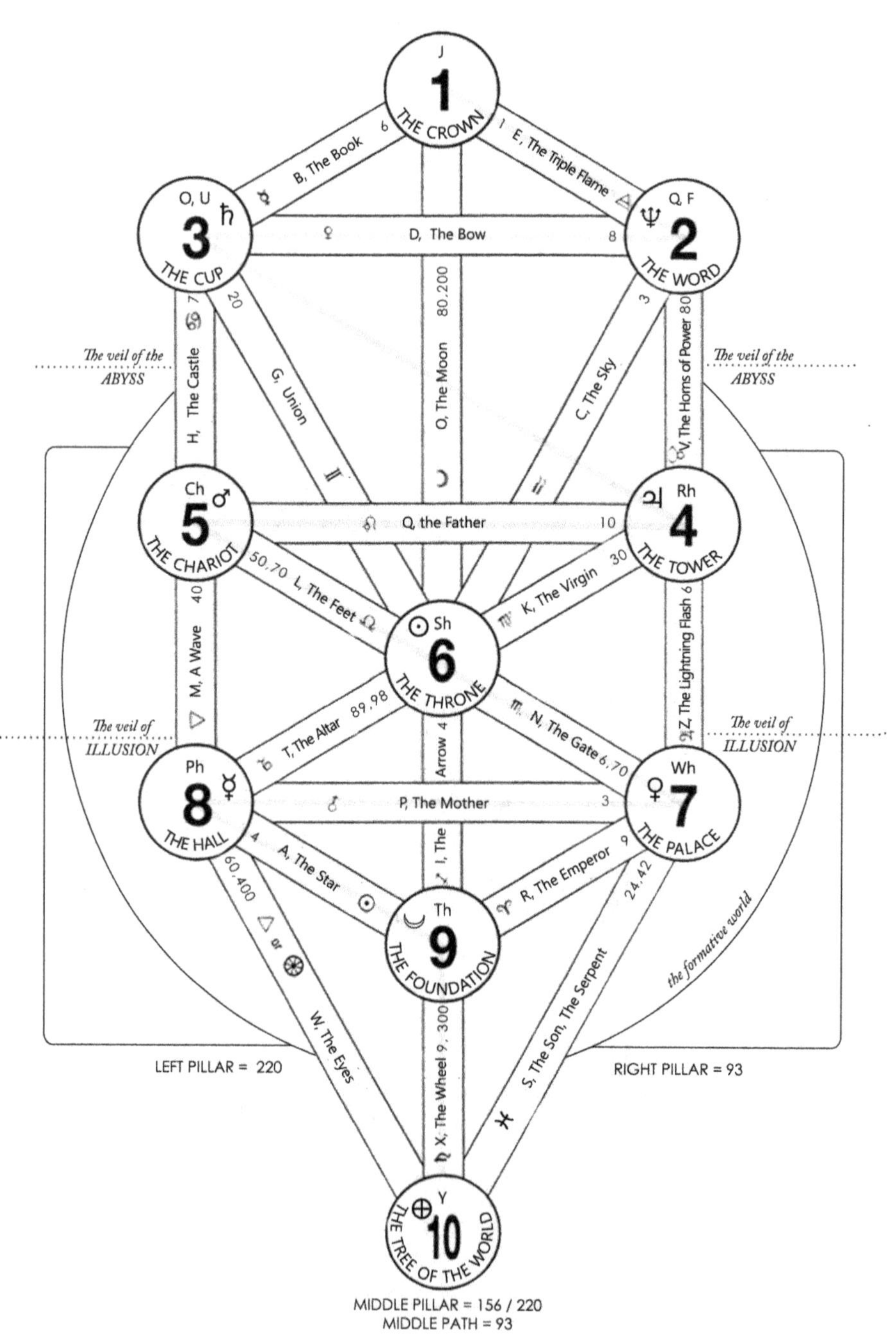

1 J — THE CROWN

3 O, U ♄ — THE CUP

2 Q, F ♆ — THE WORD

5 Ch ♂ — THE CHARIOT

4 Rh ♃ — THE TOWER

6 ☉ Sh — THE THRONE

8 Ph ☿ — THE HALL

7 ♀ Wh — THE PALACE

9 Th ☽ — THE FOUNDATION

10 Y ⊕ — THE TREE OF THE WORLD

6 — B, The Book ☿
1 — E, The Triple Flame
D, The Bow ♀ — 8
☉ 7 — 20
3
G, Union
H, The Castle
80.200 — O, The Moon ☽
C, The Sky
♈ V, The Horns of Power 80

The veil of the ABYSS
The veil of the ABYSS

♌ Q, the Father — 10
50.70 — L, The Feet ♎
K, The Virgin 30
40 — M, A Wave
♑ Z, The Lightning Flash 6

The veil of ILLUSION
The veil of ILLUSION

T, The Altar 89,98
N, The Gate 6,70 ♏
Arrow 4
P, The Mother — 3
I, The ♐
A, The Star 4
60,400
R, The Emperor ♈ 9
24,42
the formative world

W, The Eyes
X, The Wheel 9 . 300
S, The Son, The Serpent ♓

LEFT PILLAR = 220
RIGHT PILLAR = 93

MIDDLE PILLAR = 156 / 220
MIDDLE PATH = 93

The KEY to the ENGLISH QABALAH

Figure	**Value**
A	4
B	6
C_s, C_k	3, 30
D	8
E	1
f, F	2, 10
G	20
H	7
I	4
J, j	1, 5
K	30
⅃, L	50, 70
M	40
N, N_f	70, 6
Ŏ, O	80, 200
P,	3
Q	10
R	9
S, S_f	24, 42
T, T_f	98, 89
U	200
V	80
w, W	60, 400
x, X	9, 300
Y_v,Y_c	70, 6
Z	6

Introduction

HUMANITY HAS HELD in its possession the keys to the Old Glyphs for two thousand years now. These were applied and studied with much benefit, yielding first the Hebrew systems, then the Arabic and finally the Greek. In this way, the Old Glyphs formulated the Alphabets and the mystics in turn found the mapping and concordance between the Glyph and all its manifestations not in Language alone, but extending to the Physical Sciences, and to the study of Number and Proportion, that is, of Mathematics, the Father of Sciences. The texts were revisited in light of this new Knowledge. Formulae were revealed, the mysteries deciphered and Understanding flowered in souls here and there. Armed with Knowledge, these Men and Women then return to the World to resume their Work for good or for evil, but on a grander scale, empowered as they now are and cognizant of the forces at play in the Universe, of which they now possess the Lever of.

When seen from this Historical perspective, it is not incorrect to say, that the discovery of the mapping of the Glyphs is what allowed the harvesting of that vast Abyss that opened before Us with the Birth of Knowledge that is Science and the Tumult of pitting This thought against That. It was the Glyphs and their concordance that allowed for the systemization and categorization of a seemingly endless Sea of disparate and chaotic facts (events in Nature) by revealing the Source or the Tree of which those facts are the Fruit (Laws in Nature). Thus, though each Tree is Individual and grows to its distinct Image, its growth follows a common principle. And this Discovery or Line led to the birth of Western Civilization, and created its supports, the physical sciences[1] and is what has sustained humanity to this Day.

There is presently, a growing interest in the English Qabalah: English, and the Roman Script in particular, being (ostensibly) the living language of this Aeon, and thus revelatory in what concerns the New Aeon Glyphs. There is also a prescient and growing need to adjust the concordances especially those which deal with the Wheels of the Zodiac and the TARO, and how these have shifted with the Dawn of the new Aeon, and the fulfillment of the Roman Script Glyphs (or the English Qabalah), delivered fully as promised in March of 1904, through Liber CCXX among others. This rotation of the Zodiac Dial precipitates realignments of the Glyph sets and their concordances to accommodate this new Natural Order—a process which occurs every 2000 years or so.[2]

The key to the English Qabalah was discovered and declared openly for the first time and revealed to the public in 2008 by Emery of Montreal under the pseudonym of Samuel K. Vincent, in an untimely first edition of this book. We credit GFLO of

1 We lament the need for the distinction. The Social Sciences which include Psychology and Economics and which aren't sciences at all, have sullied the purity of the term by requiring that it now be prefaced by the term 'physical' in order to be meaningful.
2 See Sections on Astrology and the Procession of the Aeons for more on this.

California for his illuminated works and contribution presented here in the chapter "Cube of Space".

Since this time, research into the *Qabalah* has been focused primarily on the drive toward the application and interpreting of Class A Libers and formulae—and subsequently crown the *Qabalah* of this Age as the flower to all those traditions Past.

As the *Qabalah* continues to develop, and shear off superstition and return itself to the realm of empirical Science and direct experience from which it Sprang, it will be once again like that Lamp of Invisible Light that illumines the Student's path—a Sure and certain Means.[3]

— LLLLL, 8°=3□

3 Qabalah has always been and must always be born of observation. The Qabalah comes into the fore for the M∴T∴ as a practical necessity, while the M∴T∴ tries to Understand the concordance and the miraculous temporal synchronicities that the M∴T∴ is subject to, and is often the object, or the generator of.

* Symbol denoting the consciousness operating in BINH (or Binah, the 3rd sphere). The MT has been taken to signify *magister templi* which is a crude Latin for 'master of the temple' and is apt in this description of its material effects. The symbol is also formulaic. The officer in the 2nd sphere can be denoted (though He is not) by A∴M∴T∴ which provides a further hint: MT in the Old Key is Mem Tau = 440 and the addition of the aleph (A) implies a passage of 440 into 441 which resolves into 21. ($441=21^2$) These important matters are discussed at length later in this book and in the Tradition. Liber B vel Magi in particular, provides instruction on effecting this operation as subjective to a specific individual's path; Liber 418 maps the entire initiatory experience for all of Humanity.

This volume is intended to serve as a general introduction to English Language Gematria for the critical and modern reader, and to act as a spur to research among Students.

We discuss the discovery of this Key, and the results of its application. We provide a short demonstration of what is revealed as it were when we convert the text to Number according to the Key discovered as substantive proof of the validity of the Key. The reader can judge for him- or herself the significance of these results.

A lexicon or numerical dictionary is also provided where words and phrases of the English Language are tabulated in order of their Value. This includes a short exploration of the mathematical and mystical properties of the numbers and the operations upon them as well as the letters of the English Alphabet or the set of Roman glyphs. An exploration of Class A libers is also presented which may be of use to the Student on the Path.

We begin with some history on the Qabalah and the alphabet systems in existence today, as well as a general and critical discourse upon the Qabalah and its practices in general.

What is the Qabalah?

IT is often impossible to explain what is evident without succumbing to tautology. It is difficult to describe the wetness of water, or separate a thing that is intrinsically a property of another thing. One may ask what is the *Qabalah*? It is the Alphabet of a Language and it is the Language itself. It is a collection of terms and concordances, apparently nonsensical but verifiable in Practice, and evident in Experience.[4]

Historically, man's egocentricity is projected onto Science and the re-interpretation of Fact, until Knowledge is rooted. This Knowledge is by Necessity 're-interpreted' and so limited dimensionally by subjectivity. The situation is similar in the case of Language, and in Thought, devastatingly so.

An allegory: The sun rises and the lark sings. We hear the bird's morning song, the florid downpour of notes in an intricate melody and we think, 'The bird that sings, sings a song Nature has taught it; Nature sings through the bird.'[5] But when a Man

4 Fully and wondrously to the M.·.T.·.

5 We know that if we were to make away with an egg from the lark's nest and hatch it in isolation, that newly-hatched lark would sing the same song as though it had heard it a thousand times before. This is wired not learned behavior to use popular terminology. Nonetheless, the same arguments apply to the process of 'learning' which can be viewed as a meta-language with its own syntax and operands, very much like the Qabalah, which may be interpreted liberally or literally—get struck on the back of the head with this book and you will get 'knocked out' effectively losing your balance. See footnote 9 in this chapter,

speaks, we think it is that particular man, not Nature speaking. That the man, unlike the bird, 'writes' his song.

Worse yet, we believe that Humanity invented Language, that some particularly adroit primate took to scribbling signs either to communicate intent or mark areas or territories—very much like what the bird does with its song. In the same way, that Man did not invent Music, He did not invent Language, and the way in which Nature unfolds itself in a bird's song, so it reveals itself in Humanity's language, speech and writing. The song, like music, like language, like all forms of Intelligence are forms already inherent in Nature. It is Nature's way of blossoming, or flowering or making itself known, through its fruit, which is Life.[6] From this perspective, Language or the Roman Script or the standardized Arabic numeral set, is seen as the 'emergence of a form'. To the scientist, this is seen as a process of Natural Selection, the emergence of a dominant pattern within a competitive set; to the psychologist or philosopher as a process of revelation; and to the clear sighted as an extension of one's sensory and cognitive powers: for the emergence is nothing but the development of new Organs of Sensation which upon opening allow apprehension of what always Was.

Liber 777, a work we refer to frequently in this book, seeks a definition of *Qabalah*, and pre-emptively addresses some criticisms.[7] Though we find these definitions ultimately unsatisfactory for reasons of omission, they are accurate descriptions even if the list be incomplete.

6 We will resort to this unfortunate sort of Language now and then, and will assume the Reader to be familiar with such terminology and the summation of these ideas in such constructs as the 'Tree of Life' and Aethyrs.

7 The following passage appears in Appendix A of *777 & other Qabalistic Writings of Aleister Crowley* Aleister Crowley ed. I. Regardie (New York, USA: WEISER BOOKS 1977, rpt. York Beach, ME: Weiser, 1993)

> *Qabalah* is,
>
> a. A language fitted to describe certain classes of phenomena, and to express certain classes of ideas which escape regular phraseology.
>
> b. An unsectarian and elastic terminology by means of which it is possible to equate the mental processes of people apparently diverse owing to the constraint imposed upon them by the peculiarities of their literary expression.
>
> c. A system of symbolism which enables thinkers to formulate their ideas with complete precision, and to find simple expression for complex thoughts, especially such as include previously disconnected orders of conception.
>
> d. An instrument for interpreting symbols whose meaning has become obscure, forgotten or misunderstood by establishing a necessary connection between the essence of forms, sounds, simple ideas (such as number) and their spiritual, moral, or intellectual equivalents.
>
> e. A system of classification of uniform ideas so as to enable the mind to increase its vocabulary of thoughts and facts through organizing and correlating them.
>
> f. An instrument for proceeding from the known to the unknown on similar principles to those of mathematics.
>
> g. A system of criteria by which the truth of correspondences may be tested with a view to criticizing new discoveries in the light of their coherence with the whole body of truth.

Ultimately, there can be no rational explanation for why the Universe is the Way it is. There is only empirical evidence which itself is arguable; and the joyous act of experiencing or sensing. Reason is constructed after the perception of the event, and this reason is a simple attempt at coordinating this new data into one's knowledge map. *Dhyana* (transcendence of the Ego) is necessary before the *Qabalah* can unfold fully and *Samadhi* (transcendence of the Self) is necessary for it to be perceived without Error.[8] All rationality is a fiction and any image of the

---

8 The study and practice of the Qabalah may be sufficient to provoke these. Note that these two attainments are in a sense equivalent to the ordeal 'x' and the Crossing of the

universe, a projection; so that any description we may have of the Universe is but a definition of the limits of our comprehension. One can observe for instance, that all that exists on this Plane is attracted to the Ground. Thus if I raise a ball above my head and then remove my Hand, the ball does not remain in its position (which would seem odd if not for our conditioning), but falls, accelerating violently towards the Ground. Similarly, we see particles existing in entropy, combining in a vacuum through this force of gravity to create yet more complex particles, molecules, life. We may call this *gravity*. We may devise rationalities and electrostatic laws to explain such gravity. The Mystic may say that this is because "Love is the Law" and that all particles wish to unite with all other particles. These again are rationalities. All we know is what we observe, and even here, we cannot be certain of not being deceived by the mechanism of sensory or instrumentational apprehension itself.

What we say of bodies of mass attracting each other through gravity and thus combining and thus increasing in mass in order to exert a yet greater gravitational pull on its environment, can also be said of Energy, of Thought, and of Consciousness. We perceive synchronicity, concordance and contiguity as even identities or elements in the Field of Significance coalesce. One may even find that by looking into Time and Events as they occur in the World (any part of it), some form of organizing principle or intelligence communicates in a form that is whole and perfect, reactive and intelligent. This would imply a concordance of events, an architecture to the manifest events in time-down to the most "insignificant" details. Now, because our world is permeated with letter and number (and these being Perfect in themselves) it is natural for rational man to distill

---

Abyss, which are discussed in the section on "The Living Key" in this volume.

these components into their elemental blocks of Letter (glyph) and Number. Finally, converting to letter and number has immediate practical applications: addresses, names, titles, streets, words, etc.—their properties and functions on all planes are revealed through the perfection and concordances mentioned. This will be the Student's laboratory with all its myriad tools and instruments; and the World, entropic as it may seem, will open up like a watchpiece and reveal its internal workings to the inquisitive investigator.

History of the Qabalah

THE ORIGINS of the word *Qabalah* are not perfectly known. Qabalists themselves will tell us the word comes from the Hebrew root קבל for QBL meaning "to receive", and is said to contain in its name the formulae for receiving the fruit of the Tree of Life and successfully transcending the Knowledge of Good and Evil[9], that is to say, conditioning or conditioned knowledge, which is the task of the Adept to transcend.

---

9 A crude summary: QBL, To receive: Reception occurs through conscious study (Q: Qoph-Head) and balanced labour (L: Lamed-Ox goad); only when fortified by these two will the Student be received into the House of God (B: Beth-House). (Queen plane) Or: Reception occurs through the back of the head (Q), that is, the Word (B) is perceived darkly at first, but through the Work, is the Balance achieved (L) (King plane): *This is the very sort of nonsense that the Student of the Qabalah is urged to avoid. Such interpretation is always a creative act, not an analytic one. We would be quite justified in alternate interpretations, one of which would be that a Reception (QBL) to the Back of the Head(Q) with the Book (B) will produce imbalance (L averse).*

Factually, historians are unable to decide when the *Qabalah* was discovered. The first mention of it tells us that God "gave the *Qabalah* to Moses"; others tell us that Adam "received" it.[10] Neither of these statements provide any real help. To add to our difficulty is the fact that the *Qabalah* was not written down for centuries, but was "given" or transmitted orally by the Jewish elders or *Avot* as they were called[11]. We know for a definite fact, that the *Qabalah* predates Moses and his tablet of Ten Commandments which historians date at around the 13th century BC; for by the time Moses came along to shepherd his people away from the oases of the Nile into the deserts of Sinai, the *Qabalah* was already part of the *Aggadah*[12] and Moses had definite knowledge of it.

Some modern scholars[13] suggest that by 10 BC, as many as one million Jews were already practicing and studying the *Qabalah* communally—though this figure seems somewhat exaggerated. We do know that as early as the 5th century B.C., the *Merkavah* mystics were writing about the encrypted knowledge contained in the Book of Ezekiel. The Book of Genesis, believed to contain the secrets of the forces of Nature and the wisdom of God, had long been the object of such studies already. Across the Aegan, the Greeks were studying the mystical properties of numbers, and Pythagoras was a cult figure in the Western world.

By the first century B.C., one hundred years before Christ was born, the Jews were openly declaring that the Torah (the first five

10 It is more accurate to say, however, that the Qabalah always IS and that it is slowly revealed to the mind of man as it develops and evolves, and what pervaded and structured existence in the time of Moses did so before Adam, and likewise does so today. It is man's capacity for apprehension of the truth which grows in time, not the facts.

11 As in the case of the Books of the Old Testament.

12 Judaism's Oral Law

13 Mr. *Aryeh Kaplan* in his book "Jewish Meditation: A practical Guide" Schocken Books; 2 Rev Ed edition 1995

books of the Bible) contained encoded messages, formulae, occult significances and hidden meanings. By this time, mystics were already applying *Gematria* to the texts, converting each letter to number and summing up words, adding, dividing, multiplying, and seeking the Understanding[14] they found so elusive. Their method was simple if not crude: The number the word's letters summed to was termed the "key" to the word. Words with the same number were said to share the same key, and so could be used interchangeably in different passages. Symmetries and then Geometries appeared. Some claimed that as a result of this word play a deeper meaning to the text began to unfold; concordances were tabulated and verified; and the Formulae exposed and tested. The promise was such that the news spanned the globe. Across the continent, similar procedures were taken up by Islamic mystics.[15] Their results—the keys to the Hebrew, Arabic, Coptic and Greek alphabets—are presented later in this book.

It is only around the twelfth century when a *rishonim* (elder sage) called Isaac the Blind, wrote a book on the *Qabalah*, entitled the "Bahir", that the notion of the *sephiroth* and the "Tree of Life" and other such constructions began to materialize. Still no one thought to extend these findings to the empirical world. Despite their religiosity and their affirmations on the omnipresence of Divinity, it would appear as though they believed this presence did not extend beyond the Book—that their god could be found active within its pages alone and perfectly absent from the world once they raised their eyes from the page.

By the thirteenth century, Moses de Leon, a Spanish mystic was writing the world's first classic treatise on the *Qabalah*, the "Zohar" and signing it *Shimon bar Yochai*. It became the first

14 A technical term, referring to Binah, the 3rd Sephira on the Tree of Life.
15 Idries Shah, "T*he Sufis*" New York, DOUBLEDAY 1964

popular book on the *Qabalah* and is said to have introduced Hebrew esotericism to the western world and is responsible in many ways for the dissemination of the *Qabalah* among Christians and Western philosophers. From this point onward, despite a general ban imposed by Jewish authorities on the study of the *Qabalah* in the Middle Ages, the spread of the *Qabalah* progressed steadily. Qabalistic writing is said to have reached its peak between the 13th and 16th centuries due presumably to the unprecedented number and quality of texts that were published during this period. During these times the roster of celebrated thinkers that were attracted to the Science and which contributed directly to the body of knowledge accumulated, comprises an impressively convincing list. Among these who considered themselves Qabalists in their own words, some of the more notable perhaps are: Raymond Lully (1232-1315), the metaphysician and chemist who standardized the Catalan language and for a time was credited with the discovery of ether; Giovanni Pico della Mirandola (1463-1494), philosopher and classical scholar who wrote what is still considered today to be the manifesto of the Renaissance; Giordano Bruno (1548-1600), philosopher, astronomer, mathematician; Cornelius Henry Agrippa (1486-1535), occultist, philosopher and physician whose writings are said to have influenced Descartes, Montaigne and Goethe[16]; Robert Fludd (1574–1637), physician and philosopher who was the first to reveal the basic properties of the circulatory system; Court de Gebelin 1719-1784, whose volumes on etymology, natural history and the origins of language were among the most popular books of the 18th century, who initiated Benjamin Franklin into higher Freemasonry in Paris in the year 1771 at the Lodge *Les Neuf Soeurs* (The Nine Sisters); Isaac Newton (1643-1727) who needs no introduction; and Leibniz, Newton's

16 See his *"Materialien zur Geschichte der Farbenlehre"*

contemporary and counterpart who researched the *Qabalah* extensively and attempted to broaden its field of applicability[17]. Paracelsus one of the fathers of modern science, tells us in his *Das Buch Paragranum* to "Learn *artem Cabbalisticam*, it explains all!", while the philosopher Friedrich von Schlegel tells us, "The true esthetics is Kabbalah."

This conception that the *Qabalah* had its zenith around the time electricity was being discovered is hardly accurate however. Developments in the *Qabalah* have never truly declined. With all these top minds contributing, we should not be surprised to learn that the *Qabalah* has far outgrown the dusty cellar days of Middle Age prohibition. In its constant acquisition of new knowledge it is continually outreaching itself; and the most remarkable advances are the most recent ones.

In the 20th century for instance, we had Aleister Crowley and Allan Bennet bring syncretism to the *Qabalah*, with a remarkable attempt to synthesize the traditions, religions, systems and mystical formulae of the major cultures in the world to date.[18] Among these were included the Hebrew Qabalah, the Greek Qabalah, the Coptic and Phoenician Systems, the birth of the Enochian correspondences, the integration of the Buddhist, Islamic, Zoroastrian, Egyptian systems (and others still), and the first concordances between the Tree of Life and all of these. We can add to our roster of celebrated Qabalists, W. B. Yeats, Irish poet and Nobel Laureate; Jack Parsons co-founder of NASA's Jet Propulsion Laboratory who's work on solid rocket jet fuel propulsion enabled NASA to send man to the moon; Carl Jung and Nikola Tesla who need no introduction and so on. We can

17 See *Leibniz, Mysticism and Religion*, edited by A.P. Coudert, R.H. Popkin, G.M. Weiner, 1998 Kluwer Academic Publishers, for a quick survey.

18 *777 & other Qabalistic Writings of Aleister Crowley* Aleister Crowley ed. I. Regardie (New York, USA: WEISER BOOKS 1977, rpt. York Beach, ME: Weiser, 1993)

add Wolfgang Pauli, Einstein, Georg Cantor, Harold Bloom and others still relevant in our comprehensions of the sciences and the physical World.

The scientific community is rapidly becoming aware of the organic, self-replicating Intelligent and communicative Nature of the Universe. A conference was held in the spring of 2005 by the Universities of Stanford and Berkeley in California to explore the insights *Qabalah* yields in the field of modern physics.[19]

The 21st century has seen a remarkable expansion and adoption of the *Qabalah* by the general culture—very similarly to yoga. It is unfortunate, but as is often the case, the adoption of these exalted subjects have been appropriated by charlatans and profit-seekers and others who have very little in the way of knowledge and experience in these matters, and prostitute them for the basest of ends. Hence we see Yoga, being relegated to a 'relaxation technique' and *Qabalah* to the basest of magical superstitions championed by simpletons and popularized by coloured bracelets. These can only attract the coarsest of beings with the dullest of minds and the basest of desires (e.g. 'wear purple bracelet to gain riches'; 'wear green bracelet to cure illness'). For many, this supplies the justification for the practiced secrecy of old and the tradition of direct transmission from adept to adept. For there is the concern that more sensitive minds will be repulsed by the disorder at the Gates. But secrecy furthers not the cause of Education nor Liberty; and perhaps now more than ever, because of the loud, multitudinous din of charlatans and the consensus opinion of the general public who are very poorly educated on these subjects and so easily swayed, is the need to return these exalted matters to the realm of science more pressing than ever.

19 "*Kabbalah meets Quantum Physics*", *Kabbalah, Science and the Meaning of Life*, Laitman Kabbalah Publishers, 2006

We begin by taking inventory of the Tradition to date.

The Literal Qabalah

THERE are three distinct branches of literal *Qabalah* in the Tradition. These are generally referred to as:

I. *Notariquon*

II. *Temurah*

III. *Gematria*

We forego the first two for being unverifiable and whimsical or superstitious constructions, though we will enter upon a short description of each method here.

Notariquon

THERE are two forms of practical *Notariquon.* The first is considered legitimate or inspired, and the second which meets with some ridicule, amounts to an art form and a process of creation which makes it distinct from other forms of mostly analytical *Qabalah.*

Essentially a cousin to anagram constructs, *Notariquon* consists of matching a word to a phrase in which the first letter of each word of that phrase, when combined, spells the word. A famous Hebraic example of this is found by taking the initials of the phrase מי יולה לנו השמימה *Mi Iaulah Leno Ha-Shamayima*, "Who shall go up for us to heaven?" found in Deuteronomy, 30. 12. These form מילה or *Milah*, the Hebrew word for circumcision. Taking the final letters we get IHVH, the Tetragrammaton. *Notariquon* enthusiasts would use this to imply that Jehovah had ordained circumcision as a requirement for entrance to Heaven.

The second method is the reverse process of the first. Here the practitioner constructs the phrase from the word or Formula by taking each letter in that word as the first letter (sometimes the last, or any other position that panders to the practitioner's goals) in the corresponding Word.

A modern example would be FIAT which is taken as *Fiatus, Ignis, Aqua, Terra* equating the creative Word of Jehovah with the synthesis of the Elements. However, FIAT might equally imply *Femina Imperium Auctoritas Terrae*[20] which the Hebrew patriarchs certainly would not have liked.

Due to the multiplicity of possibilities, *Notariquon* is attacked for its empirical reliability and its results are decried as creative fantasies lacking any scientific method. This remains a legitimate criticism and a justifiable position to take on the question.

However, the utility of *notariquon* lies not in the analytic or exegetic study of Nature, but in the creative or constructive *Qabalah*, as in the application of the *Qabalah* to generate Formulae, Words of Power or even Sigils and thus deals primarily with matters of Magick and effecting Change upon Nature in accordance with one's Will—a subject outside the scope of this book.

20 *Lat*: Women have power and authority over the World.

Temurah

TEMURAH is about "commutations" or the substitution of one letter for another, and is a precursor to cryptography. For example, one can divide the alphabet in half and exchange the letters that coincide in position:

1	**2**	**3**	**4**	**5**	**6**	**7**	**8**	**9**	**10**	**11**	**12**	**13**
A N	B O	C P	D Q	E R	F S	G T	H U	I V	J W	K X	L Y	M Z

Thus, the word "ant" would be transliterated as "nag". The arrangements for letter substitutions and all the possible commutations are gathered together and are known as the "Tables of the Commutations".

Amounting to a form of crude cryptology or cipher-writing, *Temurah* deals with permutations and substitutions of the letters and assumes that either the mystics or the Holy Spirit which hath moved them to write the words would condescend to such trifles as writing in code, or that the nature of the Perfections are such that the Truth of the particular case is apparent when viewed from a particular angle only—as though Understanding would not require perfect knowledge of both the interplay of the parts and the action of the whole. The trouble once again, is that the Student will take those permutations that suit him and forego the others that spell nothing sensible or desirable, so that he will most likely find something that panders to his preconceit. In those cases where he doesn't, it becomes very easy to claim ignorance. A child will see scribbling and scratching where a man sees letters, and the Student may content himself with the notion that what he fails to see is due to his present Ignorance—a situation which Time will relieve.

Other methods also grouped under the practice of *Temurah*, are the *Thashraq*, which is writing a word backwards, and the *Aiq Bekar*, popularly known as the "Qabalah of the Nine Chambers," which groups the letters by their unit, decimal and hundreds values.

Gematria

GEMATRIA is that branch of the literal Qabalah which is the subject of this Book. We forego *Temurah* and *Notariquon* and dismiss these methods for falling outside the bounds of Science and Empiricism. They pertain primarily to the creative aspect of these Arts and primarily those that regard Magick or the projection of the Will. However, behind the idea of *Gematria* lies an equally outrageous notion: namely, that there is a simple and basic correspondence or syncreticism between Number and any phenomena—particularly words and letters. It is this *prima facie* preposterous claim that has spawned simple Numerology that most everyone is familiar with, in one sense or another; and has been the source of many another misguided superstition ever since John of Patmos wrote that famous line in his Revelations: "Here is Wisdom, Let him that hath Understanding count the number of the Beast, for it is the number of a man; and his number is six hundred and three score and six."[21].

21 Revelations 13, 18. Note that 'Wisdom' and 'Understanding' are titles of Chokmah

It has been affirmed clearly by eminent scholars in the past that a name or title and its number bear no real relation to the nature of that Person on this Plane (and by extension, no other Plane, since the Name codified is codified in the Material). Thus, because you discover that your neighbour's name adds to 666, does not mean he is the incarnation of the 'Anti-Christ', even though on the Astral Plane the suggestion is that this would be the case. This statement was generally followed by the injunction to 'not confuse the Planes'. That is, that the laws of one Plane are not necessarily applicable on another. Thus we see that Gravity which exists in the Material, has no effect on that which is not constituted by mass (e.g. energy, information and the Body of Light). Nonetheless, the laws of attraction that govern the laws of gravity hold on both, so that it would appear that the former is a manifestation of the latter, so that the previous statement is clearly an oversight. *Empirically*, with the application of the Key, continual evidence of perfect concordance on the Material Plane has been found; that formulae manifest themselves materially, and that all Creatures (human beings as well) somehow follow this Law when materialized in Place and Time regardless of the 'plane'. This is a statement which breaks with Tradition. The Student will have to verify its veracity personally.[22]

(the 2nd sphere) and Binah (the 3rd sphere) respectively. Of course, today we know that John of Patmos was thinking of Nero the Roman Emperor at the time he wrote this, and that he took the Hebrew Key as the basis from which to form his basic cryptography (Nero Caesar is NRON QSR or nun-resh-vau-nun qoph-samech-resh). He could not have openly declared the Emperor as the Enemy of their Cause, for that was treason and would invite imprisonment if not death. Prudence made him conceal the Emperor's name in code. Knowing his Brothers to be in possession of the Greek Key, while the Romans were ignorant of it, he employed this convenient fact to effect a political sleight-of-hand. If we employ the key of the Greek Qabalah we find the Emperor's name summing to that famous number. The fact that this number has come to signify the number of the Beast that comes to overthrow the House, is not an accidental result of this historical letter, for the number and its significance was already known to John and other Qabalists. John used it as proof of the emperor's Nature to convince his brethren and rouse their enthusiasm in his case against the Emperor, as we do once again Today (but after a different manner).

22 It leads immediately to our problem: the danger and lunacy of believing your

It is important to note that this correspondence goes beyond the simple Numerology that most everyone is familiar with. Nor is it a form of cryptography or code. Qabalists will claim that it is the most convenient means we have of describing and arriving at the "thing-in-itself" or the "idea" and subsequently classifying it. Because the number represents the "idea", it becomes the genetrix for all those other "images" (in this case, the symbol, letter or word) that equate or sum to it and so partake of its Nature. This is the basic assumption (premise, or axiom) behind the practice of *Gematria*: namely, the preposterous claim that because two things reduce to the same number (in this case, words or letters) they are in a sense refractions or symbols of the same "idea". There is no Reason for making such a claim except Evidence of it. For we find that not only does this preposterous

---

neighbour to be the Anti-Christ. But if we respect all Children of Men for their Word (*logos*), then every self-professed second-coming of Christ is the second-coming (for was this not the magic of the Jesus and the miracle of his Mass?) and your neighbour really is one of the many Anti-Christs running about the planet mocking all the self-crucified Christs. For just his was a potent spell, converting many and spreading his Word, so we know that for every action there is an equal and opposite reaction, so that Nature would have counter-balanced this violence with its own opposite and so re-establish the scales. Just as 'Christ' is a title given to a natural phenomenon (which we can enumerate)—a consciousness balanced in the Solar, so similarly is the Anti-Christ another title for a transcended solar consciousness given to the solar Will which engendered IT. This is necessarily so because the Anti-Christ comes afterwards: that is he is a development of the Christ and so is a symbol of the human aspiration to free itself of this Christ conditioning—even if it remain a reaction, and so an imbalance while it remains without its consort. The solution is to absorb one in the other until nothing remains. Finally, note that if there were no Christ there would be no Anti-Christ and this leads us to the ultimate aim of the Qabalah: to reduce all conception to zero; or balance any notion with its opposite. For ultimately Consciousness must ask itself: Do I number myself (i.e. numbering the phenomenon as it relates within his own consciousness) or do I number the World (independently of the observer)? In this difference lies the problem the Self seeks to transcend: Separation. For there are three possibilities to any fact, and ultimately they are identical if one unites with All. These are:

1. The Initiate is numbering him or herself or a portion of him/herself in all operations.
2. The Initiate is numbering the phenomenon.
3. The Initiate is numbering the relation between him/herself and the phenomenon.

Reason will insist upon one or the other; but they are the prismed colors of the one beam of light.

claim hold empirically, but its practical extensions are apparently without limit.

Returning to History for a moment, we see how *Gematria* in the past employed the numerical values of the Hebrew alphabet. This allowed the Student to tabulate the numerical value of words, thus enabling the comparison of words of equal value or through their multiples. As an example, one can take the Hebrew word for 'love' which is AHBH and 'unity' which is AChD. They both sum to 13 implying that the nature of Love is Unity.[23] In English, we have the same reduction of the 3 into the 1 but in the glyph 331, denoting the triune Nature of Man and Woman equal and counterpart to each other and the Power of Love to raise consciousness to the 3rd sphere (*Binah*). We have a further elucidation in the Aeon for 331 is also "Selflessness'[24] and presents a development that is evolutionary (as we shall discuss later) in the idea of Love being concordant to the idea of Selflessness.

All this is admittedly needless, for a little meditation upon the Nature of Love would produce the realization of that same Truth but more fully, and not so coldly and analytically as through Number alone. However, it is not only their equality that is of interest, but that they are equal to a particular number, which as a symbol must also be representative of the process or operation the word signifies (two open circle's (3—is a circle open at center hinge) combining to reduce to 1. 331 is also prime suggesting its final unity.[25] It is when the Question or the Object is somewhat

---

23 *777 & other Qabalastic Writings of Aleister Crowley* Aleister Crowley ed. I. Regardie (New York, USA: WEISER BOOKS 1977, rpt. York Beach, ME: Weiser, 1993)

24 A title of Kether.

25 That is, it is not a composite, or a notion comprised of other notions. If so, it would be further reducible to factors of primes, which would in turn represent the irreducible ideas of which the composite notion would be constructed from.

more complex, that these correspondences become useful; or perhaps when we are trying to move from the known to the unknown and require a test of verifiability. We provide an example by way of illustration.

A Student asks: I would like some clarification of the value of 'ck' in this system. Is it 60? Or does the existence of both c and k make one "silent" in terms of value?

The 'ck' combination is perplexing. The c is, we agree, phonetically superfluous. It may be fading; that with internet and phone texting as it is, words like neck, back, sock, will soon all be spelt nek, bak, sok... So that the hard or soft C is somehow anachronistic; and mysteriously, even counter-intuitively in the larger scheme of things, appears to be disappearing.[26]

But to answer the question: We can not take the c as silent, i.e. despite its possible disappearance, if the glyph is present in the Word or Formula, then it is present and so must be counted, until that moment that it ceases to be there. Now, do we count it hard (30) or soft (3)? Supposing we don't know, we can take sample data and look at the alternatives.

We can take the words 'sick' and 'attack'—two simple enough ideas (but any others will do). We have (58 + C) for 'sick' and (234 + C) for 'Attack'. Now, if c is soft then 'sick' is 61 (which we

26 In this way, it appears 'reasonable' to switch the usual syncretic attributions for C and K. For if C is the Cup and Aquarius and so Queens, while K the Virgin is Scorpio and so the Hermit: how is that we find the Queens waning and not the Hermit? Also the old line in Liber Al: "Tzaddi is not the Emperor - that is, while Z must still be Aries in Nature, the glyph of its manifestation on the ROTA is not "The Emperor" or ATU IV. If one takes this as a fact, integrity and symmetries inherent in the system imply further readjustments of the ROTA key to accommodate this change. For instance, very basically: if Tzaddi is not the Emperor, then some other glyph must be, and so this requires switching out a second glyph. If it switches out with the first we are done; otherwise the system cascades: it must switch out with a 3rd which would engender another replacement and so on and so forth. Perhaps at the close of the Aeon, all we that will remain of the C is its part in the Ch glyph: i.e. "She is enthroned alway". All this is pure speculation.

already know cannot be, but assuming we don't...); and 'attack' is 237. If C is hard, then 'sick' becomes 88 and 'attack', 264.

We have two possibilities:

(a) 'sick' is 61 and 'attack' is 237; or

(b) 'sick' is 88 and 'attack' is 264.

- Under the identity '61' we have: "Place" (as in "let it reside in one place"); Made He (as in Made He the Worlds); Kheph-RA; Help (ideas consistent with AIN)

- Under identity '88' we have: "He is Mad", KALI, Maim, Vice, Saw (versus See), Bind, etc...

Certainly the idea of 'sick' pertains to identity 88. 61 appears to be 'Holy' if we can resort to a colloquialism.

- For 237, we have: Drug, Gladness, Khu, Rosa...

- While for 264 we have, A Lion, Curse, Pestilence, Python, Severities, Typhon, I am the Heart (with T final).

Again, attack appears to be counted with C hard as the ideas of 264 are concordant with the idea of an attack or attacking, whereas 237 (Drug, gladness, ROSA) obviously are not. One can continue this analysis until one is satisfied, e.g.: 'rock' can be 122 or 149 depending on this C. 122 contains 'feather' and 'fly', so once again, we appear confirmed in our original hypothesis.

Finally, we can look for concordance on the Material Plane: if C were 'soft' then words like 'back', 'sack' would sound phonetically like *bask* and *sask*; while with C 'hard' they sound like *bakk*, *sakk*, which conforms to the Reality.[27]

---

27 The critical injunction for the M.·.T.·.—for one who holds the Key to All, even the M.·.T.·. must bear in mind never 'to deepen a superficie'. The material test, the most basic, is always the most certain, for in these matters we are primarily concerned with those Forces that are manifest and have a material influence on matter and energy on

The above may be no great revelation. The point to be retain however, is that *Qabalah* properly formulated will extend to all planes and encompass all matters, events and things. It matters not what we look at it, since it is everywhere.[28] For as we've intimated above, this concordance extends to all practical matters, glyphs and 'properties of things'. In this way, ideas that are classified under the same 'key' or number, are related through identity and are equated. It is more precise however, to consider them as materializations or rarefactions (depending on the case) of the idea.

The glyph of *Shin* for instance, which is enumerated at 300 and signifies "tooth" and "spirit"[29] is equivalent to the number obtained by adding up the numerical values of the letters of the words רוח אלהים (RVCh ALHIM) or *Ruach Elohim*, the spirit of the *Elohim* (ר = 200, ו = 6, ח = 8, א = 1, ל = 30, ה = 5, י = 10, ם = 40; total = 300). According to the tradition then, the letter *Shin* (ש) itself (and the number 300) is a symbol of the spirit of the *Elohim*. This was further confirmed when later generations also showed that ALHIM spelt in full also adds to 300. [30] Note also that this 300 is now fully attainable and materializable, through the activation of the X glyph, through the "Ordeal 'x'".[31]

For a more modern or practical example, we return to our original question, "What is the Qabalah?" for a final example. Seeing as this is not an English word, we seek a formula. Its

the physical plane.

28 Questions may remain, regarding coincidence, chance and apophenia which we explore in the following section.

29 The soul or Self is said to descend or flower in the body at the time of teething—or that one is the sign of the other. The mother must of course withdraw her nipple at such a time if she has not already, and so presents also an advancement or emancipation for the Child. The Will flowers at Puberty for both sexes.

30 (300 = Aleph + Lamed + He + Yod + Mem = אלפ + למד + הה + יוד + מהם = 111 + 74 + 10 + 20 + 85 = 300).

31 See Liber AL III, 22. These matters are discussed at length in the section, "On the Living Key" later in this book.

original alliteration is QBLH for there are no vowels in the Hebrew script. We discover that QBLH is 10 + 6 + 70 + 7 = 93 so that it is the 'Law' and Necessity, and it is Love (*Agapé*). We proceed further by taking the Roman Script dimension with its full spelling to arrive at Qabalah = 105 which is again ALHIM (4 + 50 + 7 + 4 + 40) and Nike (Victory). "The Qabalah" (211) is the "Hope" of "every man" which when united with Malkuth (10) is 221, another glyph for the Law and the covenant of Will[32].

558	Four Gates	
558	The Fool	
558	Divine Perfection	
558	Path of the Adepts	
558	Drawn by Doves	Sf
558	The Holy Qabalah	
558	The Primeval Things	Sf

We can proceed as far in this analysis as we like. Applying to the lexicon, we see another entry for "The Holy Qabalah"[33] that it is one with the "Primeval Things"; it is the Chariot "drawn by doves", that leads to the "Four Gates" to the Palace[34] to finally reach *Binah*—the 3rd sphere from which the perception and action of the Qabalah is made Perfect and Whole. It is the "Divine Perfection" (or its manifestation) and is a Path of the Adepts, all of which end in "The Fool" the world glyph for the man seated in *Kether*. The application of the Key suggest that all these ideas are identical in their source—that is, they are rays or precipitations of the primal undifferentiated "idea" which we

32 221 is the enumeration of "Thelema" which is Greek for Will and the banner or formula under which a new law or religion for humanity has sprung up.

33 It is lamentable that we lack more technical terminology for many of these subjects. Being appropriated as they were by a sort of religious fervor, many of these researches restrict their scope to what is religious. We are ourselves, will be forced to resort to such barbarities of language whenever we apply to History and Tradition.

34 Liber vel Legis I, 51: "There are four gates to one palace"

classify only as "558"[35] for now, to later explore or deconstruct. All we know is this 'idea' possesses this list of qualifications (the expressions equal to it by the key) which it is identical to, in both its sum and separate parts.

Such is the general exegetic method of Qabalistic *Gematria*. More concise exposition and further elucidation upon practical *Gematria* and its uses is provided in a subsequent chapter.[36]

We forego entering into this matter further, without first answering the natural cry of the rational mind to escape the question and relegate the matter to one of 'coincidence'. For the burden of proof lies heavy on the Qabalist and his Mind will be the weapon he turns on himself. For when confronted by contiguities it can not explain, the mind seeks to refute the causality with the declaration that the contiguity is a coincidence: a species of 'noise' or random event in Chance. Fortunately, we have recourse to Logic and to the laws of random numbers and of probability to advance our introduction and exploration into the *Qabalah* and its verifiability.[37]

We will return later to a discussion on the Roman Script (the letters of the English Alphabet) and the Arabic Numerals (numbers as they are represented in the West) along with their elemental significance and qabalistic correspondences. For these: the letters of the Roman Script and the Arabic Numeral, are the symbolic basis for the English Qabalah and with a minor exception, span the set of glyphs that comprise the phenomenological set of the perceivable material Universe.

35 It is pointless and in a sense, damaging to discuss the nature of the idea further, for all word and language contain in it a falsity – in the very least in this case, subjective interpretation which is not a property of the Idea itself and the very thing we attempt to shear off with the Qabalah in order to arrive at it.

36 See chapter "The Practice of the Qabalah"

37 Essentially, one applies tools of Reason to logically prove the existence of something which defies Reason! A task which dissolves the mind and any preconception.

Synchronicity & Coincidence

THOUGH WE will define synchronicity more precisely and technically for our needs, synchronicity is generally seen as the simultaneous occurrence of two 'meaningfully-connected' but 'acausal' events.

When we say 'meaningfully-connected' we denote a meaning ascribed by the observer to the event, and this is independent of whether or not the event inherently carries such meaning with it, or whether this is projected onto the event by the observer. We will later distinguish between these two.

Events are 'acausal' when they do not originate from the same cause or event. For instance, from the window my desk overlooks, we can see my neighbor's door. We notice that whenever it rains he leaves his home attired in red. The traffic signal on the corner is also always red at this time. The second of these events is acausal; the first is not. The cause of the redness of his dress is due to an ulterior fact: that his only raincoat is red; and being the sort of man he is, he would not leave his home on an overcast day without it. The redness of the traffic signal is coincidental through the intermittence of the signal.

Note that one would be correct in dismissing the redness of the traffic signal as a 'coincidence'; one would be incorrect in doing so for the first. And this is due simply to the notion of causality: that there *is* a cause, even if we know not what it is, or ascribe it incorrectly.

Now let us say, that knowing nothing of traffic signals, we repeated the experiment a hundred times and improbable as it may seem, every time my neighbour steps out the traffic signal is red. Then these two events are synchronous and acausal. They are acausal, only because we know the interior workings or the mechanics of the traffic signal to be independent of weather.

Now imagine that upon further investigation, we learn that he commutes to work. The city bus runs on a fixed schedule. He himself is meticulous and leaves his house everyday at precisely seven-thirty, so he can be at the city bus stop exactly one minute and thirty seconds later. We take apart the traffic signal and study its logic further. The traffic signal is synchronised via microchip on a controller board, and these necessarily break up time in the same units that the city bus runs on (seconds), that our neighbor's clock runs on and also that his conception of time depends on. It is natural that if he synchronizes himself to his watch; then he enters a world in which time is measured and its effects proffered out discretely. If it is red the first morning at that time, it will be red the following morning at that time, unless the traffic signal's programming has changed, his alarm clock loses time, or he fails in his usual meticulousness and leaves the home after the fifty second window of time in which the traffic signal remains red, before it switches green and begins the cycle anew.

Now we have understood why after one hundred experiments, the traffic signal was red the moment he emerged from his door. We have explained away the synchronicity and so further established the acausality. This is a critical point. In a direct chain, all causal events are contiguous, but not all contiguous events are causal. Furthermore, all causality is directional: the rain causes the use of the raincoat, and not vice-versa. Indolence of the mind often obscures this fact, and causality is mistaken for identity. Thus in an unexamined mind superstition takes root, and we often acquire the imbecile notion of reversing the chain of causality (as in for instance, wearing red in order to make it rain), especially when we have no understanding of the mechanics behind the events.

Philosophically, synchronicity does not compete with the notion of causality, but subsumes it. It maintains that just as events may be grouped by cause in time (temporal contiguity being the necessary empirical factor), they may also be grouped by meaning. By 'meaning' we understand their energy signature, and that all living things, human beings included, constitute energy fields. Thus in the same way that particles in space can be bound together invisibly by a gravity field, we can have elements in time bound together by significance or meaning intrinsic to that element.[38]

Note that the development of this line of theory leads invariably to the conclusion that such synchronistic events reveal an underlying pattern, a conceptual framework that encompasses, and is larger than any system displaying synchronicity. In this way, the existence of a larger framework is necessary to the definition of synchronicity and is necessarily presupposed by it.[39] Jung for instance, believed that synchronistic events are the manifestation of parallel events or circumstances in terms of meaning or significance reflecting this governing dynamic. The Scientist will see that the Universe is reactive and intelligent and the Mystic will see meaningful communication in such synchronous events: it will mean to him a constellation of powers

38 See Hume and other Rationalists on the notion of Causality.

39 As in the case of the neighbor and the traffic signal. A coincidence is always just a coincidence until one 'sees the meaning behind it'; that is the observer endows the event with a meaning it may not have had. The question here isn't (yet) whether this 'meaning' is illusory or not, but whether it 'informs' the event.

at least, and the *Qabalah* will be the means of deciphering the communication.

In fact, it is difficult to speak of synchronicity without evoking Jung's popular work in the exploration of this phenomenon. He is even credited with coining the term 'synchronicity' by some, and credited with the discovery of the phenomenon by others; neither of which are accurate.

Jung however, did believe (naively perhaps) that modern physics could explain synchronicity. He appealed to aspects of Relativity Theory and Quantum Mechanics and went so far as to discuss these ideas earnestly with both Albert Einstein and Wolfgang Pauli in the hopes of arriving at a cohesive scientific theory on the question. Jung was transfixed by the notion that life was not a series of random events but rather an expression of a 'deeper Order'. Together with Pauli, they referred to this Order or syncreticism as *Unus mundus*. This *Unus Mundus* implied that a human being was both embedded in an intelligent and conscious framework and (to Jung) was the focus of that framework. These were more than intellectual realizations, but implied in Jung's view, a personal transfiguration.[40]

Jung describes synchronicity as "the experience of two or more events, apparently causally unrelated, that are observed to occur together in a meaningful manner."

The following is a famous example commonly employed in the university classroom to describe a synchronous event:

> *The French writer Émile Deschamps claims in his memoirs that, in 1805, he was treated to some plum pudding by a stranger named Monsieur de Fontgibu. Ten years later, the*

40 These ideas are presented fully in Jung's Eranos lectures, which he developed and explored further with the Nobel-laureate physicist Wolfgang Pauli. Their findings were published and are available.

> *writer encountered plum pudding on the menu of a Paris restaurant and wanted to order some, but the waiter told him that the last dish had already been served to another customer, who turned out to be de Fontgibu. Many years later, in 1832, Deschamps was at a dinner and once again ordered plum pudding. He recalled the earlier incident and told his friends that only de Fontgibu was missing to make the setting complete—and in the same instant, the now senile de Fontgibu entered the room.*

This attempt at finding patterns within coincidence inevitably involves *apophenia*. Because "a meaningful manner" is a perfectly subjective term or quantifier, this statement is rampantly liable to projection error as we discuss at length in the next section on Syncreticism. Synchronicity in and of itself can not constitute Proof nor Argument for such a governing dynamic. However, a contiguous series of such events does begin to constitute strong evidence.

Before we can address these concerns however, we are faced with the unfortunate fact that these definitions of synchronicity lack any definable, deterministic terms. We would better confine ourselves to what is empirical and verifiable, and build our definitions and the scope of their applicability upon these, than attempt an all-inclusive, all-encompassing model. We define synchronicity then, as the *simultaneous occurrence of a series of events (contiguous in time) in the same location (contiguous in space) sharing a direct syncretic correspondence.*

Note this definition depends on two empirical factors:

1. Temporal contiguity of two or more events (Contiguous in space *x* contiguous in time = temporal contiguity).

2. Syncretic correspondence.

Temporal contiguity then, is a physical fact determined by events E_1 and E_2 occurring at the same time t at the same place x.

Syncretic correspondence is determined by a translational application of the Keys and tables of correspondences such as those presented in this book. Direct experience of the phenomenon should present an endless supply of 'noise' phenomenon all in direct and perfect correspondence to these.

This statement has a number of advantages over Jung's concept of synchronicity. First, it further reduces the scope of synchronistic applicability and thus reduces our data sets, making our verifiability tests more rigorous. Second, the factors are phenomenological and so quantifiable and empirically verifiable. Finally, we can infer relational definitions directly: Synchronicity depends on two or more events $(E_1,E_2,\ldots,E_n)$ occurring in temporal contiguity (same time t and place x) and in syncretic correspondence (Q).

Now, Q or syncretic correspondence is inferential: It is a variable whose function (or value in the field of time) varies with and depends upon the events $(E_1,E_2,\ldots,E_n)$, so that Q is a function of E. Thus if $p(E_i)$ denotes the probability of event E_i occurring in syncretic correspondence, then Q becomes a multiplicative probability function where the probabilities can be discrete or continuous, but certainly definable.

Thus, Synchronicity becomes a factor of $Q = 1 - \prod^{i=1}_{(i=n)} p(E_i)$

The Book of Results, Equinox, Vol I No VII, provides an elementary example of this sort of analysis:

How W. knew R.H.K.

1. Force and Fire (I asked her to describe his moral qualities).

2. Deep blue light. (I asked her to describe the condition caused by him. This light is quite unmistakable and unique; but of course her words, though a fair description of it, might equally apply to some other.)

3. Horus. (I asked her to pick out his name from a list of ten dashed off at haphazard.)

4. Recognised his figure when shown. (This refers to the striking scene at the Boulak Museum, which will be dealt with in detail.)

5. Knew my past relations with the God. (This means, I think, that she knew I had taken his place in temple, etc., and that I had never once invoked him.)

6. Knew his enemy. (I asked, "Who is his enemy?" Reply, "Forces of the waters—of the Nile." W. knew no Egyptology—or anything else.)

7. Knew his lineal figure and its colour. (A 1/84 chance.)

8. Knew his place in temple. (A 1/4 chance, at the least.)

9. Knew his weapon (from a list of 6).

10. Knew his planetary nature (from a list of 7 planets.)

11. Knew his number (from a list of the 10 units).

12. Picked him out of ("a") Five . : indifferent, "i.e." arbitrary

("b") Three. symbols.

We have no mathematical expression for tests 1, 2, 4, 5, or 6. But the other 7 tests give us the following probabilistic calculations: 1/10 x 1/84 x 1/4 x 1/6 x 1/7 x 1/10 x 1/15 which yields a 1 in 21,168,000 chance.

The above provides us with an example of how a simple probabilistic calculation can give us quantifiable means of determining synchronicity and the valence/magnitude of that synchronicity. These can be useful in providing empirical evidence to satisfy Science's or one's own burden of proof requirements. They are sufficient argument for rationalists and may provide mathematical proof via the application of limits and the law of large numbers. However, the practitioner will require more stringent standards for verifiability; that is, he/she must admit *no* error.

Qabalah & Syncreticism

IN STATISTICS, *apophenia* is known as a Type I error, or the identification of false patterns in data. It is the experience of seeing meaningful patterns or connections in random or meaningless data and has come to represent the human tendency to see patterns even when none are present. Addicts, paranoids, fanatics, scientific, political or religious bigots *et al,* exhibit this behaviour markedly and grow excited at any attempt to examine the rationality or source of their Belief. *Any* colouring of Consciousness will in fact lead to this error. Any unresolved passion, any emotion, imbalance, imperfection, weakness or strength, affects consciousness. The virtue of the *Qabalah*, and *Gematria* is that it is impossible to deceive oneself in simple calculations which can be repeatedly tested, no matter how temporarily imbalanced one may be. But the *Qabalah* is more than Number and Letter alone, but the full perception of the Universe and containing this structure and Understanding in the mind. This is why it is said that the QBLH is rightly of the M∴T∴ alone,[41] for pure spirit is Black like the Body of Space. And just as light travels through Space invisibly (that is without lighting it) until it hits upon a planet or some other gross material, so Purity presents no obstacle to the passage of Light, and because there is no reflection of Light, there is no Image.

Pareidolia for instance, is today catalogued as a type of apophenia dealing specifically with seeing images or hearing sounds in random stimuli. A common example is seeing the face of Jesus on toast, or Groucho Marx on the subway.

Finally, a third 'invisible' factor may be undisclosed to the observer. The improbability of the coincidence is destroyed if for instance, all three events took place at the same restaurant—the restaurant that a fastidious Mr. Fontgibu has been supping at every evening for the last forty years of his life. It would be no surprise in this case, if one ran into the old man every time one visited the restaurant. Or as in the case of The Book of Results, if W had the requisite knowledge of Egyptology and of P's personal matters, sufficient to answer P's questions and deceive him. All such extraneous factors abolish the integrity of the test.

These errors are to be scrupulously avoided.[42] Probabilistic

41 There is no Self beneath the Abyss and so no solidifying agent to act on one's impressions. If they are perceived at all beneath the Abyss, they are felt vaguely as 'intuitions'. Temporality and causality are affirmed beneath the Abyss though no evidence or empiricism can justify such notions. It is only above the Abyss where such constructs become visible for what they are, and the temporality or causality of things is proven by those very qualities that deny them beneath the Abyss. Furthermore the M∴T∴ possesses the Cup without which the Understanding would not be possible. All that will be seen are disconnected facts that assail the Reason and produce Wonder and Madness, which in themselves are trials of the Initiation.

42 Except in the case of the officer in BINAH, who has transcended such limitations and so is charged with giving himself to them, even if they be objects of deception and treachery, for they can not hurt the M∴T∴ and fulfill the Law. For in this way

calculation serves best as means of Argument. The practitioner will test and continue to test (as well he or she should) until he or she is convinced of a direct causality. In this way, the probability factors tend to the binary distribution (1, 0): that is, we are either certain, or we are not (regardless of how coincidental some of the events appear to be). This is of too critical an importance for the Student to neglect.

Referring again to our example from The Book of Results, had W provided the incorrect answer for question 3, the probability of the event occurring randomly would now be quantified at 1 in 2,352,000 chance. (Since the probability of answering question 3 correctly is 1/10, the probability of answering incorrectly is 9/10 and hence we have *p = 9/10 x 1/84 x 1/4 x 1/6 x 1/7 x 1/10 x 1/15*). However the probability of answering any one (and only one) of the questions incorrectly would be:

> 9/10 x 1/84 x 1/4 x 1/6 x 1/7 x 1/10 x 1/15 + 1/10 x 83/84 x 1/4 x 1/6 x 1/7 x 1/10 x 1/15 + 1/10 x 1/84 x 3/4 x 1/6 x 1/7 x 1/10 x 1/15 + 1/10 x 1/84 x 1/4 x 5/6 x 1/7 x 1/10 x 1/15 + 1/10 x 1/84 x 1/4 x 1/6 x 7/7 x 1/10 x 1/15 + 1/10 x 1/84 x 1/4 x 1/6 x 1/7 x 9/10 x 1/15 + 1/10 x 1/84 x 1/4 x 1/6 x 1/7 x 1/10 x 14/15

which is a *1* in *164, 093* chance.

Had P asked only the first 4 questions and received 3 correct answers, the probability of such an event occurring at random would be 1 in 200. Had P received only 2 correct answers the probabilities would still yield a 1 in 80 chance. These are still excellent odds for verifiability and (1 in 80 means that we would be correct 98.75% of the time in assuming the synchronous event was not random). Most prospectors would be quite justified in

alone are the 42 made to follow and Drink, and so are brought slowly to the 14th Aire wherein the Choice is presented to them, Justice is achieved and the Conquering Child is crowned.

betting the House on such a prospect. However, we seek Science and immutable Law, not Chance.

Though this may serve to satisfy most rational tests (as in the safety of air flight), for the practitioner these probabilistic calculations will hold little weight. The perfection should be such (and he would do well to insist upon it) that no error is admitted no matter how long he extends the test, no matter how convincing the mathematics. He will abandon the inquiry (or at least must revise his understanding of his object) at the first error, for in practice Synchronicity will admit no error and its perfection mathematically improbable as it will be, will quite often overshoot the bounds of even the improbable and into the fantastical or miraculous, so that no doubt can be admitted in the practitioner and the facts and their probabilities serve only for empirical record or to convince the Skeptic.[43] For there must and always will be, Voice to accompany Vision, in the same way that there must be Light where there is Fire; and so internal phenomenon must accompany external manifestation.[44]

43 We provide examples of these in the sections on "The Living Key"

44 See footnote 53. By the time the Student passes the 14th Aethyr, he/she is immersed in these Supernal realities so that their existence is perceived directly, and there remains only the training and practice that comes with the acquisition of any language. The Qabalah and the concordances, along with the application of the Key will confirm and add to the Wonder of many such operations. It may serve as a useful test. For that same Practitioner is at Play with Babalon (156) and with Chronozon (333) and with three magi (441) though he know it not certainly until the 2nd Aethyr, for the 11th head in Daath will deceive him as has been said. Nonetheless, translation of the Key and its application to Name and Place will reveal not only the Temple, but its officers to the Practitioner, even when these functions are unconscious as it were, to the officers themselves.

Synchronicity & Syncreticism in a Time-Series

INSTEAD of being a "rare" phenomenon, as some suggest, synchronicity is all-pervasive, for all events are causally connected, at least ultimately. The occasional dramatic coincidence we notice is only the materialization of subtler energies that otherwise go unnoticed. Though omnipresent, these correspondences tend to become obvious to us only in the case of the most startling coincidences. There is even a bias error ever-prevalent—for it seems to the observer that the more improbable the coincidence, the more significant the event. This presupposes an acting agent in Nature, for the more improbable the event, the more effort it takes to realize, the more extraordinary it is and so the more significant it must be to justify this lavish expenditure on part of the universe.[45] This may or may not be so; all gradations and hierarchies are errors of a particular sort. The practice of *Qabalah* balances all perceptions by virtue of its operative abstraction on the ego and the mind; and eventually corrects all errors of perception. In the very least, it offers a practical method of not only becoming more conscious of these subtle connections, but of testing and even predicting their occurrence throughout one's life. In this way, the *Qabalah* serves one to prepare for such an event, and it may serve another as a Lamp to guide one along; as a series of lamps, like points of light that trace the path; and to others, it is the path itself.

45 All the same, erecting the Himalayan mountains was much easier and much sooner accomplished that growing a single head of hair on our heads. All the same, the Himalayas will be there (presumably) after all the hairs have fallen out of our skulls. This ought to put matters in perspective.

Some discuss synchronicity in the context of a "symbolist" world view—the perception of all phenomena as interwoven by linked analogies or "correspondences." We find that if the event is meaningful, then there appears to be an intrusive, insistent intelligence behind it, as though Nature herself desired a certain result from the event that it causes to re-occur. This intelligence will respond to inquiry, and will react to attitudinal shifts in the observer. In this case, it becomes a simple matter and a further test for reliability to take in the details of one's environment as points in a time series: the name of the restaurant, it's address, the number of the gentlemen's name, and so forth, until one sees the concordances build and the significance of the event revealed. One can demand further proof which is often supplied immediately and with mathematical (*Gematria*) verifiability (equality). This power to shape Event in Time and react to projection of Thought or Glyph constitutes a multiplicative order of probabilities and is the basis of all Hermetic Art.

Such a series of events upon the same subject, contiguous in time constitute strong argument, but still no proof. As Jung puts it, "When coincidences pile up in this way, one cannot help being impressed by them—for the greater the number of terms in such a series, or the more unusual its character, the more improbable it becomes."[46] Nonetheless, one finds syncreticism an empirical fact in all but exceptional cases. Tables of syncreticism (or an attempt at such) are provided in this book.[47]

All that lives is a Field of Energy. As that Life progresses, its energy field intensifies and one's environment adapts. Though

---

46 *Synchronicity: An Acausal Connecting Principle,* Carl. G. Jung, Sonu (FRW) Shamdasani, R. F. C. HULL, 1960, p.g. 121

47 See section "The Tables". One finds 'miracles' or events of this nature increase in frequency as one advances in consciousness and aspiration. The numbers for a 10°=1° are material, large (as in the order of thousands) while those for 2°=9° are quickly reducing to one.

Science will not admit it Today, it is certain that evolution is bijectional. We understand that the organism must adapt to its environment, but we do not yet see, that the environment adapts to the organisms it supports.[48] In effect, energy alters its medium.

The Student is then urged to Open the Aethyrs should he wish experiential proof and visible manifestation of such Wonders. Liber 418 provides a subjective description of the Aethyrs and the Calls. To call upon the Enochian in the original is generally sufficient to produce an inundation of result.[49]

It appears also, that mathematical operations (summing and multiplication, for instance) have corresponding physical processes (e.g. combination of two elements for addition; one element acting upon another in chemical process as for instance fire upon wood, for multiplication) which we discuss later in this book.[50]

In this way, Gematria serves two purposes:

First, it reveals the perfection of the manifest universe.[51] It is scientific proof of an architecting intelligence in Time. The concordance of number defies all probability, which can be calculated precisely and proven empirically. When this is multiplied through all planes of concordance and then through each event in time, we reach 1/infinity for probability. It serves

48 Hence the calcification occurring every where on the material plane. The planet and its ecosystem as living fields also evolve and adapt to changes we impose upon it.

49 It is irresponsible of the author to encourage those less-experienced to call upon the Enochians. Only a high adept should do so and great care should be taken and all due preparations made. The most common mistake for the Student, is to neglect the license to depart after the call has been effected and the work completed.

50 See section on 'The Practice of the Qabalah' later in this book.

51 The wonder is such that it will provoke Samadhi in the individual and places him in Binah should he survive the ordeal with his Wit intact. The Qabalah and Gematria in particular, are the natural weapons of the M.∴T.∴. They provide certainty where there is no light of Truth; they give sign of the Word when there no Breath of Life in the Air.

then as proof undeniable to the world at large and the scientific community should they ever be interested in investigating such matters.

Second, it may be used as a test: the perfections are beyond human capacity to engineer. Hence, if ever one wishes to test the integrity of one's consciousness and to lay claim on truth versus deception, vision versus hallucination, then this is a sure and certain means even if inexplicably so for the time being. [52] If one is undergoing initiation, the officers and temple are made visible through application of the key. [53]

If for instance, the Student were to invoke Anubis and when confronted with a visible manifestation of the Being, wanted to ascertain whether or not he were hallucinating, or if he were not being led astray by some deceptive spirit... then *Gematria* is the surest means of gaining such an assurance. We begin by asking questions, and then we calculate. We may ask for names, titles, formulae and even numbers. The intricacies of the answers and their correspondences preclude any sort of prevarication,

52 Take electricity for example. I can't see it nor smell it nor hear it. I may even be ignorant of valence electrons and how electricity works. But I can tell it is there from its fruits, from the light bulb that glows; and I have power over it through my finger on the light switch and can turn it on or off at will without knowing anything of its mechanics because this has already been devised for me—much like my eye, my mind and consciousness.

53 We may take a current example by way of illustration. At the time of his initiation into the office of M∴T∴ the author had taken up residence at 983 du Couvent (french for 'of the convent' and 983, an outer number for Choronzon) in Mont-Real (Royal Mountain) with MR* (=156 and whose name transliterated actually signified Queen Mother); upon which he moved to Paris to live at 23 rue du Chevalier de la Barre (Knight of the Wand), in Mont-Martre (Mount Martyr), and then at 81 rue des Martyrs in Mont-Martre with AD (333 or 351 (Juno) - see Aires 9 through 2 - depending on which side of the Y one is on and whose name literally signified "Gift from the Moon"). At the time, he was visited by BG (also 333) and was instructing and being instructed by BM, RD, RC. (all equalling to 441 - hence the three magi who visit the Adept in Aire 6). The significance lies in the perfect concordance between text, number and syncretic physicality. Further details can be provided to any MT or Adeptus Major by appealing directly to the author.

*Names have been removed to protect the identities of those mentioned.

design or lie. It is beyond human cognitive capacity to design such perfection and concordance even if one were armed with the knowledge and all the computational power in parallel to do so.[54] One knows then that he has hit upon the true vein or current of the matter, for all planes of consciousness and of the phenomenological universe are thus informed. That is, the World is so constructed that the influence from *Kether* (for lack of a better term) is passed through the rarefying planes of concordance; and just as in a forensic audit, if one is unable to trace the event neatly to its source, then it is because the 'chain' was never formed and has its origins elsewhere—in one's being or another's, independently of Nature, a product of Error as it were and not Vision.

Hence if the numbers, symbols and formulae agree, test upon test, then one is assured. For if one is hallucinating, the hallucination could not produce such perfection, seeing as it is a mere phantom of one's mind. For the perfection of these constructions, their equivalences and symmetries are such that they are beyond one's own capacity and knowledge to produce not only instantly, but even after many hours of labour. Similarly, any being will be unable to create the concordances upon will, for they defy rationality and can only be the product of some supra-rational intellect in Nature and Time, which Humanity (foolishly or not) have always viewed as 'divine' that is to say, a force for 'good'.[55] It is a somewhat apparent fact, that those Beings charged with

54 It is not just an NP-hard problem, it is in fact logically and mathematically intractable if the equality of the correspondences among the planes is taken into account.

55 'Good' and 'evil' are perfect examples of such 'hallucinations' or projections upon the field of Truth that obscure Vision. These are relative quantifiers. Furs are 'good' in the Arctic; lethal in the Desert. Likewise, Patience and forbearance are Virtues in the 5th Aethyr; but are one's destruction in the 2nd. This 'good' is relative to Individual, Time and Place. It's only distinctive factor is that the observed quality opposes the natural operation of the environment and so provides a counter-balance and stability in one's movement. Furs counter-balance the elemental cold, but exacerbate heat. Patience focuses the rashness of the Martian fire, but allows the Spark in the 2nd to die out.

the Governance of the Planes, care not for the affairs of human beings; but only that the Work is accomplished.

In this way, *Gematria* proves useful in tests against all forms of self-delusion, including apophenia which will afflict the Student to varying degrees upon the Path as it is the mind's basic operative stance: to try and fit new fact or knowledge into its current structure. It also serves as a test of Class A Libers, for the perfections within such texts lie outside the scope of human capability to engineer, as has been said, and so add 'transcendent' authority to the origin of the text.

The mathematical calculus of probability, the continual and insistent nature of the synchronicities, the varied tests one will conduct under this Natural Science are the surest means of developing its applicability. We begin now.

The Letters[1]

1 We lament that we are forced to refer to the Qabalah itself in our definition of these glyphs and this for the sake not only of brevity, but of precision and 'fullness of Truth'. Except where it is not perfectly necessary, we describe these operations in material terms as best we can, allowing for the corruption. We call attention to the Student of the B Class of this Liber, and that capitalization implies a formulaic correspondence.

The Roman Script

—The less advanced Student may omit the *Notes* section under each letter: they are suggested material for meditation.

N.B. Formulae are capitalized.

(Classes B, C, D; entries Class B, Notes, Classes C & D)

A

THE STAR | Value: 4

A is the Star: that Fire Visible in the Sky corresponding each one to a Living Soul on Earth. It is that Point of Light that shines in the Darkness of Night. It is that which is fixed above the revolving Earth to guide the Traveller. Its sound when prolonged is the Song of Ecstasy (*Aaaaaa*!). When punctuated with H, or the Light, it is the sound of discovery (*aha*!) so that the A in itself concentrates already that Light into the Wheel, whereas the I, is the Ray, the Hollow Tube wherein was hidden the stolen Fire of Heaven. By extending the middle bar, it becomes the Pentagram. In this way the A, the Star, can be seen as the concentration of this Light and I as the projectile Light[2]. And these are both the feminine and masculine forms of 4.

Notes

The letter A takes as its origin the letter *aleph,* which in the Old Key was the first and enumerated as 1. The revelation of the Aeon and the Aethyrs reveals three positions (1, 2 and 3 or E, F and C) preceding the A in the new system[3]. Together, these three engender and provide the framework for the manifestation of the Star. They are: the Triple Flame and Light (E), the Separation of Space (F) and The Night-Sky (C) without which there could be no suns.

Finally note that the lower case 'a' suggests an ear[4] in Form, and the common manner of drawing an ear is an 'a' with a loop around one end of it. The Student will note that "the ear' equals 111 when T is taken as final, and that 111 is the full enumeration of *aleph* in the old key.

2 'A' is also the Arrow after a certain mystery (see Liber 418), wherein its projectile nature is also evinced.

3 The proper ordering of the glyphs by their value is presented at the end of the chapter.

4 The organ of Spirit.

One can proceed with such analyses to determine the precise manner in which the glyphs have transitioned. To provide another example, we take the next letter: B, the Book, which in the old Key is *beth,* which is *beth-heh-tau* which spelt in full as ואט הה תיב = (2 +10 + 400) + (5 + 5) + (9 + 1+ 6) = 438 = 8 + 200 + 200 + 30 = Book, etc. Indications of this nature abound. The student may profit greatly from meditation upon them.

B

THE BOOK | Value: 6

B is the first of three "Stable" glyphs whose value is 6[5], The lower case "b" denotes the 6 in its shape,[6] which corresponds to its numerical value. 'B' uppercase, is The Book, fanned Open, which as can be seen by its Shape is Open to All. By another Means, IT is also the Breasts of Babalon, also Open to All, and Him Alone. Traditionally associated with the "Word" it denotes the Word Spoken[7] (not the Word living, or made Flesh) and is that Falseness and Illusion which is the Highest truth below the Veil of the Abyss and lights the happy, balanced, golden character of Tiphareth.

Notes

Mystically, B is the glyph for the Conversation of the HGA. Its appearance in Formulae such as BABALON for instance, announces the Conversation as the catalyzing initial step, which is again revisited[8]

5 The others are Z, Nf

6 *b* and 6: symbols denoting a wheel taking its light from above.

7 Note: The Name Babalon = Breasts of Babalon = 441 a number necessary to the birth of a Magus. [The Name Babalon = 106 + 115 + 156 = 221 + 156 = THELEMA + BABALON, pre-418; but post-418, we have N non-final as per 2nd Aire where N continueth, so that Babalon = 220, and now, "The Name Babalon" = 221 + 220 = 441], [Breasts of Babalon = 106 + 175 + 90 + 176 (L balanced) = 441]. See the Living Key chapter in this book for more on this and similar matters.

8 In the 8th Aethyr.

before Balance is achieved and ON is opened, and the N is set to vibration[9] as is described in Book 418 and Liber Trigrammaton in this book. Finally observe that B in the old Key is *beth,* which spelt in full equals Book.[10]

C

THE WOMB | Value: 3, 30

C is the glyph of NUIT. It is the over-arching of the Night Sky (even the Crescent of the Moon, after another manner); it is the Womb and in a sense represents the Cup manifest in one of its more immediate and practical incarnations. For the first Sky of Man is the wall of the Womb, and the Gash in the Sky from which the Light pours in is the Yoni, and all these symbols are interchangeable here.

As a Yoni, or a Womb, or a Cup, it is necessarily modified in character by that which is poured into it, or that which it contains. Hence we see that the C glyph takes on two distinct phonetic existences: It can be Soft or Yielding, as in the word *Celebration*; or Hard and Active as in the word *Cat.*

As a general rule, the C is Soft when followed by one of the male vowels, E or I as in the words *cease, cent, ice,* or *dice.* In this case, C takes the value of 3, which is also P, the Pregnant Goddess.

9 See Book 418 and Liber Trigrammaton included in this book for more on these exalted matters. Note that we can arrive at an explication of formulae via the description of the letters: BABALON which is the 7-fold word of BINH to equilibrate the 4-fold of Chokmah (KAOS) can be now seen as B: Knowledge of the HGA (in the 20th Aethyr); A: The Light Established; B: Conversation of the HGA (in the 9th Aethyr) A: The Light Established; L: The Balance Achieved; O: The Egg of Spirit Formulated (The Process Completed) and N: The Gate or the Way made Open. Finally observe that etymologically, Babalon signifies the Gate (babal) to ON. And note that historically ON was known as Heliopolis to the Greeks.

10 Beth is *beth-heh-tau* spelt in full as ואט הה תיב = (2 +10 + 400) + (5 + 5) + (9 + 1+ 6) = 438 = 8 + 200 + 200 + 30 = Book, etc. See Notes on Letter A.

When followed by one of the *female* vowels A, O or U, it is usually 'hard'. Examples are *case, cane, cone, copper, etc.* In this case C takes on the Value of 30 which is K, its homophone, holy to DIANA the Huntress, and even BABALON.

Notes

C was born of a modified G. Tz or *tzaddi* of the Hebrews (which was later abbreviated in sound to 's' and 'z') also plays role in the adoption of this glyph particularly when c is 'soft' as in the words "once" or "face".[11]

Hard C, Soft C—This is a simple case of phonetics, the hard c and k being homophones are given the same value[12]. In fact, the letter C has no distinct phonetic existence. When soft as in the word "cedar" it is phonetically, an *S*; when hard as in "case" it is phonetically equivalent to a *K*.

D

THE BOW | Value: 8

D is the BOW that makes swift the ARROW. This is the birth of all motion. The A is light fixed in a Star, the B is a vibration, the C is that which receives and bears the Vibration. With D we have the first indication of movement, and it is the *primum mobile*, that which is All Motion, but Moves Not. It's value is 8 and by its shape we have a hint of this infinite stillness in motion contained in its double loop and centre-fold.

11 See Section on *The Living Key* later in this book.

12 However, the attentive Student will note either the addition of a k to a word terminating in c (as in magick) and the growing tendency of people to replace c with a k in alternate spellings of a name or catch-phrase. In this way, "kool" is cooler than "cool" and "Karla" is sexier than "Carla". Most Ad and PR firms exploit this truth. Instinctively aware of this development, they use its power to attract attention. Finally, by employing it, and disseminating its use, advertisers themselves contribute to the advance of this evolution.

E

THE TRIPLE SWORD | Value: 1

E is the Light, the Breath and the Fire in One. The First of the Letters, it is the Foundation of all other glyphs and replaces the *aleph* as the First. It is the source of all that is intelligible and has the power of softening the other vowels as well as consonants, while hardening itself. [13]

F

THE AXE | Value: 2, 10

F is the first of the "lost" father letters, now re-instated with the English Key. It is from F, that U is born; and together they gave birth to the V which in turn fathered the W[14]. And IT required P, the Pregnant Goddess in order to accomplish This.[15]

Notes

Once considered an axe, at other times a club; and a pin to the Hebrews: F is in reality the source of which all these are the result or fruit. F is Force. F is breath. F is one of three fricatives in the English Language. The others are S and Th which like the F require air to be forcefully expelled between the upper teeth and the lower lip (labio-dental fricative).

13 E.g. hardening itself: bed vs. beed; hardening other vowels: bad vs. bade, grim vs. grime, nod vs. node, fuzz vs. fuze, softening consonants: case vs. cease, etc.
14 See letters U,V and W in this chapter for more on this mystery.
15 The Student will note the transition in the Latin of the *p* into the *f* of English as in *pater* for father, *pedis* for foot. The Greeks overcame the difficulty by appending an h to the P, hence the ph equivalent to the English F in Greek-derived words such as *phonograph, telephone, physics,* etc.

The nature of this force is double, or as is said, it is double-wanded. As 2, it is the force that divides. It is the Axe or the hatchet which makes 2 of 1 (*e.g.* in the act of splitting a single log in two). And this 'f' is the division between the Waters Above and the Waters Below the Firmament; it is the Aethyr, or the Aire by which Vision, Hearing, Distance and in a sense, Time, are made Possible.[16]

When Initial it is 10, which is Ph its homophone (3 + 7), and is the female counterpart to the 2 (the 1 0, that is the Lingam standing by the Yoni), the Pregnant Goddess (P) enthroned (H).

G

THE WHEEL | Value: 20

Union, Coitus, the pairing of the Beloved and the Lover, Summing: all these are symbols pertinent to G. In shape it denotes the Lingam and Yoni conjoined (the C taking in the horizontal I) and also the Child in its Womb. Its very Nature destroys duality and its numerical glyph of *(2 0)* denotes this Union that is the Reduction to 0 through the Union of the opposite (the 2 reducing to the 0, which is the Great Work). The Wheel is the Circle Squared and all androgynous gods, and all Child gods preside over its operation. For this reason, it is among the first vocalizations infants or primates or most beasts make. It is one of the primal letters and corresponds to primal conditions and forces. It requires no teeth and no tongue to pronounce, but only the action of the throat and so it is one of the sounds children first articulate, as in the "goo-goo ga-ga" of the folklore.

16 This reveals further revisions in the old formulae. IAO, which was revealed to be FIAOF to correct the short-sightedness of IAO, which was enumerated at 93, is in actually 220, the generalized law and not a specific formula.

Notes

G is the Union, and it is out of this Union that was born the C. The K and the Q (homophones of hard C) were necessary products and constituents of this operation, which later contributed to the birth of J. But it was G, the Union, which was the process by which all these were created. G has a history unlike any other letter. It seems that when Gladness left the world, it took the G with IT. It was G that held the third position ever since the inception of the first alphabets before 2000 B.C. Despite this, the G disappeared for 500 years in the Middle Ages, eclipsed by the rise of the hard C, its Daughter which was used in G's stead. That C is a direct descendent of G is the reason why C retains all of G's properties (e.g. turning soft before all the male vowels, and hard before the female vowels.) Later, when the letter G returned, it did so with an accretion and development which it seemed to have been gestating for those five centuries. For it was by uniting with the I (or the E) that the soft G (as in *Georgia*) was born. Before then, there had been no equivalent in the Latin script. And it was this G which, in its Union with the male vowels, contributed to the creation of J—a sound in English identical to the soft G. (*e.g.*: Georgia and Jorja are phonetically equivalent).

Generally, G is soft before E, I, and Y (the male vowels) and hard otherwise, and that G often makes the I "long" as in *sign* (long i) which otherwise would have been *sin* (short I). It is not improper to say in this case, that the G excites the I, the Phallus, thus making it 'long' or 'hard'. This holds for all GN digraphs, and is also the case for the GH[17] digraph (*e.g.* si*gh*t (long i) would otherwise be *sit* (short i). Note also that the uppercase G, is the C (the yoni) taking in the horizontal I (the projectile) while lower case g which denotes two circles: the taking in from above and from the right, and the wrapping of the tail onto itself of what would otherwise have been a 'p' (note: all symbols associated with the third position: c, g, p). Observe that in both the upper and lower case, the letter in shape suggests a taking "into" a circle.

17 Otherwise the GH glyph denotes a process of F (e.g. as in Tough)

H

THE CASTLE, THE THRONE | Value: 7

H is Light in Extension. IT is the Castle and the Throne, as IT is the Chariot and the Armoured Charioteer. For that Castle is the House of the Moon. It is Love and denotes in its shape the Constant Union of two pillars or Ones. Its Number is 7 and denotes Victory, for Love is the Law, and so IT is a Fortress (H) for it Defends Life, and IT is a Throne (h) because it is exalted in the Soul of Man. Its Sound is like the Sigh, and because it is Love, it combines perfectly with more letters than any other in the English set (often softening them in the process), and in so-doing creates a new glyph with its distinct phoneme. Among these we can list, *Ch, Gh, Ph, Rh, Sh, Th, Wh*. Observe that the H is silent in those glyphs where it is ineffectual (Rh) or unnecessary (Gh).[18]

The uppercase H denotes a Castle with its two towers in shape, while the lowercase h, denotes the Throne.

Notes

The H is often silent in those glyphs where it is either ineffectual (e.g.: RH) or unnecessary (e.g.: GH). H conceals the Union so that Love's formula is already fulfilled; while R is Birth or the Phallus exhausted implying either satiation or impotence.

18 G is Union so that Love's formula is already fulfilled; while R is Birth or the Phallus exhausted implying either impotence or satiation.

I

A COLUMN | Value: 4

I is the Ray, while A is the Star. I is the projectile and A is the wheel.[19] These two are the male and female counterparts of 4.[20] Its Shape indicates Perfection and the Unity, whereas the A indicates the culmination or the harmony of this perfection. Both reduce the 4 to the 1: that is, the elements are synthesized herein. I is the Ray, the Beam of Light that pierces. It is the Sword of Arthur and other Fables, and the Column of Samson. All these are interchangeable here for each of them denote the Lingam or the Phallus and their Sovereign place in the Body as Sun and Genitor.

Notes

It is in fact, the softening[21] of the I, which is responsible for many additions of letters and the transition from Latin to the Romance Languages. This 'I' in the English gives birth to J (through union with G) and the Y sounds, and to H sounds in Spanish and modified G in French and Italian. The introduction of the letter J into English usage can be traced to Spanish influence, in which the softening of the I became a H. Thus original *Iesus* in Spanish (or Hay-Zeus), becomes Jesus, the letter J in Spanish denoting the English H sound. Similarly, the I in French and Italian took on a soft g instead of a j, as in *gesu.* The Hebrew glyph *Yod,* transliterated as I, also plays a contribution in J's usage in English. An example is *Hallelujah*, where j retains its original 'I' phoneme.

19 Another interpretation: I is the shaft of the Arrow, A it's Barb and L it's tail. Together they comprise LAILA.

20 Note the formula LAILA already known which balances the two. Observe also that LAILA = HADIT$_f$.

21 Read "the exhausting".

J

THE HORN OF PLENTY, A HOOK | Value: 1, 5

J is the Last. As the Last, it is also the First; for the First and the Last are One on the Wheel. Its Shape denotes a turning of a corner, and contains in it, like the Crescent, a portion of the Circle. This letter was Born from the Union of G acting upon the male I[22] and phonetically equates to the softened G and this action upon the I produces an "arching" of its lower Parts to transform into the J. The projectile which once pierced, now drags, pulls and suspends, and becomes a Hook to Gore the Flesh, a Plough to till the Earth, and a Rake to Reap.[23] It is the fruits of the Labor of this Hook, this Plough, this Rake that fills the Horn of Plenty.

Notes

The Letter J is the last of the letters to be included in the modern English Alphabet (V comes just before). It is also one of only of two affricates in the collection of English Language sounds (the other is Ch as in *Chain*, but not hard as in *Chaos*.)

It is in the 17th Century that J makes its first appearance in the English Language. It took 150 years after that, before it was accepted. Until then, J was viewed not as a letter in itself but as a mere variant of I. In fact, J succeeds I in order of the English Alphabet because it was essentially born of it. The same holds for the letter V which was born of the U, and so was inserted after it. Consonants are typically inserted after their mother (or father) vowels.

---

22 See Letter I - Notes

23 As the Hook, it has the Power to fasten itself to an object and is the traditional means of catching large Fish and especially of baiting Fish. Observe the prominence of the letter in most Christian formulae (Christ as the Son is 'S' or Piscean - the Fish. Note his many miracles involving Fish: His 'walking on water', his multiplying fish and loaves; his own declaration as a 'fisher of men') : from Jehovah, Joseph, Jesus, Joshua, Job, John, James, etc.

K

THE VIRGIN | Value: 30

Of the Three homophones: the K, Q and the hard C, the K has always been favoured by the Poets. Its very existence is at War with two other letters with which the K must Fight for survival.

In shape, the letter K denotes the Arrow hitting its target. IT is also the Goddess seated on Her Throne (seen from above), her Legs or Arms Open in Love—and so there is Success in the Operation, for in Shape it is also the God without standing with an erect Lingam. Its value is 30, that of the hard C, which is the C materialized (30 = 3 × 10 = C × 10, 10 being Malkuth), that is the Yoni fulfilled. It's glyph in numeral, again denotes this process: 30 or 3 0 is the C (3) materializing (0—the Egg of the Universe). Note the progressive materialization of the same Element: from C, to hard C, to K, to Q: the Sky, (the Sea), the Womb, the Yoni, the Lingam, the Spermatazoon.

Notes

K, Q and hard C, are homophones, and are once more male and female perspectives of the One idea which is summarized in 30.

The complexity of C, which is phonetically sometimes a K, sometimes an S, has meant that newly created or adopted words with a hard C sound in the English Language are increasingly spelt with a K as the choice of preference. This is done in order to avoid confusion[24] and suggests that the K is Rising and will eventually gain ascendency over the C.

24 In fact, the Caesars in Rome were not pronounced "the Seezers" but the Keezers. Had the English adopted the K, they would have avoided this error as they did in their equivalent title 'Kaiser'. We see that the Russian with czar, have got but half way. Note that Kaiser and Czar share the same etymological root to Caesar.

There is some Confusion in the History of this Letter as regards the Mystical Tradition.[25] The letter K has traditionally been the glyph for the Hand perhaps indicating onanism and its necessary relation to a virginal status in a sexually mature being. The Hand, a symbol of man's will and his sovereignty over the Animal, is also the main instrument of auto-eroticism.[26]

As a rule, this letter is taken to be 30 by the key. This is problematic in certain instances where it is silent as in the words *Knowledge* and *Unknown*. We leave this to the discretion of the Qabalist. The Author has preferred to take the following line of reasoning: that if it is present in the word, it is significant and will continue to be so, until that day it disappears.

---

25 History can be of assistance here, for the development of the Alphabets is traceable. Its origins were in Egypt. The Semitics adopted it, and developed upon it. From the Semitics it found its way to the Phoenicians, who gave it to the Greeks and to the Hebrew of the Jews. From the Greek, it found its way eventually to Latin which is the script of the English Language.

26 This may denote humanity's material emancipation from the sexual drive, for he or she now has an immediate means of satisfying the compulsion without the requirement of a mate and all the social dynamics, preparations and responsibilities such a prospect invokes. We know that the original Egyptian glyph for the Hand stood for the first letter of the Egyptian word for Hand (*dirite*) which corresponds to the modern letter D, and was identical to it in Sound. However, the Phoenician word for hand began with the voiceless velar plosive, which is the sound of the modern K. When they adopted the hand glyph (in shape it resembled an upright hand) they adjusted their system to compensate. In this way, the Hand glyph became associated with the K. This development was already in place by the time the Hebrews took the Phoenician alphabet to devise their own. When arriving at the 11th position, they adopted *kaph*, which is the word for the Palm of a hand and begins with a K. This transition from Hand to Palm and finally to Virgin corresponds to revelatory stages of our comprehension of this glyph. A further hint may be taken from the Egyptian papyri, primarily the creation myths: *I gathered together my members, and afterwards had union with my hand, and my heart came unto me from out of my hand, and the seed fell into my mouth, and I emitted from myself the gods Shu and Tefnut (The Book of Overthrowing Apep*, British Museum). By this act, Kephra creates Shu and Tefnut. Note also that this operation is said to have taken place at Heliopolis, or ON to the Egyptians. (See The Letter N)

L

BALANCE | Value: 50, 70

L is the Balance without which there could be no Movement. It resembles a Leg and a Foot in Shape: that is, the *lower parts* of Man, his motive power.

If the L is balanced it will sum to 70 which is the EYE in the old key; otherwise it denotes 50, the old glyph for Death.

Notes

The Squaring of the Circle or its Failure are mysteries that correspond to the letter L, which can take two values, the Upright and the Averse depending on the letters immediately following and preceding it. Whether this letter is Averse or Upright is decided by whether the particular Balance is established or Not.

Technically, the L is said to be Balanced if it is supported on either side by the same vowel (as in *Palace* or *Element*). Otherwise, L is said to be Averse. [27]

We devote a specific section in this book[28] for a discussion of this matter.

27 Dr. John Dee and Edward Kelley first make mention of a special property of this letter, back in the 17th century. Their research suggested that L can sometimes be an "*N that extendeth*"—N which in the Old Key was the glyph for Death, which is now known to be a Gate—that this state of Death or lingering about the Threshold or Gate, can Prolong itself *unnecessarily.* For the failure to Square the Circle would imply Death, a release of energy into Piscean realms over which the letter N (or the Hebrew *nun* which in his time, equalled 50) presides. Kelley records in his journal that "Avé" explained that Dee must make up the name PARAOAN. Dee asks, "What shall become of the "L" aversed?" Avé replies "In EXARPH there wanteth an "L." Though Dee could not anticipate this: the implication here is that when L is averse, it takes on the Value (and operation) for N in the old Key. See *Dr. John Dee, A True and Faithful Relation,* CASAUBON, London, England, 1659

28 See "The Living Key" Section in this Book.

M

A WAVE, A VALLEY | Value: 40

M denotes the Great Sea. It is the Water that Binds and Nourishes. Its elastic Flow, its power of permeability, its ability to adopt the form of its container, its very Ebb and Flow—all mimic the powers and Principles of Life. And as IT is a vehicle for Life, it is necessarily a precondition for IT. [29]

One of the Mother letters in the Old Key, its shape denotes a Wave or a Valley carved by a River, and has traditionally been associated with the element Water. Mystically, it has been the symbol of self-sacrifice, of motherhood and the Hanged Man in the Book TARO. Also, to pronounce 'm' requires compressing both lips shut, and thus it has also been associated with Silence in the Tradition.

Notes

M is sometimes a syllabic consonant: it is considered by some to be a vowel in certain cases. An example would be chasm, where a vowel is implied between the *s* and the *m.* It is the most ubiquitous letter in the English language and many others as well. As a glyph, it has persisted throughout the Aeons, and its function and properties have remained immune to Change. It's value remains 40, and being the 13th letter, it also divides the Key[30], and is a hinge on which the System turns for its numerical value changes Not throughout the Aeons. All formulas for transcending Death require this M as indicated by the passwords and formulae and Godnames presiding over this Place.[31]

29 Water as ubiquitous as it is, is still a great mystery to modern chemistry and physics. It defies many a physical law or property. Water binds two of the most combustive or fiery elements (Hydrogen and Oxygen) into some thing wet. These two elements exist naturally as gases yet are bound together my electrostatic and gravitational forces into something not quite gaseous and not quite solid. It conducts electricity but is electrostatically inert. It will not contract, but expand if you attempt to slow its atomic motion.

30 There are 26 letters in the English Alphabet.

31 See M**N (of the OTO III° rite and other Masons which now instead of 93 is

N

A GATE | Value: 6, 70

N is a Gate, which is the Threshold; and it is the glyph, which in the past has been traditionally associated with Death—that Death that is Regeneration or New Life. It takes on two possible values: 6 or 70 depending on which side of the gate One is ON[32]. And that Gate that is N, is the Gate that the Key ON (which is 150) opens, and which opened from one side is 156 (150 + N_f) and from the other 220 (150 + N) which are both BABALON so that the Gate is also the Key.[33]

Notes

For the purposes of Gematria, the letter N takes two values depending on its position[34]. Its value is 70 except when it terminates a word or a phrase (appears as the last letter) as in "Man" or "Babylon". In this latter case, it takes on the value of 6 and becomes a Z, which is the Lightning Flash[35], by falling on its side[36]. This addition contains a new key to the Mysteries of Death, which loses its Aspect of Terror for Humanity, and is discussed in greater length under the letter Y. Later we will see how the letter Y, the Tree of the World, which is the Tree of Life, ultimately culminates in one of the two possible values for N[37] which is the Gate that the balancing of the L (*i.e.* the squaring of the circle) opens.

enumerated at 120 which makes better sense - as per ON and the Aethyrs), MAUT, MAT, AIMA, NEMO—not one of which is male (NEMO is neither).

32 Babalon etymologically equivalent to the Gate (Babal) ON and BABAL ON = 156 with N final, and 220 otherwise. Passage through the second Aire opens this Gate and so sets the letter into vibration. See LIber 418.

33 For Babal = 70 = N

34 It is the first letter to take a final value. The other two are S and T, as will be seen shortly. A discussion on the significance of final values is presented separately.

35 Z = 6 suggests the lightning bolt in shape.

36 The Falling of N on its Side, or the N final, which is 6. In shape, an N is a Z on its side and vice-versa.

37 See Letters Y and L.

THE MOON | Value: 80, 200

The O is the Moon, the reflective nature of Water and the Egg of Spirit. It is also the Universe or the reflective nature of Consciousness. The Cup is implied in both cases, and so reflection (=projection) is the basis of the operation. Like the Cup, the Moon is Full when directly facing the Sun. Only then does it Receive fully of its Light and is wholly Illumined. It shines Golden in the Day like the Cup, which is 200[38] and *Resh* in the old Key, a glyph receptive to the Sun. And in the Sky at Night, it is the Splendour into the Kingdom which is 8 (the 8th sphere—Splendour) into 10 (the Kingdom or Material Plane) or 80. These two states correspond phonetically to the long and short phases of this vowel.[39]

Notes

O can be 80 or 200, which correspond to its two phonetic phases. At 80 the Egg is Fertilized, the Eye is Established, the Yoni is Fulfilled.[40] At 200, the Earth is Parched, the Eye is Closed, the Yoni is in Travail. As 200 it is solar—impregnated with the force of 120, while at 80 it is Mercurial in character as evidenced by the Horns.[41]

38 See Letter U and Resh in the old Key: a glyph receptive to the Sun.
39 It is 80 when short as in song, and 200 when long as in stone.
40 These symbols being interchangeable here.
41 The symbol for Mercury is the symbol of Venus crowned with the Crescent Moon, or Horns of Power.

P

THE MOTHER | Value: 3

Traditionally, the symbol of War and of Priesthood, it is She who stands guard. The Pregnant Goddess embodies not only the generative life, but also that attitude of the bearing Mother, who is Armed and Mighty to defend and empowered to do All to direct the Future or the Outcome of the Battle.

Notes

Note that P shares the value of 3 with soft C, a manifestation of the same in Lunar Form. See also, R the Birth which shows the I emanating from the womb of P; and H which when paired with P denotes the female counterpart to this Power: Ph and F which are equivalent in Sound & Value, for P + h = 3 + 7 = 10 = F which is equivalent to IT in Sound & Value.

P is a bilabial plosive, so that with every P that is articulated in a word a kiss is given, for making the sound 'p' requires joining the lips together. Observe also the plethora of young goddesses, nymphs and maidens in mythology that champion the letter: Pallas, Persephone, Pasiphae, Perse, Philia, Phoebe, Psyche, etc.

THE LION | Value: 10

Q, the Lion or the Spermatazoon, was first a Monkey. The Sumerians drew the body of the animal with a tail. The letter today retains this tail. Later when the Semitics appropriated the symbol from the Phoenicians, they named it "qoph" which signified "the back of the Head", that is, the primal subconsciousness of man, his animal soul or paleo-cortex. It is all of these: IT is the evolutionary motive power within the individual, and that buried force that propels its growth both within its life and throughout the Aeons, and so also that which made the Ape overcome or rise above itself. This progression from Ape to Lion portrays this evolutionary or aeonic development in the primal character of Man.

Notes

Q is the power of generation which when applied to another element raises it to a higher wheel or plane and manifests the Egg of Spirit beneath it ready for fertilization. (Q = 10, 156 × Q = 1560). It is THAT which reproduces itself into the Egg of Spirit in Its original Perfection (n × 10 = n0, for any integer n).

Note that Q manifests the Father and the Goddess for Q = F (the Father) = 10 = Ph (The Mother) = Ch (The Graal). Q summarizes then, the Secret of the FreeMasons and the Miracle of the Mass, and in its sound, models the mechanics by which this process is achieved[42]. For observe that except in rare cases, the Q is always followed by the U, which aptly denotes the Cup. And this denotes the Universal process which to Halt in order to arrive at One free of the other can only be effected with great pains.

As a final note, Q shares this power of generation with two compound glyphs, Ch and Ph which are also 10 (soft C = 3 and H = 7) and are that female half to counterbalance the male Q or F.

42 Q sounds like Kw (e.g. kwick for quick, or kwark for quark). A further hint: KW = 90 = 30 × 3 that is the Hard C (30 akin to the Arrow) transitioning upon the soft c (3, akin to the Pregnant Goddess), that is *cc* as in su*cc*ess. Also W=60 is the Spirit, concentrated with force upon a point, K=30. Such meditations should provide ample material for experiment.

R

THE EMPEROR | Value: 9

R, the Emperor is the establishment. It manifests institutional authority and political government and symbolizes all that resists Change.[43] R is the abortive Birth: the I emanating from the Pregnant Goddess (P) and hitting Ground. Its glyph is 9 which illustrates not only this re-birthing but also that particular refusal to change under combination with other elements. Thus the recursive sum on the digits of the product of 9 with any other number is again 9[44]; so that whatever is born of 9 is 9 again and Progress that is Life itself, is halted. In this way, what is Born of the R or Authority is born Dead, and that Authority survives only by replicating and assimilating.

Finally, R is the Phallus, flaccid or exhausted as its shape denotes both in the lower case (r, flaccid) and the uppercase (R, fallen); and by its number 9, which also resembles the profile of the flaccid male genitalia (the testicles and *lingam* in profile). In all cases, the ultimate impotence of Authority is implied.

---

43 Any establishment, institution or government relies on the upholding of the status quo on which they were founded or have existed, even if that status quo be deleterious to its constituting members. Change is its only threat and any new development or invention or improvement is bound to be interpreted as disruptive unless that development goes directly to enhancing the means of governance. As long as the status quo -whatever it is, once established- persists, then all is well in the Empire, but whenever the 'people' cry and gather under a new passion, or truth or justice, then Authority exerts itself.

44 E.g.: 9 * 146 = 1314; 1 + 3 + 1 + 4 = 9. Consider $9 x m_1m_2m_3...m_k$ where x denotes multiplication and $m_1,m_2,m_3...m_k$ denote the digits of any integer number. Then if $n_1n_2n_3 ... n_j = 9 x m_1m_2m_3...m_k$ then the recursive sum of $n_1n_2n_3 ... n_j$ always equals 9. We omit the proof, but can take any two numbers by way of example for clarification: 9 x 23 = 207 and 2 + 0 + 7 = 9; or 9 x 146 = 1314 and 1 + 3 + 1 + 4 = 9; a final example: 9 x 63 = 567 and 5 + 6 + 7 = 18 and 1 + 8 = 9). Finally note how the suffix 'er' denote a superlative (e.g. quick and quicker), again repeats the idea with an incremented degree of materialization (quicker manifests the idea of 'quick' further). Note 'er' = 10: the Malkuth or the material plane. The same applies for the prefix 're' which denotes a repetition or reinforcement.

Notes

Note also how this R is troublesome rendering impotent the W, which is the Vision and the Voice[45] and eliminates that Fire by which Light and Heat and Sight are possible.

Traditionally, a Solar glyph, we now know that the Sun, a Star, like other Stars is but One in the Body of Nuit. It's phasing from 200 to 9 in the new key, denotes the end or impotence of the cosmocentric ideal, and the paternal, authoritarian systems of old. The new key gives U the Cup for 200, and reveals a new perspective for R, the Osirian Gods, which are now Exhausted.

S

THE SERPENT, THE SON | Value: 24, 42

The Letter S has two phases. When final it is the Serpent of Knowledge and Delight and it is 42 in number[46] and has the power of pluralizing any object. Otherwise it is 24 and denotes the Son on the Cross, or the Rosy Cross, who is the Son Crucified in the Name of the Father, the Sun-Solar Beast and the Angel of Tiphareth materialized—for these ideas are all interchangeable here and are resolved to One.[47]

Notes

The letter S holds a special place in the English Lexicon as the main symbol for denoting plurality. There is a distinction to be made therefore in the S that terminates the word as it is, (e.g.: *chaos)* and the S that

45 The W is silent when compounded with R. We have the words *wrong, wreck, write, wrap,* etc, as an illustration. See Letter W.

46 A number associated with the Second Aethyr and the tablet of the 42 names of God incarnate in the Accusers whom the Adept must baffle.

47 To later be reversed. For the Man hangs on the Tree, while it is the Serpent which Climbs it.

although terminating the word is not *of* it, but is suffixed to denote pluralization (e.g.: *words*). The letter S therefore takes on two values depending on its position. As S final it takes the value of 42 (21 into 2) versus 24 (12 into 2).

Perhaps the most tortuous of the glyphs, the letter S sometimes denotes a clear hiss as in words like *Super* or *Supper* or *Case*. In others this hiss is constrained by bringing the tongue to rest upon the palate, as in the words *Sure* and *Sugar*, which appear to compound an *h* to *s*. Other times yet, this hiss is entirely constrained until by force of pressure[48] it releases thundering and rumbling in the throat, turning it essentially into a *z* especially when terminating a word as in *towards* and *days*, or sometimes in the middle of the word : *rose, nose* (versus the example of *doze* and *dose*).

T

THE TABLE, THE ALTAR | Value: 89, 98

T is the Table upon which the Banquet is laid; and T is the Altar where the Sacrifice is made. When final it is the Altar, and takes the value of 89. Otherwise, it is 98, and a Table. Both imply Stability and a grounding in the Four. And this grounding can be beneficial or detrimental given the particular case.

Notes

These two values denote new introductions into the Key—as these values have never before in History had a single symbol attributed to them. These glyphs then, denote universal revelations particular to this Aeon and represent as such, advances in the evolution of the species as a whole. These are demoted / promoted from 90 or the Tzaddi in the old key and deal with questions concerning the ROTA, ATU IV and other critical

48 The pressurized release vibrates the air between the palate and the tongue which creates the sound corresponding to the letter. One can feel this.

matters discussed at length later in this book[49], and elsewhere by other adepts.[50]

The T final is distinct. The T elsewhere in a word denotes an explosive release of energy; but it takes on an entirely different character at the end of the word. It is the most sudden and violent of the terminations and denotes in this case an implosion, or the *reverse* effect, the value of which is the corresponding reversal of the digits of its usual numerical attribution.[51] It takes the value of 89, a prime, traditionally associated with the "Wrong" kind of Silence[52]. Otherwise it is taken as 98 in value.

U

THE CUP (THE URN) | Value: 200

So much has been said and hinted at concerning this glyph, that there is little to add for what may be of practical use. Legends of the Graal[53], of the Cup of Babalon and others are essentially representations of this glyph in form of legend and folk-tale.

However, some oversights are prevalent, and certain other practicalities are often overlooked by rasher Students. Note for instance, that the Cup as IT is, possesses not only the Power

49 See Notes on the Procession of the Aeons. Essentially, these two forms of T arise from a split of T and Tz. Simple addition can verify this for us: Tzaddi = 90, which is transliterated as Tz and contains not only the 'T' but also the 'Z', the Lightning Flash, which the Key now releases as an independent variable, so that we have Tf → Tzaddi; and T → Tzaddi + Z. Now Tzaddi = 90 and Tzaddi + Z = 97 which together are 187 = T + Tf.

50 See the Book of Thoth for example.

51 T = 98, T final = 89

52 That of those who are drowned before the vine is planted - technically called the Black Brothers. Being the Name of a thing, we'll leave it to the interested Student to calculate its Number. The 'right' kind of silence would correspond to a free-flow of Will, and would be more akin to an inner peace which may manifest itself vociferously depending on the Need.

53 The Graal is Nemo and refers to the initiate at such a stage. It does not denote a historical fact, but a process continually present and incarnating in the Universe.

to contain and restrain liquids into Shape (that is, give them Form), but also all ground or powdered solids (or ash as in the case of the Urn). In the case of the liquid (the most immediate application), the Student will notice that the Cup must be still, that is Fixed, for Reflection on the liquid's surface to be possible. The slightest vibration sends the liquid in the Cup to Motion, and the rippling of the liquid distorts the Image into hellish and obscene caricatures of the True Reflection. The importance of this fact can not be overstated.

Notes

U often succeeds Q. Note that the U is prevalent everywhere without the Q, but that Q, has trouble appearing without the U at its Side. Q and Ch represent the male and female counterparts of That which the U contains. They are each 10, and there union is 20 (the G – the Yoni satisfied), which together with the Cup or U, is 220, The Law.

Observe also that U = Q x G.

THE HORNS OF POWER | Value: 80

Resembling Horns in shape, V is the glyph of that which Born of the Skull, gores the Flesh and uproots the Tree. It's value is 80, which is that of the soft O, or the new or crescent Moon, its corresponding female glyph. Note that both glyphs resemble these horns in shape.[54]

54 The difference between these letters and their correspondents on the pole of the sexes, is in their shape at the root. U and C are right angle images of each other, and differ from the V only at the base, which in the latter case resolves to a point and in the case of the

Notes

A fricative like the F, and one of the last letters along with the J to be included into the standardized listing of the English Alphabet, it's original usage was that of an initial U. Thus whenever the letter u appeared at the beginning of a word (*e.g.* upon) it was written with a 'v' (vpon). Born of its mother vowel the U, it was placed immediately after it.

THE EYES | Value: 60, 400

Another late addition to the language, this letter at the beginning of a Word always denotes the free flow of Energy as evinced by its sound – the Mouth opening wide and the air passing unrestricted (as in Wah, Weh, Wuh, etc) and expresses the free flow of force of the letter F which fathered it.

Its value is that of 60, that is *Tiphareth* or Human Consciousness into *Malkuth*, the material plane. It is the source of Intelligent Life and mystically corresponds to Vision and Voice, whose two V's constitute the W.

Called the "Double U", when activated, it takes on the value of 400[55] which is the totality of the Universe, and as Tau IT is the Crucifixion, and in Shape IT denotes the two Eyes of Horus, like pins, or hot brands in Thine Head, that see into the Horizon and are fixed on Eternity, and are like two Cups[56] that pour forth the Golden Light to Brighten the World.

W is silent when it precedes R, which is the exhaustion, or the

U is a continuous, smooth arc.
55 U + U = 200 + 200 = 400 = W
56 U is the Cup, which reflects light and allows for Vision.

Sleep of *Shi-Lo-Am* for the righteous[57] wherein the Eye of the Mind is ostensibly shut.

Notes

The W is in a sense unique to English. There are only four other European languages that employ W in words native to their language, and these five use the letter to denote yet other sounds that not known in English. This is suggestive of the glyph's modernity. For the German and the Polish, the W is closer to the voiced labio-dental fricative of the letter , thus employing the teeth and the tongue to restrict the free-flow of air evinced in the English. Instead, the Polish employ a symbol very much like the averse L (Ł) to denote the */w/* sound as we have it in English. In Cyrillic, the W sound is denoted with a y shaped glyph, while in Welsh, the W can represent a vowel as well as a consonant, and in Finland the "W" hasn't been born of the V yet, and is still viewed as a mere variant of "V" and not a separate letter.[58]

Note also that two hard *c*s or two *k*s (arrow hitting their targets each constituting a pin), or a '*ck*', denote a '*w*' which in all four cases are 60, denoting this double fixing, or the pinning of the separate poles wherein the Wheel turns.

THE WHEEL, THE CROSS | Value: 9, 300

As a cross, the 'x' is the counterpart to the R and the ideas summarized in the numeral 9, especially as these relate to what has been said concerning the exhaustion of the Osirian Gods,

57 A foul word and not to be interpreted in its usual sense : Righteousness implies Separation not Love.

58 This is always the case when the effect of a glyph is perceived but not isolated or understood: Humanity seeks to relate the unknown to something it knows. Until it separates the action of its combination with other elements, it sees the new glyph as modifications or variations of an existing glyph.

i.e. the resurrecting gods, garnered under the symbol of the Cross. As the Wheel, the 'X' is 300 which is Spirit[59], that which harmonizes and consecrates the four elements[60] into one. For this Wheel contains the Cross on its Axle, but now the Cross moves and Spins like the whirling Sword (the original Aleph) whenever that Wheel in set in motion and so causes Change.[61]

Notes

The letter X, a very modern addition and problematic, is sometimes a Z (xylophone) sometimes a *ks* (tax) yet others like a *gz* (exert, execute), *gsh* (luxurious), and *ksh* (noxious). Via the Greek, it came to the English language where it originally denoted a sound identical to Z.

Y

THE TREE OF THE WORLD | Value: 6, 70

Y enjoys the special distinction of being the only letter which can be both vowel (*e.g.* cry) and consonant (*e.g.* yellow). Here we see that Y, the Tree of Life, the forked road suggested by its Shape, ends in one of two ways: in that Death which is Balanced Life (70 = N = L balanced), or into Tiphareth which is Harmony and Beauty (N_f = 6). In both cases, the Letter Y or the Tree of Life, ends in N (the old glyph for death). Yet, this is the Glad Word for Humanity: how the active glyphs (L, Y, N) coalesce into these two: the 70 and 6, wherein Beauty and Love are exalted.

59 300 = Shin, Spirit, symbolized by a Wheel. See pages 17-18.

60 See Ordeal 'x' discussed in The Living Key chapter in this book.

61 It has been the claim of an enlightened School that an ordeal awaits the Student upon the Path concerning this letter. This ordeal, which the Adept chooses to take up or not, once having passed, results in the transfiguration of the "Five Wounds" into Wheels. For these "winners of the Ordeal X" as it is written, the X is set at 300 for what remains of their physical Life.

And that Path which is fixed and leads unto *Tiphareth*, or Sol, is the consonant Y whose value is 6. It is the illusory word which Man, the Son is subject to, and incarnates. So it is also B, which is the Book. The light of RHK here, is like the lightning flash (Z)[62], which is only seen distantly, but soon trembles in the Breast (the falling of N on its side[63]) all of which are 6.

And that path which leads to the open EYE and is the Balance, is Y vowel and takes the value of 70, which is N, which is a Gate and Eye and Death. For this Gate is the Gate to the Palace of Understanding or *Binah*, and this Eye is the Eye of Shiva. The passing through the Gate N or the opening of the Eye of Shiva, destroys the Universe. And this is the Balanced L which is the key to the Gate that is N.[64]

Notes:

To perceive the Universe without Error—and this is the meaning of the "Eye of Shiva" or its Opening—requires that the Initiate Cease. This Universe (of the 6), being a Mirror or a Looking Glass, reflects the Image of that which envelops the Eye, and is False unless what looks is No Longer, is Dead, or in this Life, Empty of Light.[65] Otherwise, All that is Seen is one's own Reflection.

The y is called "the greek I" in many languages (*I griega*, Spanish; *i greca,* Italian, *i grec,* French, *i grego,* Portuguese) or sometimes *epsilon.* Phonetically, it is kin to the Spanish double *ll* which is kin to the *j* in Germanic languages. The Y is a Greek discovery, a gift of the Classical Period and symbolic of that Age. The glyph was absorbed into the

62 B = Z = 6, and Z suggests the lightning bolt in shape.

63 Or N final which is 6. Note that N is identical in shape to Z, when turned 90 degrees in any direction - "the falling of N on its side." See the letter N, and the balancing of the Ls.

64 N in shape denotes a gate.

65 See formulae for NOX: The pure spirit is pure darkness in the same way the Sun does not light up the Space it travels through unless it hits upon a planet or some coarser material: so pure Understanding is Darkness, for it passes the light unto Others and in this way, is invisible and illuminating at once.

Qabalistic systems later on as a welcome development when it was found that the double *l* had not as elemental constituents two *l*'s, but was in itself such an element. These two halves then united at the centre, and extended as one down to the root, hence morphing the two bar shape of the double *l* (like two pillars), into the forked shape of the modern Y.

The consonant Y therefore is kin to the double LL[66] and in some cases where the phonetics appears clear and spelling may be in transition—a judicious application of the rule is advised.

In the English language however, the inclusion and subsequent integration of the Y glyph in the language takes an unexpected turn. Here the symbol is used to denote the contraction of two separate letters "T" and "H" and the accompanying sound. Today we still see remnants of this as in Ye Olde English. This symbol "Y" denoting a "Th" was called *thorn.* However, when coming across a Ye as in Ye Olde Pub, an Anglophone will pronounce it *yee* and not *thee* as was originally intended and practiced.

Z

THE LIGHTNING FLASH | Value: 6

While S is that Serpent that Climbs the Tree of Life, Z is that Lightning Flash that shoots from the Crown when IT is Storm-Laden[67]. Traditionally seen as a sword that divides, it explodes from ON High, and in an instant, irresistible in its Force, traverses the Spheres to discharge its Might on the Ground of Earth.

66 A misguided attempt at balancing the glyph.

67 It can shatter the Tree with its blast, set it to Fire and otherwise consume it on its traversal. The only means of withstanding the Lightning Flash is to be electrical oneself. Only in this way, does the Lightning Flash charge the Body of Light, for any obstacle on its path is destroyed including the 'non-electric' parts of the Initiate.

Compound Glyphs

IT – The Miracle of the Mass. **(= 93)**

ST – The Son (S) on the Cross or on the Altar (T) or the Serpent (S_f)on the Tree (T_f). **(= 131)**[68]

QU – The Eagle is in the CUP **(= 210)**

H Glyphs

(H - The Castle—The Chariot 418 in the ROTA key):

CH is the crescent Moon or the Cup or Holy Graal (C) enthroned or exalted (H). It is the High Priestess and the Symbol of the Great Work accomplished. **(= 37)** [69]

PH – The Mother (P - The Pregnant Goddess) enthroned (H - The Throne) **(= 10)** Observe the equivalence to a phase of CH.

RH – The Emperor (R) on his Throne (H) **(= 16)**

SH – The Son (S) Enthroned (H) and the Serpent (Sf) Crowned **(= 31; = 49)**

TH – The Cross (T) as a Weapon (H). **(= 96)**

WH – The Watchtowers **(= 67, 407)**

---

68 Note: Its value is 131 which is S final and T final (42 + 89). 131, the surrounding of the 3, Alchemically, the fire, the Serpent on the Altar (crucible) conjoined.

69 Note: The value of CH is 10 or 37, depending on whether it is soft (as in chance) or hard (as in chaos). As 37 it is the Chariot of the old glyphs and 418 fully spelt, a formula denoting the Great Work. It is that Chariot of which it is spoken, "There is no Power which endureth except in this my Chariot that descendeth from Babalon," and this Ch is the hard c paired with the h, whose enumeration is 30 (hard c) and 7 (h) which united makes 37. Note then, the power which descends from Babalon which lies in Binah, which is the 3, which into 37 is 111 (111 = 37 × 3) and so spans the triune numbers which in themselves are balanced and so Endure.

Male vowels: E, I, Y_v

Female Vowels: A, O, U, Y_c

The Grand Equivalences

70 = Y = N : *The Tree of Life is the Gate of Death.*

6 = Y = N : *The Gate of Death is the Tree of Life.*

200 = O = U : *The full Moon is a Cup.*[70]

3 = C = P : *All Goddesses are Mothers. The Mother is the Goddess.*

30 = C = K : *The Mother is the Daughter.*[71]

The Great Divides

⅃, L : *The Averse and the Upright.*

w W : *Blindess / Vision*

S S_f : *Beneath the Great Waters / Above the Great Waters*

T T_f : *Sacrifice / Preservation*

Y, Y_c : *Choice.*

Ŏ, O: *Action / Passivity*

N, N_f : *Life / Death.*

N is a Gate, implying it swings both Ways. It is N going In, and N_f going Out. [72]

70 In that IT is fixed and receives fully of the Light; but this moon is of a different Order: Full Moon = 788 (Babalon as Venus presiding over Mercury) while Cup = 233 (Mercury as Chokmah presiding over Babalon as Binah) [-- see section on Three Wheels] though both these imply an exchange between the Word (Mercury or Chokmah) and Babalon.

71 See the old formula for the TETRAGRAMMATION.

72 Note that this is of no help to the Student. In and Out are meaningless terms without their context; and there is no context. These are mysteries revealed to the Student in the

Astrological Attributions

- Please refer to Notes on Astrology later in this book.[73]

(Class C Document)

2nd Aire. It is a matter of Choice fulfilling the Law.

73 These attributions depend upon several considerations the primary of which is the transition to the Aeon III and the revolutions of the Zodiac wheel, especially as regards Aries *The Ram,* Aquarius *The Water-Bearer* (The Age of the Aeon); ATUs *The Emperor, The Star* and *The Chariot*; and the letters R, x and H as they transition from the Aeon and pre- to post-418. Also observe that in particular phases: Ch = Q = F = Ph, Y = N, P = C, etc. denoting some form astrological equivalence.

☉ **A, the Star,** is that Star particular to our System, that concentration of Fire and Light that bestows Life and Beauty.

☿ **B, the Book**, which are the **Breasts of Babalon**, is the vessel of the Word, which is Hermes or Mercury, the 2nd (reflected in the 8th - HOD) as Baphomet.[74]

♒ **C, the Womb and Sky**, is Aquarius, the Water-Carrier, which is the Womb or the Sky which rains upon the Earth.

♀ **D, the Bow**, is Venus as The Empress (and so Babalon as Huntress), the 3rd (reflected in the 7th: Netzach), which is Love and the Victory (Netzach) of the propelling, penetrating force of the Arrow.

🜁 **E, the Triple Flame**, is that triple Sword which is AIR.

♆ **F, the Hook**, is Neptune ruler of the Great Sea (*Binah*), master of the Trident that reduces three to one. Note, the hook is the traditional means of catching Fish.

♊ **G, the Union**, is Gemini ruled by Mercury as boy Cupid and contains the projectile Arrow of Sagittarius into the Sky womb of Aquarius.

♋ **H, the Throne**, is not only the Fortress & Throne, but the Chariot & the 4 Pillars & Elements surrounding it & the Armoured Charioteer of that Castle, the House of the Moon, Cancer, the *Genitor* which has a hardened protective covering ITself.

74 BREASTS (175) + OF (90) + BABALON (176, with L balanced) = 441 = 21^2, the operational number of a Magus, affirming this identity. See *Liber B vel Magi* for more on this.

♐ **I, the Arrow/Lingam/Column**, is Sagittarius, the projectile of the Archer (Cupid/Mercury).

♅♇ **J, the Horn of Plenty**, the Hook, the Scythe is that which sows and reaps all and corresponds to the Primum Mobile and to Pluto (one of the Fathers Lost).

♍ **K, the Virgin**, is Virgo the Virgin wading in Water (the element ruling over this house).

♎ **L, the Foot/Balance**, is Libra the scales over which Venus presides.

▽ **M, the wave or valley**, is Water - its Element form.

♏ **N, the Gate**, is Scorpio, another house over which Water presides.

☽ **O, the Moon**, is Luna in both her phases.

♂ **P, the Mother,** the symbol of War and of Priesthood, denotes Mars. She is Gaia or Earth, storm-laden and burdened,[75] the expectant goddesss who stands guard and carries with Her the Treasure and the motive of War.

♌ **Q, the Lion**, is Leo, which is constituted by Fire, and whose symbol has the shape of the spermatazoon.

♈ **R, the Emperor**, the exhausted Phallus, is Aries, the Ram, that Animal noble and fierce in the lofty heights, but docile like the Lamb once fettered. It's motto is Vita and may also denote nascent Life.[76]

75 See letter Y that shares in this attribution in one of its phases. She is our Mother who hath Borne Us and given Us of her Body for nourishment.

76 ITs key in the ROTA is The Emperor, which portrays the Principle of Government

♓ **S, the Serpent or the Son**, is Pisces, a fish that walks on the Water.

♑ **T, the Altar or Table**, is Capricorn the Goat, the first of sacrificial animals: the first altars being the mountain tops where these lofty creatures enjoy grazing.

♄ **U, the Cup** is Saturn as the Great Sea *Binah*.

♉ **V, the Horns of Power**, is Taurus, which cavorts in the Earth and is ruled by Venus. He is the Bull who comes at Spring and ploughs the Earth and Redeems it.

△ **W, is Fire**, which is Light that gives Sight and Heat which gives Life. It is the cause of all expansive force in the Universe and the principle property of all Suns.

♄ **X, the Cross and Wheel** is Saturn as Time on the Path.

⊗,∇ **Y, the Tree of the World**, is *Malkah* the Elemental Earth in her redeemed and abased forms, and Gaia or Earth, our Mother who hath Borne Us and given Us of her Body for nourishment. She is Life and the Symbol of Life and conceals in her Body the perfection and all the Fruits of the Tree of Life.

♃ **Z, the Lightning Flash**, is Jupiter's lightning bolt and the destructive onrush of fire that breaks down the Doors to the Palaces within the Spheres.

---

in action and properly describes the cycle of the phallus or the brute male force. Note the cross in its lower parts formed by the Emperor legs, implying the impotence of material authority (See Tf = 89 in the new Aeon and the transition of Tzaddi and the Black Brothers which this Card conceals in its Lower Parts: the T of the Emperor's crossed legs) and the coming of Chaos, for this Emperor is the one seated within the Tower of the ROTA key of Mars.

Liber Trigrammaton

(English Alphabet Attributions)

(Class B Document)

Here is Nothing under its three forms. It is not, yet informeth all things.

E - The Triple Light, the Triple Flame, J- The Hook, The Horn of Plenty

Now cometh the glory of the Single One, as an imperfection and stain.

f– Breath

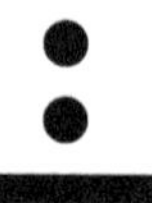

But by the Weak One the Mother was it equilibrated.

Soft C, P – The Mother

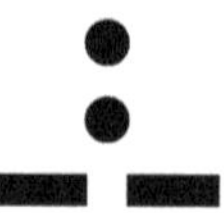

Also the purity was divided by Strength, the force of the Demiurge.

I – The Projectile

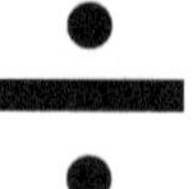

And the Cross was formulated in the Universe that as yet was not.

A – The Five Fold Star

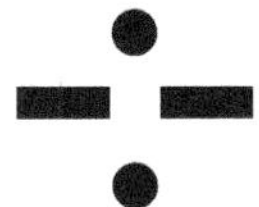

But now the Imperfection became manifest, presiding over the fading of perfection.

Z, Nf - The Lightning Flash

Also the Woman arose, and veiled the Upper Heaven with her body of stars.

B – The Book[2] , Y consonant

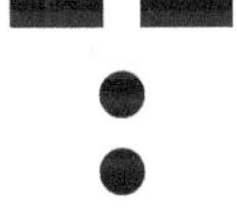

Now then a giant arose, of terrible strength; and asserted the Spirit in a secret rite.

H – The Fortress

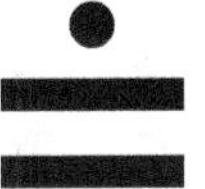

And the Master of the Temple balancing all things arose; his stature was above the Heaven and below Earth and Hell.

D – The Bow[3]

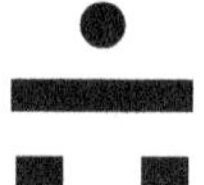

Against him the Brothers of the Left-hand Path, confusing the symbols. They concealed their horror [in this symbol];

x - The Cross

for in truth they were

R - The Phallus exhausted

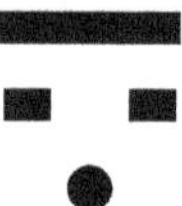

The master flamed forth as a star and set a guard of Water in every Abyss.

Q – The Lion, F – An Axe

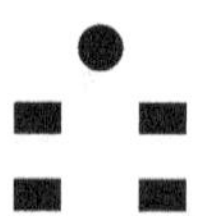

Also certain secret ones concealed the Light of Purity in themselves, protecting it from the Persecutions.

G – Union

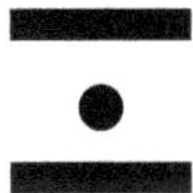

Likewise also did certain sons and daughters of Hermes and of Aphrodite, more openly

K (hard C) – The Virgin

But the Enemy confused them. They pretended to conceal that Light, that they might betray it, and profane it.

S – The Serpent

Yet certain holy nuns concealed the secret in songs upon the lyre.

M – The Wave, The Valley

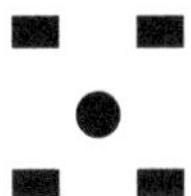

Now did the Horror of Time pervert all things, hiding the Purity with a loathsome thing, a thing unnameable.

Sf – The Son

Yea, and there arose sensualists upon the firmament, as a foul stain of storm upon the sky.

L averse[4]

And the Black Brothers raised their heads; yea, they unveiled themselves without shame or fear.

w – Vision[5]

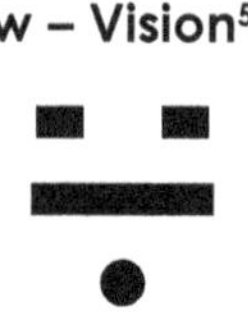

Also there rose up a soul of filth and of weakness, and it corrupted all the rule of the Tao.

T-final (The Altar)[6]

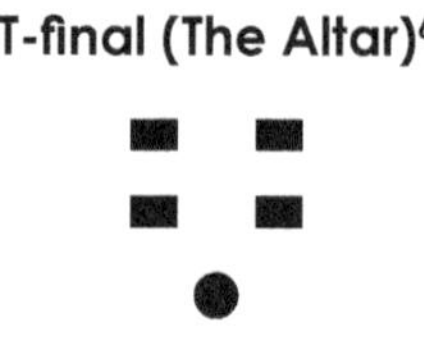

Then only was Heaven established to bear sway; for only in the lowest corruption is form manifest.

L upright – Balance – A Foot

Also did Heaven manifest in violent light,

N – The Gate, Y (vowel)

And in soft light.

O – The Moon

Then were the waters gathered together from the heaven,

V – The Horns of Power[7]

And a crust of earth concealed the core of flame.

T – The Table

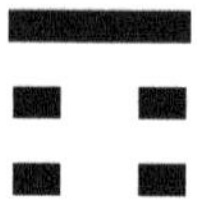

Around the globe gathered the wide air,

U – The Cup

And men began to light fires upon the earth.

W – The Eyes (Spirit)

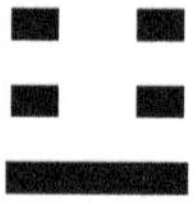

Therefore was the end of it sorrow; yet in that sorrow a sixfold star of glory whereby they might see to return unto the stainless Abode; yea, unto the Stainless Abode.

X – The Wheel[8]

Notes

1 The manner of manifestation.
2 The Book is Knowledge, the Fanning (unfolding) of the Pages are the breasts of Our Lady concealed in the shape of the letter.
3 That which propels the Arrow across the Abyss.
4 L for Foot denotes Balance.
5 The eyes in lower case denoting blindness.
6 Actually the "Wrong Kind of Silence" - an external silence or passivity which creates internal noise. It is the internal silence that is sought. The perfect whirling of the wheel or working of the machine produces no noise.
7 The shape suggests rain, funnelling or draining of water.
8 W and X switch positions as per the chapter discussing the Discovery of the Key, via ST : w=60=samech (S), W = 400 = Tau (T); while X=300=Shin (S) and x=9=teth (T).

The Trees

WE NOW apply the English Key in its Static form to the Tree of Life and similar constructions and see what revelations it yields. This is done for two reasons: (1) Despite being an anachronistic construction as has been said[1], we can appeal to it as a test of the integrity of our Key and the System we are developing. Science is developed on the discoveries of the past. Just as quantum mechanics contains and explains Newtonian mechanics, whose laws are a particular case of quantum mechanics when applied to large system dynamics, so New Truth and Law must explain and comprise the Old. The universal truths are never destroyed, only further elucidated. (2) We shall in this way, be able to construct from it later a syncretic system of concordances on the edifice of the science and Knowledge of the Past.

1 It is a system better replaced with that of the Aethyrs. For one thing, the Tree of Life is geocentric and ill-ordered. The Tree of Life has as a basis the sephiroth or spheres of influence which the planets in the solar system are material manifestations of. The planet Earth is the 10th sphere. Now if the implication is that one moves in direction towards the sun, the nearest or first object we encounter on our trajectory is the moon. We label it 9th sphere. The next object is Venus not Mercury—an astronomical error dating 2000 years. [However, we know Mercury to be associated experientially with 8 and Venus with 7 so that some other order (one of influence or passage) is here implied.] After Mercury, is the Sun, or the 6th. Passing the Sun, one expects to encounter Mars, Jupiter, Saturn and Neptune in that order, respectively the 5th, 4th, 3rd and 2nd spheres. At the head of it all is the Crown, or the Divine Effulgence, the 1st sphere.

THE TREES are formed by branches or paths, nodes or sephiroth, columns and planes. The tree has 32 paths in total; 10 spheres or objective paths (sephiroth)[2] and 22 subjective rays linking the spheres. The 22 paths correspond traditionally to the 22 glyphs of the Hebrew script and the 22 cards of the ROTA major arcana, while the spheres or sephiroth correspond to the cosmic bodies in the solar system.

Before we proceed in constructing our Tree on the model of the Past, we correct some of the deficiencies in the old Aeon Tree of Life. The Student will note that the Sephiras in the original construction of the Tree of Life do not have letters associated to them; only the Paths do. The new Aeon has given us the compound glyphs. And as these are generated by 'H', we place it at the Crown which is *Kether*; its astrological concordance is switched back to the old Aeon, seeing as the Tree of Life is rooted in the soil of the Aeon past.[3]

We would expect the assignment of the remaining Letters into the Tree via their astro-cosmological attributions to yield symmetries and properties concordant to new Aeon revelations we have so far. We verify the obvious first: We test the names against those constructions they represent, Understanding that Perfection and so Truth are not to be found here if even these first casual tests Fail.

---

2 There is an 11th sphere that is not a sphere about which much has been said. This sphere has been called Daath by the Hebrew brethren and termed "Knowledge". It is said to denote the Abyss by some or the portal into the averse Tree by others.

3 It is important to note that the Tree of Life has taken very many different forms or constructions over the Past and the development of History. The established form in use today was proposed in the 17th century alone. Still there remains some argument and contention over the attribution of the paths today.

We note for instance that:

(1) The Sum of the Sephiras, that is the Letters of all three Pillars when summed, are equal to the gematria for "Tree of Life";
(2) Gematria for 'Middle Pillar' is equivalent to the sum of the Sephiras in the Middle Pillar;
(3) Both Left- and Right-hand paths are equivalent to 111, and when summed are equivalent to a phase of the Middle Pillar, etc.

A short demonstration follows. We develop the tables of correspondence fully in a subsequent section.

We include a second Tree, occult in its Nature, rooted as it is in New Aeon soil, to further test the integrity of our system. In this Tree we associate the letters via their astro-cosmological attributions directly. It is upon this Tree that we will develop our system of concordances.

Note that each sephira contains in itself, the formulae for its transcendence, usually its opposite or stabilizing factor. Hence *Binah* or the 3rd sphere which is assigned to Saturn or old Man Time, the first of the Fathers, is attributed the most exalted of the feminine glyphs: U, the CUP and C, the SKY. Likewise, the 'male' sephira possess female formulae and vice-versa. The formulae denote the means of transcending the sphere—that is overcoming its limiting gravity. Thus Ch counters Mars, Ph counters Mercury, Wh is the result and issue of Venus, and to possess them is to pass through unhindered. These are the passwords. Similarly, in the sphere of Sol we see the action of Pisces (S), in Luna that of Capricorn (T) and so on.

Notes

C's hard, O's full, F's active.

Demonstration

(1) The Sum of the Sephiras, that is the Letters of all three Pillars when summed, are equal to the gematria for "Tree of Life" which is equivalent to the Middle Path:

(Left Pillar = 77) + (Right Pillar = 93) + (Middle Pillar = 204) = 384 = 'Tree of Life' = 109 + 210 + 65 = OIX (middle Path) = 80 + 4 + 300

(2) Gematria for 'Middle Pillar' is equivalent to the sum of the Sephiras in the Middle Pillar:

"*Middle Pillar*" = (40 + 4 + 8 + 8 + 50 + 1) + (3 + 4 + 50 + 50 + 4 + 9) = 231 = H + Sh + Th + Y (the middle pillar)

(3) Both Left- and Right-hand paths are equivalent to 111, and when summed are equivalent to a phase of the Middle Pillar.

Left Path = B + J + M + W = 6 + 5 + 40 + 60 =111
Right Path = E + V + Z + S = 1 + 80 + 6 + 24 = 111
Middle Pillar = H + Sh + Th + Y = 7 + 49 + 96 + 70 = 222

(4) The Letters of the middle path combined with the letters of either the right-hand or left-hand path and summed are equal to a phase of the middle pillar:

H + Sh + Th + Y = 7 + 31 + 96 + 70 = 204 = 93 + 111, i.e. the middle path plus either the left or right pillar

Etc.

Observations

PATHS

Left Path : B + J + M + W = 6 + 5 + 40 + 60 =111
Right Path : E + V + Z + S = 1 + 80 + 6 + 24 = 111
Middle Path : O + I + X = 93 / 213 / 384

PILLARS

Left Pillar : C + Ch + Ph = 30 + 37 + 10 = 77
Right Pillar : F +Rh + Wh = 10 + 16 + 67 = 93
Middle Pillar:

- T final: H + Sh + Th + Y = 7 + 31 + 96 + 70 = 204 (= 93 + 111, i.e. the middle path plus either the left or right pillar)
- S final: H + Sh + Th + Y = 7 + 49 + 105 + 70 = 231 = "Middle Pillar" = (Note: In this case, the sum of all sephiras are 231 + 77 + 93 = 401 when F is active and C is hard, and S final)
- S & T final: H + Sh + Th + Y = 7 + 49 + 96 + 70 = 222 = 111 + 111, i.e. the sum of both left and right paths.

The TREE of LIFE

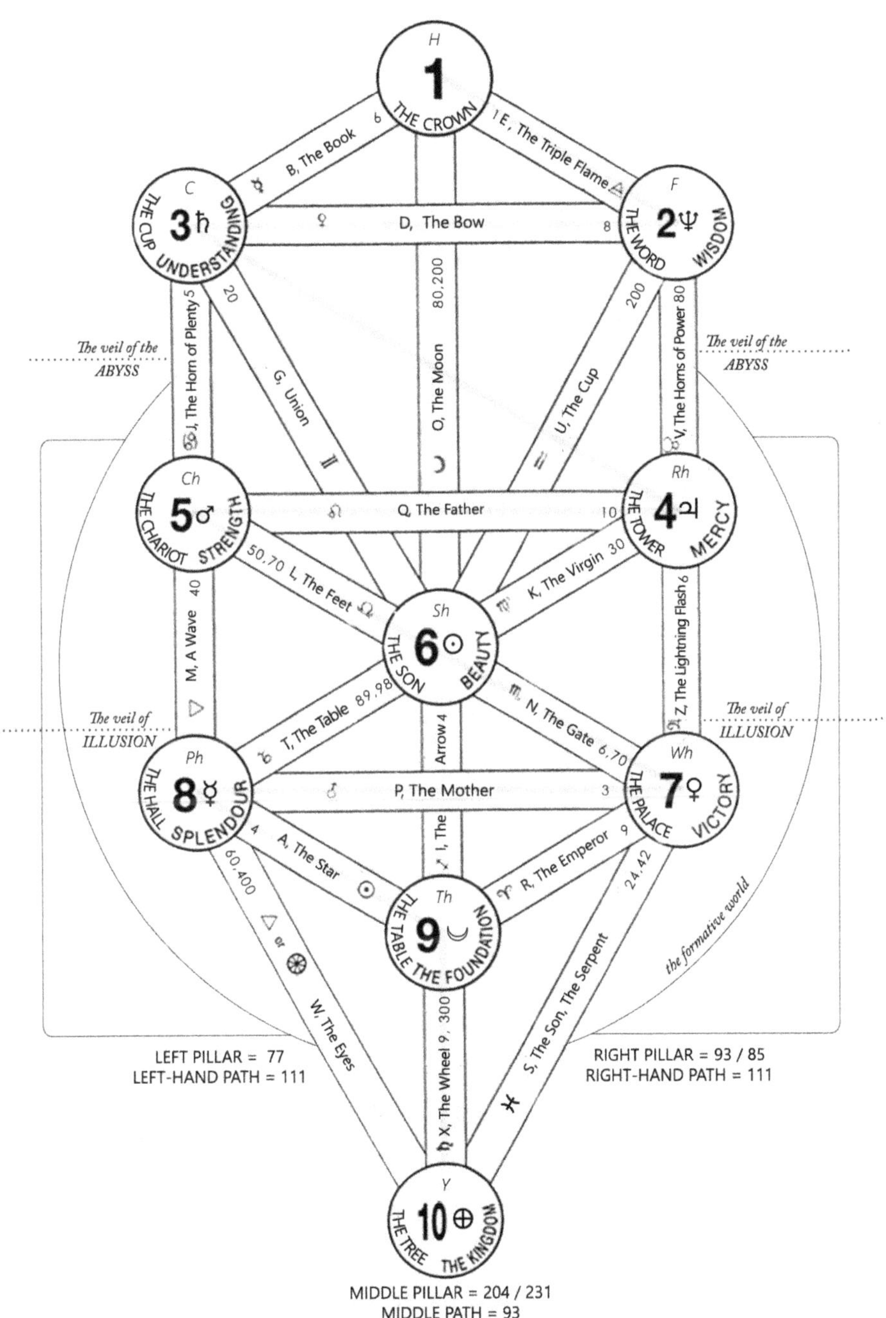
H
1
THE CROWN
6
B, The Book
1 E, The Triple Flame
C
3
THE CUP
UNDERSTANDING
D, The Bow
8
F
2
THE WORD
WISDOM
80,200
20
200
J, The Horn of Plenty 5
V, The Horns of Power 80
The veil of the ABYSS
The veil of the ABYSS
G, Union
O, The Moon
U, The Cup
Ch
5
THE CHARIOT
STRENGTH
Q, The Father
10
Rh
4
THE TOWER
MERCY
50,70
L, The Feet
K, The Virgin 30
40
M, A Wave
Sh
6
THE SON
BEAUTY
Z, The Lightning Flash 6
T, The Table 89,98
N, The Gate 6,70
Arrow 4
The veil of ILLUSION
The veil of ILLUSION
Ph
8
THE HALL
SPLENDOUR
P, The Mother
3
Wh
7
THE PALACE
VICTORY
4
A, The Star
I, The
R, The Emperor
9
60,400
24,42
Th
9
THE TABLE
THE FOUNDATION
the formative world
W, The Eyes
X, The Wheel 9, 300
S, The Son, The Serpent
LEFT PILLAR = 77
LEFT-HAND PATH = 111
RIGHT PILLAR = 93 / 85
RIGHT-HAND PATH = 111
Y
10
THE TREE
THE KINGDOM
MIDDLE PILLAR = 204 / 231
MIDDLE PATH = 93

Notes:

C's & O's soft.

Demonstration

(1) The Sum of the Sephiras, that is the Letters of all three Pillars when summed, are equal to the gematria for "The World Tree"

(Left Pillar = 220) + (Right Pillar = 93) + (Middle Pillar = 220) = 533 = 'The World Tree'

(2) The World Tree conceals / contains the Tree of Life: Sum of the Sephiras,

Middle Path = O + I + X = 93 / 213 / 384 = 'Tree of Life'

(3) The Middle Pillar phases alternate between Victory and establishment of the Law:

Middle Pillar = J + Sh + Th + Y = 5 + 49 + 96 + 6 = 156
Middle Pillar = J + Sh + Th + Y = 5 + 49 + 96 + 70 = 220

(3) The Law is fulfilled in all cases:

Sh (The Son Enthroned) is replaced by ST (The Son on the Cross) when Y = 6: J + STf + Tfh + Y = 5 + 24 + 89 + 96 + 6 = 220;

(4) The Lightning Flash through the Supernals avows the same:

THE LIGHTNING FLASH through the supernals : J = 1, E = 1, F = 10, D = 8, U = 200 = 220

Observations

SEPHIRA

Left Pillar = U + Ch + Ph = 200 + 10 + 10 = 220
Right Pillar = F + Rh + Wh = 10 + 16 + 67 = 93
(Y - The Tree is 6 on the left; 70 on the right:)
Middle Pillar = J + Sh + Th + Y = 5 + 49 + 96 + 6 = 156
Middle Pillar = J + Sh + Th + Y = 5 + 49 + 96 + 70 = 220

PATHS

Left Path = B + H + M + W = 6 + 7 + 40 + 60 =113
Right Path = E + V + Z + S = 1 + 80 + 6 + 24 = 111
Middle Path = O + I + X = 93 / 213 / 384 = 'Tree of Life'

PLANES

1st plane : H + G + O + C + V = 7 + 20 + 200 + 3 + 80 = 31 X 10
2nd plane : M + L + G + O + C + K + Z = 40 + 50 + 20 + 80 + 3 + 30 + 6 = 229
3rd plane : M + T + I + N + Z = 40 + 98 + 4 + 70 + 6 = 228
4th plane : W + A + I + R + S = 400 + 4 + 4 + 9 + 24 = 441 = 21 x 21
5th plane
w + x + S = 60 + 9 + 24 = 93
w + x + Sf = 111
w + X + S = 60 + 300 + 24 = 384 = 'tree of life' = OIX (middle path)

Note :
Planetary Glyphs, pentagrams, and hexagrams and elementary triangles can be derived from the Tree of Life.

The WORLD TREE

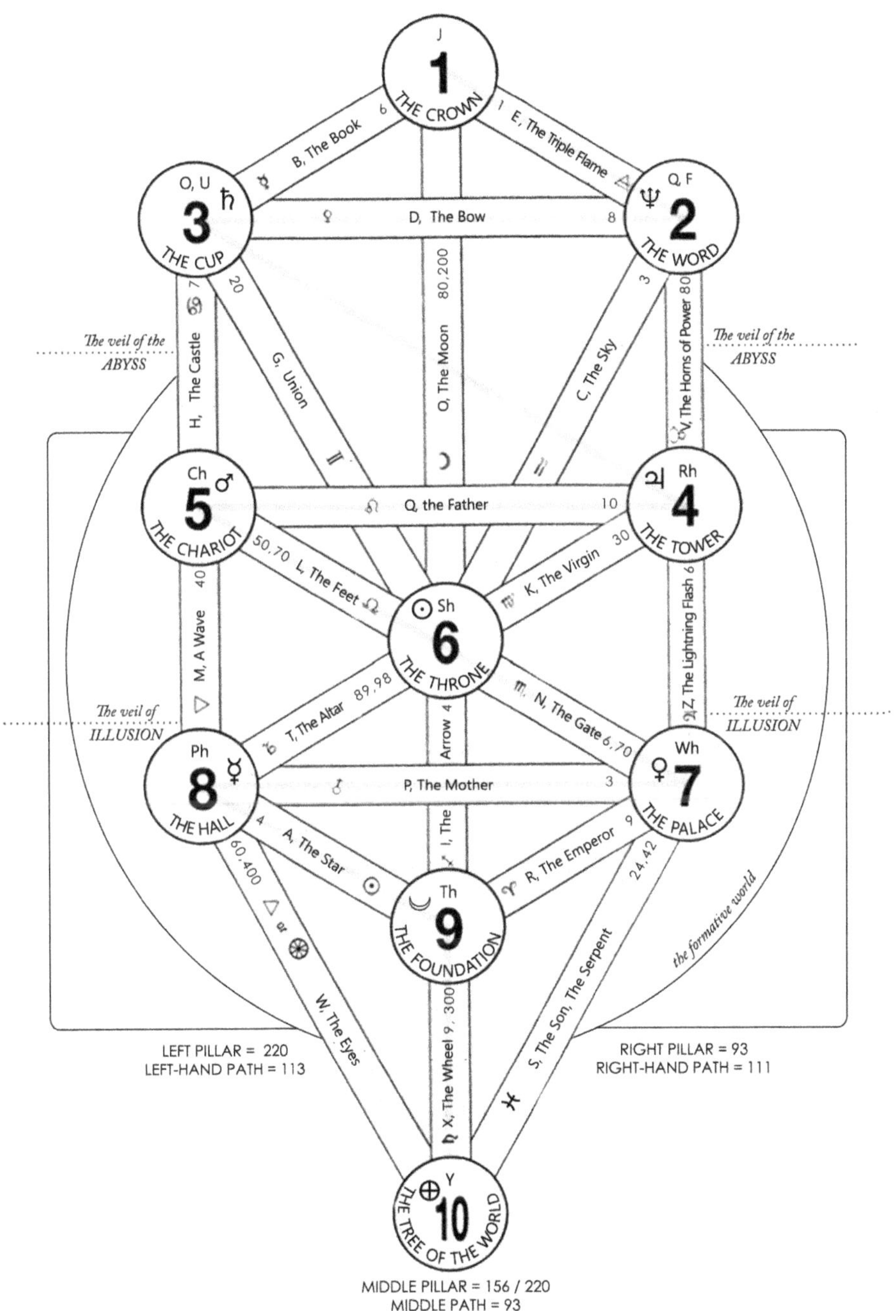
1
THE CROWN
J
2
THE WORD
Q, F
3
THE CUP
O, U
4
THE TOWER
Rh
5
THE CHARIOT
Ch
6
THE THRONE
Sh
7
THE PALACE
Wh
8
THE HALL
Ph
9
THE FOUNDATION
Th
10
THE TREE OF THE WORLD
Y
B, The Book
E, The Triple Flame
D, The Bow
O, The Moon 80,200
G, Union
C, The Sky
H, The Castle
V, The Horns of Power 80
Q, the Father
L, The Feet
K, The Virgin
M, A Wave
Z, The Lightning Flash
T, The Altar 89,98
N, The Gate 6,70
Arrow 4
P, The Mother
I, The
A, The Star
R, The Emperor
W, The Eyes
X, The Wheel 9, 300
S, The Son, The Serpent
The veil of the ABYSS
The veil of the ABYSS
The veil of ILLUSION
The veil of ILLUSION
the formative world
LEFT PILLAR = 220
LEFT-HAND PATH = 113
RIGHT PILLAR = 93
RIGHT-HAND PATH = 111
MIDDLE PILLAR = 156 / 220
MIDDLE PATH = 93

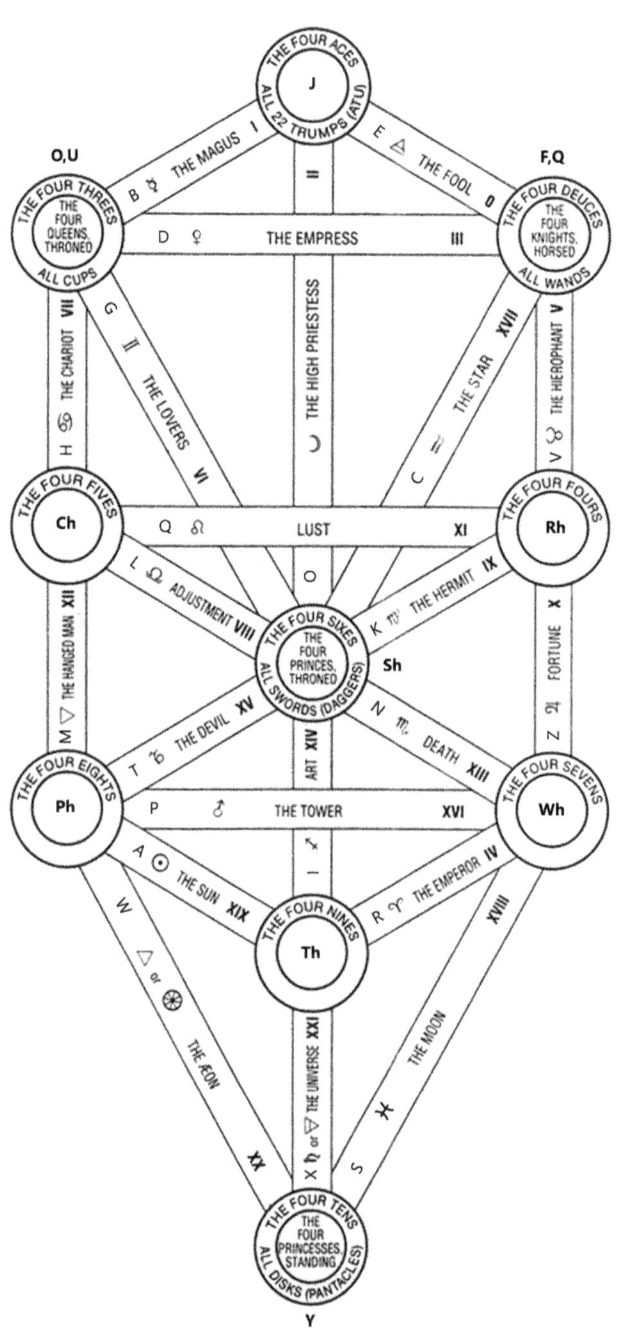
THE FOUR ACES
J
ALL 22 TRUMPS (ATU)
O,U
THE FOUR THREES
THE FOUR QUEENS, THRONED
ALL CUPS
F,Q
THE FOUR DEUCES
THE FOUR KNIGHTS, HORSED
ALL WANDS
B ☿ THE MAGUS I
E 🜁 THE FOOL 0
II
D ♀ THE EMPRESS III
THE HIGH PRIESTESS ☽
H ♋ THE CHARIOT VII
G ♊ THE LOVERS VI
C ♒ THE STAR XVII
V ♉ THE HIEROPHANT V
THE FOUR FIVES
Ch
THE FOUR FOURS
Rh
Q ♌ LUST XI
O
L ♎ ADJUSTMENT VIII
K ♍ THE HERMIT IX
THE FOUR SIXES
THE FOUR PRINCES, THRONED
ALL SWORDS (DAGGERS)
Sh
M 🜄 THE HANGED MAN XII
Z ♃ FORTUNE X
T ♑ THE DEVIL XV
N ♏ DEATH XIII
ART XIV
THE FOUR EIGHTS
Ph
THE FOUR SEVENS
Wh
P ♂ THE TOWER XVI
I ♐
A ☉ THE SUN XIX
R ♈ THE EMPEROR IV
THE FOUR NINES
Th
W 🜂 or ☸ THE ÆON XX
XVIII
THE MOON ♓ S
X ♄ or 🜃 THE UNIVERSE XXI
THE FOUR TENS
THE FOUR PRINCESSES, STANDING
ALL DISKS (PANTACLES)
Y

The Numbers

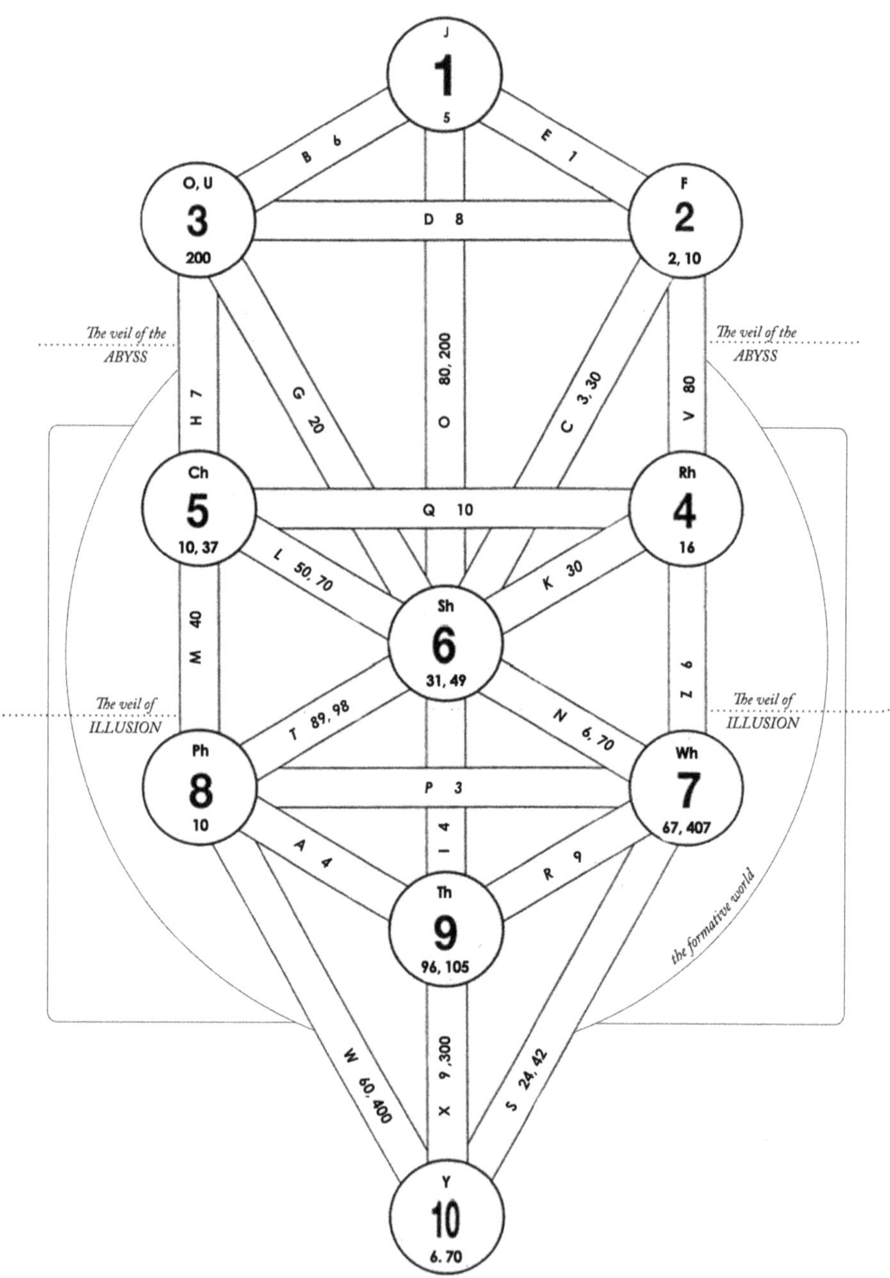

J
1
5
O, U
3
200
F
2
2, 10
B 6
E 1
D 8
The veil of the
ABYSS
The veil of the
ABYSS
H 7
G 20
O 80, 200
C 3, 30
V 80
Ch
5
10, 37
Rh
4
16
Q 10
L 50, 70
K 30
Sh
6
31, 49
M 40
Z 6
The veil of
ILLUSION
The veil of
ILLUSION
T 89, 98
N 6, 70
Ph
8
10
Wh
7
67, 407
P 3
I 4
A 4
R 9
Th
9
96, 105
the formative world
W 60, 400
X 9, 300
S 24, 42
Y
10
6. 70

What is a Number?

THERE exists a philosophy of mathematics and a Science on the theory of Numbers that has discussed this question and de-constructed our notions of Number, and lain bare the deficiencies of our Understanding on this matter better than we can hope to do so here. We remind the Student however, that in mathematics itself, even a thing so simple as Number is defined according to its scope and needs. Thus in Geometry, a number represents a Length or a Ratio or a Quantity. In Arithmetic, it is always an identity; in Calculus, the limit of a function. In mathematical and philosophic theory, every number is infinite in itself and contains within it the possibility for engendering all other Identities by combining with other Numbers. Even the transcendental numbers which cannot be expressed finitely, can be written down as the operation between two numbers to some degree.[1] Thus Π, though incomprehensible as a string of numbers, is simply the circumference of the Circle divided by its diameter and expressible as a simple ratio of two quantities. Though the result is mathematically a fiction, we allow it into our calculations, for we witness Circles in Nature and know this

1 This is not the case with irrational numbers such as $\sqrt{2}$.

ratio to exist in Reality, though it does not in our current Field of integral Number.[2]

For our purposes, we are not so much concerned with Number as we are with the subset of positive integers and their prime factorizations. There are a number of reasons for this:

1. First, *all Number (except the irrational numbers) can be expressed as the operation of one integer upon another;* and
2. *Every integer can be expressed as a finite product of primes.*[3]

---

2 There are an infinite number of transcendental numbers like pi. We know of only very few however. The discovery of these numbers correspond to the revolution of the Aeons and are the single most important discoveries of our entire History. Without pi, the physical world as we have shaped with architectural structures and machinery would not be possible. Physics and the sciences as they relate to change on the field of time would not be possible without e or the exponential number; and modern electronics and physics would not be possible without the discovery of i. There are an infinite variety of such transcendental numbers, though it remains today extremely difficult to prove that a number is transcendental.

3 The proof is elementary: A number is either (a) prime or (b) composite.

(a) If it is prime, it's only factors are itself and 1, both prime, and so *QED.*

(b) If it is not prime, then it is composite. We argue by contrapositive:

If not all numbers can be expressed as a finite product of primes then there exists a non-empty set S of all such numbers. We define:

Let S be the set of all number not expressible as a finite product of primes.

Furthermore, because the set S is non-empty, there exists at least one m such that m is an element of S. And of all the elements we can select the smallest element of S. (If S consists of one element only, we take this element as *m*). We define:

Let m be the least element in the set of S.

Now because m belongs to S, so it cannot be prime, otherwise it would be expressible as a product of 1 and itself, both primes. So m is composite. That is $m = q \times r$, for some *q, r*. Now because, *q* and *r* divide *m*, they are both less than m $(q, r < m)$. Because *q* and *r* are smaller than *m*, they cannot be in the set S, seeing as m is the *least* element (the smallest element) in S and there are no smaller numbers in it. Thus, *q* and *r* are both expressible as a finite product of primes, and $r = r_1 \times r_2 \times \ldots \times r_n$ and $q = q_1 \times q_2 \times \ldots \times q_s$ with *pi* and *qi* all prime, so that $m = q \times r = r_1 \times r_2 \times \ldots \times r_n \times q_1 \times q_2 \times \ldots \times q_s$ all prime so that m itself is a finite product of primes, which contradicts our

We note that, regardless of what number is or how we may define it, we represent these identities through a series of glyphs, and that every integer is in itself a Glyph. The set of glyphs is in fact the Arabic Numerals which we use here in the West, namely the set {0, 1, 2,..., 9}, consisting of 10 elements including the null element (0). Each of these elements is a glyph in itself, an irreducible identity which all other Integers are a composites of, both as mathematical expressions of quantities and as glyphs. Thus, though one-hundred twenty-three is a number in itself, as a glyph, we represent it as composite of three glyphs in precise sequence 1-2-3 or 123. This set of 10 glyphs {0, 1, . . . , 9} spans the integer space, is the basis for the modern decimal system and constitutes the Spheres of Manifestation in increasing degrees as exhibited in the *sephiroth* of the Tree of Life.

Before discussing the properties and definitions for the glyph set, we examine first its operation and modes of use.

---

defintion of *m*. Hence *m* cannot exist and the set S of all integers not expressible as a finite product of primes is empty. *QED*.

This argument actually consititues the Euclidean proof for the prime factorization of integers. In fact, all modern cryptography and IT encryption algorithms depend upon this simple result.

The Decimal System

THE ARABIC numeral set and the decimal numerical system are the accepted standards on the planet today by which one can affirm quantity or classify a given identity. It is called the *decimal* system because it consists of ten elements (0 to 9) arranged in increasing powers of 10^n, $n \in I$ from left to right. Thus 3213.56 is no more than $3 \times 10^3 + 2 \times 10^2 + 1 \times 10^1 + 3 \times 10^0 + 5 \times 10^{-1} + 6 \times 10^{-2}$. However, the decimal system was not the first of the numerical systems employed nor by any means the more practical or best-suited. There is some belief that the decimal systems arises from the fact that human beings have ten fingers. History presents evidence that suggests the decimal system was introduced as a very deliberate and enforced standard that did not arise naturally and gain preponderance throughout the world through the process of natural selection as some historians have argued.

The first numerical system is believed to be a binary one, composed therefore, of two elements. One element we shall call A for simplicity, which represents the unit, and the second element B representing the quantity 2. (These may have been scratches of different shapes on cave walls.) Thus, in this binary system the quantity of 7 would be represented by BBBA or three B's and one A—an additive system, unlike the modern binary system which consists of powers of base 2 and would represent 7 as 1001 ($1 \times 2^3 + 0 \times 2^2 + 0 \times 2^1 + 1 \times 2^0$). All quantities would be represented in a similar manner under such a system. This would do if one were keeping tracking of a small herd or counting tribe members. To represent any large quantity however would be impossible. Referring to our example, to write 3213 would require one thousand six hundred and six Bs written sequentially, followed by an A: The entire cave wall would be covered and it would take all season to scratch into the rock. As man evolved, his capacity and need for number and calculation increased. New systems were developed primarily using the fingers and toes as counting instruments. From the finger-and-toe counting came the quinine (5-base) and base-20 systems, remnants of which we still see today in many languages, as in the eighty of the French which is denoted as "four twenties" (*quatre-vingts*).

Among other notable systems was the 60-based system mostly used by the Mesopotamians around 1700 BC. The virtue of such systems such as the base-60 are that they are divisible by many more numbers. 60 is divisible by 2, 3, 4, 5, 6, 10, 12, 15, 20, and 30, whereas 10 is divisible only by 2 and 5. Therefore it is impossible to pay one third of a dollar and frequently for one third of any quantity. This becomes problematic if one is bartering or selling by pieces or weight. Hence the persistence of pricing by the dozen by bakers and other craftsmen and why Americans hold on to the imperial system[4]. Similarly, a quarter of an hour would have no meaning if clocks were on a decimal system. If you are trying to calculate fractional components of the sky for instance (astronomy) or on the clock or calendar, you will get reducible fractions and simple expressions. This means

4 The metric system is a decimal system: 10 millimeters makes a centimeter, 100 centimeters makes a meter, 1000 meters makes a kilometer. The imperial system is a hodge-podge of 12-base system and a 60 base system: 12 inches make a foot, 36 feet make a yard, 1760 yards make a mile. A quarter of an inch or a foot or a mile are whole integers, while a quarter of anything in the decimal system is necessarily a fractional quantity. Hence your baker would have to break bread to close the deal.

that in a base-60 system arithmetic problems worked out in even numbers much more than they would in a decimal system.

Meanwhile, in other parts of the world developments were being made parallel to those mentioned above. But it was the Hindus of India infamous for their contribution of the 0 or null element into the set of integers as well as their negative counterparts, who were elaborating upon the world's first decimal system. This system had not been accepted readily due to the inconveniences mentioned, but somehow the Greeks came into contact with it. Pythagoras[5] in the 6th century B.C. knew of it and it was partially due to his influence that the Greeks took on the decimal system as its state standard. It was not long after, through their contact with merchants and suppliers who were forced to adopt their system of counting, as well as the influence of their reputed culture, that the decimal system began to spread.

The *Tetractys*

FOLLOWING the example of the Pythagoreans, we begin by considering the universe to be "nothingness", devoid of all but space, a great egg, a 0. We take a point in this universe, and this is our number 1, the unity. (A point is defined mathematically as having no magnitude, only position.)

5 Anecdotally, Pythagoras was known as the "father of numbers" in his day, and is quoted as stating that "number is the ruler of form and idea and the cause of gods and demons." He lectured his students from behind a veil and forbade everyone he knew from eating beans. They used the symbol of the pentagram (five-pointed star) to denote their order, to recognize themselves, and gain public recognition. The Pythagoreans were all vegetarians and did not believe in personal possessions. They would help a man raise his burden onto his back, but would not help him lay it down. Pythagoreans were okay to handle black cocks, but never a white cock. Despite all this, Pythagorean mathematics had a definite mystical component.

From this universe we then extract a second point. By virtue of the relationship between their respective positions of the two points, we now have a line, and what we denote by the idea "2".[6]

We then take a third point outside this line and by virtue of the relationship in position between our third point and the infinite amount of points on the line (2), a plane is formed. (A plane can be defined as an infinite number of lines with proportional linear coefficients, and as a line is no more than an infinite number of points, it follows that a plane is an infinite number of points spread along a flat surface—the two-dimensional). This is the Pythagorean 3.

Taking a fourth point above this plane, and again taking this relation between the respective positions of this fourth point and all the other points in the flat surface beneath it—and a solid is formed, that is, 3-dimensional space is spanned. And it is in three dimensions that we perceive our material reality. Thus the Pythagorean 4, and it is the symbol of the physical world to the Pythagoreans for this very reason. So we have the futher division of the material plane into four elements, four seasons, four cardinal points, etc.[7]

In summary, we have:

> **One point:** the field, generator of dimensions.
>
> **Two points**: generator of a line of dimension one
>
> **Three points**: generator of a triangle of dimension two
>
> **Four points**: generator of a tetrahedron, of dimension three.

6 Mathematicians never shy of transcending logic through contradiction to remind us that a line is no more than an infinite number of points who themselves have no magnitude but when combined do. However, this is a subtlety that Pythagoreans did not pick up on at the time.

7 For elements we have fire, air, earth, water—see section on tables for their attributions and the concordance between these different sets.

A central belief of the Pythagoreans was that one could come to know Divinity through an understanding of numbers and geometry.

Taking the number of 4 as representative of physical existence, they pondered on how man should reach the Unity, the source, the Indivisible Creator, the Perfect. Drawing four points on a line, and then 3 above it, and 2 above it, filtering finally to one, forming a triangle they called the *tetractys*:

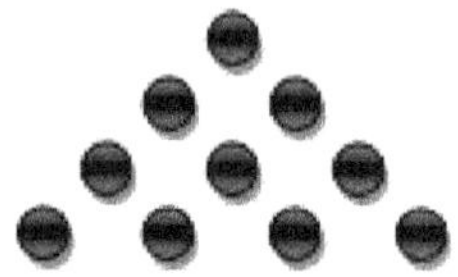

Figure 3 - The Tetractys

Notice that no matter which direction we approach the *tetractys* from, the four dots (the elemental or physical) are encountered first and filtered successively to the Unity. By casting off one dot at a time, the coarser becomes the finer until the source is reached. The solid collapses into the plane, the plane onto the line, and the line onto its point of origin.

The Pythagoreans took this as the symbol of what they saw as the human aspiration: the ascension from the physical to the heavenly unity. Counting the total number of points, we have 4 + 3 + 2 + 1 = 10, and so the Pythagoreans took the decimal system over all others as the system most in harmony with their purpose and humanity's goals. One would think, that having ten fingers, for this reason alone man would have favoured the decimal system. But the decimal does not divide neatly into thirds or fourths, making commercial exchange difficult and simple division cumbersome; and the historical evidence suggests that out of this mystical consideration alone, was the decimal system adopted by the ruling classes and scholars. It subsequently found its way into Greek culture in general and in particular as a numerical standard in Athens. It was here, at the time and place of the birth of Western Civilization that through its influence as a commercial and intellectual centre and the point of gathering for merchants and scholars the world over, that the decimal system came to spread to the rest of the Western World.

Note how the Tetractys contains the Tree of Life in its basic construction, with its sephiroth organized along planes.

Numeral	Mystical Interpretation	Derivation
0	Nuit, the Yoni, the Egg, the receptacle, the all-absorbing, no reflection.	
1	Hadit, reproducing after itself, the all-reflecting.	From 0 by extension
2	Hadit aware of itself through reflection, thought, sound, reverberation.	From 1 by reflection 1/1 (or by revolution of the line around its end)
3	Hadit within and a part of Nuit, aware of itself, all-relation.	From 1 and 2 by addition
4	Hadit manifest (and profane), aware of itself as independent to all relation.	From 2 by multiplication.
5	Hadit aware and active upon the field of relation.	From 2 and 3 by addition.
6	Hadit in perfect relation, passive and balanced.	From 2 and 3 by multiplication.
7	Hadit unites through a particular relation. Union.	From 2 and 3 by multiplication.
8	Hadit perceives itself materially in this relation.	From 3 and 4 by addition, also $8 = 2^3$.
9	Hadit wills this relation.	From 2 and 3 by multiplication, also $9 = 3^2$.
10	Hadit (1) separate from Nuit (0) for the possibility of Union.	From 1 + 2 + 3 + 4.

Interpretation of the Arabic Numeral Glyphs

0. The Egg of the Universe, The Yoni.
1. The Light, The Arrow, The Lingam.
2. The Light concealing itself. The light hits and illumines an Object)
3. A Circle that will not be (open at the centre hinge), the below reflecting the above (two half circles: the self-reflection of the 2.)
4. The Bow and Arrow.
5. A ploughshare, The lowered horns, The image of the 2 reflected: **25**
6. A taking into the circle from above.
7. A crutch, a walking stick, a support.
8. Two circles above and below informing each other.
9. A taking into the circle from below.

The glyph of 0, and the Idea it represents listed in this chapter under its various forms is seen to be the source and return of all things.

Other Interpretations

THESE interpretations arising as they do from the Old System are necessarily tainted by interpretations symptomatic of the Nihilism contained in the old Law and the religious viewpoint held in the past. As such we have the idea not of a Manifest Universe but of a Creation. Furthermore this degeneration is seen as progressive for as one moves away from the Unit, one moves away from Purity and the Godhead—so that the higher the number, or the more material the manifestation, the more corruptible it is seen to be.

Mystical:

0. The Infinite - the Circle - the Point.
1. The Unity - the Positive - the Finite - the Line. Supernal Being.
2. The Dyad - the Superfices. The Demiurge. Supernal Will.
3. The Triad, the Solid. Matter. Supernal Intelligence.
4. The Quaternary, Matter or the Solid manifest in Time
5. The Quinary, Force and Motion. The Supernal Will manifest into or acting upon Matter.
6. The Senary - Consciousness.
7. The Septenary - Desire.
8. The Ogdoad - Intellect.
9. The Ennead - Ego
10. The Decad - the Body.

Hermeneutical:

0. The Cosmic Egg.
1. The Self.
2. The God.
3. The Goddess.
4. The Father - Material Authority.
5. The Mother - Active Power.
6. The Son - harmonizing 1 throughout 5.
7. Emotion - The lower reflection of the Mother.
8. Reason - The lower reflection of the Father.
9. Animality - The lower Reflection of the Son.
10. Matter - The lower reflection of the Daughter.

Psychological:

0. Consciousness
1. Being, Id
2. The Self; that which perceives "I" apart from the "not I"
3. The Soul; Id, and the Super-ego.

4-9. The Intellectual Self and its functions:

 4. Memory.
 5. Will.
 6. Imagination.
 7. Desire.
 8. Reason.
 9. Animal being.

6. The Conscious Self. The illusory Ego.

9. The Unconscious Self, and his nervous, circulatory, digestive (and to an extent, his respiratory) systems.

10. The Body - containing 1 through 9 on the lower plane of the Elemental.

Mathematical:

0. Space
1. The point (position, but no extension); 0th dimension, $\mathbb{R}^0$
2. Two points and their connection, creates a line; 1st dimension, $\mathbb{R}^1$
3. A line and a point external to it providing a flat plane; 2nd dimension, $\mathbb{R}^2$
4. A point outside the plane, creating 3 dimensional space, $\mathbb{R}^3$
5. The finite three dimensional solid and a point of relation outside of it (Vectorials)
6. The Equation, The Formulae
7. Union or Addition
8. Geometry & Algebra
9. Derivative and Integral Calculus
10. All operations, operators and operands.

Integer Properties
(N=1 to 2000)

THE LEXICON appended to this work tabulates the integers along with their list of factors and properties if any. Among these properties we include:

1. Prime or composite (Prime numbers indicated; otherwise the integer is composite.)[1]
2. Whether the number be the termination of a series (e.g. $276 = \Sigma 23$)
3. Whether the integer is a perfect number or not.
4. A perfect square.
5. Any other special properties.

Prime Numbers

A PRIME number is a positive integer which has only two divisors: one and itself. There are an infinite number of primes as Euclid proved over 2000 years ago in his *Elements*. (We omit the proof and leave it to the interested reader; it is quite elegant.)

1 It is important to note, that any composite number is in fact a finite product of primes, and can be expressed as such. These considerations are valuable when investigating the nature of a particular number.

Prime numbers enjoy a special place in mathematics as the basic units from which all other numbers can be spanned through the field of multiplication. This means essentially that all integer numbers can be broken down into a list of primes that when multiplied together equal that integer. Furthermore this sequence of primes is unique to that number, a signature of sorts, a fingerprint or a DNA trace. Take for example, the number 222, this number (like any number) breaks down into a *unique* list of prime factors, namely: 37 × 3 × 2. Similarly, 345 is composite for 23 × 5 × 3 and 6 782 545 = 5 × 7 × 11 × 79 × 223.

This is called a *one-to-one* mapping: no two numbers can share the same multiplicative list of primes.[2]

We can see then that prime numbers constitute the building blocks for other numbers. However it would be an error to consider 222 simply as 37 the idea of *Kether* refracted into Tiphareth (human consciousness). 222 can also be expressed as 111 × 2 (the *Aleph* or Word into *Chokmah*) or 74 × 3 (the Ox-Goad pulling at *Binah*). In fact 222 is an "identity" in itself, and all these product expressions of it are its properties.

The first 100 prime numbers are listed here.

2 3 5 7 11 13 17 19 23 29 31 37 41 43 47 53 59 61 67 71 73 79 83 89 97 101 103 107 109 113 127 131 137 139 149 151 157 163 167 173 179 181 191 193 197 199 211 223 227 229 233 239 241 251 257 263 269 271 277 281 283 293 307 311 313 317 331 337 347 349 353 359 367 373 379 383 389 397 401 409 419 421 431 433 439 443 449 457 461 463 467 479 487 491 499 503 509 521 523 541.

2 Proof should be obvious to the student. Argue by contrapostive: Axiomatically, it is impossible to multiply the same list of numbers and arrive at different results.

Perfect Numbers

A PERFECT number is an integer which is the sum of its positive proper divisors (all divisors except itself). Qabalistically, this implies it is the perfect unity/identity of its perfect parts (divisors).

The first five perfect numbers are : 6; 28; 496; 8,128; 33,550,336. They grow in magnitude very quickly as can be seen from this short list. Humanity only knows of 43 perfect numbers. In the meantime, it is not known whether there are (or are not) any other perfect numbers besides the ones known; and if so, if this list be finite or infinite. This remains an unsolved problem in mathematics.

Mystical Numbers of the Planets

Summation of the Integers

THE NUMBER 10 equals to the summation of all the integers up to and including 4. That is, $10 = 1 + 2 + 3 + 4$ or $\sum^{4}_{i=1} i = 10$. This idea of 10 then, contains in itself the notion of the sequential development of the ideas represented by the numerals 1, 2, 3, 4 (the unit, reflection, relation, and their integration as a whole). Now the 4th sphere is the sphere of Jupiter. And so 10, which is the summation of all the integers up to an including 4, contains all the ideas necessary for the manifestation of 4th sphere, which mathematically is the 3rd dimension, or the material plane, which is 10 or Malkuth. We say then that 10 is a "mystical" number for Jupiter. Similarily 21, is a mystical number for SOL, or the SUN (the 6th sphere), seeing as 21 is the summation of the first 6 integers. Qabalistically, this implies a kernelling of all the states engendering the identity or so a Perfect Path.

We present now the summation of the first 100 integers, along with their planetary attributions. Among these numbers the student will note an unusual density in the collection of significant initiatory events or formulaic values (e.g.: 21, 78, 91, 120, 210, 276, 496, 666, 780, 1035, etc.).

1	1		**26**	351		**51**	1326		**76**	2926	
2	3	♆	**27**	378		**52**	1378		**77**	3003	
3	6	♄	**28**	406		**53**	1431		**78**	3081	
4	10	♃	**29**	435		**54**	1485		**79**	3160	
5	15	♂	**30**	465		**55**	1540		**80**	3240	
6	21	☉	**31**	496		**56**	1596		**81**	3321	☽
7	28	♀	**32**	528		**57**	1653		**82**	3403	
8	36	☿	**33**	561		**58**	1711		**83**	3486	
9	45	☽, ♄	**34**	595		**59**	1770		**84**	3570	
10	55	⊗	**35**	630		**60**	1830		**85**	3655	
11	66		**36**	666	☉	**61**	1891		**86**	3741	
12	78		**37**	703		**62**	1953		**87**	3828	
13	91		**38**	741		**63**	2016		**88**	3916	
14	105		**39**	780		**64**	2080	☿	**89**	4005	
15	120		**40**	820		**65**	2145		**90**	4095	
16	136	♃	**41**	861		**66**	2211		**91**	4186	
17	153		**42**	903		**67**	2278		**92**	4278	
18	171		**43**	946		**68**	2346		**93**	4371	
19	190		**44**	990		**69**	2415		**94**	4465	
20	210		**45**	1035		**70**	2485		**95**	4560	
21	231		**46**	1081		**71**	2556		**96**	4656	
22	253		**47**	1128		**72**	2628		**97**	4753	
23	276		**48**	1176		**73**	2701		**98**	4851	
24	300		**49**	1225	♀	**74**	2775		**99**	4950	
25	325	♂	**50**	1275		**75**	2850		**100**	5050	⊗

Elemental Gematria Theory

A SET is a collection of things. In mathematics, we deal primarily with sets of numbers; in *Qabalah* with letters or words. The most common sets in mathematics are the sets **natural numbers** and the **integers**.

In this case, we will be looking at sets of letters (the English Alphabet) and sets of Natural Numbers (1,2, 3,... etc). We define them as follows:

Let **Q** be the set of English Letters, that is **Q** = {A, B, C,..., Z}.

Let **N** be the set of Natural Numbers. **N** = {1, 2, 3, 4, ... } = the natural numbers[3].

These are the only two sets we will be interested in for this discussion.

Some definitions follow.

3 "0" is sometimes included in the set of natural numbers.

Elemental Sets & Operations on Elemental Sets

BY definition, a *set* is a collection of *elements*. Sets can be combined with other sets or elements. One can add to a set, and subtract from it. One can multiply two sets or multiply a set by a single element. One can in fact, define any sort of function, relation or mapping one likes between two sets: that is, we can associate any pair of elements (one from each) according to any rule or whim we choose.

If A is a set, and x is an element in A, then we write: $x \in A$.

For example, the English Alphabet is a set of letters. 'b' is a letter in the English Alphabet, therefore, b ∈ {English Alphabet} or b ∈ **Q** where Q is the set of English Letters.

If A is a set, and x is not an element in A, then we write: $x \notin A$.

For example, the number 13 is an element of N, the natural numbers but not of Q the set of English Letters. Therefore, 13 ∉ **Q**, but 13 ∈ **N**.

The Algebra of Sets

WE introduce some of the basic notation and operations on sets.

Supposing A and B are sets, then

If every element in **A** is also contained in **B** then we say that **A** is a **subset** of **B** (**A ⊂ B**).

Note : A and B are equal if and only if $A \subset B$ and $B \subset A$.

$A \cup B$: The **union** of **A** and **B**, is the set of all elements that are either in A or in B or in both.

$A \cap B$: The **intersection of A** and **B** is the set of all elements that are in both sets A and B.

$A \setminus B$: is the set of all elements from A that are not in B.

Finally, two sets are said to be *disjoint* if **$A \cap B$** = 0 (the empty set). Note that **Q** and **N** are disjoint, the former being a set of letters and the latter one of numbers so that they share no common term between them.

Generally, the *associative*, *commutative*, and *distributive* laws of arithmetic hold true for operations upon Sets as well as operations upon their Elements.

The foundation of mathematical science was laid in the simplicity of these three laws. Their importance should not be overlooked. We state them here for the Student's consideration.

We illustrate with the case of natural numbers (though these laws apply equally to sets) before proceeding with examples in English *Gematria*.

1. The *Associative Law* states that it matters not the order in which we sum things (if we are looking at the parts of a whole):

Associative law : $(a + b) + c = a + (b + c) = a + b + c$, $\forall$ a, b, c $\in$ **N.**

e.g. a =4, b =8, c = 3

$(a + b) + c = (4 + 8) + 3 = 12 + 3 = 15$
$a + (b + c) = 4 + (8 + 3) = 4 + 11 = 15$
$a + b + c = 4 + 8 + 3 = 15$

2. The *Commutative Law* states that in matters not what is first or last, right or left, when a union of the two (or more) is the aim and result:

Commutative law : $a + b = b + a$, $\forall$ a, b $\in$ **N**

e.g.: $4 + 8 = 8 + 4$

3. The *Distributive Law* states a law of immense practical importance : namely that the effect of one element's combined operation upon a composite is equal to the sum of the separate effects of that element's operation into the composite's constituent parts:

Distributive law : $a \times (b + c) = (a \times b) + (a \times c)$, $\forall$ a, b, c $\in$ **N.**

e.g. a =4, b =8, c = 3

$a \times (b + c) = 4 \times (8 + 3) = 4 \times 11 = 44$

$(a \times b) + (a \times c) = (4 \times 8) + (4 \times 3) = 32 + 12 = 44$

We find that though these laws hold in neater worlds of Arithmetic, Algebra and Calculus they do not always hold for physics and certainly not for *Gematria*.

In our case, if we take **Q** to be the set of English Glyphs, then the *associative*, and *distributive* laws hold for **Q** as well. The *commutative law* will ***not*** hold in the case of final values. For instance,

Associative law : $(a + b) + c = a + (b + c) = a + b + c$, $\forall$ a, b, c $\in$ **Q.**

e.g.: a = "The" , b = "Law", c = "Thelema"

(a + b) + c = (The + Law) + Thelema = 220 + 221 = 441

a + (b + c) = The + (Law + Thelema) = 106 + (114 + 221) = 441

a + b + c = The + Law + Thelema = 106 + 114 + 221 = 441

Commutative law : a + b = b + a $\forall$ a, b, c $\in$ **Q**

e.g.: a = "The Name" , b = "BABALON"

a + b = (The Name) + Babalon = 221 + 156 (n final) = 377

b + a = Babalon + The Name = 220 + 221 = 441

So that,

Babalon, the Name ≠ The Name Babalon

Relations and Functions on Sets

THE English key is a function (or a mapping) from the set of English Alphabet Glyphs to a subset of the Natural Numbers. This means that for the sets Q and N, there exists a collection of ordered pairs *(q, n)* such that $q \in$ **Q** and $n \in$ **N**. This is called a relation, and this relation and its ordered pairs is what is illustrated in table I – The English Key at the beginning of this book.

We denote this relation by the following: $f(Q) \mapsto N$.

Mathematically, if **Q** and **N** are two sets, then a **function** *f* from **Q** to **N** is a relation between **Q** and **N** such that for each $q \in$ **Q** there is one and only one associated $n \in$ **N**. The set **Q** is called the **domain** of the function, **N** is called its **range**.

Using the English Key mapping function as an example, we have : *f(e)=1, f(a)=4, f(me)=41,* etc. and see that Q here is the set of Roman Script letters, while N is its range; that is f maps Q into N.

We now introduce some theorems. First we show that for every number in existence, there exists at least one letter combination that will sum to that number, so that there is no number without expression.

Theorem I

Let f be the mapping of the English Key denoted by $f(\mathbf{Q}) \mapsto \mathbf{R}$ where **Q** is the set of English Alphabet letters and $\mathbf{R} \subset \mathbf{N}$.

Then f is **additive**, that is

$$f(a + b) = f(a) + f(b), \quad \forall\, a, b \in Q$$

Proof: by Induction (*omitted here*).

Theorem II

Let **N** be the set of Natural Numbers and let $f(\mathbf{Q}) \mapsto \mathbf{R}$ be the English Key mapping where **Q** is the set of English Alphabet letters and $\mathbf{R} \subset \mathbf{N}$, then the relation $f(\mathbf{Q}) \mapsto \mathbf{R}$ is a function.

Proof

A function f from **Q** to **N** is a relation between its domain Q and its range N such that for each $q \in \mathbf{Q}$ there is one and only one associated $n \in \mathbf{N}$.

If we take final and initial, soft and hard values for separate instances of the domain variable, then from table I, we can see that each glyph corresponds to one and only one number. The proof follows.

Theorem III

Let **N** be the set of Natural Numbers and let $f(\mathbf{Q}) \mapsto \mathbf{R}$ be the English Key mapping where **Q** is the set of English Alphabet letters and $\mathbf{R} \subset \mathbf{N}$. Then for all $\mathbf{n} \in \mathbf{N}$, there exists at least one finite combination of $q_1, q_2, \ldots, q_r \in \mathbf{Q}$, such that

$$f(q_1, q_2, \ldots, q_r) = f(q_1) + f(q_2) + \ldots + f(q_r) = n.$$

Proof.

0 is an element of Q. E=1 so that Q contains the unit. The rest follows from induction.

$$f(0) = 0,\ f(e) = 1,\ f(q_{k+1}) = f(q_k) + f(e) = f(q_k + e)$$

The principle of Mathematical Induction states that if S is a subset of N such that, (1) $1 \in S$ and, (2) if $k \in S$ then $k + 1 \in S$ is True, then S = N.

If we substitute S for R, where $\mathbf{R} = \{ f(q_1, q_2, \ldots, q_r) \}$, the set of values attained from applying the transformation $f(\mathbf{Q}) \mapsto \mathbf{R}$ upon all possible letter combinations in **Q**; and let **N** be the Natural numbers, then we see that:

(a) $R \subset N$

(b) $f(e)=1$ so that $1 \in R$ and the first condition is verified.

(c) If $k \in R$, then by definition, there exists some combination of $q_1, q_2, \ldots, q_r \in \mathbf{Q}$ such that $f(q_1, q_2, \ldots, q_r) = k$. We can always add the unit element $f(e) = 1$. By theorem I, we have $k+1 = f(q_1, q_2, \ldots, q_r) + f(e) = f(q_1, q_2, \ldots, q_r, e)$ so that $k + 1 \in R$.

Therefore, R = N.

Q.E.D.

Corollary I

The elemental set **Q** of English Key glyphs spans the space of Natural Numbers, so that **Q** is a *basis* for **N**.

This is essentially a restatement of Theorem II in algebraic terminology. Namely that the set of **Q** is sufficient to span the Natural Numbers: for any n $\in$ **N**, there exists a set of coefficients $a_1, a_2, a_3..., a_1 \in N$ such that $a_1 f(q_1) + a_2 f(q_2) + a_3 f(q_3) + \ldots + a_j f(q_j) = n \in N$, where $a_i f(q_i)$ is the value of the letter $q_i \in Q$ in the set of English glyphs.

In laymen's terms, any positive integer can be expressed by a combination of letters and their corresponding numbers according to the English Key mapping.

The Tables

The astute Student will note that phases of the letters are not here attributed. This difficulty will be dealt with later, but can be interpolated from combining the tables that here follow. For instance, the Moon has two phases though they are not here denoted. One would expect the Moon when full like the Cup (0 = 200) to be attributed to the High Priestess, while O = 80 to the Moon ROTA while still retaining its character throughout.

Value	English	Hebrew		Greek		Arabic	
		Figure	Name	Figure	Name	Figure	Name
1	E, J	א	*Aleph*	α	*Alpha*	ا	*alif*
2	F	ב	*Beth*	β	*Beta*	ب	*bä*
3	C_s, P	ג	*Gimel*	γ	*Gamma*	ج	*jim*
4	A, I	ד	*Daleth*	δ	*Delta*	د	*dâl*
5	j	ה	*Heh*	ε	*Epsilon*	ه	*hâ*
6	B, Z, N_f	ו	*Vau*	ϝ	*Digamma*	و	*wâw*
7	H	ז	*Zayin*	ζ	*Zeta*	ز	*zâ*
8	D	ח	*Cheth*	η	*Eta*	ح	*hâ*
9	R, x	ט	*Teth*	θ	*Theta*	ط	*tâ*
10	Q, F	י	*Yod*	ι	*Iota*	ي	*yâ*
20	G	כ ך	*Kaph*	κ	*Kappa*	ك	*käf*
24	S						
30	C_k, K	ל	*Lamed*	λ	*Lambda*	ل	*läm*
40	M	מ ם	*Mem*	μ	*Mu*	م	*mîm*
42	S_f						
50	L_{av}	נ	*Nun*	ν	*Nu*	ن	*nűn*
60	w	ס	*Samekh*	ξ [s]	*Xi (Sigma)*	س	*sîn*
70	L, N, Y	ע	*Ayin*	ο		ع	*äyn*
80	Ŏ, V	פ ף	*Peh*	π	*Pi*	ف	*fa*
89	T_f						
90		צ ץ	*Tzaddi*	φ	*Omicron*	ص	*sâd*
98	T						
100		ק	*Qoph*	ρ	*Rho*	ق	*qäf*
200	O.U	ר	*Resh*	σ	*Sigma*	ر	*râ*
300	X	ש	*Shin*	τ	*Tau*	ش	*shîn*
400	W	ת	*Tau*	υ	*Upsilon*	ت	*tä*
500		ך	*Kaph*	[ϕ]	*Phi*	ث	*thä*
600		ם	*Mem*	χ	*Chi*	خ	*khâ*
700		נ	*Nun*	ψ	*Psi*	د	*dal*
800		ף	*Peh*	ω	*Omega*	ض	*dâd*
900		ץ	*Tzaddi*			ظ	*za*
1000						غ	*ghain*

The KEY to the ENGLISH QABALAH

Figure	Value
A - *The Star*	4
B - *The Book*	6
C_s, C_k - *The Womb*	3, 30
D - *The Bow*	8
E - *The Triple Flame*	1
f, F - *The Axe*	2, 10
G - *Union*	20
H - *The Castle*	7
I - *The Arrow*	4
J, j - *The Hook*	1, 5
K - *The Virgin*	30
⅃, L - *The Balance*	50, 70
M - *The Sea*	40
N, N_f - *The Gate*	70, 6
Ŏ, O - *The Moon*	80, 200
P - *The Goddess*	3
Q - *The Lion*	10
R - *The Emperor*	9
S, S_f-*The Son, The Serpent*	24, 42
T, T_f- *The Table, The Altar*	98, 89
U - *The Cup*	200
V - *The Bull*	80
w, W - *Vision*	60, 400
x, X - *The Wheel*	9, 300
Y_v,Y_c - *The Tree*	70, 6
Z - *The Lightning Flash*	6

The English Key

Value	Figure
1	E, J
2	f
3	C_S, P
4	A, I
5	j
6	B, Z, N_f
7	H
8	D
9	R, x
10	Q, F
20	G
24	S
30	C_K, K
40	M
42	S_f
50	˩
60	w
70	L, N,Y
80	Ŏ, V
89	T_f
98	T
200	O, U
300	X
400	W

The Hebrew Key

Name	Figure	Value	Transl.
Aleph	א	1	A
Beth	ב	2	B
Gimel	ג	3	G
Daleth	ד	4	D
Heh	ה	5	H
Vau	ו	6	V
Zayin	ז	7	Z
Cheth	ח	8	Ch
Teth	ט	9	T
Yod	י	10	I
Kaph	ך כ	20, 500	K
Lamed	ל	30	L
Mem	ם מ	40, 600	M
Nun	נ	50, 700	N
Samekh	ס	60	S
Ayin	ע	70	O
Peh	ף פ	80, 800	P
Tzaddi	ץ צ	90, 900	Tz
Qoph	ק	100	Q
Resh	ר	200	R
Shin	ש	300	Sh
Tau	ת	400	Th

The Greek Key

Glyph	Value
[σ]	200
[ϕ]	500
ω	800
[ε]	
χ	600
α	1
β	2
γ	3
δ	4
ε	5
ϝ	6
ζ	7
η	8
θ	9
ι	10
κ	20
λ	30
μ	40
ν	50
ξ [σ]	60
ο	70
π	80
ψ	700
φ	90
ρ	100
τ	300
υ	400

The Arabic Key

Glyph		Value
ا	alif	1
ب	bä	2
ج	jim	3
د	dâl	4
ه	hâ	5
و	wâw	6
ز	zâ	7
ح	hâ	8
ط	tâ	9
ي	yâ	10
ك	käf	20
ل	läm	30
م	mîm	40
ن	nűn	50
س	sîn	60
ع	äyn	70
ف	fa	80
ص	sâd	90
ق	qäf	100
ر	râ	200
ش	shîn	300
ت	tä	400
ث	thä	500
خ	khâ	600
د	dal	700
ض	dâd	800
ظ	za	900
غ	ghain	1000

The Coptic Key

Glyph		Value	Trans.
Ϭϭ	*Gima*		Sz
Ϯϯ	*Ti*		Tt
Ⲏⲏ	*Heta*	8	Æ
Ⲫⲫ	*Phi*	500	Ph
Ⲱⲱ	*Ö*	800	ōō (long o)
Ⲉⲉ	*Ei*	5	E
Ϥϥ	*Fai*	90	f, v
Ϫϫ	*Janja*	.	J
Ⲥⲥ	*Sémma*	200	S
Ⲁⲁ	*Alpha*	1	A
Ⲃⲃ	*Beta*	2	B
Ⲅⲅ	*Gamma*	3	G
Ⲇⲇ	*Dalda*	4	D
Ϩϩ	*Hori*		H
Ⲩⲩ	*He*	400	U
Ⲍⲍ	*Zéta*	7	Z
Ϧϧ	*Khei*		Ch
Ⲑⲑ	*Théta*	9	Th
Ⲓⲓ	*Yota*	10	I,y, ee
Ⲕⲕ	*Kappa*	20	K
Ⲗⲗ	*Lauda*	30	L
Ⲙⲙ	*Mé*	40	M
Ⲛⲛ	*Nr*	50	N
Ⲝⲝ	*Ksi*	60	X
Ⲟⲟ	*Ow*	70	O
Ⲡⲡ	*Pi*	80	P
	Psi	700	Ps
	Khi	600	Q
Ⲣⲣ	*Ro*	100	R
Ϣϣ	*Shai*	900	Sh
Ⲧⲧ	*Taw*	300	T

Tarot & ROTA Key Attributions

	Glyph		Tarot Card Attributions	Proper Tarot Card Titles	Correct Design of Tarot Trumps.
A	The Star	☉	The Sun	The Lord of the Fire of the World.	The Sun
B	The Book	☿	The Juggler	The Magus of Power.	A fair youth with winged helmet and heels, equipped as a Magician, displays his art; or Ra-Hoor-Khuit, in blue and golden headdress, right-hand uplifting, left-handing casting down; the desert and ocean behind him.
C	The Sky	♒	The Star	The Daughter of the Firmament. The Dweller between the Waters.	The figure of a water-nymph disporting herself
D	The Bow	♀	The Empress	The Daughter of the Mighty Ones.	Crowned with stars, a winged goddess stands upon the moon; or Nuit.
E	The Triple Flame	🜂	The Fool	The Spirit of Αιθηρ	A child on a lotus or Hoor-Paar-Kraat.
f,p	Force	♂	The House of God	The Lord of the Hosts of the Mighty.	A tower struck by forked lightning
F	The Father	♆	4 Kings, Wands		
G	Union	♊	The Lovers	The Children of the Voice: the Oracle of the Mighty Gods.	A prophet, young, and in the Sign of Osiris Risen; or the Sun (Beast or Lion) and Moon (Babalon or Crowned Woman) conjoined.
H	The Throne	♋	The Chariot	The Child of the Powers of the Waters: the Lord of the Triumph of Light.	A young and holy king under the starry canopy.
I	The Lingam	♐	Temperance	The Daughter of the Reconcilers, the Bringer-Forth of Life.	The figure of Diana huntress
J	The Horn of Plenty	♅			
K	The Virgin	♍	Hermit	The Prophet of the Eternal, the Magus of the Voice of Power.	Wrapped in a cloak and cowl, a man walks, bearing a lamp and staff; or Aiwass.
L	The Foot	♎	Justice	The Daughter of the Lords of Truth. The Ruler of the Balance.	A conventional figure of Justice with scales and balances
M	A Wave	🜄	The Hanged Man	The Spirit of the Mighty Waters.	The figure of a hanged or crucified man; or Jesus.
N	A Gate	♏	Death	The Child of the Great Transformers. The Lord of the Gate of Death.	A skeleton with a scythe mowing men. The scythe handle is a Tau; or a Pyramid under a night sky.
O	The Moon	☽	The High Priestess	The Priestess of the Silver Star.	A crowned priestess sits before the veil of Isis between the Pillars of Set;, or Babalon.
P	The Mother	⊗	4 princesses, Disks		
Q	The Lion	♌	Lust	The Daughter of the Flaming Sword.	A smiling woman holds the open jaws of a fierce and powerful lion
R	Birth	♈	The Emperor	The Son of the Morning, chief among the Mighty.	A flame-clad god bearing equivalent symbols, sitting with legs crossed in Tf.

	Glyph		Tarot Card Attributions	Proper Tarot Card Titles	Correct Design of Tarot Trumps.
S	The Son	♓	The Moon	The Ruler of Flux and Reflux. The Child of the Sons of the Mighty.	The waning moon
T	A Table	♑	The Devil	The Lord of the Gates of Matter. The Child of the Forces of Time.	The figure of Pan or Priapus; or Baphomet.
U	The Cup	♄	4 Queens, Cups		
V	The Horns	♉	The Hierophant	The Magus of the Eternal.	A man throned between two pillars; or Hadit, the winged globe.
W	The Eyes	△	The Angel or Last Judgement	The Spirit of the Primal Fire.	Israfel blowing the Last Trumpet. The dead arising from their tombs; or The Arrow of the 5th Aethyr.
X	The Wheel	♄	The Universe	The Great One of the Night of Time.	The symbols of the Squaring of the Circle
Y	The Tree	🜃	4 Princes, Swords		
Z	The Lightning Flash	♃	Wheel of Fortune	The Lord of the Forces of Life.	A wheel of six shafts, whereon revolve the Triad of Hermanubis, Sphinx, and Typhon

PanTheonic Attributions

	Astro-logical & Planetary	Egyptian Gods.	Practical Attribution (Egyptian Gods)	Greek Gods.	Roman Gods.
A	☉	Ra and many others	Ra	Helios, Apollo	Apollo [[Ops]]
B	☿	Thoth and Cynocephalus	Thoth	Hermes	Mercury
C	♒	Ahepi, Aroueris	Nuit	[Athena] Ganymede	Juno [[Æolus]]
Ch, Kh	Sphere of Mars	Horus, Nephthys	Horus	Ares, Hades	Mars
D	♀	Hathor	Hathoor	Aphrodité Athena	Venus
E	🜁	Nu [[Hoor-pa-kraat as ATU 0]]	Mout	Zeus	Jupiter [[Juno, Æolus]]
f,P	♂	Horus	Menthu	Ares, [[Athena]]	Mars
F,Ph	♆ Sphere of the Zodiac	Amoun, Thoth, Nuith [Zodiac]	Isis [As Wisdom]	Athena, Uranus [[Hermes]]	Janus [[Mercury]]
G	♊	Various twin Deities, Rekht, Merti, [[Heru-Ra-Ha]]	The twin Merti	Apollo the Charioteer	Castor and Pollux, [Janus] [[Hymen]]
H	♋	Khephra	Hormakhu	Demeter [borne by lions]	Mercury [[Lares and Penates]]
I	♐	Nephthys		Apollo, Artemis (hunters)	Diana (as Archer) [[Iris]]
J	♅ Sphere of Primum Mobile	Ptah, Asar un Nefer, Hadith [[Heru-Ra-Ha]]	Ptah	Zeus, Iacchus	Jupiter
K	♍	Isis [as Virgin]	Heru-pa-Kraath		[Attis], Ceres, Adonis [[Vesta, Flora]]
L	♎	Ma	Maat	Themis, Minos, Aeacus and Rhadamanthus	Vulcan [[Venus, Nemesis]]
M	▽	Tum, Ptah, Asar (as Hanged Man), Hekar, Isis [[Hathor]]		Poseidon	Neptune [[Rhea]]
N	♏	Merti goddesses, Typhon, Apep, Khephra	Hammemit	Ares [[Apollo the Pythean, Thanatos]]	Mars [[Mors]]
O	☽	Chomse	Chomse	Artemis, Hekaté	Diana
p, Y_c	⊗ Sphere of the Elements	Seb. Lower (i.e. unwedded) Isis and Nephthys. [[Sphinx]]	Osiris	Persephone, [Adonis], Psyché	Ceres
Q,Ph	Sphere of Mercury	Anubis	Thoth	Hermes	Mercury
Q	♌	Ra-Hoor-Khuit, Pasht, Sekhet, Mau	Horus	[Attis]	Venus (repressing the Fire of Vulcan)

	Astro-logical & Planetary	Egyptian Gods.	Practical Attribution (Egyptian Gods)	Greek Gods.	Roman Gods.
R	♈	Men Thu	Isis	[Heré]	Mars, Minerva
Rh	Sphere of Jupiter	Amoun, Isis [[Hathoor]]	Amoun	Poseidon [[Zeus]]	Jupiter [[Libitina]]
S	♓	Khephra (as Scarab)	Anubi	Poseidon [[Hermes Psychopompos]]	Neptune
Sh	Sphere of Sol	Asar, Ra [[On, Hrumachis]]	Ra	Iacchus, Apollo, Adonis [[Dionysus, Bacchus]]	Apollo [[Bacchus, Aurora]]
T	♑	Khem (Set)	Set	Pan, Priapus [Erect Hermes and Bacchus]	Pan, Vesta, Bacchus
Th	Sphere of Luna	Shu[[Hermanubis]]		Zeus, Diana of Ephesus [[Eros]]	Diana[[Terminus, Jupiter]]
U	Sphere of Saturn	Maut, Isis, Nephthys	Nephthys	Cybele, Demeter, Rhea, Heré, [[Psyché, Kronos]]	Juno, Cybele, Hecate, &c.
V	♉	Asar, Ameshet, Apis	Osiris	Castor and Pollux, Apollo the Diviner [[Eros]]	Venus [[Hymen]]
W	△	Thoum-Aesh-Neith, Mau, Kabeshunt, Horus, Tarpesheth.	Mau	Hades	Vulcan, Pluto
Wh	Sphere of Venus	Hathoor	Hathoor	Aphrodité, Niké	Venus
X	♄	Sebek, Mako		[Athena]	Saturn [[Terminus, Astræa]]
Y_v	🜃	Satem, Ahapshi, Nephthys, Ameshet		[Demeter] [[Gaia]]	Ceres
Z	♃	Amoun-Ra	Amoun-Ra	Zeus	Jupiter, [Pluto]

Flora & Fauna Attributions

	Astro-logical & Planetary	Animals, Real and Imaginary.	Plants, Real and Imaginary.	Vegetable Drugs.	Mineral Drugs.
A	☉	Lion, Sparrowhawk [[Leopard]]	Sunflower, Laural, Heliotrop [[Nut, Galangal]]	Alcohol	. . . .
B	☿	Swallow, Ibis, Ape [[Twin Serpents, fish,hybrids]]	Vervain, Herb Mercury, Major-lane, Palm [[Lime or Linden]]	All cerebral excitants	Mercury
C	♒	Man or Eagle (Cherub of Air), Peacock	[Olive], Cocoanut	All diuretics	. . . .
Ch,Kh	Sphere of Mars	Basilisk	Oak, Nux Vomica, Nettle [[Hickory]]	Nux Vomica, Nettle [[Cocaine, Atropine]]	Iron, Sulphur
D	♀	Sparrow, Dove [[Sow]]	Myrtle, Rose, Clover [[Fig, Peach, Apple]]	All aphrodisiacs	. . . .
E	🜁	Eagle, Man (Cherub of Air) [[Ox]]	Aspen	Peppermint	. . . .
f, P	♂	Horse, Bear, Wolf [[Boar]]	Absinthe, Rue	. . . .	. . . .
F	♆Sphere of the Zodiac	Man	Amaranth [[Mistletoe, Bo or Pipal Tree]]	Hashish [[Cocaine]]	Phosphorus
G	♊	Magpie, hybrids [[Parrot, Zebra, Penguin]] Crab, Turtle, Sphinx [[Whale, all beasts of Transport]]	Hybrids, Orchids	Ergot and ecbolics	. . . .
H	♋	Lion (Cherub of Fire)	Lotus	Watercress	. . . .
I	♁	Centaur, Horse, Hippogriff, Dog	Rush	. . . .	. . . .
J	♅Sphere of Primum Mobile	God [[Swan, Hawk]]	Almond in Flower [[Banyan]]	Elixir Vitæ	Aur. Pot.
K	♍	Virgin, Anchorite, any solitary person or animal [Rhinoceros]	Snowdrop, Lily, Narcissus [[Mistletoe]]	All anaphrodisiacs	. . . .
L	♎	Elephant [[Spider]]	Aloe	Tobacco	. . . .
M	▽	Eagle-Snake-Scorpion (Cherub of Earth)	Lotus, all Water Plants	Caseara, all purges	Sulphates
N	♏	Scorpio, Beetle, Crayfish or Lobster, Wolf [[all Reptiles, Shark, Crablouse]]	Cactus [[Nettle, all poisonous plants]]	. . . .	. . . .
O	☽	Dog [[Stork, Camel]]	Almond, Mugwort, Hazel, Moonwort, Ranunculus [[Alder, Pomegranete]]	Jupiter, Pennyroyal, & all emmenogogues	. . . .
p, Y_c	⊗Sphere of the Elements	Sphinx	Willow, Lily, Ivy [[Pomegranete, all cereals]]	Corn	Mag. Sulph.

	Astro-logical & Planetary	Animals, Real and Imaginary.	Plants, Real and Imaginary.	Vegetable Drugs.	Mineral Drugs.
Ph	Sphere of Mercury	Hermaphrodite, Jackal [[Twin serpents,Monoceros de Astris]]	Moly, Anhalonium Lewinii	Anhalonium Lewinii [[Cannabis Indica]]	Mercury
Q	♌	[[Cat, Tiger, Serpent]]	Sunflower	All carminatives and tonics	. . . .
R	♈	Ram, Owl	Tiger Lily, Geranium [[Olive]]	All cerebral excitants	. . . .
Rh	Sphere of Jupiter	Unicorn	Olive, Shamrock [[Opium Poppy]]	Opium	. . . .
S	♓	Fish, Dolphin [[Beetle, Dog, Jackal]]	Unicellular Organisms, Opium [[Mangrove]]	All narcotics	. . . .
Sh	Sphere of Sol	Phœnix, Lion, Child [[Spider, Pelican]]	Acacia, Bay, Laurel, Vine [[Oak, Gorse, Ash, Aswata]]	Stramonium, Alcohol, Digitalis, Coffee	. . . .
T	♑	Goat, Ass [[Oyster]]	Indian Hemp, Orchis Root, Thistle [[Yohimba]]	Orchis [Satyrion]	. . . .
Th	Sphere of Luna	Elephant [[Tortoise, Toad]]	[Banyan], Mandrake, Damiana [[Ginseng, Yohimba]]	Orchid Root	Lead
U	Sphere of Saturn	Woman [[Bee]]	Cypress, Opium Poppy [[Lotus, Lily, Ivy]]	Belladonna, Soma	Silver
V	♉	Bull (Cherub of E)	Mallow [[all giant trees]]	Sugar	. . . .
W	△	Lion (Cherub of Fire)	Red Poppy, Hibiscus, Nettle	. . . .	Nitrates
Wh	Sphere of Venus	lynx [[Raven, all carrion birds]]	Rose [[Laurel]]	Damiana, Cannabis Indica [[Anhalonium]]	Arsenic
X	♄	Crocodile	Ash, Cypress, Hellebore, Yew, Nightshade [[Elm]]	. . . .	Lead
Y_v	🜃	Bull (Cherub of Earth)	Oak, Ivy [[Cereals]]	. . . .	Bismuth
Z	♃	Eagle [[Praying Mantis]]	Hyssop, Oak, Poplar, Fig [[Arnica, Cedar]]	Cocaine	. . . .

Formulae & Utilities

	Astro-logical & Planetary	Precious Stones	Perfumes	Weapons	Formulae
A	☉	Crysolith	Olibanum, Cinnamon, all Glorious Odours	The Lamen or Bow and Arrow	IAO : INRI
B	☿	Opal, Agate	Mastic, White Sandal, [[Nutmeg]], Mace, Storax, all Fugitive Odours.	The Wand or Caduceus	. . . .
C	♒	Artificial Glass [[Chalcedony]]	Galbanum	The Censer or Aspergillus	. . . .
Ch, Kh	Sphere of Mars	Ruby	Tobacco	The Sword, Spear, Scourge, or Chain	AGLA. ALHIM
D	♀	Emerald, Turquoise	Sandalwood, Myrtle, all Soft Voluptuous Odours	The Girdle	AGAPE
E	🜁	Topaz	Galbanum	The Dagger or Fan	. . . .
f,P	♂	Ruby, any red stone	Pepper, Dragon's Blood, all Hot Pungent Odours	The Sword	. . . .
F	♆ Sphere of the Zodiac	Star Ruby, Turquoise	Musk	Lingam, the Inner Robe of Glory [[The Word]]	VIAOV
G	♊	Alexandrite, Tourmaline, Iceland Spar	Wormwood	The Tripod	. . . .
H	♋	Amber	Onycha	The Furnace [[The Cup or Holy Graal]]	ABRAHADABRA.
I	♐	Jacinth	Lign-aloes	The Arrow	ON
J	♅ Sphere of Primum Mobile	Diamond	Ambergris	Swastika or Fylfot Cross, Crown [[The Lamp]]	. . . .
K	♍	Peridot	Narcissus	The Lamp and Wand (Virile Force reserved), the Bread [[Lotus Wand]]	. . . .
L	♎	Emerald	Galbanum	The Cross of Equilibrium	. . . .
M	🜄	Beryl or Aquamarine	Onycha, Myrrh	The Cup and Cross of Suffering, the Wine [[Water of Lustration]]	. . . .
N	♏	Snakestone	Siamese Benzoin, Opoponax	The Pain of the Obligation [[The Oath]]	AUMGN
O	☽	Moonstone, Pearl, Crystal	Menstrual Blood, Camphor, Aloes, all Sweet Virginal Odours	Bow and Arrow	ALIM

	Astro-logical & Planetary	Precious Stones	Perfumes	Weapons	Formulae
p, Y_c	⊗Sphere of the Elements	Rock Crystal	Dittany of Crete	The Magical Circle and Triangle	VITRIOL
Ph	Sphere of Mercury	Opal, especially Fire Opal	Storax	The Names and Versicles and Apron	. . . .
Q	♌	Cat's Eye	Olibanum	The Discipline (Preliminary) [[Phœnix Wand]]	TO MEGA THERION
R	♈	Ruby	Dragon's Blood	The Horns, Energy, the Burin	. . . .
Rh	Sphere of Jupiter	Amethyst, Sapphire [[Lapis Lazuli]]	Cedar	The Wand, Sceptre, or Crook	IHVH
S	♓	Pearl	Ambergris [[Menstrual Fluid]]	The Twilight of the Place and Magic Mirror	. . . .
Sh	Sphere of Sol	Topaz, Yellow Diamond	Olibanum	The Lamen or Rosy Cross	ABRAHADABRA IAO: INRI
T	♑	Black Diamond	Musk, Civet (also Saturnian Perfumes)	The Secret Force, Lamp	ON
Th	Sphere of Luna	Quartz	Jasmine, Ginseng, all Odoriferous roots	Perfumes, Sandals	ALIM
U	Sphere of Saturn	Star Sapphire, Pearl	Myrrh, Civet	Yoni, the Outer Robe of Concealment [[The Cup, the Shining Star]]	BABALON. VITRIOL
V	♉	Topaz	Storax	The Labour of Preparation [[The Throne and Altar]]	. . . .
W	△	Fire Opal	Olibanum, all Fiery Odours	The Wand or Lamp, Pyramid of Fire [[The Thurible]]	. . . .
Wh	Sphere of Venus	Emerald	Benzoin, Rose, Red Sandal	The Lamp and Girdle	ARARITA
X	♄	Onyx	Assafœtida, Scammony, Indigo, Sulphur (all Evil Odours)	A Sickle	. . . .
Y	🜃	Salt	Storax, all Dull and Heavy Odours	The Pantacle or [[Bread and Salt]]	. . . .
Z	♃	Amethyst, Lapis Lazuli	Saffron, all Generous Odours	The Sceptre	. . . .

4 Elements	12 Houses	10 Planets
🜁 E	♒ C	☉ A
▽ M	♊ G	☿ B
△ W	♐ I	♀ D
🜃 Y	♍ K	♂ P
	♎ L	♅ J (one of the Fathers Lost).
	♏ N	☽, in both her phases, O.
	♌ Q	⊗ Y
	♋ H	♆ F
	♓ S	♄ U
	♑ T	♃ Z
	♉ V	
	♈ R	

Hebraic Glyph Set

Hebrew	Name	English Tr.
אלף	Aleph	Ox
בית	Beth	House
גמל	Gimel	Camel
דלת	Daleth	Door
הה	Hé	Window
וו	Vau	Nail
זין	Zain	Sword
חית	Cheth	Fence
טית	Teth	Serpent
יוד	Yod	Hand
כף	Kaph	Palm

Hebrew	Name	English Tr.
למד	Lamed	Ox-Goad
מים	Maim	Water
נון	Nun	Fish
סמך	Samekh	Prop
עין	Ayin	Eye
פה	Pé	Mouth
צדי	Tzaddi	Fish-hook
קוף	Qoph	Back of head
ריש	Resh	Head
שין	Shin	Tooth
תו	Tau	Tau

Hebrew Trans-literation	Hebrew Names and Letters	English Transliteration	The Spheres and Houses	Roman Script	The Tree of Life.
אוף	Ain	Nothing			
און סוף	Ain Soph	No Limit			
אוד און סוף	Ain Soph Aur	Limitless L.V.X			. . . .
כתר	Kether	Crown*	Sphere of Primum Mobile	H	1st Plane, Middle Pillar
חכמה	Chokmah	Wisdom	Sphere of the Zodiac	F.Q	2nd Plane, Right Pillar
בינה	Binah	Understanding	Sphere of Saturn	C	2nd Plane, Left Pillar
חסד	Chesed	Mercy	Sphere of Jupiter	Rh	3rd Plane, Right Pillar
גבורה	Geburah	Strength	Sphere of Mars	Ch, Kh	3rd Plane, Left Pillar
תפארת	Tiphareth	Beauty	Sphere of Sol	Sh	4th Plane, Middle Pillar
נצח	Netzach	Victory	Sphere of Venus	Wh	5th Plane, Right Pillar
דה	Hod	Splendour	Sphere of Mercury	Ph	5th Plane, Left Pillar
יסוד	Yesod	Foundation	Sphere of Luna	Th	6th Plane, Middle Pillar
מלכור	Malkuth	Kingdom	Sphere of the Elements	Y	7th Plane, Middle Pillar
אלף	Aleph	Ox	Air	E	Path joins 1 – 2
בת	Beth	House	Mercury	B	" 1 – 3
גמל	Gimel	Camel	Luna	O	" 1 – 6
דלת	Daleth	Door	Venus	D	" 2 – 3
הה	Hé	Window	Aries	R	" 2 – 6
וו	Vau	Nail	Taurus	V	" 2 – 4
זי׳	Zain	Sword	Gemini	G	" 3 – 6
חית	Cheth	Fence	Cancer	H	" 3 – 5
טית	Teth	Serpent	Leo	q	" 4 – 5
ישד	Yod	Hand	Virgo	K	" 4 – 6
כע	Kaph	Palm	Jupiter	Z	" 4 – 7
למד	Lamed	Ox Goad	Libra	L	" 5 – 6
מי׳	Maim	Water	Water	M	" 5 – 8
נו׳	Nun	Fish	Scorpio	N	" 6 – 7
סמ	Samekh	Prop	Sagittarius	I	" 6 – 9
ין׳	Ayin	Eye	Capricorn	T	" 6 – 8
פה	Pé	Mouth	Mars	f, P	" 7 – 8
צדי	Tzaddi	Fish-hook	Aquarius	U	" 7 – 9
קוע	Qoph	Back of head	Pisces	S	" 7 – 10
ריש	Resh	Head	Sol	A	" 8 – 9
שי׳	Shin	Tooth	Fire	W	" 8 – 10
תו	Tau	Tau (as Egyptian)	Saturn	X	" 9 – 10

5	*And the Cross was formulated in the Universe that as yet was not.* **J- The Hook, The Horn of Plenty** ● ▬ ▬ ●	5. The reception of the M.T. among the Brethren of the A A; the manifestation of the Arrow.	♅	☋♆ South Node CAUDA DRACONIS KETU (♄ ♂) DRACONIS
6	*But now the Imperfection became manifest, presiding over the fading of perfection.* **N_f – The Gate, B – The Book**[2] ▬▬ ● ●	6. A shadowing-forth of the grade of Magus.	♏,☿ (N),(B)	🜁
	Also the Woman arose, and veiled the Upper Heaven with her body of stars. **Z, - The Lightning Flash, Y_c - The Tree** ▬ ▬ ● ●	7. The Virgin become the Bride, the great Reward of the Ceremony. Also an adumbration of the Further Progress.	♃, 🜃 (Z), (Y)	🜃

* It is to be noted that the "forces" whether they be elemental, planetary or cosmic pertaining to each letter, do not necessarily coincide with the manifestations of the Aethyrs, but may overlap a number of consecutive Aethyrs (this will be indicated in the table below) or otherwise precede the Aethyr itself as a necessary sensorium or medium to the Aethyr's manifestation.

Note: The first column is Witnessed from the perspective of Kether; the second from Malkuth, i.e. one is ascending in degrees of manifestation while the other descends.

TRIGRAMMATON and the AETHYRS

Value	TRIGRAMMATON	AETHYR*	Letter	Trigram
1	*Here is Nothing under its three forms. It is not, yet informeth all things.* **E - The Triple Light, the Triple Flame** ● ● ●	1. The final manifestation. All leads up to the Crowned Child, Horus, the Lord of the New Æon.	🜁	⊛
2	*Now cometh the glory of the Single One, as an imperfection and stain.* **F– Breath** ● ● ▬	2. The understanding of the Curse, that is become a Blessing. The final reward of the M.T., his marriage even with Babalon Herself. The paean thereof.,	♂,♆	△
3	*But by the Weak One the Mother was it equilibrated.* **Soft C, P – The Pregnant Goddess** ● ● ▪ ▪	3. The Magician. Exhibition of the Guards to the Higher Knowledge.	♒, ⊗ (C) (P)	▽
4	*Also the purity was divided by Strength, the force of the Demiurge.* **I – The Projectile, A – The Five Fold Star** ● ▬ ●	4. Further concerning the Magus. The marriage of Chaos (I) with the purified Virgin (A).	♐, ☉	☊♅ North Node C A P U T DRACONIS RAHU (♃ ♀)

10	*The master flamed forth as a star and set a guard of Water in every Abyss.* **F, Q, CH, PH** **F – An Axe, Q – The Lion, CH, PH** 	13. The emergence of Nemo into the world; his work therein. This is the first mystery revealed to an M.T. *A guard of water in every abyss, the four watchtowers: F, Q, Ch, Ph. The Frontier is guarded by the Four Watchtowers here represented elementally by F, Q, Ch and Ph. (Air, Fire, Water, Earth)*	♂, ♌	♊, ▽ of 🜁
20	*Also certain secret ones concealed the Light of Purity in themselves, protecting it from the Persecutions.* **G – Union** 	14. The Shrine of Darkness. Final initiation into grade of M. T. *See Liber 418 for this doctrine on Understanding as Darkness and how Emptiness prevents the formation of images and how mass, which is resistance, is required in order to reflect light and so illuminate the environment. "… and so perfect Understanding is darkness."* *To understand is ultimately to unite. It is to be noted however, He who seeks BINH, must Understand All (that is stand-under) and so passes under, that is He goes underground. He submerges according to his element, crashing through the Crust of Earth, into the Waters that are the Deserts that are the Caverns which are Peaks in Hell. For all is seen from the averse until the 2nd Aethyr. (See the letter M, or the 17th to 19th Aethyrs.)*	♊	♑
30	*Likewise also did certain sons and daughters of Hermes and of Aphrodite, more openly* **K– The Virgin, C_k –The Mother Goddess** 	15. The mystic dance by Salome. The new Temple, the signs of the grades are received and the A.E. rejected. *… did certain sons (K) and daughters (C) (see w or CK =60)*	♍	♎, △ of 🜁

7	*Now then a giant arose, of terrible strength; and asserted the Spirit in a secret rite.* **H – The Fortress** ● ▬▬ ▬▬	8. The fuller manifestation of the Holy Guardian Angel. *(Note the compound glyphs that later arise: CH, PH, SH, TH, WH)*	♋	♐ ▽ of △
8	*And the Master of the Temple balancing all things arose; his stature was above the Heaven and below Earth and Hell.* **D – The Bow**[3] ● ▬▬ ▬ ▬	9. The M.T. hath passed the Abyss, and is led to the Palace of the Virgin redeemed from Malkuth unto Binah.	♀	♍, ▽ of △
		10. The Abyss.		
9	*Against him the Brothers of the Left-hand Path, confusing the symbols. They concealed their horror [in this symbol];* **x - The Cross** ● ▬ ▬ ▬▬	11. Now cometh the Frontier of the Holy City; the M.T. is taken into the Abyss.	♄	♓, ▽ of 🜃
	for in truth they were **R - The Phallus exhausted** ▬▬ ▬ ▬ ●	12. The Second Mystery: the cup-bearer of Babalon the beautiful. The Holy Grail manifested to the M.T., with the first knowledge of the Black Brothers. *(They have withheld their blood from her Cup, and so remain as they were, exhausted and not reborn, having attempted to preserve the shell of the dead ego, that is Choronzon.)*	♈	♓

49	**SH** **The Resurrection**	19. Now cometh forth the Angel who giveth instruction, in the lowest form. The Hegemone in the Ceremony of Magister Templi which the Seer is about to undergo. *Via SH, the balance is established even if aversely (for he Hangs upside down and so sees everything aversely). See following the 2nd aethyr in which this is finally revealed.*		
50	*Yea, and there arose sensualists upon the firmament, as a foul stain of storm upon the sky.* **L averse**[4] ▬ ▪ ▪ ●	*L averse is equivalent to Nun = 50, the number of the gates of Understanding and the glyph for Death. This should be suggestive to the Aspirant as to the law directing the flow of life and of death.*	___	♌
60	*And the Black Brothers raised their heads; yea, they unveiled themselves without shame or fear.* **w – Vision**[5] **(CK)** ▪ ▪ ▬ ●	20. A guide is given to the Seer, his Holy Guardian Angel. And this is attained by a mastery of the Universe conceived as a wheel The Hiereus in the Ceremony of Magister Templi. *The act of unveiling not only reveals the concealed face, but also uncovers the eyes and yields Vision.* *Note how the male current is absent here. The passivity required for perfect receptivity in BINH for Understanding to be achieved now bars the aspirant from the crown. He must move.*	△	♒
67	**wh**	21. This seems to be the Vision of God face to face that is the necessary ordeal for him who would pass the Abyss, as it were. A commission to be the prophet of the Æon arising is given to the Seer. The God is the Hierophant in the Ceremony of Magister Templi		

* *via distribution of the sum operator—a mathematically unlawful operation despite being a physical reality. A perfect example of a boundary experience where conventional science fails and investigation yields undiscovered results.*

24	*But the Enemy confused them. They pretended to conceal that Light, that they might betray it, and profane it.* **S – The Serpent**	16. The sacrifice is made. The High Priestess (image of Babalon) (hard C ♀) cometh forth upon her Beast (K– The Virgin ♂) and maketh this.	♓	♈, △ of △
31	**SH** **The Serpent Crowned**	*CH, KH : The symbol of balance: "the Wisdom of Him that sets his Balance in the ever-changing Airs". Note 37: a ram's head and a goat's, horns entangled, caught in their leap, their bodies arching over the gates to a garden. 37 spans all triune numbers and is the foundation of Aleph and a number of Kether. (111 = 37 x 3; 222 = 37 x 6; etc.)*		
37	**CH, KH** **The Lovers Enthroned**			
40	*Yet certain holy nuns concealed the secret in songs upon the lyre.* **M – The Wave, The Valley**	17. The symbol of the Balance is now given unto the Aspirant. *Certain holy nuns: See above; CH, KH the High Priestess enthroned engenders the Symbol of Balance : 40, the Hanged Man. (note: the transition from 401 to 441, ie. From (20x20) + 1 into (20+1) x (20+1)* requires the addition of 40 = M.* *Note: Balance = 8 + 4+ 70+4+70+3+1 = 156 + 4 = 160 = M x 4 that is, onto the material plane; and note the procession that rests upon this pivot: S, SH, (CH, KH), M, Sf, SfH = 260 = M + 220 (The Law), so that M divides S and Sf via K, the Virgin and Hard C, the Mother where both are established and enthroned with Power (KH,CH). See Sf and Sh below.* *Note: the Procession of the Qabalah through the Aeons pivots through this point. *See notes on the Procession of the Aeons.*	▽	♋, △ of ▽
42	*Now did the Horror of Time pervert all things, hiding the Purity with a loathsome thing, a thing unnameable.* **S_f –The Son**	18. The Vault of preparation for the Ceremony of M.T The Veil is the Crucifixion, symbol of the dead Æon. The first ordeal is undergone. *S becomes Sf, through M (or S is hung in M and so becomes Sf). In this process, he is united to the Angel, H, in both phases as SH (=31) and SfH (=49)*	♓	♏

80	*And in soft light.* **O – The Moon** ☲	24. Now appears his mate, the heavenly Venus, the Scarlet Woman (0), who by men is thought of as Babalon (0) as he is thought of as Chaos (V).	☽	☉
	Then were the waters gathered together from the heavens, **V – The Horns of Power**[7] ☱	*Note the transition from O-C and V-K, in this union of Opposites. See Aethyr 16.*	♉	♀
93	**IT**	25. Appearance of the Lion God of Horus, the child of Leo that incarnates him. The first Angel is Isis its mother.		
98	*And a crust of earth concealed the core of flame.* **T – The Table** ☶	*Note: Tf+IT+T=89+93+98=280, the severities associated with Pe (Mars).*	♑	♂
96, 105	**TH**	26. The death of the past Æon, that of Jehovah and Jesus; ends with adumbration of the new, the vision of the Stele of Ankh-f-n-khonsu, whose discovery brought about in a human consciousness the knowledge of the Equinox of the Gods, 21. 3. 04.		
131	**ST**			

89	*Also there rose up a soul of filth and of weakness, and it corrupted all the rule of the Tao.* **T_f (The Altar)**[6]	*L – The Balance divides T and Tf.*	♑	♉
70	*Then only was Heaven established to bear sway; for only in the lowest corruption is form manifest.* **L – Balance – A Foot**	22. Here is the First Key to the formula of Horus, a sevenfold arrangement. A shadow of Horus declares his nature.* *The Gate to 'the great god ON' – the Balancing of the Ls (NOTE: L AVERSE + L = 50 + 70 =120 = (Aeon II ON or Nun + Ayin)* *L upright and the establishment of the Balance in Air: "It is the letter I in this Æthyr that gives this vision, and L is its purity, and N is its energy.* "LIBER CDXVIII, THE CRY OF THE 22NDÆTHYR, WHICH IS CALLED LIN. Note I, the yod, is to be interpreted as Y here.	♎	♄
	Also did Heaven manifest in violent light, **N – The Gate, Y_v, The Tree**	23. Here appear the Cherubim, the other officers of the new Temple, the earth (Y) and water(N)* assistants of the fire and air Beast and Scarlet Woman. **Scorpio is Water sign.*	♏ 🜄 (N), (Y)	☿

* A hint of the seven-fold arrangement: These are the seven permutations of L, Y and N in the body (and distributed throughout the tablet). See Chapter on the three wheels: Y the vision, the 1st wheel; L the purity, the 2nd; N the energy, the third:

1. At first, there is no vision (∄ Y), the purity is concealed (∄ L) and the energies are dormant (N = Nf = 6): Y,L,N = 0, 0, 6 Σ = 6
2. The passive energies awaken the sensorium, the veil is perceived, and the vision is darkness (Y=Yc): Y,L,N = 6, 0, 6 Σ = 12
3. The energies are awakened (N=N=70): Y,L,N = 6, 0, 70 Σ = 76
4. The veil is momentarily lifted (Y = Yv=70). The flooding of light and in that light the perception and intellection of Duality. The imbalance or the impurity is perceived as consumed and exhausted in the explosion. (N =Nf =6): Y,L,N = 70, 50, 6 Σ = 126

N.B.: 6 + 12 + 76 + 126 = 220

5. The swooning after the ecstasy: the energies are dormant. The vision recedes (Y=Yc=6): Y,L,N = 6, 50, 6 Σ = 62
6. The balance is established (L = 70): Y,L,N = 6, 70, 6 Σ = 82
7. There is no vision, no voice, (∄ Y) for there is no separation. The Godhead is established silently, invisibly : L, N = 70, 6, Σ =76

200	*Around the globe gathered the wide air,* **U – The Cup**	27. Hecate appears—her son, the son of a Virgin, a magus, is to bring the Æon to pass. And she, the herald, her function fulfilled, withdraws within her mystic veil.	♄	☽
210	**QU**			
400	*And men began to light fires upon the earth.* **W – The Eyes (Spirit)**	28. Now is a further and clearer shadowing-forth of the Great Mystery of the Æon which is to be led up to by the Æthyrs. *Observe how the W and X are interchanged in position as per Liber Al vel Legis. This process is essentially processed through the S and T, the union of which is concealed in the glyph ST=131. We have two cases for interpreting this ST in the old Aeon. ST as (1) Samech, Tau or as (2) Shin, Teth. But this is (1) Samech = 60 and Tau = 400)or (w,W) ; and (2) Shin = 300 and Teth = 9 or (X,x). These glyph substitutions imply a grand scale operation in the procession of the Aeons.*	△	♃
300	*Therefore was the end of it sorrow; yet in that sorrow a sixfold star of glory whereby they might see to return unto the stainless Abode; yea, unto the Stainless Abode.* **X – The Wheel**[8]	29. The disturbance of Equilibrium caused by the Coming of the Æon.	♄▽	⊕
	WH	30. Without the cube—the material world—is the sphere system of the spiritual world enfolding it. the Cry seems to be a sort of Exordium, and external showing forth of the coming of the new Æon, the Æon of Horus the crowned child.		

The Cube of Space

(the Material Plane)

Note

We are grateful to the adept GFLO, the author of this chapter containing his original and invaluable works. This high and exalted work contains the tables and constructs which trace the development of the glyphs through increasing degrees of manifestation. First, the trigrams can be viewed as operational signs of these properties as they manifest into the Supernals. These are later filtered down and undergo varied Change before they reach a particular Sephira or Aethyr. Finally the Cube itself represents the Material Plane including this World, perfectly and concisely.

The Cube of Space - The Hexahedron

NOTE: Each edge is the sum of the two sides that meet at that edge & each corner is the sum of the three sides that meet at that corner.

The CUBE of SPACE (Hexahedron)

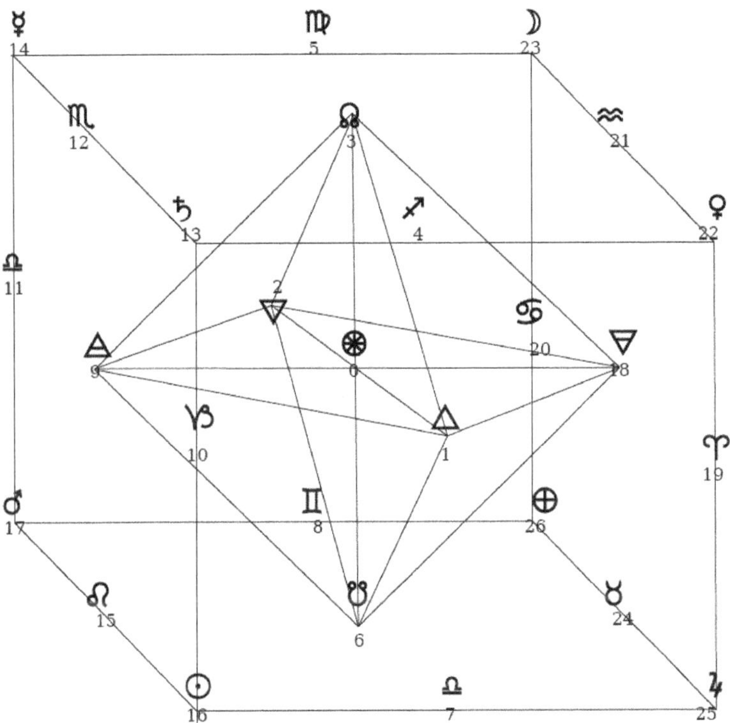

NOTE: The 8 Triangular Faces are the sum of the 3 Corners of each Triangle. The 12 Edges are the sum of the Corners it lies between. The 6 Corners are placed opposite each other. The Corners of the Octahedron connect with the Faces of the Cube & the Faces are turned towards the Corners of the Cube. These are the only two geometric three-dimensional forms, each known as a Dual (Twin) Polyhedron Platonic Solid, that exhaust the proportional characteristics of 6, 8 & 12 in all (including, of course, the Space Within, the 0). These can also be applied to other Platonic Solids, 5 in all, with similar mathematical properties, yet these attributions seem redundant with the larger solids (Dodecahedron, Icosahedron or even the Archimedean solid Cuboctahedron which is well within the proportions of the Cube) or incomplete as a system with the smaller one (Tetrahedron).

The Octahedron (Top Half)

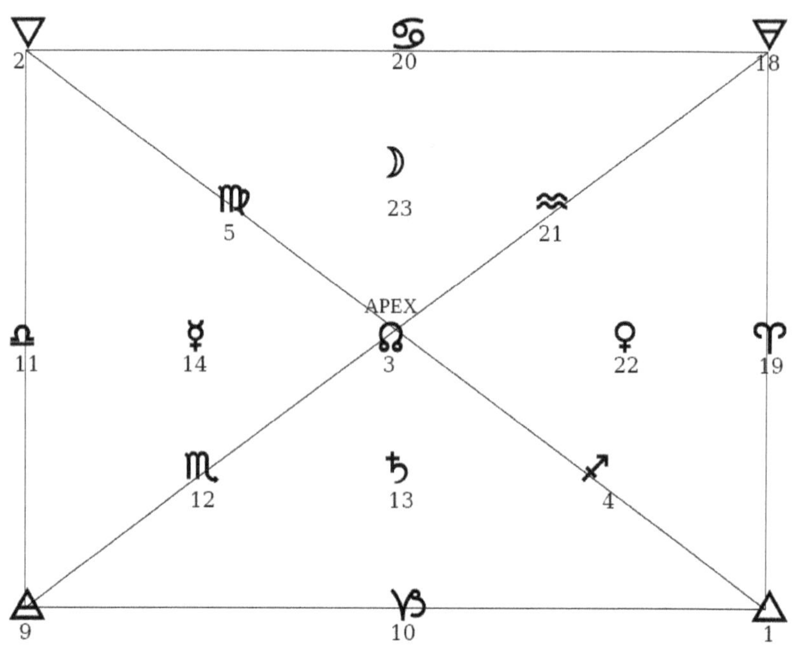

The Octahedron (Bottom Half)

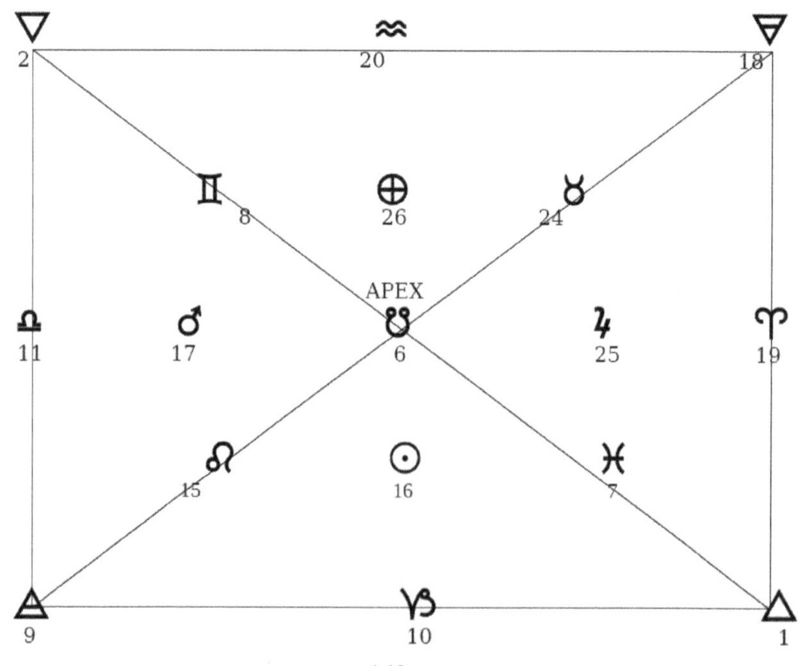

The Sun on the Cross

(or The Cube Unfolded)

Here the ❃ is free from the constraints of the Cube of Space.

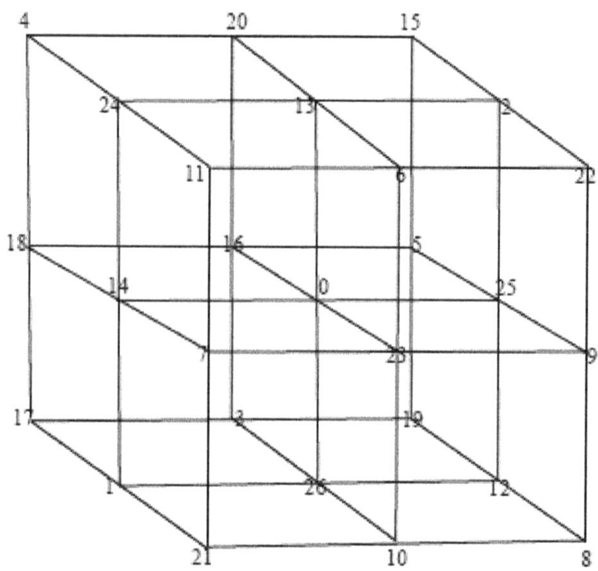

This cube consists of all numbers from 0 to 26. The sum of the 3 numbers in each of the 9 rows & 9 columns equals the magic constant 39. Each level, horizontally or vertically, is equal to 117. The 6 faces of this Magic Cube has the sum of 3*39 = 117 & 6 sides of the Cube of Space sums to 39; 117+ 39 = 156. All of the displaced opposites are identical to the Cube of Space. 39 is the reflection of 93 by the guidance of 54, AL (39 + 54 = 93).

The Magick Cube of Space = 708

Magick Cube of Space = 602 = Liber Trigrammaton. Empress & the Hierophant

Magic Cube of Space = 572 = HOOR-PAAR-KRAAT

The Magic Cube of Space = 678 = Eight and One in Eight. Worship then the Khabs

Magic Cube = 335 = Triple Light (E, the Center). Influx. Gnostic. Metaphysical.

Magick Cube = 365, the central number of 729 (27*27)

The Magic Cube = 441 = The Triple Light. One Light. Tetrahedron.

117 = Sphinx

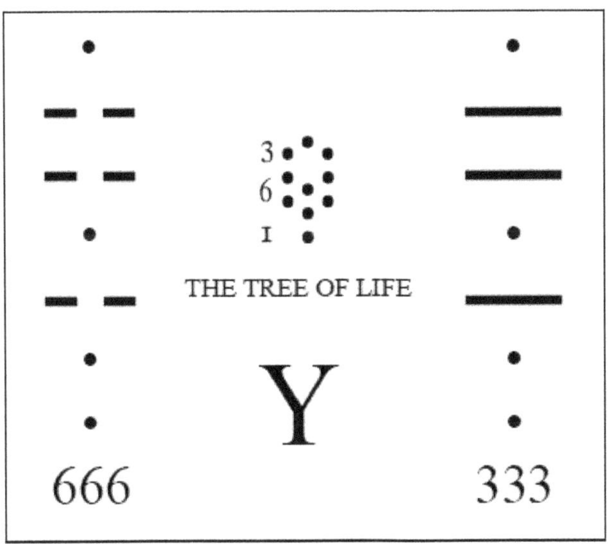

Note:
6+6+6 = 18 → ⚋ • • → E→ Y, The Tree of Life or The Tree of the World

The Y in its form if traced upon the Tree joins the Yin (Binah & Hokmah) and the Tao at the center (Tifareth) and the Tao below the center (Malkuth). These are the 4 Elements of the Minor Arcana.

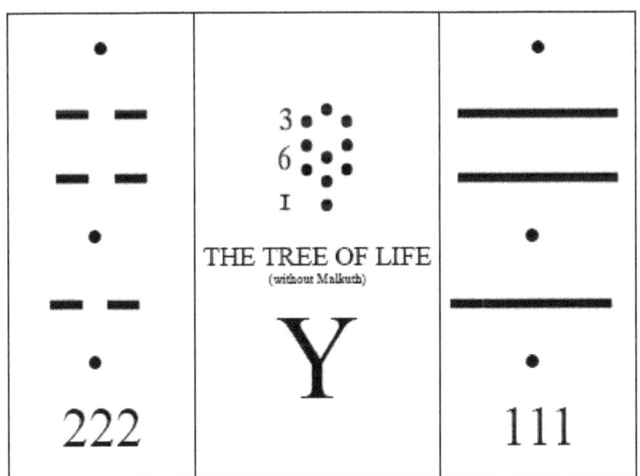

NOTE: 111+222 = 333
111+222+333 = 666

The 81 Tetragrams of T'ai Hsüan Ching

85	86	87	89	90	91	93	94	95
101	102	103	105	106	107	109	110	111
117	118	119	121	122	123	125	126	127
149	150	151	153	154	155	157	158	159
165	166	167	169	170	171	173	174	175
181	182	183	185	186	187	189	190	191
213	214	215	217	218	219	221	222	223
229	230	231	233	234	235	237	238	239
245	246	247	249	250	251	253	254	255

Note: According to the tradition of the I Ching NUCLEAR HEXAGRAMS are formed from the four central lines of each Hexagram leaving out the bottom & top lines which are replaced by the 2nd and 5th lines while the 3rd and 4th are doubled in between them so that the order appears as lines 2, 3 & 4 as the lower Trigram and lines 3, 4 & 5 as the upper Trigram from the bottom up. Because only four lines are being used to generate these Nuclear Hexagrams, there are 81 in all. This of course suggests a further correspondence of not only the 81 lines of Liber Trigrammaton and the Stanzas of Dzyan, but also the 81 insights of the Tao Te Ching (Book of the Way and its Virtue) and the 81 Tetragrams of the T'ai Hsüan Ching (Tai Xuan Jing / Canon of Supreme Mystery / The Great Dark Mystery) of Yang Hsiung (Yang Xiong). This set of 81 is part of a larger set of 256 that number 0–255 using the four digits of 0, 1, 2 & 3; so there are 175 more Tetragrams not displayed here. In the base 4 or quaternary numeral system such as this each level is a multiple of 4 and thus from bottom up we have 1, 4, 16 & 64. Note that this Book is also known as The Elemental Changes. These appear in the original order the author intended and from this it is obvious that he has numbered them in consecutive order from the least to greatest quaternary value as 1-81. Attribution should be as simple as matching the corresponding order found in the table titled THE KEY.

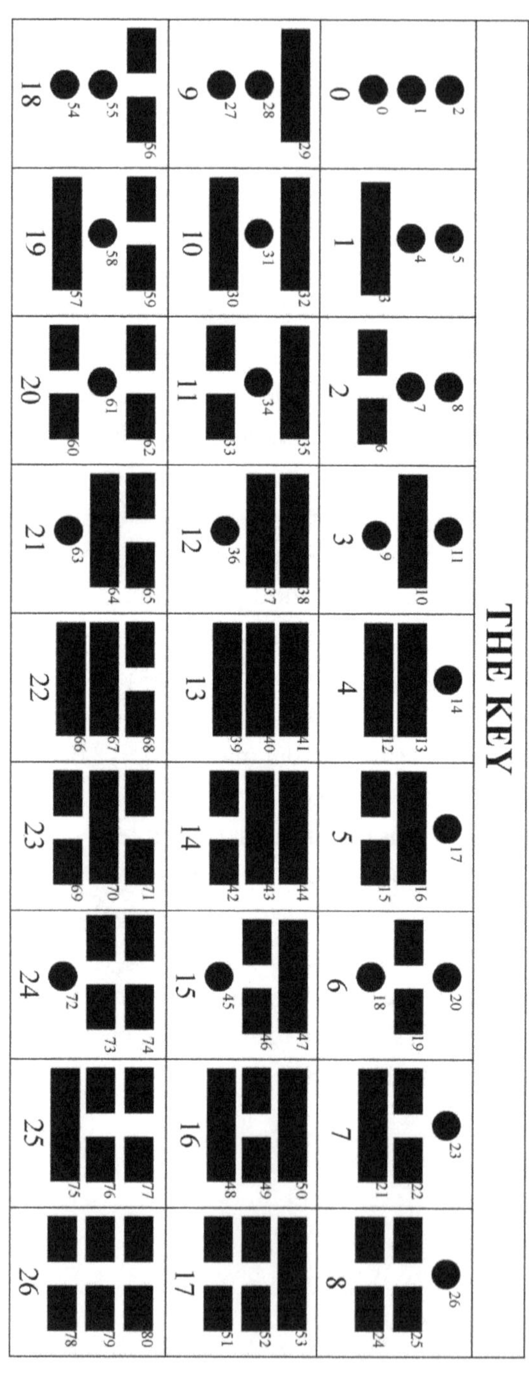
THE KEY
0
1
2
3
4
5
6
7
8
9
10
11
12
13
14
15
16
17
18
19
20
21
22
23
24
25
26

Brief examination of the 3 by 3 cells as 9 individual cells:

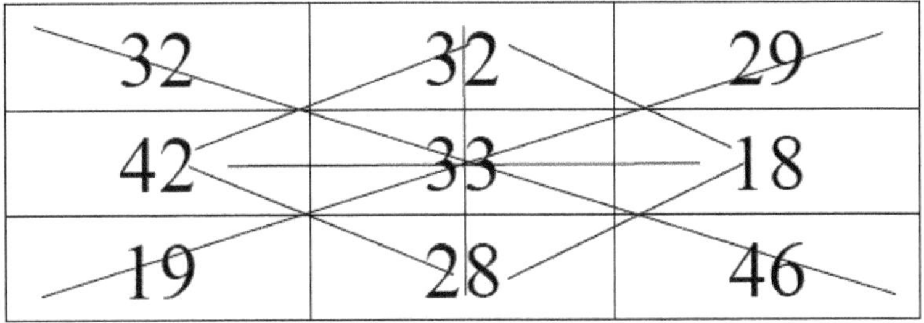

32	32	29
42	33	18
19	28	46

Note:
-upper right – bottom left = 111 (ANKH, the reversed Hexagram of 93)
-bottom left – upper right = 81 (The number of lines in the 27 trigrams)
-the "X" = 159 (ELEVEN)
-the "+" = 186 (Zenith, Lighten, Man-Child)
-the "◊" = 120 (AIWASS)

The Trigrams transforms the Square into a 3 by 3 within a 9 by 9 simultaneously which implies a manipulation of 93. If you rotate the Square 90° to the right or 180° reversed the Magic Sum is 141. A 90° turn to the left and the Magic Sum is 93. The Magic Sum of 0–80 on a 9 by 9 Square is 360. The analysis (and construction) of magic squares is more logical, and the results make more sense, when the smallest number is 0—instead of 1. 360 represents the degrees of a Circle which calls to mind the letter O, attributed to the Moon. 360 is also the value of AL in the form of a Hexagram if read from the bottom up. The implications are numerous. In a sense, the Circle has been Squared. This Square appears to be the only (or at least few in number) unique & natural arrangement possible with any significance. There are perhaps other parallel equivalents of the corresponding English Glyphs.

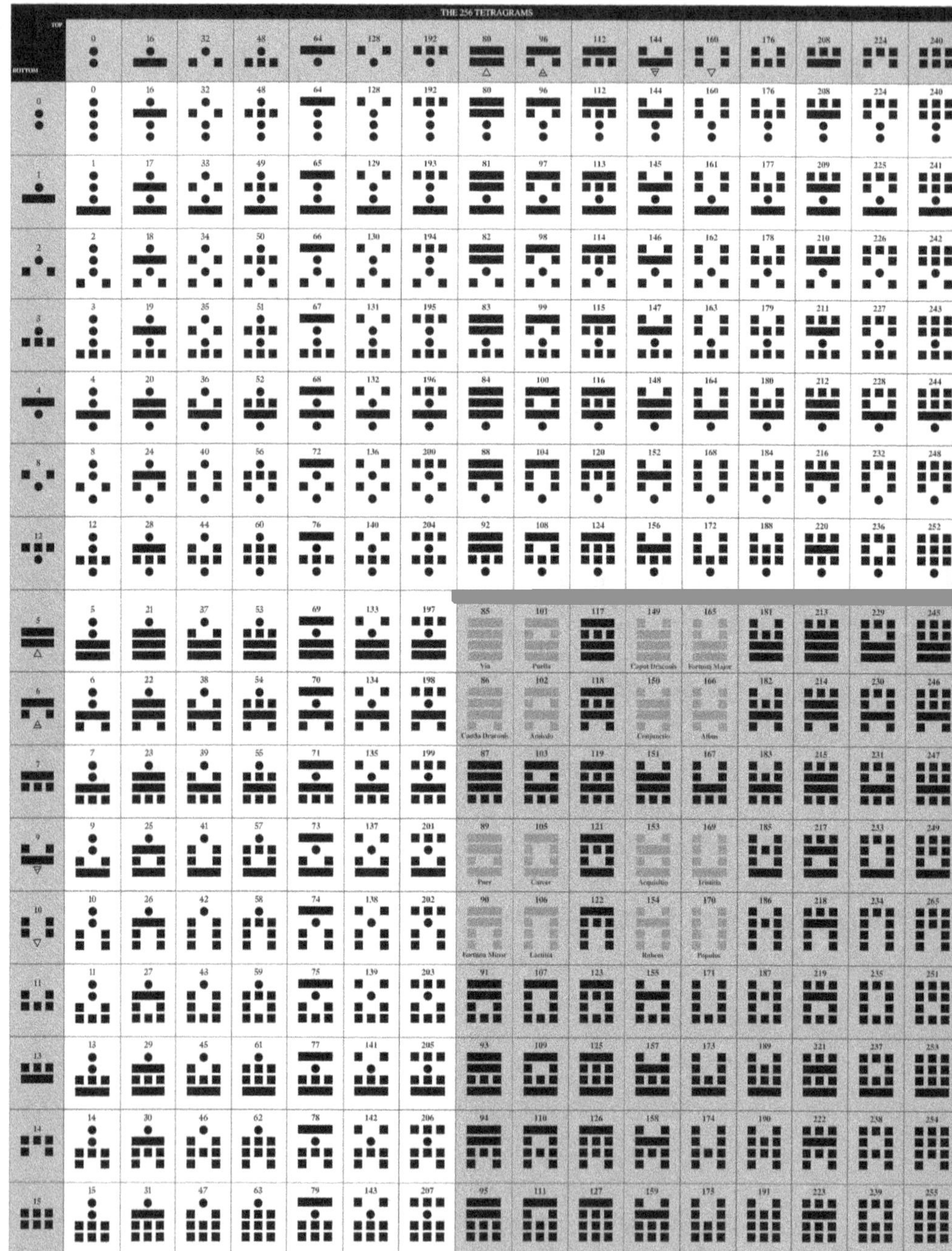

THE 256 TETRAGRAMS

TOP / BOTTOM	0	16	32	48	64	128	192	80	96	112	144	160	176	208	224	240
0	0	16	32	48	64	128	192	80	96	112	144	160	176	208	224	240
1	1	17	33	49	65	129	193	81	97	113	145	161	177	209	225	241
2	2	18	34	50	66	130	194	82	98	114	146	162	178	210	226	242
3	3	19	35	51	67	131	195	83	99	115	147	163	179	211	227	243
4	4	20	36	52	68	132	196	84	100	116	148	164	180	212	228	244
8	8	24	40	56	72	136	200	88	104	120	152	168	184	216	232	248
12	12	28	44	60	76	140	204	92	108	124	156	172	188	220	236	252
5	5	21	37	53	69	133	197	85 Via	101 Puella	117	149 Caput Draconis	165 Fortuna Major	181	213	229	245
6	6	22	38	54	70	134	198	86 Cauda Draconis	102 Amissio	118	150 Conjunctio	166 Albus	182	214	230	246
7	7	23	39	55	71	135	199	87	103	119	151	167	183	215	231	247
9	9	25	41	57	73	137	201	89 Puer	105 Carcer	121	153 Acquisitio	169 Tristitia	185	217	233	249
10	10	26	42	58	74	138	202	90 Fortuna Minor	106 Laetitia	122	154 Rubeus	170 Populus	186	218	234	265
11	11	27	43	59	75	139	203	91	107	123	155	171	187	219	235	251
13	13	29	45	61	77	141	205	93	109	125	157	173	189	221	237	253
14	14	30	46	62	78	142	206	94	110	126	158	174	190	222	238	254
15	15	31	47	63	79	143	207	95	111	127	159	175	191	223	239	255

The Magic Square of 9 (The Moon)

The Magic Square of 9												
		423										
78		141			141			141				78
	39	66	39	36	66	39	36	66	39	36	63	
	12	36	77	28	69	20	61	12	53	4	36	
93	39	5	37	78	29	70	21	62	13	45	39	141
	42	46	6	38	79	30	71	22	54	14	66	
	12	15	47	7	39	80	31	63	23	55	36	
93	39	56	16	48	8	40	72	32	64	24	39	141
	42	25	57	17	49	0	41	73	33	65	66	
	12	66	26	58	9	50	1	42	74	34	36	
93	39	35	67	18	59	10	51	2	43	75	39	141
	42	76	27	68	19	60	11	52	3	44	66	
	15	42	39	12	42	39	12	42	39	12	39	
78		93			93			93				78
		279										

Note:
The +, 17 squares = 78 = AIWAZ
The + (both ways) = 156
The □, 32 squares = 156
The X, 17 squares (both ways or all 4 corners of) = 156 = BABALON, KAOS
The X (down) = 54 = AL
The X (upwards) = 102 = Sigil
The Swastika (right), 29 squares = 141 = HEKATE
The Swastika (left) = 119 = PHTAH
The † = 105 Σ14 = TH, Ten, I am Life
279 + 423 = 702 = The Sky of NU, Trinity of Triads

Liber Trigrammaton, The Cube of Space & Attributions

Letter, Value & Trigram	Oriental Attribution		Occidental Attribution	Cube of Space
E, J -1 0 ● 2 ● 1 ● 0 0 Here is Nothing under its three forms. It is not, yet informeth all things.	空 (AETHYR/ VOID)		☸	CENTER
(Upper) ● 2 Heaven Nothingness	○ 無極 WU CHI		△↔▽	EAST/ WEST AXIS
(Middle) ● 1 Man Unboundedness	☉ 吳念 WU NIEN		☊ ↕ ☋	VERTICAL AXIS
(Lower) ● 0 Earth Emptiness	☯ 太極 - - 道德 TAI CHI- -TAO-TEH		🜁↔🜃	NORTH/ SOUTH AXIS

Letter, Value & Trigram	Oriental Attribution		Occidental Attribution	Cube of Space
f - 2 27 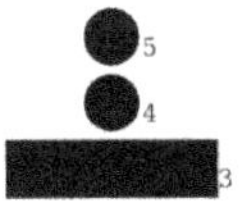 5 4 3 1 **Now cometh the glory of the Single One, as an imperfection and stain.**	火♂ FIRE upward expansive 南 SOUTH	Old Yang 丙, 丁 ♂ Vermilion Bird of the South: Summer Tai Yang =9	△	EAST/ FRONT
softC, P - 3 54 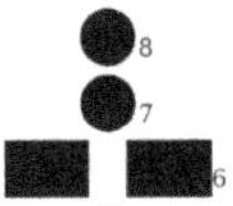 8 7 6 2 **But by the Weak One the Mother was it equilibrated.**	水☿ WATER downward stillness 北 NORTH	Old Yin 壬, 癸 ☿ Black Tortoise (& Snake) or Warrior of the North: Winter  Tai Yin =6	▽	WEST/ REAR
I, A - 4 81 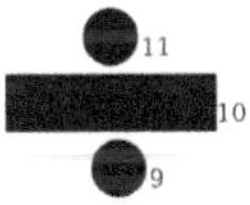 11 10 9 3 **Also the purity was divided by Strength, the force of the Demiurge.**	土 ♄ EARTH ABOVE centering, stabilizing & conserving 風 WIND ☽	Middle Yang 戊 ♄ The Yellow Dragon or Qilin of the Center: Change of Seasons	☊♅ **North Node** **CAPUT** **DRACONIS** **RAHU**	ABOVE/ HEIGHT
j - 5 162 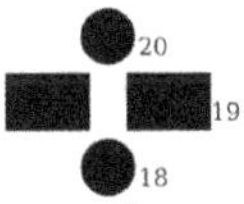 20 19 18 6 **And the Cross was formulated in the Universe that as yet was not.**	土♄ EARTH BELOW centering, stabilizing & conserving	Middle Yin 己 ♄ The Yellow Dragon or Qilin of the Center: Change of Seasons	☋♆ **South Node** **CAUDA** **DRACONIS** **KETU**	BELOW/ DEPTH

Letter, Value & Trigram	Oriental Attribution		Occidental Attribution	Cube of Space
B, N_f - 6 243 29 28 27 9 **But now the Imperfection became manifest, presiding over the fading of perfection.**	木♃ WOOD outward strength and flexibility 東 EAST	Young Yang 甲, 乙 ♃ Azure Dragon of the East: Spring Shao Yang =7	🜁	SOUTH/ RIGHT
Z, Y - 6 486 56 55 54 18 **Also the Woman arose, and veiled the Upper Heaven with her body of stars.**	金♀ METAL inward contracting 西 WEST	Young Yin 庚, 辛 ♀ White Tiger of the West: Autumn Shao Yin =8	🜃	NORTH/ LEFT
H - 7 108 14 13 12 4 **Now then a giant arose, of terrible strength; and asserted the Spirit in a secret rite.**	馬/ 马 (午) ☉ FIRE 丙 **-BING**	**June** **HORSE** 馬 **+△** **Yang**	**December** ♐ Mutable ▽ of △	EAST ABOVE
D - 8 135 17 16 15 5 **And the Master of the Temple balancing all things arose; his stature was above the Heaven and below Earth and Hell.**	兔/ 兎 (卯) ☿ SMALL WOOD 乙 **-YI**	**March** **RABBIT** **(HARE, CAT)** 兔 **−▲** **Yin**	**September** ♍ Mutable ▽ of 🜃	WEST ABOVE

Letter, Value & Trigram	Oriental Attribution		Occidental Attribution	Cube of Space
R, x - 9 189 23 22 21 7 Against him the Brothers of the Left-hand Path, confusing the symbols. They concealed their horror [in this symbol]; for in truth they were	雞/ 鸡 (酉) ♀ SMALL METAL 辛 -XIN	September ROOSTER (HEN, CHICKEN, COCK) 鸡 –▼ Yang	March ♓ Mutable ▽ of ▽	EAST BELOW
F, Q - 10 216 26 25 24 8 The master flamed forth as a star and set a guard of Water in every Abyss.	鼠 (子) ☽ WATER 壬 -REN	December RAT (MOUSE) 鼠 +▽ Yin	June ♊ Mutable ▽ of 🜁	WEST BELOW
K, C - 30 270 32 31 30 10 Also certain secret ones concealed the Light of Purity in themselves, protecting it from the Persecutions.	羊 (未) ♂ SMALL EARTH 己 -JI (YIN FIRE) 丁 -DING	July GOAT (RAM, SHEEP, LAMB) 羊 EARTH –△ Yang	♑ Cardinal △ of 🜃	SOUTH EAST
G - 20 297 35 34 33 11 Likewise also did certain sons and daughters of Hermes and of Aphrodite, more openly.	龍/ 龙 (辰) ⊕☊♅- ♃ BIG EARTH 戊 -WU BIG WOOD 甲 -JIA	April DRAGON 龍 EARTH +▲ Wood Yang	October ♎ Cardinal △ of 🜁	SOUTH WEST

Letter, Value & Trigram	Oriental Attribution		Occidental Attribution	Cube of Space
S - 24 513 59 58 57 19 But the Enemy confused them. They pretended to conceal that Light, that they might betray it, and profane it.	狗/ 犬 (戌) ♄-♂ SMALL EARTH 己 -JI (BIG METAL) 庚 -GENG	October DOG 犬 EARTH +▼ Metal Yin	April ♈ Cardinal △ of △	NORTH EAST
M - 40 540 62 61 60 20 Yet certain holy nuns concealed the secret in songs upon the lyre.	牛 (丑) ⊕♅♆- ♀ BIG EARTH 戊 -WU (YIN WATER) 癸 -GUI	January OX (WATER BUFFALO, COW) 牛 EARTH −▽ Yin	July ♋ Cardinal △ of ▽	NORTH WEST
S_f - 42 324 38 37 36 12 Now did the Horror of Time pervert all things, hiding the Purity with a loathsome thing, a thing unnameable.	蛇 (巳) ♂ SMALL EARTH 丁 -DING	May SNAKE 蛇 −△ Yang	November ♏ Fixed 🜁 of ▽	SOUTH ABOVE
Ł - 50 405 47 46 45 15 Yea, and there arose sensualists upon the firmament, as a foul stain of storm upon the sky.	虎 (寅) ♃ BIG WOOD 甲 -JIA	February TIGER 虎 +▲ Yang	August ♌ Fixed 🜁 of △	SOUTH BELOW

Letter, Value & Trigram	Oriental Attribution		Occidental Attribution	Cube of Space
w - 60 567 65 64 63 21 And the Black Brothers raised their heads; yea, they unveiled themselves without shame or fear.	猴 (申) ♄ BIG METAL 庚 -GENG	**August** **MONKEY** 猴 +▼ **Yin**	**February** ♒ Fixed 🜁 of 🜁	NORTH ABOVE
T_f - 89 648 74 73 72 24 Also there rose up a soul of filth and of weakness, and it corrupted all the rule of the Tao.	豬/ 猪 (亥) ⊕♉♆- ♀ BIG EARTH 戊 -WU (YIN WATER) 癸 -GUI	**November** **PIG** **(BOAR, HOG ELEPHANT)** 猪 −▽ **Yin**	**May** ♉ Fixed 🜁 of 🜃	NORTH BELOW
L - 70 351 41 40 39 13 Then only was Heaven established to bear sway; for only in the lowest corruption is form manifest.	乾 Qián, Khien, Chyán is the HORSE 庚 -GENG ♀ ☽	BIG METAL +▼ +🜁 Heaven, Sky Father Late Autumn & Early Winter Night	♄ ⊛ ▽ This is the creative Saturn, the hidden God, and the Daäth of the apex of the upper triangle of the hexagram is in reality a concentration of the Trinity of the Supernals. ~777	SOUTH EAST ABOVE
N, Y - 70 378 44 43 42 14 Also did Heaven manifest in violent light.	巽 Xùn, Sun, Hsun is the CHICKEN or FOWL (SHEEP) 乙 -YI ♃ ☽	SMALL WOOD −▲ −🜁 Wind, Air Eldest Daughter Late Spring & Early Summer Late Morning	☿ 🜁	SOUTH WEST ABOVE

Letter, Value & Trigram	Oriental Attribution		Occidental Attribution	Cube of Space
Ō, Ȯ - 200 432 ☲ 50 49 48 16 And in soft light.	離 Lí is the PHEASANT 丙 -BING ♂	FIRE +△ Lightening Middle Daughter Mid-Summer Midday, Noon	☉ △	SOUTH EAST BELOW
V, Ŏ - 80 594 ☱ 68 67 66 22 Then were the waters gathered together from the heaven.	兌 Duì, Tui is the GOAT 辛 -XIN ♀ 癸 -GUI ☿	SMALL METAL −▼ −▽ Lake, Valley, Marsh Youngest Daughter Autumn, Fall Evening	♀ 🜃	NORTH EAST ABOVE
T - 98 459 ☶ 53 52 51 17 And a crust of earth concealed the core of flame.	艮 Gèn, Kèn is the DOG 己 -JI ♄ 丁 -DING ♂	SMALL EARTH −🜃 −△ Mountain, Hill, Volcano Youngest Son Late Winter & Early Spring Early Morning	♂ △	SOUTH WEST BELOW
U - 200 621 ☵ 71 70 69 23 Around the globe gathered the wide air.	坎 Kǎn, Khǎn is the PIG 壬 -REN ☿	WATER +▽ Cloud, Rain, Springs, the Abyss Middle Son Mid-Winter Midnight	☽ 🜁	NORTH WEST ABOVE

Letter, Value & Trigram	Oriental Attribution		Occidental Attribution	Cube of Space
W - 400 675 77 76 75 25 **And men began to light fires upon the earth.**	震 Zhèn, Khèn, Chèn is the DRAGON 甲 -JIA ♃	BIG WOOD +▲ Thunder Eldest Son Spring Midmorning	♃ ▽	NORTH EAST BELOW
X - 300 702 80 79 78 26 **Therefore was the end of it sorrow; yet in that sorrow a sixfold star of glory whereby they might see to return unto the stainless Abode; yea, unto the Stainless Abode.**	坤 Kūn, Khwǎn is OXEN or CATTLE 戊 -WU ♄ 甲 -JIA ♃ 癸 -GUI ☿	BIG EARTH +🜃 + – ▲↔▽ ☊↔☋ Mother Late summer, Early Fall, ripening season Afternoon	⊕ 🜃	NORTH WEST BELOW

SUGGESTIVE OBSERVATIONS FOR ATTRIBUTIONS

E, J

Like the Hebrew letter Shin, the 'E' is also a glyph of the triple tongue of flame. The idea of the ternary shown by the 3 horizontal strokes is modified by the value of the trigram and letter as 0 and 1. One being the concentrated form of 0 it therefore implies the doctrine of the Negative Trinity. 'J' is the Horn of Plenty and also a Fish-Hook and its capital value of 5 implies Man (pentagram) and the 5th element which is also the First. 1/5 = 0.2 which implies 0 = 2

f

"*the fiery god Horus took the place of the airy god Osiris in the East as Hierophant*" -Book of Thoth

A withering or sprouting plant or seedling. The letter 'f' therefore signifies the root or antecedent of any action. It is the creative spark or impulse, like a seed planted in Spring which is just ready to sprout. This beginning is symbolized by Fire.

C, P

'C' is the Barren Womb or empty Chalice and 'P' is the Pregnant Goddess and a Needle's Eye. Pregnancy involves the growth of the embryo nourished by the amniotic fluid (water). Vessels are of the element of Water which implies receptivity, reflection, stillness and fluidity. The 'C' also resembles a Tidal Wave and a Crescent Moon which is a tattva symbol of Water. As a Scythe or Sickle it suggests harvesting.

I

'I' is the ego or self. The nominative case of the pronoun of the first person; the word with which the subject designates or identifies itself.

A

'A' is the Pyramid of Light. By definition, it is an adjective or indefinite article, and signifying one or any, but less emphatically: a determining or causal element or factor relative to a subject or object. As a prefix it means 'not' or 'without', 'in the process of' or ' a particular state of'. The 'A' not only resembles a Star, but also a Masonic Compass, a technical drawing instrument that can be used for inscribing circles or arcs.

Z, Nf

'Z' resembles the thunderbolt of Zeus, god of Air. Both thunder and lightning are caused primarily by the forces of Air. "The true form of the Sword is the flaming sword, the lightning flash, which strikes down from Kether through the Sephiroth as a zig-zag flash. " -Liber 777

B, Y

The Book of Knowledge is made from the Tree of this World which grows out of the element of Earth & She is a Woman. Was it not Eve who gave the fruit to Adam & he did eat? This Book & the Pages thereof are also the Breasts of Our Lady. It is here that the Pentacle or "the Coin redeemeth". The 'Y' shape suggests the division of that which is perfect only in unity, the dual contending forces, struggling.

L

The Foot and the Framing Square partake naturally of the earth element and measurement which has an affinity with Saturn and is also mathematically the first magic Square. It is the successful squaring of the circle and the balance of Stability.

N, Y

The letter 'Y' is phonetically equivalent to the word "Why?" (see AL II:30-33) and signifies the misuse of Reason. As a Fork in the Road it is the division of Unity by the Dyad. Note that the Dog (of Reason) is partly associated with Mercury and symbolizes the lower nature of intelligence. 'N' as the Gate signifies boundaries. In ancient Greece, the Hermae statues had a ritualistic purpose and were placed at crossings, country borders and boundaries. The Romans called him Mercury & Terminus, in his landmark aspect. The 'Y' also resembles the Caduceus and the Tree of the World. The 'N' points above and below.

Ō, Ȯ

'O' is the Circle of the Sun in simplest form. Its phonetic symbol of pronunciation places the point or line, which are identical, out from the center and above it. Also if the line was placed within the Circle it would resemble the Greek letter Theta attributed to Leo, the House of the Sun. 'O' is an emotional or impassioned exclamation of expression. 200 = Satan

V, Ŏ

The 'V' resembles the Roman numeral 5 as the Key of the TARO assigned to Taurus, the Horns of Power, signifying its ruler Venus. V is Lucifer or Venus ascending (morning star) and 'Ŏ' is Venus descending (evening star). V also signifies a vagina or an inverted triangle. Eighty = 200 The horns are a fertility symbol.

T

Phonetically the 'T' is violently explosive and a forceful "release of energy." The cross is an instrument of torture for serious offences. The idea was to prolong the agony, not to make the victim more comfortable. The "flail," "scarlet" and "fire" are of Mars. 'T' as a Table -Rectangular tables were used at feasts, and the seating assignments normally reflected the feudal hierarchy. Also the shape of the letter suggests the hilt, and the lower part of the blade and is the magickal weapon of Mars as the active and militant energy of the magician and symbolical of the warrior caste. The tongue is the double edged sword of the mouth (Pe). Note also that the final form is Horus the Spirit Guide of the 18th Aethyr. The Chinese ideogram "DING" resembles the 'T' as the pictograph for "nail" and means "to strike." Compare with the DOG/ARIES attribution of 11th Aethyr. 98 = Sin

U

The connection here is obvious. Gimel means camel and the shape of the U suggests the curve between the camel's hump. The shape suggests a Cup, Chalice, Graal, Cauldron, Urn etc. and any receptacle or container. Note that the path of Gimel crosses the Abyss which the Trigram signifies.

X

'X' resembles the hub and 4 (Jupiter) spokes of a wheel and is the Roman numeral for the TARO titled "Fortune" or "The Wheel." The Hebrew letter Kaph as the palm of the hand symbolized the hub of the Wheel. 300 = Jehovah. Note that Zeus is a thunder god.

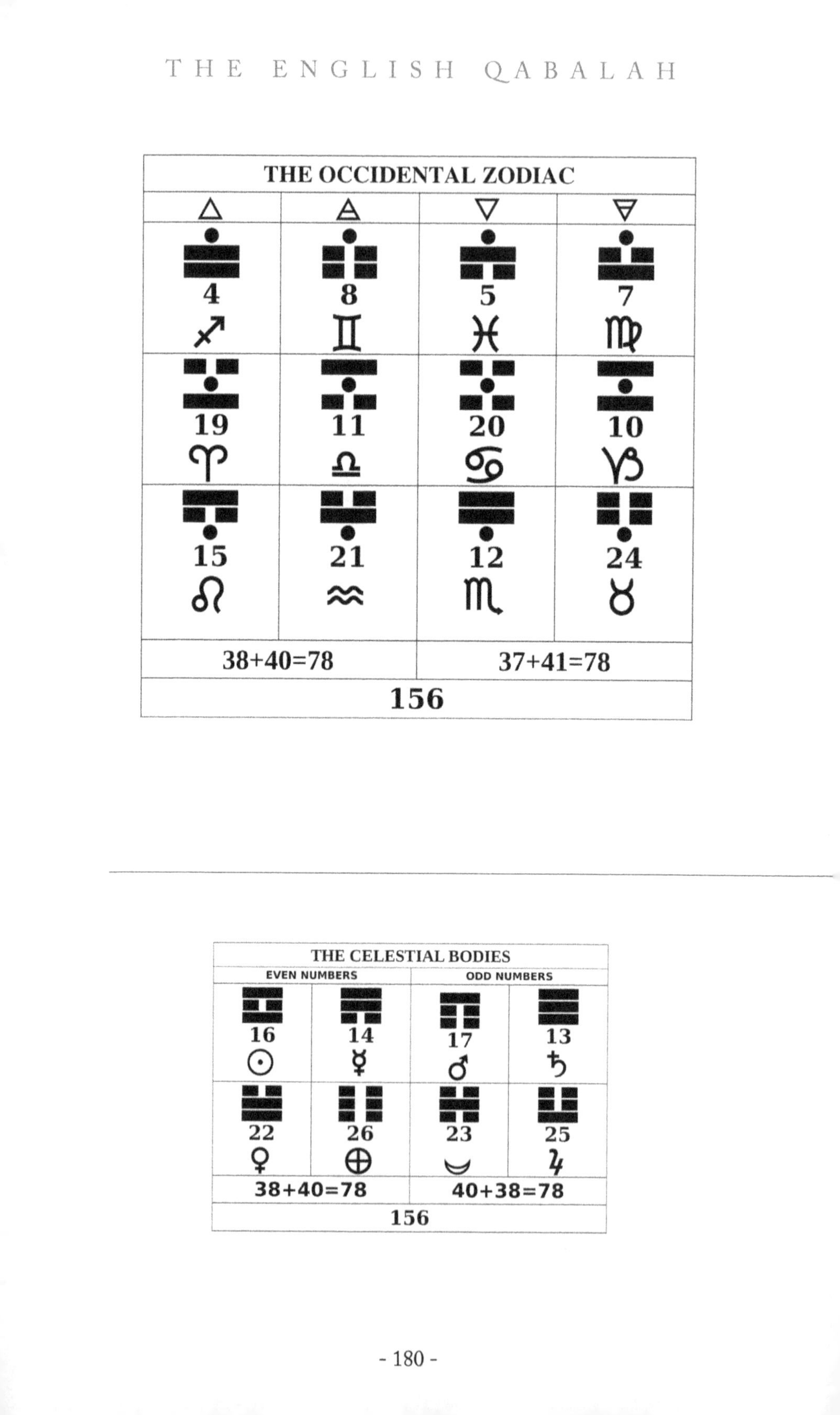

THE OCCIDENTAL ZODIAC			
△	🜁	▽	🜃
4 ♐	8 ♊	5 ♓	7 ♍
19 ♈	11 ♎	20 ♋	10 ♑
15 ♌	21 ♒	12 ♏	24 ♉
38+40=78		37+41=78	
156			

THE CELESTIAL BODIES			
EVEN NUMBERS		ODD NUMBERS	
16 ☉	14 ☿	17 ♂	13 ♄
22 ♀	26 ⊕	23 ☽	25 ♃
38+40=78		40+38=78	
156			

THE ORIENTAL ZODIAC			
ODD NUMBERS		EVEN NUMBERS	
▼	▲	△	▽
7	5	4	8
19	11	10	20
21	15	12	24
47+31=78		26+52=78	
156			

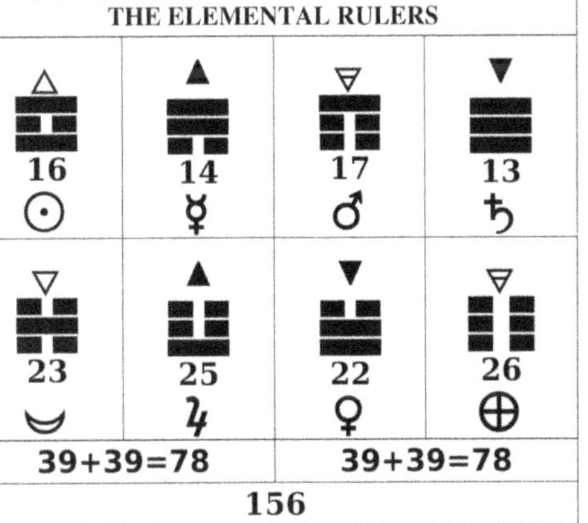

THE ELEMENTAL RULERS			
△ 16 ☉	▲ 14 ☿	🜃 17 ♂	▼ 13 ♄
▽ 23 ☽	▲ 25 ♃	▼ 22 ♀	🜃 26 ⊕
39+39=78		39+39=78	
156			

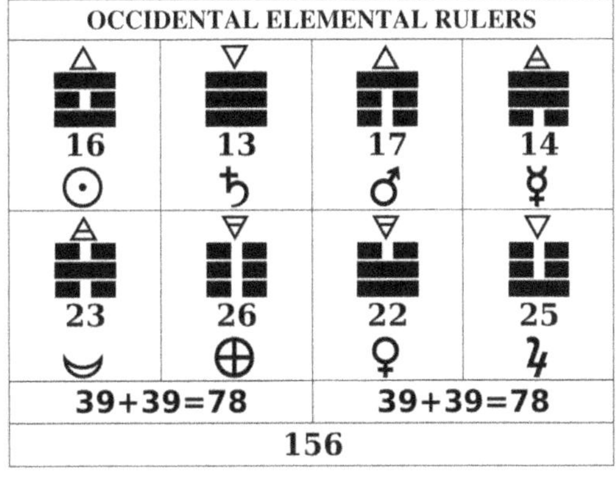

OCCIDENTAL ELEMENTAL RULERS			
△ 16 ☉	▽ 13 ♄	△ 17 ♂	🜁 14 ☿
🜁 23 ☽	🜃 26 ⊕	🜃 22 ♀	▽ 25 ♃
39+39=78		39+39=78	
156			

THE ORIENTAL TETRAGRAMMATON					
THE HSIANG (SI XIANG)	GEOMETRY	THE TIEN TAO	PLANETARY TRIGRAMS	PENTAGRAMMATON	RELATIONSHIP
Old (Mature) Yang ⚌ △	● ● Vertical Line	亨 Heng Expansion Summer	☉ ♂	י△	Father Knight
Young Yang ⚎ 🜁 WOOD	● ● ● Upright Triangle	元 Yuan Eminent Spring	♃ ☿	ו🜁	Son Prince King
The Tao ● ⊕	● Circle or Point			ש🜀	
Young Yin ⚍ 🜃 METAL	● ● ● Inverted Triangle	利 Li Harvest Autumn	♄ ♀	ה🜃	Daughter Maiden Princess
Old (Mature) Yin ⚏ ▽	● ● ● ● Square	贞 Zhen Determinati on Winter	☽ ⊕	ה▽	Mother Queen

Ruling Element	Trigram	Polarity	Sign(s)
Metal ♀	**13♄**	**Positive Metal**	**Monkey, Dog** ♒,♈
	22♀	**Negative Metal**	**Rooster** ♓
Water ☿	**23◡**	**Positive Water**	**Rat** ♊
	26⊕	**Negative Water**	**Ox, Pig** ♋, ♉
Wood ♃	**25♃**	**Positive Wood**	**Tiger, Dragon** ♌,♎
	14☿	**Negative Wood**	**Rabbit** ♍
Fire ♂	**16☉**	**Positive Fire**	**Horse** ♐
	17♂	**Negative Fire**	**Snake, Goat** ♏,♑
Earth ♄	**26⊕**	**Positive Earth**	**Dragon** ♎
	17♂	**Negative Earth**	**Dog** ♈
Wind ◡	**13♄**	**Positive Air**	**Monkey, Dog** ♒,♈
	14☿	**Negative Air**	**Rabbit** ♍

The Link Between the Eastern and Western Elements

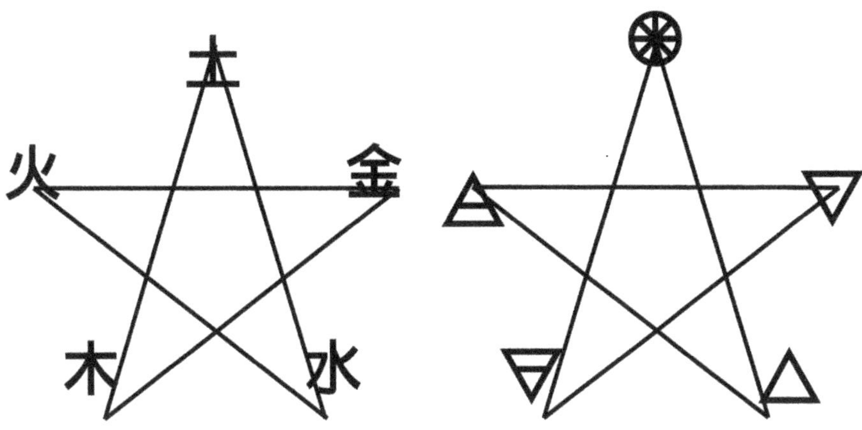

1 Note that the Oriental attributions of the Trigrams follow the Wu cycle in its progression & the Ke cycle in its reverse. Note that Earth, as the transitioning element is represented by 2 central Trigrams.

2 Note that in the Oriental idea of Earth (土) is similar to the Occidental idea of Spirit & so likewise is Wood (木) with Air & Metal (金) with Earth (Occidental). Of course Fire (火) & Water (水) are identical to their Occidental equivalents. If one follows the Occidental Pentagram in a Circle clockwise or counter-clockwise it will be seen that these elements trace the exact same path as the Wu (Insulting) & Ke (Destruction) cycles, but in the form of a pentagram. If one follows the Occidental elements in the form of a pentagram it will be seen that these elements trace the exact same path as the Sheng (Creation) cycle both ways, but in the form of a circle.

Court Card	Trigram	Geomancy	Tetragram	Tetragram	Geomancy	Trigram	Court Card
PRINCESS OF CUPS 🜃 OF 🜄	M	Via 15 ♋ decrease	85	170	Populus 30 ♋ increase	M	**QUEEN OF CUPS** 🜄 OF 🜄
PRINCESS OF DISKS 🜃 OF 🜃	J	Cauda Draconis 16 ☋	86	169	Tristitia 29 ♒	w	**PRINCE OF SWORDS** 🜃 OF 🜁
QUEEN OF WANDS 🜄 OF 🜂	S	Puer 17 ♈	89	166	Albus 28 ♊	F, Q	**KNIGHT OF SWORDS** 🜂 OF 🜃
PRINCE OF WANDS 🜁 OF 🜂	Ł	Fortuna Minor 18 ♌ S. decline	90	165	Fortuna Major 27 ♌ N. decline	Ł	**PRINCESS OF WANDS** 🜃 OF 🜂
QUEEN OF SWORDS 🜄 OF 🜁	G	Puella 19 ♎	101	154	Rubeus 26 ♏	S_r	**PRINCE OF CUPS** 🜁 OF 🜄
PRINCE OF DISKS 🜁 OF 🜃	T_f	Amissio 20 ♉	102	153	Acquisitio 25 ♐	H	**KNIGHT OF WANDS** 🜂 OF 🜂
QUEEN OF DISKS 🜄 OF 🜃	K, C	Carcer 21 ♑	105	150	Conjunctio 24 ♍	D	**KNIGHT OF DISKS** 🜂 OF 🜃
KNIGHT OF CUPS 🜂 OF 🜄	R, x	Laetitia 22 ♓	106	149	Caput Draconis 23 ☊	I, A	**PRINCESS OF SWORDS** 🜃 OF 🜁

THE ORDER OF THE 729 HEXAGRAMS

BOTTOM \ TOP	⊛ E, j	△ f	▽ ₛC, P	☊ I, A	☋ J	△ B, N_f	▽ Z, Y_c	♐ H	♍ D	♓ R, x	♊ F, Q	♑ K, C	♎ G	♈ S	♋ M	♏ S_f	♌ Ł	♒ w	♉ T	♄ L	☿ N, Y	☉ Ö, Ò	♀ V, Ŏ	♂ T	☽ U	♃ W	⊗ X
⊛ E, j	0	27	54	81	162	243	486	108	135	189	216	270	297	513	540	324	405	567	648	351	378	432	594	459	621	675	702
△ f	1	28	55	82	163	244	487	109	136	190	217	271	298	514	541	325	406	568	649	352	379	433	595	460	622	676	703
▽ ₛC, P	2	29	56	83	164	245	488	110	137	191	218	272	299	515	542	326	407	569	650	353	380	434	596	461	623	677	704
☊ I, A	3	30	57	84	165	246	489	111	138	192	219	273	300	516	543	327	408	570	651	354	381	435	597	462	624	678	705
☋ J	6	33	60	87	168	249	492	114	141	195	222	276	303	519	546	330	411	573	654	357	384	438	600	465	627	681	708
△ B, Nf	9	36	63	90	171	252	495	117	144	198	225	279	306	522	549	333	414	576	657	360	387	441	603	468	630	684	711
▽ Z, Y_c	18	45	72	99	180	261	504	126	153	207	234	288	315	531	558	342	423	585	666	369	396	450	612	477	639	783	720
♐ H	4	31	58	85	166	247	490	112	139	193	220	274	301	517	544	328	409	571	652	355	382	436	598	463	625	679	706
♍ D	5	32	59	86	167	248	491	113	140	194	221	275	302	518	545	329	410	572	653	356	383	437	599	464	626	680	707
♓ R, x	7	34	61	88	169	250	493	115	142	196	223	277	304	520	547	331	412	574	655	358	385	439	601	466	628	682	709
♊ F, Q	8	35	62	89	170	251	494	116	143	197	224	278	305	521	548	332	413	575	656	359	386	440	602	467	629	683	710
♑ K, C	10	37	64	91	172	253	496	118	145	199	226	280	307	523	550	334	415	577	658	361	388	442	604	469	631	685	712
♎ G	11	38	65	92	173	254	497	119	146	200	227	281	308	524	551	335	416	578	659	362	389	443	605	470	632	686	713
♈ S	19	46	73	100	181	262	505	127	154	208	235	289	316	532	559	343	424	586	667	370	397	451	613	478	640	694	721
♋ M	20	47	74	101	182	263	506	128	155	209	236	290	317	533	560	344	425	587	668	371	398	452	614	479	641	695	722
♏ S_f	12	39	66	93	174	255	498	120	147	201	228	282	309	525	552	336	417	579	660	363	390	444	606	471	633	687	714
♌ Ł	15	42	69	96	177	258	501	123	150	204	231	285	312	528	555	339	420	582	663	366	393	447	609	474	636	690	717
♒ w	21	48	75	102	183	264	507	129	156	210	237	291	318	534	561	345	426	588	669	372	399	453	615	480	642	696	723
♉ T_f	24	51	78	105	186	267	510	132	159	213	240	294	321	537	564	348	429	591	672	375	402	456	618	483	645	699	726
♄ L	13	40	67	94	175	256	499	121	148	202	229	283	310	526	553	337	418	580	661	364	391	445	607	472	634	688	715
☿ N, Y	14	41	68	95	176	257	500	122	149	203	230	284	311	527	554	338	419	581	662	365	392	446	608	473	635	689	716
☉ Ö, Ò	16	43	70	97	178	259	502	124	151	205	232	286	313	529	556	340	421	583	664	367	394	448	610	475	637	691	718
♀ V, Ŏ	22	49	76	103	184	265	508	130	157	211	238	292	319	535	562	346	427	589	670	373	400	454	616	481	643	697	724
♂ T	17	44	71	98	179	260	503	125	152	206	233	287	314	530	557	341	422	584	665	368	395	449	611	476	638	692	719
☽ U	23	50	77	104	185	266	509	131	158	212	239	293	320	536	563	347	428	590	671	374	401	455	617	482	644	698	725
♃ W	25	52	79	106	187	268	511	133	160	214	241	295	322	538	565	349	430	592	673	376	403	457	619	484	646	700	727
⊗ X	26	53	80	107	188	269	512	134	161	215	242	296	323	539	566	350	431	593	674	377	404	458	620	485	647	701	728

On The 81 Tetragrams of the Elemental Changes

The titles and commentary on the Tetragrams were provided by TO MH in the year of 1912 e.v. in Liber CLVII and are here appended without comment.

Center
1
85

1. THE NATURE OF THE TAO.

1. The Tao-Path is not the All-Tao. The Name is not the Thing named.

2. Unmanifested, it is the Secret Father of Heaven and Earth manifested, it is their Mother.

3. To understand this Mystery, one must be fulfilling one's will, and if one is not thus free, one will but gain a smattering of it.

4. The Tao is one, and the Teh but a phase thereof. The abyss of this Mystery is the Portal of Serpent-Wonder.

Full Circle
2

86

2. THE ENERGY- SOURCE OF THE SELF.

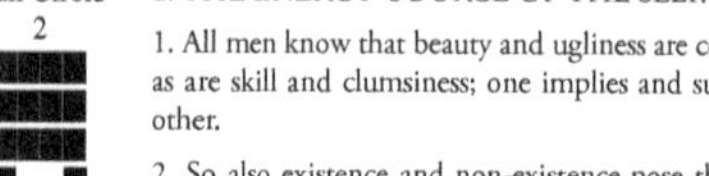

1. All men know that beauty and ugliness are correlatives, as are skill and clumsiness; one implies and suggests the other.

2. So also existence and non-existence pose the one the other; so also is it with ease and difficulty, length and shortness; height and lowness. Also Musick exists through harmony of opposites; time and space depend upon contraposition.

3. By the use of this method, the sage can fulfil his will without action, and utter his word without speech.

4. All things arise without diffidence; they grow, and none interferes; they change according to their natural order, without lust of result. The work is accomplished; yet continueth in its orbit, without goal. This work is done unconsciously; this is why its energy is indefatigable.

Mired
3

87

3. QUIETING FOLK.

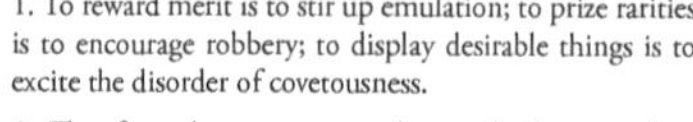

1. To reward merit is to stir up emulation; to prize rarities is to encourage robbery; to display desirable things is to excite the disorder of covetousness.

2. Therefore, the sage governeth men by keeping their minds and their bodies at rest, contenting the one by emptiness, the other by fullness. He satisfieth their desires, thus fulfilling their wills, and making them frictionless; and he maketh them strong in body, to a similar end.

3. He delivereth them from the restlessness of knowledge and the cravings of discontent. As to those who have knowledge already, he teacheth them the way of non-action. This being assured, there is no disorder in the world.

Barrier
4
89

4. THE SPRING WITHOUT SOURCE.

1. The Tao resembleth the emptiness of Space; to employ it, we must avoid creating ganglia. Oh Tao, how vast art Thou, the Abyss of Abysses, thou Holy and Secret Father of all Fatherhoods of Things!

2. Let us make our sharpness blunt; let us loosen our complexes; let us tone down our brightness to the general obscurity. Oh Tao, how still art thou, how pure, continuous One beyond Heaven!

3. This Tao hath no Father; it is beyond all other conceptions, higher than the highest.

Keeping Small
5
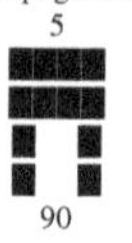
90

5. THE FORMULA OF THE VACUUM.

1. Heaven and earth proceed without motive, but casually in their order of nature, dealing with all things carelessly, like used talismans. So also the sages deal with their people, not exercising benevolence, but allowing the nature of all to move without friction.

2. The Space between heaven and earth is their breathing apparatus: Exhalation is not exhaustion, but the complement of Inhalation, and this equally of that. Speech exhausteth; guard thyself, therefore, maintaining the perfect freedom of thy nature.

Contrariety
6
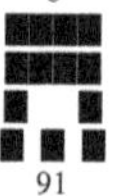
91

6. THE PERFECTING OF FORM.

1. The Teh is the immortal enemy of the Tao, its feminine aspect. Heaven and Earth issued from her Gate; this Gate is the Root of their World-Sycamore. Its operation is of pure Joy and Love, and faileth never.

Ascent
7
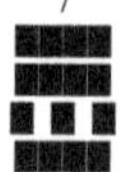
93

7. THE CONCEALMENT OF THE LIGHT.

1. Heaven and Earth are mighty in continuance, because their work is delivered from the lust of result.

2. Thus also the sage, seeking not any goal, attaineth all things; he doth not interfere in the affairs of his body, and so that body acteth without friction. It is because he meddleth not with personal aims that these come to pass with simplicity.

Opposition
8

94

8. THE NATURE OF PEACE.

1. Admire thou the High Way of Water! Is not Water the soul of the life of things, whereby they change? Yet it seeketh its level, and abideth content in obscurity. So also it resembleth the Tao, in this Way thereof!

2. The virtue of a house is to be well-placed; of the mind, to be at ease in silence as of Space; of societies, to be well-disposed; of governments, to maintain quietude; of work, to be skillfully performed; and of all motion, to be made at the right time.

3. Also it is the virtue of a man to abide in his place without discontent; thus offendeth he no man.

Branching Out
9
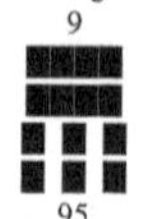
95

9. THE WAY OF RETICENCE.

1. Fill not a vessel, lest it spill in carrying. Meddle not with a sharpened point by feeling it constantly, or it will soon become blunted.

2. Gold and jade endanger the house of their possessor. Wealth and honors lead to arrogance and envy, and bring ruin. Is thy way famous and thy name becoming distinguished? Withdraw, thy work once done, into obscurity; this is the way of Heaven.

Distortion
10

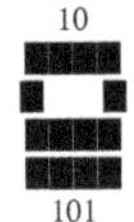

101

10. THINGS ATTAINABLE.

1. When soul and body are in the bond of love, they can be kept together. By concentration on the breath it is brought to perfect elasticity, and one becomes as a babe. By purifying oneself from Samadhi one becomes whole.

2. In his dealing with individuals and with society, let him move without lust of result. In the management of his breath, let him be like the mother-bird. Let his intelligence comprehend every quarter; but let his knowledge cease.

3. Here is the Mystery of Virtue. It createth all and nourisheth all; yet it doth not adhere to them; it operateth all, but knoweth not of it, nor proclaimeth it; it directeth all, but without conscious control.

Divergence
11

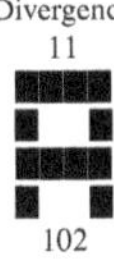

102

11. THE VALUE OF THE UNEXPRESSED.

1. The thirty spokes join in their nave, that is one; yet the wheel dependeth for use upon the hollow place for the axle. Clay is shapen to make vessels; but the contained space is what is useful. Matter is therefore of use only to mark the limits of the space which is the thing of real value.

Youthfulness
12

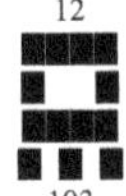

103

12. THE WITHDRAWAL FROM THE EXTERNAL.

1. The five colors film over Sight; The five sounds make Hearing dull; The five flavours conceal Taste; occupation with motion and action bedevil Mind; even so the esteem of rare things begetteth covetousness and disorder.

2. The wise man seeketh therefore to content the actual needs of the people; not to excite them by the sight of luxuries. He banneth these, and concentrateth on those.

Increase
13

105

13. THE CONTEMPT FOR CIRCUMSTANCE.

1. Favor and disgrace are equally to be shunned; honour and calamity to be alike regarded as adhering to the personality.

2. What is this which is written concerning favour and disgrace? Disgrace is the fall from favour. He then that hath favour hath fear, and its loss begetteth fear yet greater of a further fall. What is this which is written concerning honour and calamity? It is this attachment to the body which maketh calamity possible; for were one bodiless, what evil could befall him?

3. Therefore let him that regardeth himself rightly administer also a kingdom; and let him govern it who loveth it as another man loveth himself.

Penetration
14

106

14. THE SHEWING- FORTH OF THE MYSTERY.

1. We look at it, and see it not; though it is Omnipresent; and we name it the Root-Balance.

We listen for it, and hear it not, though it is Omniscient; and we name it the Silence.

We feel for it, and touch it not, though it is Omnipotent; and we name it the Concealed.

These three Virtues hath it, yet we cannot describe it as consisting of them; but, mingling them aright, we apprehend the One.

2. Above, it shineth not; below, it is not dark. It moveth all continuously, without Expression, returning into Naught. It is the Form of That which is beyond Form; it is the Image of the Invisible; it is Change, and Without Limit.

3. We confront it, and see not its Face; we pursue it, and its Back is hidden from us. Ah! but apply the Tao as in old Time to the work of the present; know it as it was known in the Beginning; follow fervently the Thread of the Tao.

Reach
15

107

15. THE APPEARANCE OF THE TRUE NATURE.

1. The adepts of past ages were subtle and keen to apprehend this Mystery, and their profundity was obscurity unto men. Since then they were not known, let me declare their nature.

2. To all seeming, they were fearful as men that cross a torrent in winter flood; they were hesitating like a man in apprehension of them that are about him; they were full of awe like a guest in a great house; they were ready to disappear like ice in thaw; they were unassuming like unworked wood; they were empty as a valley; and dull as the waters of a marsh.

3. Who can clear muddy water? Stillness will accomplish this. Who can obtain rest? Let motion continue equably, and it will itself be peace.

4. The adepts of the Tao, conserving its way, seek not to be actively self-conscious. By their emptiness of Self they have no need to show their youth and perfection; to appear old and imperfect is their privilege.

Contact
16

109

16. THE WITHDRAWAL TO THE ROOT.

1. Emptiness must be perfect, and Silence made absolute with tireless strength. All things pass through the period of action; then they return to repose. They grow, bud, blossom and fruit; then they return to the root. This return to the root is this state which we name Silence; and this Silence is Witness of their Fulfilment.

2. This cycle is the universal law. To know it is the part of intelligence; to ignore it bringeth folly of action, whereof the end is madness. To know it bringeth understanding and peace; and these lead to the identification of the Self with the Not-Self. This identification maketh man a king; and this kingliness groweth unto godhood. That godhood beareth fruit in the mastery of the Tao. Then the man, the Tao permeating him, endureth; and his bodily principles are in harmony, proof against decay, until the hour of his Change.

Holding Back
17

110

17. THE PURITY OF THE CURRENT.

1. In the Age of Gold, the people were not conscious of their rulers; in the Age of Silver, they loved them, with songs; in the Age of Brass, they feared them; in the Age of Iron, they despised them. As the rulers lost confidence, so also did the people lose confidence in them.

2. How hesitating did they seem, the Lords of the Age of Gold, speaking with deliberation, aware of the weight of their word! Thus they accomplished all things with success; and the people deemed their well-being to be the natural course of events.

Waiting
18

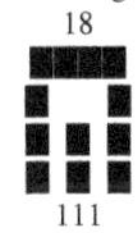

111

18. THE DECAY OF MANNERS.

1. When men abandoned the Way of the Tao, benevolence and justice became necessary. Then also was need of wisdom and cunning, and all fell into illusion. When harmony ceased to prevail in the six spheres it was needful to govern them by manifesting Sons.

When the kingdoms and races became confused, loyal ministers had to appear.

Following
19

117

19. RETURNING TO THE PURITY OF THE CURRENT.

1. If we forgot our statesmanship and our wisdom, it would be an hundred times better for the people. If we forgot our benevolence and our justice, they would become again like sons, folk of good will. If we forget our machines and our business, there would be no knavery.

2. These new methods despised the olden Way, inventing fine names to disguise their baneness. But simplicity in the doing of the will of every man would put an end to vain ambitions and desires.

Advance
20

118

20. THE WITHDRAWAL FROM THE COMMON WAY.

1. To forget learning is to end trouble. The smallest difference in words, such as "yes" and "yea", can make endless controversy for the scholar. Fearful indeed is death, since all men fear it; but the abyss of questionings, shoreless and bottomless, is worse!

2. Consider the profane man, how he preeneth, as if at feast, or gazing upon Spring from a tower! But as for me, I am as one who yawneth, without any trace of desire. I am like a babe before its first smile. I appear sad and forlorn, like a man homeless. The profane man hath his need filled, ay, and more also. For me, I seem to have lost all I had. My mind is as it were stupefied; it hath no definite shape. The profane man looketh lively and keen-witted; I alone appear blank in my mind. They seem eagerly critical; I appear careless and without perception. I seem to be as one adrift upon the sea, with no thought of an harbor. The profane have each one his definite course of action; I alone appear useless and uncomprehending, like a man from the border. Yea, thus I differ from all other men: but my jewel is the All-Mother!

Release
21

119

21. THE INFINITE WOMB.

1. The sole source of energy is the Tao. Who may declare its nature? It is beyond Sense, yet all form is hidden within it. It is beyond Sense, yet all Perceptibles are hidden within it. It is beyond Sense, yet all Perceptibles are hidden within it. It is beyond Sense, yet all Being is hidden within it. This Being excites Perception, and the Word thereof. As it was in the beginning, is now, and ever shall be, its Name operateth continuously, causing all to flow in the cycle of Change, which is Love and Beauty. How do I know this? By my comprehension of the Tao.

Resistance
22

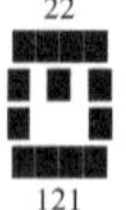

121

22. THE GUERDON OF MODESTY.

1. The part becometh the whole. The curve becometh straight; the void becometh full; the old becometh new. He who desireth little accomplisheth his Will with ease; who desireth many things becometh distracted.

2. Therefore, the sage concentrateth upon one Will, and it is as a light to the whole world. Hiding himself, he shineth; withdrawing himself, he attracteth notice; humbling himself, he is exalted; dissatisfied with himself, he gaineth force to achieve his Will. Because he striveth not, no man may contend against him.

3. That is no idle saw of the men of old; "The part becometh the whole"; it is the Canon of Perfection.

Ease
23

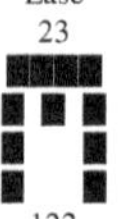

122

23. THE VOID OF NAUGHT.

1. To keep silence is the mark of one who is acting in full accordance with his Will. A fierce wind soon falleth; a storm-shower doth not last all day. Yet Heaven and Earth cause these; and if they fail to make violence continue, how much less can man abide in spasm of passion!

2. With him that devoteth him to Tao, the devotees of Tao are in accord; so also are the devotees of Teh, yea, even they who fail in seeking those are in accord.

3. So then his brothers in the Tao are joyful, attaining it; and his brothers in the Teh are joyful, attaining it; and they who fail in seeking these are joyful, partaking of it. But if he himself realize not the Tao with calm of confidence, then they also appear lacking in confidence.

Joy
24

123

24. EVIL MANNERS.

1. He who standeth a-tiptoe standeth not firm; he who maketh rigid his legs walketh ill. He who preeneth himself shineth not; he who talketh positively is vulgar; he who boastheth is refused acceptance; he who is wise in his own conceit is thought inferior. Such attitudes, to him that hath the view given by understanding the Tao, seem like garbage or like cancer, abhorrent to all. They then who follow the Way do not admit them.

Contention
25

125

25. IMAGES OF THE MYSTERY.

1. Without Limit and Perfect, there is a Becoming, beyond Heaven and Earth. It hath nor motion nor Form; it is alone, it changeth not; it extendeth all ways; it hath no Adversary. It is like the All-Mother.

2. I know not its Name, but I call it the Tao. Moreover, I exert myself, and call it Vastness.

3. Vastness, the Becoming! Becoming, it flieth afar. Afar, it draweth near. Vast is this Tao; Heaven also is Vast; Earth is vast; and the Holy King is vast also. In the Universe are Four Vastnesses, and of these is the Holy King.

4. Man followeth the formula of Earth; Earth followeth that of Heaven, and Heaven that of the Tao. The formula of the Tao is its own Nature.

Endeavor
26

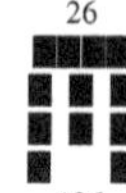

126

26. THE NATURE OF MASS.

1. Mass is the fulcrum of mobility; stillness is the father of motion.

2. Therefore the sage King, though he travel afar, remaineth near his supplies. Though opportunity tempt him, he remaineth quietly in proper disposition, indifferent. Should the master of an host of chariots bear himself frivolously? If he attack without support, he loseth his base; if he become a raider, he forfeiteth his throne.

Duties
27

127

27. SKILL IN THE METHOD.

1. The experienced traveler concealeth his tracks; the clever speaker giveth no chance to the critic; the skilled mathematician useth no abacus; the ingenious safesmith baffleth the burglar without the use of bolts, and the cunning binder without ropes and knots. So also the sage, skilled in man-emancipation-craft, useth all men; understanding the value of everything, he rejecteth nothing. This is called the Occult Regimen.

2. The adept is then master to the zelator, and the zelator assisteth and honoreth the adept. Yet unless these relations were manifest, even the most intelligent observer might be perplexed as to which was which. This is called the Crown of Mystery.

Change
28

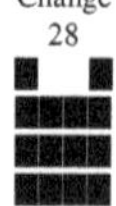

149

28. THE RETURN TO SIMPLICITY.

1. Balance thy male strength with thy female weakness and thou shalt attract all things, as the ocean absorbeth all rivers; for thou shalt formulate the excellence of the Child eternal, simple, and perfect.

Knowing the light, remain in the Dark. Manifest not thy Glory, but thine obscurity. Clothed in this Child-excellence eternal, thou hast attained the Return of the First State. Knowing splendour of Fame, cling to Obloquy and Infamy; then shalt thou remain as in the Valley to which flow all waters, the lodestone to fascinate all men. Yea, they shall hail in thee this Excellence, eternal, simple and perfect, of the Child.

2. The raw material, wrought into form, produceth vessels. So the sage King formulateth his Wholeness in divers Offices; and his Law is without violence or constraint.

Decisiveness
29

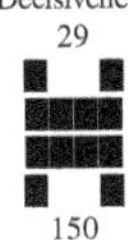

150

29. REFRAINING FROM ACTION.

1. He that, desiring a kingdom, exerteth himself to obtain it, will fail. A Kingdom is of the nature of spirit, and yieldeth not to activity. He who graspeth it, destroyeth it; he who gaineth it, loseth it.

2. The wheel of nature revolveth constantly; the last becometh first, and the first last; hot things grow cold, and cold things hot; weakness overcometh strength; things gained are lost anon. Hence the wise man avoideth effort, desire and sloth.

Bold Resolution
30

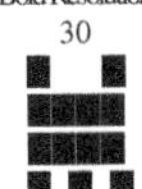

151

30. A WARNING AGAINST WAR.

1. If a king summon to his aid a Master of the Tao, let Him not advise recourse to arms. Such action certainly bringeth the corresponding reaction.

2. Where armies are, are weeds. Bad harvests follow great hosts.

3. The good general striketh decisively, once and for all. He does not risk by overboldness. He striketh, but doth not vaunt his victory. He striketh according to strict law of necessity, not from desire of victory.

4. Things become strong and ripe, then age. This is discord with the Tao; and what is not at one with the Tao soon cometh to an end.

Packing
31

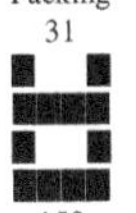

153

31. COMPOSING QUARREL.

1. Arms, though they be beautiful, are of ill omen, abominable to all created beings. They who have the Tao love not their use.

2. The place of honour is on the right in wartime; so thinketh the man of distinction. Sharp weapons are ill-omened, unworthy of such a man; he useth them only in necessity. He valueth peace and ease, desireth not violence of victory. To desire victory is to desire the death of men; and to desire that is to fail to propitiate the people.

3. At feasts, the left hand is the high seat; at funerals, the right. The second in command of the army leadeth the left wing, the commander-in-chief, the right wing; it is as if the battle were a rite of mourning! He that hath slain most men should weep for them most bitterly; so then the place of the victor is assigned to him with philosophical propriety.

Legion
32

154

32. THE WISDOM OF TEH.

1. The All-Tao hath no name.

2. It is That Minute Point yet the whole world dare not contend against him that hath it. Did a lord or king gain it and guard it, all men would obey him of their own accord.

3. Heaven and Earth combining under its spell, shed forth dew, extending throughout all things of its own accord, without man's interference.

4. Tao, in its phase of action, hath a name. Then men can comprehend it; when they do this, there is no more risk of wrong or ill-success.

5. As the great rivers and the oceans are to the valley streams, so is the Tao to the whole universe.

Closeness
33

155

33. THE DISCRIMINATION (VIVEKA) OF TEH.

1. He who understandeth others understandeth Two; but he who understandeth himself understandeth One. He who conquereth others is strong; but he who conquereth himself is stronger yet.

Contentment is riches; and continuous action is Will.

2. He that adapteth himself perfectly to his environment, continueth for long; he who dieth without dying, liveth for ever.

Kinship
34

157

34.THE METHOD OF ATTAINMENT.

1. The Tao is immanent; it extendeth to the right hand as to the left.

2. All things derive from it their being; it createth them, and all comply with it. Its work is done, and it proclaimeth it not. It is the ornament of all things, yet it claimeth not fief of them; there is nothing so small that it inhabiteth not, and informeth it.

All things return without knowledge of the Cause thereof; there is nothing so great that it inhabiteth not, and informeth it.

3. In this manner also may the Sage perform his Works. It is by not thrusting himself forward that he winneth to his success.

Gathering
35

158

35. THE GOOD WILL OF THE TEH.

1. The whole world is drawn to him that hath the likeness of the Tao. Men flock unto him, and suffer no ill, but gain repose, find peace, enjoy all ease.

2. Sweet sounds and cates lure the traveler from his way. But the Word of the Tao; though it appear harsh and insipid, unworthy to hearken or to behold; hath his use all inexhaustible.

Strength
36

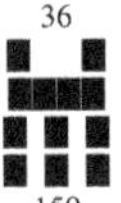

159

36. THE HIDING OF THE LIGHT.

1. In order to draw breath, first empty the lungs; to weaken another, first strengthen him; to overthrow another, first exalt him; to despoil another, first load him with gifts; this is called the Occult Regimen.

2. The soft conquereth the hard; the weak pulleth down the strong.

3. The fish that leaveth ocean is lost; the method of government must be concealed from the people.

Purity
37

165

37. THE RIGHT USE OF GOVERNMENT.

1. The Tao proceedeth by its own nature, doing nothing; therefore there is no doing which it comprehendeth not.

2. If kings and princes were to govern in this manner, all things would operate aright by their own motion.

3. If this transmutation were my object, I should call it Simplicity. Simplicity hath no name nor purpose; silently and at ease all things go well.

Fullness
38

166

38. CONCERNING THE TEH.

1. Those who possessed perfectly the powers did not manifest them, and so they preserved them. Those who possessed them imperfectly feared to lose them, and so lost them.

2. The former did nothing, nor had need to do. The latter did, and had need to do.

3. Those who possessed benevolence exercised it, and had need it; so also was it with them who possessed justice.

4. Those who possessed the conventions displayed them; and when men would not agree, they made ready to fight them.

5. Thus, when the Tao was lost, the Magick Powers appeared; then, by successive degradations, came Benevolence, Justice, Convention.

6. Now convention is the shadow of loyalty and good will, and so the herald of disorder. Yea, even Understanding is but a Blossom of the Tao, and foreshadoweth Stupidity.

7. So then the Tao-Man holdeth to Mass, and avoideth Motion; he is attached to the Root, not to the flower. He leaveth the one, and cleaveth to the other.

Residence
39
167

39. THE LAW OF THE BEGINNING.

1. These things have possessed the Tao from the beginning: Heaven, clear and shining; Earth, steady and easy; Spirits, mighty in Magick; Vehicles, overflowing with Joy; all that hath life; and the rulers of men. All these derive their essence from the Tao.

2. Without the Tao, Heaven would dissolve Earth disrupt, Spirits become impotent; Vehicles empty; living things would perish and rulers lose their power.

3. The root of grandeur is humility, and the strength of exaltation in its base. Thus rulers speak of themselves as "Fatherless," "Virtueless,' "Unworthy," proclaiming by this that their Glory is in their shame. So also the virtue of a Chariot is not any of the parts of a Chariot, if they be numbered. They do not seek to appear fine like jade, but inconspicuous like common stone.

Law
40
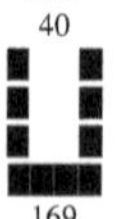
169

40. OMITTING UTILITY.

1. The Tao proceeds by correlative curves, and its might is in weakness.

2. All things arose from the Teh, and the Teh budded from the Tao.

Response
41

170

41. THE IDENTITY OF THE DIFFERENTIAL.

1. The best students, learning of the Tao, set to work earnestly to practice the Way. Mediocre students now cherish it, now let it go.
The worst students mock at it. Were it not thus mocked, it were unworthy to be Tao.
2. Thus spake the makers of Saws: the Tao at its brightest is obscure. Who advanceth in that Way, retireth. Its smooth Way is rough. Its summit is a valley. Its beauty is ugliness. Its wealth is poverty. Its virtue, vice. Its stability is change. Its form is without form. Its fullness is vacancy. Its utterance is silence. Its reality is illusion.
3. Nameless and imperceptible is the Tao; but it informeth and perfecteth all things.

Going to Meet
42

171

42. THE VEILS OF THE TAO.

1. The Tao formulated the One.

The One exhaled the Two.

The Two were parents of the Three.

The Three were parents of all things.

All things pass from Obscurity to Manifestation, inspired harmoniously by the Breath of the Void.

2. Men do not like to be fatherless, virtueless, unworthy: yet rulers describe themselves by these names. Thus increase bringeth decrease to some, and decrease bringeth increase to others.

3. Others have taught thus; I consent to it. Violent men and strong die not by natural death. This fact is the foundation of my law.

Encounters
43

173

43. THE COSMIC METHOD.

1. The softest substance hunteth down the hardest; the unsubstantial penetrateth where there is no opening. Here is the Virtue of Inertia.

2. Few are they who attain: whose speech is Silence, whose Work is Inertia.

Stove
44

174

44. MONITORIAL.

1. What shall it profit a man if he gain fame or wealth, and lose his life?

2. If a man cling to fame or wealth, he risketh what is worth more.

3. Be content, not fearing disgrace. Act not, and risk not criticism. Thus live thou long, without alarm.

Greatness
45

175

45. THE OVERFLOWING OF TEH.

1. Despise thy masterpieces; thus renew the vigor of thy creation. Deem thy fullness emptiness; thus shall thy fullness never be empty. Let the straight appear crooked to thee, thy Craft clumsiness; thy Musick discord.

2. Exercise moderateth cold; stillness heat. To be pure and to keep silence, is the True Law of all that are beneath Heaven.

Enlargement
46

181

46. THE WITHDRAWAL FROM AMBITION.

1. When the Tao beareth away on Earth, men put swift horses to night-carts. When it is neglected, they breed chargers in the border marches.

2. There is no evil worse than ambition; no misery worse than discontent; no crime greater than greed. Content of mind is peace and satisfaction eternal.

Pattern
47

182

47. THE VISION OF THE DISTANT.

1. One need not pass his threshold to comprehend all that is under Heaven, nor to look out from his lattice to behold the Tao Celestial. Nay! but the farther a man goeth, the less he knoweth.

2. The sages acquired their knowledge without travel; they named all things aright without beholding them; and, acting without aim, fulfilled their Wills.

Ritual
48

183

48. OBLIVION OVERCOMING KNOWLEDGE.

1. The scholar seeketh daily increase of knowing; the sage of Tao daily decrease of doing.

2. He decreaseth it, again and again, until he doth no act with the lust of result. Having attained this Inertia all accomplisheth itself.

3. He who attracteth to himself all that is under Heaven doth so without effort. He who maketh effort is not able to attract it.

Flight
49

185

49. THE ADAPTABILITY OF THE TEH.

1. The wise man hath no fixed principle; he adapteth his mind to his environment.

2. To the good I am good, and to the evil I am good also; thus all become good. To the true I am true, and to the false I am true; thus all become true.

3. The sage appeareth hesitating to the world, because his mind is detached. Therefore the people look and listen to him, as his children; and thus doth he shepherd them.

Vastness
50
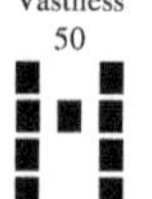
186

50. THE ESTIMATION OF LIFE.

1. Man cometh into life, and returneth again into death.

2. Three men in ten conserve life; three men in ten pursue death.

3. Three men also in ten desire to live, but their acts hasten their journey to the house of death. Why is this? Because of their efforts to preserve life.

4. But this I have heard. He that is wise in the economy of his life, whereof he is warden for a season, journeyeth with no need to avoid the tiger or the rhinoceros, and goeth uncorsleted among the warriors with no fear of sword or lance. The rhinoceros findeth in him no place vulnerable to its horn, the tiger to its claws, the weapon to its point. Why is this? Because there is no house of death in his whole body.

Constancy
51
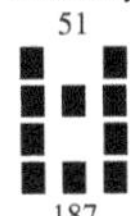
187

51. THE TEH AS THE NURSE.

1. All things proceed from the Tao, and are sustained by its forth-flowing virtue. Every one taketh form according to his nature, and is perfect, each in his particular Way. Therefore, each and every one of them glorify the Tao, and worship its forth-flowing Virtue.

2. This glorifying of the Tao, this worship of the Teh, is constantly spontaneous, and not by appointment of Law.

3. Thus the Tao buddeth them out, nurtureth them, developeth them, sustaineth them, perfecteth them, ripeneth them, upholdeth them, and reabsorbeth them.

4. It buddeth them forth, and claimeth not lordship over them; it is overseer of their changes, and boasteth not of his puissance; perfecteth them, and interfereth not with their Ways; this is called the Mystery of its Virtue.

Measure
52

125

52. THE WITHDRAWAL INTO THE SILENCE.

1. The Tao buddeth forth all things under Heaven; it is the Mother of all.

2. Knowing the Mother, we may know her offspring. He that knoweth his Mother, and abideth in Her nature, remaineth in surety all his days.

3. With the mouth closed, and the Gates of Breath controlled, he remaineth at ease all his days. With the mouth open, and the Breath directed to outward affairs, he hath no surety all his days.

4. To perceive that Minute Point is True Vision; to maintain the Soft and Gentle is True Strength.

5. Employing harmoniously the Light Within so that it returneth to its Origin, one guardeth even one's body from evil, and keepeth Silence before all men.

Eternity
53
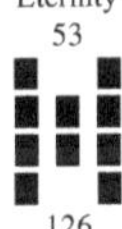
126

53. THE WITNESS OF GREED.

1. Were I discovered by men, and charged with government, my first would be lest I should become proud.

2. The true Path is level and smooth; but men love by-paths.

3. They adorn their courts, but they neglect their fields, and leave their storehouses empty. They wear elaborate and embroidered robes; they gird themselves with sharp swords; they eat and drink with luxury; they heap up goods; they are thievish and vainglorious. All this is opposite to the Way of Tao.

Unity
54

127

54. THE WITNESS OF WISDOM.

1. If a man plant according to the Tao it will never be uprooted; if he thus gather, it will never be lost. His sons and his son's sons, one following another, shall honour the shrine of their ancestor.

2. The Tao, applied to oneself, strengtheneth the Body, to the family, bringeth wealth; to the district, prosperity; to the state, great fortune. Let it be the Law of the Kingdom, and all men will increase in virtue.

3. Thus we observe its effect in every case, as to the person, the family, the district, the state, and the kingdom.

4. How do I know that this is thus universal under Heaven? By experience.

Diminishment
55

213

55. THE SPELL OF THE MYSTERY.

1. He that hath the Magick powers of the Tao is like a young child. Insects will not sting him or beasts or birds of prey attack him.

2. The young child's bones are tender and its sinews are elastic, but its grasp is firm. It knoweth nothing of the Union of Man and Woman, yet its Organ may be excited. This is because of its natural perfection. It will cry all day long without becoming hoarse, because of the harmony of its being.

3. He who understandeth this harmony knoweth the mystery of the Tao, and becometh a True Sage. All devices for inflaming life, and increasing the vital Breath, by mental effort are evil and factitious.

4. Things become strong, then age. This is in discord with the Tao, and what is not at one with the Tao soon cometh to an end.

Closed Mouth
56
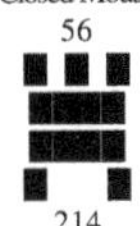
214

56. THE EXCELLENCE OF THE MYSTERY.

1. Who knoweth the Tao keepeth Silence; he who babbleth knoweth it not.

2. Who knoweth it closeth his mouth and controlleth the Gates of his Breath. He will make his sharpness blunt; he will loosen his complexes; he will tone down his brightness to the general obscurity. This is called the Secret of Harmony.

3. He cannot be insulted either by familiarity or aversion; he is immune to ideas of gain or loss, of honour or disgrace; he is the true man, unequalled under Heaven.

Guardedness
57
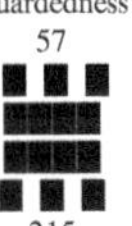
215

57. THE TRUE INFLUENCE.

1. One may govern a state by restriction; weapons may be used with skill and cunning; but one acquireth true command only by freedom, given and taken.

2. How am I aware of this? By experience that to multiply restrictive laws in the kingdom impoverisheth the people; the use of machines causeth disorder in state and race alike. The more men use skill and cunning, the more machines there are; and the more laws there are, the more felons there are.

3. A wise man has said this: I will refrain from doing, and the people will act rightly of their own accord; I will love Silence, and the people will instinctively turn to perfection; I will take no measures, and the people will enjoy true wealth; I will restrain ambition, and the people will attain simplicity.

Gathering In
58
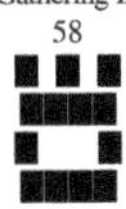
217

58. ADAPTATION TO ENVIRONMENT.

1. The government that exerciseth the least care serveth the people best; that which meddleth with everybody's business worketh all manner of harm. Sorrow and joy are bedfellows; who can divine the final result of either?

2. Shall we avoid restriction? Yea; restriction distorteth nature, so that even what seemeth good in it is evil. For how long have men suffered from misunderstanding of this.

3. The wise man is foursquare, and avoideth aggression; his corners do not injure others. He moveth in a straight line and turneth not aside therefrom; he is brilliant but doth not blind with his brightness.

Massing
59

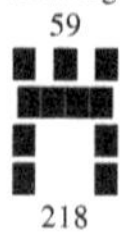

218

59. WARDING THE TAO.

1. To balance our earthly nature and cultivate our heavenly nature, tread the Middle Path.

2. This Middle Path alone leadeth to the Timely Return to the True Nature. This Timely Return resulteth from the constant gathering of Magick Powers. With that Gathering cometh Control. This Control we know to be without Limit and he who knoweth the Limitless may rule the state.

3. He who possesseth the Tao continueth long. He is like a plant with well-set roots and strong stems. Thus it secureth long continuance of its life.

Accumulation
60

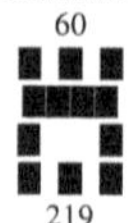

219

60. THE DUTY OF GOVERNMENT.

1. The government of a kingdom is like the cooking of fish.

2. If the kingdom be ruled according to the Tao, the spirits of our ancestors will not manifest their Teh. These spirits have this Teh, but will not turn it against men. It is able to hurt men; so also is the Wise King; but he doth not.

3. When these powers are in accord, their Good Will produceth the Teh, endowing the people therewith.

Embellishment
61

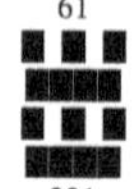

221

61. THE MODESTY OF THE TEH.

1. A state becometh powerful when it resembleth a great river, deep-seated; to it tend all the small streams under Heaven.

2. It is as with the female, that conquereth the male by her Silence. Silence is a form of Gravity.

3. Thus a great state attracteth small states by meeting their views, and small states attract the great state by revering its eminence. In the first case this Silence gaineth supporters; in the second, favour.

4. The great state uniteth men and nurtureth them; the small state wisheth the good will of the great, and offereth service; thus each gaineth its advantage. But the great state must keep Silence.

Doubt
62

222

62. THE WORKINGS OF THE TAO.

1. The Tao is the most exalted of all things. It is the ornament of the good, and the protection and purification of the evil.

2. Its words are the fountain of honour, and its deeds the engine of achievement. It is present even in evil.

3. Though the Son of Heaven were enthroned with his three Dukes appointed to serve him, and he were offered a round symbol- of-rank as great as might fill the hands, with a team of horses to follow, this gift were not to be matched against the Tao, which might be offered by the humblest of men.

4. Why did they of old time set such store by the Tao? Because he that sought it might find it, and because it was the Purification from all evil. Therefore did all men under Heaven esteem it the most exalted of all things.

Watch
63

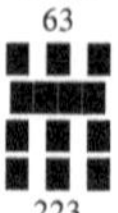

223

63. FORETHOUGHT AT THE OUTSET.

1. Act without lust of result; work without anxiety; taste without attachment to flavour; esteem small things great and few things many; repel violence with gentleness.

2. Do great things while they are yet small, hard things while they are yet easy; for all things, how great or hard soever, have a beginning when they are little and easy. So thus the wise man accomplisheth the greatest tasks without undertaking anything important.

3. Who undertaketh thoughtlessly is certain to fail in attainment; who estimateth things easy findeth them hard. The wise man considereth even easy things hard, so that even hard things are easy to him.

Sinking
64

229

64. ATTENDING TO DETAILS.

1. It is easy to grasp what is not yet in moti withstand what is not yet manifest, to break what yet compact, to disperse what is not yet coheren against things before they become visible; attend to before disorder ariseth.

2. The tree which filleth the embrace grew from a shoot; the tower nine-storied rose from a low found the ten-day journey began with a single step.

3. He who acteth worketh harm; he who graspeth f it a slip. The wise man acteth not, so worketh no he doth not grasp, and so doth not let go. Men ofte their affairs on the eve of success, because they are prudent at the end as in the beginning.

4. The wise man willeth what others do not wil valueth not things rare. He learneth what others lea and gathered up what they despise. Thus he is in with the natural course of events, and is not overb action.

Inner
65

230

65. THE PURITY OF THE TEH.

1. They of old time that were skilled in the Tao soug to enlighten the people, but to keep them simple.

2. The difficulty of government is the vain knowle the people. To use cleverness in government is to sc the kingdom; to use simplicity is to anoint it.

3. Know these things, and make them thy law and example. To possess this Law is the Secret Perf of rule. Profound and Extended is this Perfectio that possesseth it is indeed contrary to the rest, b attracteth them to full accordance.

Departure
66

231

66. PUTTING ONE'S SELF LAST.

1. The oceans and the rivers attract the streams by skill in being lower than they; thus are they m thereof. So the Wise Man, to be above men, spe lowly; and to precede them acteth with humility.

2. Thus, though he be above them, they feel no bu nor, though he precede them, do they feel insulted.

3. So then do all men delight to honour him, and not weary of him. He contendeth not against any therefore no man is able to contend against him

Darkening
67

233

67. THE THREE JEWELS.

1. They say that while this Tao of mine is great, ye inferior. This is the proof of its greatness. If it wer anything else, its smallness would have long been kr

2. I have three jewels of price whereto I cleave; gentl economy, and humility.

3. That gentleness maketh me courageous, that eco generous, that humility honoured. Men of today ab gentleness for violence, economy for extravag humility for pride: this is death.

4. Gentleness bringeth victory in fight; and holde ground with assurance. Heaven wardeth the gentle by that same virtue.

Dimming
68

234

68. ASSIMILATING ONE'S SELF TO HEAVEN.

1. He that is skilled in war maketh no fierce ges the most efficient fighter bewareth of anger. He conquereth refraineth from engaging in battle; he w men most willingly obey continueth silently wit Work. So it is said: "He is mighty who fighteth n ruleth who uniteth with his subjects; he shineth w will is that of Heaven."

Exhaustion
69
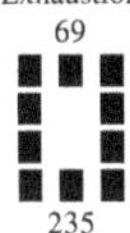
235

69. THE USE OF THE MYSTERIOUS WAY.

1. A great strategist saith: "I dare not take the offensive. I prefer the defensive. I dare not advance an inch; I prefer to retreat a foot." Place therefore the army where there is no army; prepare for action where there is no engagement; strike where there is no conflict; advance against the enemy where the enemy is not.

2. There is no error so great as to engage in battle without sufficient force. To do so is to risk losing the gentleness which is beyond price. Thus when the lines actually engage, he who regretteth the necessity is the victor.

Severance
70
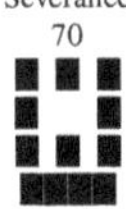
237

70. THE DIFFICULTY OF RIGHT APPREHENSION.

1. My words are easy to understand and to perform; but is there anyone in the world who can understand them and perform them?

2. My words derive from a creative and universal Principle, in accord with the One Law. Men, not knowing these, understand me not.

3. Few are they that understand me; therefore am I the more to be valued. The Wise Man weareth sack-cloth, but guardeth his jewel in his bosom.

Stoppage
71

238

71. THE DISTEMPER OF KNOWLEDGE.

1. To know, yet to know nothing, is the highest; not to know, yet to pretend to knowledge, is a distemper.

2. Painful is this distemper; therefore we shun it. The wise man hath it not. Knowing it to be bound up with Sorrow, he putteth it away from him.

Hardness
72
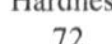
239

72. CONCERNING LOVE OF SELF.

1. When men fear not that which is to be feared, that which they fear cometh upon them.

2. Let them not live, without thought, the superficial life. Let them not weary of the Spring of Life!

3. By avoiding the superficial life, this weariness cometh not upon them.

4. These things the wise man knoweth, not showeth: he loveth himself, without isolating his value. He accepteth the former and rejecteth the latter.

Completion
73
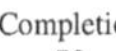
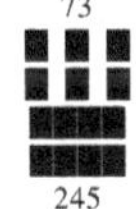
245

73. ESTABLISHING THE LAW OF FREEDOM.

1. One man, daring, is executed; another, not daring, liveth. It would seem as if the one course were profitable and the other detrimental. Yet when Heaven smiteth a man, who shall assign the cause thereof? Therefore the sage is diffident.

2. The Tao of Heaven contendeth not, yet it overcometh; it is silent, yet its need is answered; it summoneth none, but all men come to it of their free will. Its method is quietness, yet its will is efficient. Large are the meshes of Heaven's Net; wide open, yet letting none escape.

Closure
74
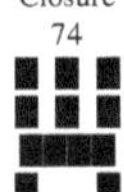
246

74. A RESTRAINT OF MISUNDERSTANDING.

1. The people have no fear of death; why then seek to awe them by the threat of death? If the people feared death and I could put to death evil-doers, who would dare to offend?

2. There is one appointed to inflict death. He who would usurp that position resembleth a hewer of wood doing the work of a carpenter. Such an one, presumptuous, will be sure to cut his own hands.

Failure
75
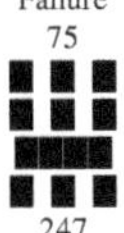
247

75. THE INJURY OF GREED.

1. The people suffer hunger because of the weight of taxation imposed by their rulers. This is the cause of famine.

2. The people are difficult to govern because their rulers meddle with them. This is the cause of bad government.

3. The people welcome death because the toil of living is intolerable. This is why they esteem death lightly. In such a state of insecurity it is better to ignore the question of living than to set store by it.

Aggravation
76
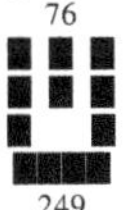
249

76. A WARNING AGAINST RIGIDITY.

1. At the birth of man, he is elastic and weak; at his death, rigid and unyielding. This is the common law; trees also, in their youth, are tender and supple; in their decay, hard and dry.

2. So then rigidity and hardness are the stigmata of death; elasticity and adaptability, of life.

3. He then who putteth forth strength is not victorious; even as a strong tree filleth the embrace.

4. Thus the hard and rigid have the inferior place, the soft and elastic the superior.

Compliance
77
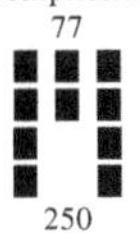
250

77. THE WAY OF HEAVEN.

1. The Tao of Heaven is likened to the bending of a bow, whereby the high part is brought down, and the low part raised up. The extreme is diminished, and the middle increased.

2. This is the Way of Heaven, to remove excess, and to supplement insufficiency. Not so is the way of man, who taketh away from him that hath not to give to him that hath already excess.

3. Who can employ his own excess to the weal of all under Heaven? Only he that possesseth the Tao.

4. So the Wise Man acteth without lust of result; achieveth and boasteth not; he willeth not to proclaim his greatness.

On the Verge
78
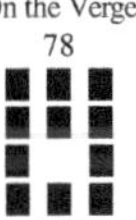
251

78. A CREED.

1. Nothing in the world is more elastic and yielding than water; yet it is preeminent to dissolve things rigid and resistant; there is nothing which can match it.

2. All men know that the soft overcometh the hard, and the weak conquereth the strong; but none are able to use this law in action.

3. A Wise Man hath said: "He that taketh on the burden of the state is a demigod worthy of sacrificial worship; and the true King of a people is he that undertaketh the weight of their sorrows."

4. Truth appeareth paradox

Difficulties
79
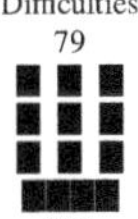
253

79. TRUTH IN COVENANT.

1. When enemies are reconciled, there is always an aftermath of illwill. How can this be useful?

2. Therefore, the Wise Man, while he keepeth his part of the record of a transaction, doth not insist on its prompt execution. He who hath the Teh considereth the situation from all sides, while he who hath it not seeketh only to benefit himself.

3. In the Tao of Heaven, there is no distinction of persons in its love; but it is for the True Man to claim it.

Laboring
80
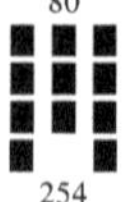
254

80. ISOLATION.

1. In a little kingdom of few people it should be the order that though there were men able to do the work of ten men or five score, they should not be employed. Though the people regarded death as sorrowful, yet they should not wish to go elsewhere.

2. They should have boats and wagons, yet no necessity to travel; corslets and weapons, yet no occasion to fight.

3. For communication they should use knotted cords.

4. They should deem their food sweet, their clothes beautiful, their houses homes, their customs delightful.

5. There should be another state within view, so that its fowls and dogs should be heard; yet to old age, even to death, the people should hold no traffic with it.

Fostering
81

255

81. THE SHEWING- FORTH OF SIMPLICITY.

1. True speech is not elegant; elaborate speech is not truth. Those who know do not argue; the argumentative are without knowledge. Those who have assimilated are not learned; those who are gross with learning have not assimilated.

2. The Wise Man doth not hoard. The more he giveth, the more he hath; the more he watereth, the more is he watered himself.

3. The Tao of Heaven is like an Arrow, yet it woundeth not; and the Wise Man, in all his Works, maketh no contention.

The Practice of Qabalah

THE PRIMARY goal of Analytic *Qabalah* is to reduce all composite phenomena to its elemental constituent parts.[1] Purple, for instance, is made by combining red with blue. Purple then, can be said to be the composite phenomenon which a Qabalist might (if convenient) see as comprised of the two irreducible elements *red* and *blue*. Thus, practically, if ever the Qabalist have need of red, when he has only purple, then he has only to extract its blue.

Understand that what is said of Colour, is also true of Sound, of Mind, Consciousness and Matter or Physical Reality.

In practice, *Qabalah* is a broad science spanning many disciplines. Like Hesse's *Glass Bead Game* it can be applied to any human endeavor.[2] Adding to this richness is the fact that we have a choice as to which elemental constituents we distill the composite phenomena to. This can be number, word, color, musical note, vibration frequencies, etc. This makes sense the further one proceeds with the investigation seeing as all entities at this level are connected and the terms we use to represent them, simple conveniences: It is a question of the particular language or symbol system one wishes to use and the particular sensorium through which one encounters the phenomenon. In this way, energy of one particular sort, transmitted in identical frequency with identical amplitudes, etc. portrays a signature.

---

1 The goal of the Adept is to further reduce all such elemental constituents to zero. Otherwise, he cannot perceive clearly: If, for instance in our example, he is tainted with red, then all manifestation of blue would appear to him as purple.

2 For we ourselves, our consciousness and our construction are products of IT.

This to hearing will be a note, to our eyes a color, to our minds a thought.

The advantage of *Gematria Qabalah* however (the principle subject of this chapter), is that it distills and then classifies the phenomena according to number. Number has the advantage of transcending language and cultural differences (universality) and is also precisely definable. Perhaps the greatest gain to be achieved in our choice of number as element is that we can perform operations on numbers (addition, multiplication, *et cetera*). In this way, we can ask and answer simple questions, and so project or experiment with the possibilities inherent in Nature:

> What will happen if one combines two elements? – *Add the numbers.*
>
> What will happen if one makes one element to react with another? —*Multiply the numbers.*
>
> What is the sum effect of an elements' place in the Universe?—*Perform Integral Calculus on its modifications over the field of Time.*[3]

Because all entities are connected and all elements (or their descriptions) whether it be in terms of vibration or number, are simply expressible terms of the same idea, we can develop a correspondence between all these basic elements.[4]

---

3 We provide detailed examples of such analyses in the chapter, "Considerations on The Tree of Life"

4 For an admirable work on this and tables of such correspondences, please refer to the *Sephir Sephiroth*, for a past Aeon example. Preliminary tables of correspondence are also included in this present Work.

AT THIS juncture, it will be clear to the discerning reader that beneath this open and declared axiomatic assumption of the correspondence between the elemental constituents, lies an even more shocking claim: namely, that the universe is so designed and structured that if a human being could discover the one-to-one (*injective*) or one-to-many (*surjective*) mapping between the phenomenological universe and the set of integers say, then he will have arrived at the Key to unlock the Universe; for that human being will have hit at the intelligible source of all things, and in this way proceeding through investigation, be able to unlock the keys to all Sciences declared or occult: for to know a law of Music say, would be to discover the corresponding law in Biology or Chemistry—whatever it may be—after that law in Music is distilled to its essence and then reformulated in the field of application according to its language, be it biological, chemical or otherwise.

Rather than attempt to discover the *surjective* function or mapping for all phenomena, *Gematria* Qabalists restrict themselves to finding the *surjective* mapping between words (graphical representation of thought) and their numerical equivalents. The incredible claim made at this point is that this correspondence holds all the way down to the letter-level. That is, we can find a mapping between the letters and the numbers and sum up words and list out numerical concordances and in this way come to proof undeniable of the intelligent, active and living nature of the Time and Space we exist in. The symmetries and concordances are not only beyond the ability of human construction or invention, but these apparent 'coincidences' defy the laws of probability and can be proven mathematically to be not random. Furthermore, this phenomenon besides being systematic and determined, can be shown to be reactive and party to some natural force that defines all phenomenon, physical or otherwise.

Now, the Alphabet is already in itself an elemental set that spans language—any word is expressed as a finite combination of the 26 glyphs. In this way the Universe has done most of the work for us in the sense that it has already reduced the language to the element set that spans the entire space of the language. What we have in an alphabet system then, is the elemental constituents themselves, already organized and tabulated.[5] All that remains for the Qabalist is to find this mapping of the letters to the numbers, and from there it shall be possible to propagate the entire system.

We leave these matters for a later chapter where they are discussed in full in the section "The Discovery of the Key".

5 It is no matter if this determination of an alphabet is a product of Man, Culture or 'accident'. For there are no arbitrary events in the Universe. Man, culture, accidents are all fruits or products of the architecting intelligence of Nature and so are expressions of that Intelligence or Consciousness. One 'knows' such a thing instinctively and holds the memory of having perceived it once the brain has recovered from the experience of Samadhi.

The Living Key

UNTIL NOW, we have presented and discussed only the Static Key. We have only hinted at those glyphs which are 'phased' according to Being or Plane; and have not explored their operations nor their apparent necessity. The Static Key is a true picture of the Universe in its architectural form as it manifests ITself to the Animal Senses and Consciousness in discrete units of Time. However, the discrete model is inadequate and leads to the False assertion that matters are written in Stone, the laws unyielding or the facts immutable or fixed and unchanging. We find evidence to support the idea that the Intelligence of the Universe is very much Alive and Reactive. It operates its Influence through "doors" which Evolution successively Makes Open. These doors or Perceptive Organs in the Sensual Body of the Universe have their correspondents in the Letters and in the Sensorium.

The first of these, the more obvious and encountered in the Outermost Abyss, is the L which cometh on the Left Hand as Averse, and on the Right as Upright. IT is for NEMO to Balance the Two and destroy Daath[1]*. The W is the second whose action occurs early in the Path, and like the F is universal in Operation so that it colours the sky*

1 Together (L averse, 50 and L upright, 70) these are 120, the old numeration to the Gate ON and the number in the English Key of the III° word of Outer Orders (as in the O.T.O., most advanced religions and Masonic bodies) which conquer Death. We remind the Student, that the formula is an elemental one and so must be four-fold. Therefore, it is a four-letter word. It begins with M and must terminate in N.

of that Path, and brings Wonder to the heart but touches not the Man, and Works ITs Way imperceptibly. The C throughout will be modified in character as to the Nature of the Operation. The same holds for the O glyph which is modified according to its attunement to the Solar, that is the Consciousness of the Student.[2] *Above all these lies the E, which is the Light by Which Made He the World.*

COSMOLOGICALLY, the new Aeon has opened portals through which the Human consciousness is now able to traverse intact. In the broadest terms, this means that new regions in the perceptible universe are now accessible to the human mechanism. Unchartered territory is slowly being explored by the more restless of us, and these are able to return to us with conscious, intelligible rendering of what was once only seen darkly or distantly.

All this discovery has brought about revelations; new continents to map and new systems to explicate and elucidate our old constructions. In particular, the structure of the Tree of Life as it has been known is unsatisfactory in the Light of this new Knowledge. Its two dimensional structure is at first too crude a simplification, and the concept of the paths crossing the different Veils is cumbersome at best, as there is no direct evidence for this, and in some cases direct evidence against them. Furthermore, the word 'path' implies a traversal, whereas the rays linking the Sephira are perhaps more accurately seen as influences bearing upon that State. It is in this Light especially, that the current structure of the Tree of Life fails in providing an accurate representational model of the perceptual Universe.

2 O, the Moon, shines not with her Light, but with that of the Sun.

The Aethyrs with their system of concentric rings seems more suitable a model. This task we will leave to more enlightened scholars for now.

Of immediate practical interest are the glyphs as they map out in concordances across the Planes; and of particular interest to Us are the transformations these glyphs undergo along these Planes after initiatory, aeonic or cataclysmic experience. Among these we can note:

1. the "Ordeal x"[3] ;
2. the accomplishment of 418, conversation with HGA
3. the Three Ordeals in One[4]; and
4. the successful crossing of the Abyss.[5]

These matters deal exclusively with the Man and the Woman as individual Souls, each a Star fixed on its particular Path, and even that Path ITself, insomuch as it is an individual Journey. As for matters cosmological and universal, outside the province of human control, of historical and trans-human paradigm change, we have the Aeonic shifts throughout Time. In this case, we have the Age of Aquarius, or the Aeon of Horus, and the inception of a New Law and the fulfillment of the Roman Script Glyphs as promised and delivered fully and without exception on March 1904, through Liber CCXX among others, though this was not seen nor written down or communicated publicly until the 21st century in this very Work. This last cosmic paradigm shift has precipitated revisions and realignments of the Glyph set

3 See Liber Al III, 22.

4 "Yea Than, Yea Theli, Yeah Lilith" See LIBER LXV,

5 Though initiatory ordeals persist after the crossing of the Abyss, and though these may be more acute in some cases, the Adept has established his footing in BINH, and is become the vehicle for his Star and so has transcended the possibility of Error; in this Way, She (the Adept in BINH) can do no Wrong.

and their concordances to accomodate this new natural Order. It provoked the emergence of new Glyphs corresponding to evolutionary developments to occur throughout the Aeon.[6]

In order to discuss how these developments are revealed through the Glyphs and the English Key, an introduction into the principles of Astrology, the Zodiac and the progression of the Aeons will be required. We call the Student's attention to the "Notes on Astrology" and "On the Procession of the Aeons" chapters in this book. Of particular interest are the transitions in the glyph set from that of the Aeon of Osiris to that of Horus, particularly as to the technicalities of their astrological attributions and elemental concordances which are discussed and presented in tables in this book. Before we can explore these matters, we must enter upon a short discussion on the discinction between the Active or Passive, and Balanced or Imbalanced letters. We illustrate with some examples.

It will be noted by the passing observer that some of these letters of the Roman Script are mapped to two different numbers. There are eleven such letters: C, F, J, L, N, O, S, T, W, X, Y, the balancing of which requires an eleven-fold formula.[7] Which particular value any of these letters takes will depend upon various conditions.

The student should be aware of the distinction to be made between textual values and actual values accorded to the Phenomenon at hand. Though a particular glyph may appear active or balanced textually, this is so only as far as the operation of the formulae are

6 We have for instance the appearance of E, J, W, F; and the emancipation and empowerment of all feminine glyphs; we have the injunction that "Tzaddi is not the Star" and so a call for a realignment of the ROTA wheel.

7 There must be an endless variety. We are aware of three suitable: RA HOOR KHUIT, ASAR UN NEFER, HOOR PA KRAAT.

concerned in the universal case. In the particular case, to the intitiate and the immediate environment, the glyph can never appear except in that state for which he or she has won the right to experience it. These matters are touched upon later in this chapter.[8]

A letter may be active or passive: These are: F, W, J and X and are characteristically male glyphs, hence the dual state of "active" and "passive" which indicates tumescence, physical, spiritual or otherwise. In text, a letter is said to be active if it is capitalized, at the beginning of the Word or in any part of IT.

A letter may be final: These are S, T and N. A letter is said to be 'final' if it terminates the Word. In some cases a combination of final values can terminate the word as in $Les_f s_f$.

A letter may be balanced: L; or imbalanced: ⅃. Textually, the L is balanced if it is flanked on both sides by the same letter.

A letter may be soft or hard: These are the variant cases of the C and O: C, C_k, O and Ŏ and are female glyphs according to the distinct phases of full or soft and crescented (horned) or hard. The soft letter is yielding, while the hard letter is cutting. One takes from without and revolves IT within; the other projects outward. One is the sign of the Mother and the other of Horus, the Child. In text, the C is soft when it is phonetically an S and hard when it is phonetically a K. Similarly, O is soft when equivalent to 'aw' and full when equivalent to the 'U'.

A letter maybe a vowel or a consonant: Y_c, Y_v. The letter Y in the English Language sometimes masquerades as an I when the occasion calls for it.

All that has been said, is for the Static Key. For the Student on the Path, it must be kept in mind that initation, Aethyrs, and

8 See Section Pre- and Post-418.

other factors override phonetics and other considerations. These matters are now discussed at length.

Active/Passive Values

AN activated glyph denotes the conscious and manifest equivalent of the dormant subconcious element.

We have already seen how activating the W, further manifests Being into Perceptive Existence, so that Aiwaz for instance, which is 78 and emanates from *Kether* becomes 418, the Great Work Accomplished which is the union of the 5 and the 6 and denotes the establishment of this force from *Kether*, materially in the individual. Note:

AIwAZ is 4 + 4 + 60 + 4 + 6 = 78 (= 156/2) while

AIWAZ is 4 + 4 + 400 + 4 + 6 = 418 (= HAD × 22)[9] and,

AIwASS is 4 + 4 + 60 + 4 + 42 + 42 = 156 while

AIWASS is 4 + 4 + 400 + 4 + 42 + 42 = 496 (= $\Sigma 31$).

Note that AIWAZ runs from Kether down and employs Z - the Lightning Flash; while AIWASS runs from Malkuth up and requires S, the Serpent that climbs the Tree and S, the Son that is crucified on it. In this case, with 'w' inactive he is BABALON = KAOS = 156 the perfect Unity. By activating along the 'w' we have 496 which contains and summarizes all the ideas from the unity to 31, (496 = $\Sigma 31$) which is 'AL' in the old key and 'Sh' in the new, "a secret key to this Law".

9 Note that these summations are verified in the Greek, Hebrew and Coptic as well: αιϝασσ (alpha, iota, digamma, iota, sigma,sigma - the same holds true for the Coptic) =1+10+1+6+200+200 = 418 = AIWAZ = 4 + 4 + 400 + 4 + 6; In Hebrew, איוָאס = 1+10+6+1+60 = 78 = AIwAZ = 4+4+60+4+6

Here we see that activating the 'W' in both cases increments the degree of manifestation. W denotes the Eyes, and whether it is the manifestation of the Object that makes it visible (W) or the Vision that manifests the Object is a meaningless question here. "If to be conscious of a thing is to call it into existence" is a question possible only if that consciousness be divided and that Vision cease (w). This materialization is accomplished via the addition of a digit (60 to 400) so that AIWAZ is the influence of Kether (78) which provokes the accomplishment of 418.

For a more accessible example, we can take the word "wisdom":

"His wisdom" (371) without the W activated, is the empty wisdom that is "bitterness", and "imperfection", it is a "must" or is the rule of many or "most" and it is often belligerent: 'to war": all terms equal to the key of 371.

371		
	Bitterness	SSf
	Duant	Tf
	His Wisdom	
	Imperfection	Nf
	Most	ST,Tf
	Must	ST,Tf
	No Difference	
	To War	

Activating the W, we have "His Wisdom" summing to 711 which also equals the phrases "One Knowledge" and "One is the Magus", confirming all these as properties as rightful emanations from the Crown or 1st sphere.

711		
	His Wisdom	*W*
	One is the Magus	*Sf*
	One Knowledge	

The student should take care and apply these activating properties of these glyphs in his calculations and operations wherever suitable.

Final Values

USE of the final value in formulae or words denotes a termination of the process. Similarly, in the cases where the initial value is employed, this would denote a continuation of the process. Take for example:

(a) Until that moment that he is emitted from Her womb (figuratively speaking) and the process is terminated, we have BABALON = 4 + 6 + 4 + 6 + 50 + 80 + 70 = 220, i.e. He is submitted to this formula as decreed by The Law (= 220) and the N continues. Only when the process is complete and the N final do we have BABALON_f = 4 + 6 + 4 + 6 + 50 + 80 + 6 = 156 which is the Perfect Unity.

(b) Similarly as active perpetual force AIWASS is 4 + 4 + 60 + 4 + 24 + 24 = 120 (the Key to Vault – see Liber 418, 12th Aire) but at the termination of the process he becomes as AIWAS_fS_f = 4 + 4 + 60 + 4 + 42 + 42 = 156 or BABALON_f, the Perfect Unity yet again.

Averse/Upright Values

THESE are equivalent to the Balanced and the Imbalanced Glyphs.

For the sake of Analytic *Gematria*, and the Establishment of the Static Key, the L is said to be Balanced or Upright, if it is supported on both sides by the same vowel. Otherwise, it is said to be averse and "continueth", that is, IT dies Not. The upright L has value of 70, and the averse, 50. These shifts (the addition of a 20, which is Union or the glyph of the Squaring of the Circle) are important paradigm adjustments with significant material effects.

The balancing of the L presupposes the termination of certain other glyphs. We provide Liber Al, I, 24 as an example: "I am Nuit, and my word is *six and fifty.*"

> "Six and fifty" = 42 + 4 + 9 (six, with S final) 4 + 6 + 8 (and) 10 + 4 + 10 + 98 + 6 (fifty) = 55 + 18 + 112 = 201 = Thelema (L imbalanced); but
>
> "*six*" = 24 + 4 + 9 = 37 with S non-final and "*Fifty*" = 10 + 4 + 2 + 98 + 70 = 184 with T final; while "*FiFty*" = 10 + 4 + 10 + 89 + 70 = 183, with T non-final] which are 220 = "The Law" and 221 = "Thelema" (with L balanced) respectively.[10]

Practically, L balanced and L imbalanced refer to states of the perceptible universe as they appear to the initiate pre- and post-418. We remind the reader that these come to Him on the Left Hand as Averse and on the Right Hand as Upright, and that together they are 120 ($L+L_{av}$ = 50 + 70) which is the Key to the Gate ON[11]. IT is for NEMO to Balance the two and destroy Daath by opening this Gate[12]. We present the technicalities of these transitional states and provide examples in the following section.

10 "The Law" and "Thelema" are technical terms particular to the document, as are the numbers 93, 220, 221, 440, 441, 666.

11 ON = Ayin and Nun = 70 + 50 = L and L averse = 120 and the enumeration of Aiwass in one of His phases.

12 It is improper and unnecessary to discuss these matters further. They are delineated in great detail elsewhere in the Tradition. See Book 418 for example as an exhaustive treatment of the subject by a High Adept.

Pre- and Post- 418

ACCOMPLISHMENT of 418[13] and the successful traversing of the Abyss, alters the perceptual universe significantly. Glyphs before invisible are now manifest, formulae are reversed or balanced and in some cases replaced.[14]

Upon entering the supernals or past the 3rd Aethyr the following is 'true' in that it is perceived. Note, this does not mean the Student can not avail himself of Pre-418 glyphs, though they no longer act on him. It is because he stands outside this World (the pre-418 world) that he can 'move' it. As Archimedes' (inventor of the lever) stated: "Give me a place to stand on, and I shall move the world." A lever requires a fulcrum resting on some other object; and so a human being cannot move an object without using some other fixed object or plane.

He is to take care of the rarefication and transformation of the glyphs as they pass through the Waters (see Cheth, 418, abraHADabra, The Chariot, et al). To pass X, or the old Shin for 300, is to have it manifest into 9 for those who have not won the "Ordeal X" (See Liber Al III, 22).

13 418 is the Qabalastic formula for uniting the 5 with the 6, that is the union between the perfected human being and his or her divine nature in the present incarnation, often referred to as 'The Great Work'. It requires traversing the Tree of Life, crossing the Abyss and all the adventures generally described in the Legends and perfectly and completely in Liber 418.

14 The ROTA card attributions are not altered upon a completion of 418, but the nature of their influence or bearing on the particular state are. There is no better suited example than that of the Chariot which remains the Fortress and the Charioteer that brings about the accomplishment of 418. He is Cancer officer of the Moon, Lord of the Waters, armoured like the Crab and accomplishes the Great Work. But once this is accomplished (post-418), the moon has waned, and this force is now Jupiterean and disposing.

Post-418 Conditions :

- (A∴M∴T∴) There are no more double values.
- (M∴T∴) L's are necessarily balanced. (L averse is no more. 50 the number of the gates of Death is dropped from the system: Death is no more. All N's final as per the 2nd Aire.[15]
- The Ordeal X is undergone (all X's are activated , i.e. X is 300) and 'Shin' or the 5 spoked Wheel of Spirit is operational.
- The ordeal 'x' is accomplished : X's are now active and Saturnian from Aries. (The R remains in Aries)
- The Moon has waned. That false light is behind one's Shadow. (All O's cresecented)
- The Y is necessarily 70, otherwise the old Aeon Goat has not been sacrificed, the Eye has not been opened and the Man is at most at 6 or Tiphareth in the old system (SOL).
- All N's final (see second note)
- The goddesses (C, P) pass from Water to Aquarius (from elemental to zodiacal). The Balance of the Sexes and emergence of Goddess consciousness.
- (M∴T∴) L is now Libra above the supernals (whereas it is Martian beneath them).
- (M∴T∴) N, the Gate of Death and Y the Tree of Life also take on revised attributions/concordances upon successful completion of 418. These are discussed in detail elsewhere in this book. A summary is as follows:
    - N's are now final and so in the house of Scorpio (The phasing of Mercury has been accomplished).
    - Y is always 70 and so Earth (in it's elemental form)
- E, J make their appearance
- Q is mature and is replaced by F in the 'schema'.

We take the birth name of the Scribe of Liber vel Legis as an

15 "In the letter N the Voice of the Aethyr is ended." Liber 418, 2nd Aethyr.

example of results that may be obtained by the play of these forces. Such analyses work with the Name of any Human Being and we hope that this illustration will serve as an example of the depth of analysis that the Student can take in the application of *Gematria*, and the symmetry to be discovered along the planes: *the system remains integral confirming initial results when we proceed along these axes (in this case, L, C, W).* [16]

Pre-418

Edward Alexander Crowley=Alastair[17] Crowley=Ra Hoor Khu=666

> Edward Alexander Crowley = (1 + 8 + 60 + 4 + 9 + 8) + (4 + 50 + 1 + 9 + 4 + 70 + 8 + 1 + 9) + (30 + 9 + 200 + 60 + 50 + 1 + 70) = 90 + 156 + 420 = 666
>
> Alastair Crowley = (4 + 70 + 4 + 42 + 89 + 4 + 4 + 9) + (30 + 9 + 200 + 60 + 50 + 1 + 70) = 666
>
> Ra Hoor Khu = 13 + (7 + 200 + 200 + 9) + (30 + 7 + 200) = 666[18]

But note that if we take S and T as non-final (i.e. continuing or reverberating) we get:

> Aleister Crowley = (4 + 50 + 1 + 4 + 24 + 89 + 1 + 9) + (30 + 9 + 80 + 60 + 50 + 1 + 6) = 182 + 236 = 418

---

16 See Footnote 1 of the chapter entitled "The Tree of Life & The Harmony of the Spheres" on Nu for another example

17 A variant of the name used by the adept himself to sign his poetic works. See also "Alastair and the Spirit of Solitude"; and note that he had yet to accomplish 418 at the time he was employing this pseudonym.

18 This number is likely to excite the fear of some of the more superstitious. It has been linked in the lore with a contrary force, as in an *Anti*-Messiah. This is correct in the sense that He is the Harbinger of new Truth and Law, and in this sense, Destroys the Old by erecting the New, and so is seen as inimical by the proponents of all those who are against Nature and Progress and Motherhood. The three wheels into the 6 confirm this as a perfectly balanced Solar diety. Not only is 6 the number of the Sphere of Sol (Tiphareth) so that each wheel is turned and attuned to Sol, 666 is the mystical number of Sol for it is the sum of all integers up to and including 6 into 6 (that is the synthesis of all paired ideas below it united into Sol, for $666=1+2+...+6^2$). [Note: 6 itself as a glyph denotes the 'taking in from above'.] See section on the Mystical Number of the Planets.

Dura-418: Finalizing the Glyphs

Edward Alexander Crowley = 602 = Ankh Af Na Khonsu *(N.B. Ankh Af Na Khonsu was the name given to the scribe by Aiwass)*;

Taking N as final (See Liber 418, 2nd Aire, 418 Accomplished) we have :

> Edward Alexander Crowley = (1 + 8 + 60 + 4 + 9 + 8) + (4 + 50 + 1 + 9 + 4 + 6 + 8 + 1 +9) + (30 + 9 + 200 + 60 + 50 + 1 + 70) = 90 + 92 + 420 = 602
>
> Ankh Af Na Khonsu = (4 + 70 + 30 +7) + (4 + 2) + (70 + 4) + (30 + 7 + 80 + 70 + 24 + 200) = 111 + 6 + 74 + 411 = 602

Post-418: Balancing the Glyphs

Assuming the L's to have been balanced (in the initiate's name only), we arrive at:

> Aleister = 220 = The Law;
> Crowley = 440 = Horus = Perdurabo = Great Work
> (Aleister = 4 + 70 + 1 + 4 + 42 + 89 + 1 + 9 = 220
> The Law = (98 + 7 + 1) + (50 + 4 + 60)= 220
> Crowley = (30 + 9 + 200 + 60 + 50 + 1 + 70) = 440
> Horus = 7 + 200 + 9 + 200 + 24 = 440)

Thus the name now denotes the Law of Horus (or the Union of these two concepts : The Law, and Horus).

Activating the Glyphs

Activating W and balancing the L, we have

> Crowley = 30 + 9 + 200 + 400 + 70 + 1 + 70 = 780 (= Aiwaz into Malkuth, 78 x 10), and
>
> Aleister Crowley = 220 + 780 = 1000, while by softening the C and the O we have:
>
> Edward Alexander Crowley = (1 + 8 + 400 + 4 + 9 + 8) + (4 + 70 + 1 + 9 + 4 + 6 + 8 + 1 + 9) + (3 + 9 + 80 + 400 + 70 + 1 + 6) = 1111, the secret fourfold glory of the scribe's Name as mentioned in the Book.

All such dynamic aspects of the Key are omitted from the lexicon as is the Tradition. The lexicon contains then, the static key of these forces as they are, dormant though reactive, awake though unactivated.

The Tree of Life
& The Harmony of the Spheres

It may prove convenient to witness the progression of certain formulae as they pass through increasing degrees of manifestation, materialization or condensation. To provide an illustration: the scale 56, 156, 256,..., 1056 can be seen as denoting the operation of 56 (NU in the old key, ISIS in the new)[19] as it progressively modifies itself through the successive degrees of manifestation.[20] Taking the Tree of Life and the old system structure for sake of

19 A deeper meaning is here implied, for her *Word* is six and fifty, not her *Name*, though the latter coincides with the numeration in the old key. (NU is Nun + Vau = 50 + 6.) The exact quote is "*I am Nuit, and my word is six and fifty.*" Liber Al I, 24. Note, NU is 56 in the old Key; Nuit is NU (3^3 x 10) + IT (93) in the new. Her word is "six and fifty" not "56" (that is, it is spelt out, not enumerated); and it is her *word* not her Name. Note: "Six and fifty" = 42 + 4 + 9 (six, with S final) 4 + 6 + 8 (and) 10 + 4 + 10 + 98 + 6 (fifty) = 55 + 18 + 112 = 201 = Thelema (L imbalanced).
Also note the injuction in the next line, "Divide, add, mulitply and understand." (Liber Al, I. 25) for "six" + "fifty" yields further clues, for "six" + "fifty" yields 220 (= The Law) and 221 (= Thelema, with L balanced) respectively, so that her Word is alternately "Thelema" (in two varaiant cases, pre- and post-418) and "The Law":
[*six* = 24 + 4 + 9 = 37] and [*Fifty* = 10 + 4 + 2 + 98 + 70 = 184 with T final; while *FiFty* = 10 + 4 + 10 + 89 + 70 = 183, with T non-final] which together yield 220 = The Law = 98 + 7 + 1 50 + 4 + 60; and 221 = Thelema (with L balanced) = 98 + 7 + 1 + 70 + 1 + 40 + 4 respectively, so that her Word is alternately "Thelema" (in two variant cases, pre- and post-418) and "The Law". See Notes on the Living Key, Pre- and Post-418 conditions later in this chapter for a discussion on final and non-final values *et al.*
20 See the Mystical Properties of the Numbers for the significance of these modifiers; and also the Tree of Life and the *sephiroth* they correspond to.

illustration, it is not incorrect to think then of 56 itself, as the operation of this formula or current into the *Ain Soph Aur*[21]. The result 056 = 56 creates no change, which is sensible, for one would not expect the *Ain Soph Aur* to modify the energies travelling across it. With 156 we now see the operation of this "current" of "force" in *Kether*, its first manifestation in full purity (though manifest and hence profane), which is the numerical glyph and formulae (KAOS = BABALON = 156) for the energies passing through the two paths descending from *Kether* (*aleph* and *beth*). Similarly, with 256, we now see this current manifest in *Chokmah*, or the second sphere of Being.

But to know of a current or energy signature's operation *into* or *upon* these planes, we multiply them. Hence, if we are asking the question: What is NU (or how is She manifest? how will she be in such a Place?) we look at her number on the appropriate scale. (e.g. 7th plane of desire, we have 756 and its concordant attributes). If instead, we ask what happens to a particular world or level of consciousness when NU appears (that is, what does her Work consist of? How is the object modified when this energy is applied to it?), we look at the product between these two. Hence 0 x 56 denotes the effect of the current or the Goddess on the *Ain Soph Aur* which is again the null element or 0. In fact, any number multiplied by zero reduces to zero which implies that whatever current or energy it may be, it will have no effect whatsoever on the *Ain Soph Aur.*[22] Once again, this stands to reason, as one would not expect the *Ain Soph Aur* to be modified by what passes through it (though the sun rages it can not brighten the darkness of space around it until it comes into contact with an object, something to react upon, as in a planet,

21 "Limitless light": a technical term referring to the boundless energies that enswathes the manifest Universe (and NOT only outside it as traditionally represented).
22 There is nothing material in the Ain Soph Aur for the energy to graft onto.

and suddenly its light is visible even if it be a galaxy away).

To see the operation of this current into *Kether* then, we multiply it by the unit and so encounter the first, undifferentiated manifestation of the thing itself. Similarly 112 summarizes[23] the operation of the current into *Chokmah* which is equivalent to a form of Hadit (with T non-final)—once more, as stands to reason.

All this is more or less useless to the Student setting out upon practical experimentation. For *Kether* or the *Ain Soph Aur,* even *Malkuth* must appear as distant, abstract concepts. Nonetheless, as the Tree of Life is a model for the Cosmos, so it is a model for Consciousness for these two are one and the same ultimately. If it is a model for Mind, then it is a model for the Body of Man. The microscosm is the macrocosm and so on. This being said, we proffer that it may be more pratical a model to view such a progression along the lines of operations upon the "Three Wheels". This alters the interpretation of the number. Whereas 156, was the action of 56 from *Kether*, and 256 the action of 56 from *Chokmah*, we will view the numbers essentially as the two lower wheels "attuned to" 5 (the sphere of Mars, and 6 (the sphere of Sol) repectively, while in the case, of 156, we have the results of this attunement, while the highest wheel is in *Kether* (or *Chokmah*, as in the case of 256). We explore these matters in the following sections.[24]

23 But does not define!

24 See also the example "His wisdom" vs "His Wisdom". One might say of the former that "he is all about the victory" of his wisdom.

Orders of Magnitude

SINGLE DIGITS typically imply pure ideas, useless in practical matters but crucial in setting up the proper field. For instance, it would be vain to attempt to construct a formula for immediate action with the first wheel in three, which is *Binah* and which, with Saturn presiding, is the province of delayed reaction: the system is in a state of quasi-coma while it undergoes profound Change and re-organization in the Athanoor.

Whereas Single digits denote pure and primal forces, double digits denote ideas still not practical, but fundamental or basic to manifestation. Acting as intermediary, they supply the medium for propulsion between the two wheels, and in one way or another because of its position effects the necessary balances.

Three digit numbers refer to a full manifestation within the Human Consciousness entailing, the Idea, The Image, and its Reflection in the Mind.

Four digit numbers refer to material manifestations both within and outside the Being.[25]

The above statements apply to Formulae alone.

25 Note that numerically, orders of magnitude are acheived by multiplication into Malkuth, the Material Plane, the 10th sphere or 10. Thus 200 the Cup, can be seen as the materialization of 20 the Union. Linguistically, consider the suffix "er" in the English Language which denotes an accentuation of a property. An object may be hard, soft. "Harder" and "softer", that is hard + 10 or soft + 10 denote a futher materialization of the ideas "hard" or "soft" respectively. Consider also the various transitions from verb to noun which rely on the same mechanism: a thing that sifts is a sift+*er*, a person who wins is a 'winn*er*'; he who sighs is a sigher (sigh+*er*); but he who lies is a li+*ar*.

The Three Wheels
- Magick & Qabalah

THE THREE WHEELS are practical constructs. They have no physical existence though their counterparts have a place in the human body. They correspond vaguely to a number of notions, historically felt, intuited or imagined. Some of these are:

Chakras: *Sahasrara, Anahata, Muladhara*

Sephiroth: *Kether, Tiphareth, Malkuth*

Human Body: *The Brow, The Heart, The Hand and/or Gentials*

States of Perfection: *Sat, Chit, Ananda*

Mystically: *Soul, Mind, Body*

Materially: *Spirit, Man, Animal*

In certain texts, these wheels are alternately referred to as 'wounds' in others as 'cups' or 'bodies' and even sensory organs. In fact they correspond to all these separate components that enter into the building up of the sensorium. To perceive a Plane, one must first develop the 'Body of Light' so as to be able to Travel or Be there. Afterwards one must grow the 'eyes' to see, and the ears to hear. Until that moment, all is Darkness and Silence; for as we observe in Nature's Law: whether of the Womb or of Space, Life invokes Darkness.[26] If by act of Will one remains and survives for a Season in this Place, then the Body of Light further adapts to its environment until it is perfectly formulated and established

26 Note that these properties are reversed upon hitting the Source of Life. See Liber 418 and in particular, the notion of the emptiness of Spirit and of Energy reacting on Matter.

there. This disparity or dissonance between the physical and the Body of Light now acts with increasing force upon the Balance of the system. The physical nervous system continually adapts itself in attempting to accomodate these energies. Once the new Energy channels are established, the physical tissue is itself now irrigated through this new Energy source. The physical body completes the Change and the new sensorium with its Organs of Perception and its Powers of discernment are perfectly developed and established and begin to drink and live of their own accord, as the physical ear and eye do, without encumbering Mind or necessitating Will.

Some practical considerations arise. Let us propose the following:

The Higher Wheel corresponds to the eternal aspect of Man, the Self, the Architecting Consciousness which is Beyond Limitation, and the perception of which is called Enlightenment, and the Union with which is called Bliss.

The Middle Wheel is the Consciousness including the Self's ego if IT is still alive, and the Mind.

The Lower Wheel is the Animal Self, the passions and drives.[27]

The proper functioning of all three Wheels is necessary. The doctrine of denying the Lowest Wheel (and in some cases the two lower wheels) as promulgated in some religions or disciplines, can only lead to imbalance, poor health, diminished intellect and gross error. Denying one's highest wheel, leads to profound misery; and in the passionate, to madness. Accelerating or stopping one wheel over another is a violence one commits upon the System and Nature and should be done for definite purpose and duration only.

27 As the M.∴T.∴ will observe, these are three distinct beings in actuality; each with their own bodies, habitats, and wills. He is become Three which is One.

By way of illustration, we observe that single digit numbers refer to all that flows into or from the first wheel. A high, unmanifest force, it descends no further than the Subconscious and leaves the Consciousness and Body unaffected. However, the system tends to Harmony, and now that the spinning of the Higher Wheel is altered, the system itself must adjust: for all wheels seek to spin with identical or complementary frequencies (that is rhythmic multiples).[28]

Triune numbers like 111, 222, etc., reflect a fundamental operation of the human structure to tend to Balance. Historically, this triune division in man's constitution has been referred to as the "trinity", the "supernals", "the id, the superego the ego, and a plethora of other trinitarian constructions. Loosely, we can refer to these functions however we like so long as we preserve a certain order and know what they refer to in the Body itself.

With development Man will lose whatever it is that interferes with the proper operation of these "three wheels". At each turn, he is like the Titan torn upon the Wheels. He will lose his ego, personality even, tendencies and all psychological conditioning as various parts of himself he will sheathe.

Typically the initiate will have all three wheels flowing into a particular receptacle before he is stable enough to pass into *Kether* and withstand the swirlings that emanate from this sphere. In this way, a number like 444 suggests all three wheels flowing into Chesed which JUPITO presides over; and a number like

28 Thus, the 112 wishes to become a 111, which appears easier for the man to accomplish than to revert to a 222—it requires altering only the lowest wheel (essentially releasing it from the energies of *Chokmah*, and transcending them to the energies of *Kether*.) But once He is 111, he can manifest himself as 222 quite easily by dividing his consciousness: once again "listen to Himself" and Observe Himself instead of Being that Motion as he was in 111, i.e. he lays his Hand on the Higher Wheel and thus divides it: the two lower wheels if this state is not corrected, would divide themselves further to repair the imbalance.

888, suggests the Magus who sports it, applies all his energies to MERCURIUS.

The complexity of the initiate's name and number is slowly reduced throughout his career until this perfection and grace is revealed in one final number, which ceases to mean anything.[29]

For analytical purposes: it is important to note that triune numbers of the form 111 or 222, etc. are spanned by 37: that they are multiples of 37 (= Ch, the old glyph for CHETH) in the order of 3. (111 = 37 x 3 x 1; 222 = 37 x 3 x 2; 333 = 37 x 3 x 3; 444 = 37 x 3 x 4, etc). 37 is the 'key' or root of all such balancing acts[30]. This would indicate a Practical Formula or Law, that in order to have the three Wheels and the system balanced in unison there is first a necessary condition: that the first wheel be tuned to the energies of *Binah*, and the second to that of *Netzach*, the sphere of Venus or Victory, while the lowest sphere is abandoned or relinquished to the control of the first two. However, this practice may be dangerous. In essence, it is the means by which a Nemo is formulated and IT is the Operation of "Ch"—or "this my chariot that descendeth from Babalon" and is a process best left to Nature's architecting.

The discerning mind now asks, "What is this famed Chariot from which all power descends?" We can refer to the Lexicon for an answer and then to the doctrine of the Three Wheels for

29 See Perdurabo's birth name and mottoes in light of the key for an example.

30 A deep mystery: The glyph of 37 can be summarized in the following Idea: (The student can verify the Vision by tracing the glyph and stepping into it.) 37 is the horns of a Ram (3) and those of a Goat (7). The first climbed the Mount from the East and the other from the West coming to the summit simultaneously. Both leapt to the attack and butting, locked their horns, leaving only their hind legs on the Earth. Their bodies arched over, is the Gate to a circular Garden atop the Hill which is thy Refuge. Note that this Garden is the famed Garden that harbours the Fount of Life; and that precipitating its Vision: travelling there and developing the sensorium is what calls for the Ram and the Goat and the opening of the Eye coincides with the locking of Horns and the establishment of the Gate.

a practical application. Thus we can see that Chariot (37 + 4 + 9 + 4 + 200 + 89) is 343. that is the central wheel crosses the abyss establishing itself in *Chesed*, the 4th sphere, while the other two are pinned onto *Binah* from which he hangs. Likewise, the Charioteer (37 + 4 + 9 + 4 + 200 + 98 + 1 + 1 + 9), that is, the one conscious and directing the Chariot, is 363, and here the central wheel descends to the 6th sphere, *Tiphareth*, the Sun, or balanced consciousness. Observe also that Charioteer = Chariot + 20 (G, the Union) which implies the Charioteer operates in unison with His Chariot.

In this way, if the Initiate had need of Courage (Courage = 464) at any moment in time, he hath only to turn his three wheels to the 4th, 6th, 4th spheres respectively. Similarily, if he ever had need of Strength, then he had only turn his wheels to the 3rd, 3rd, and the 6th spheres respectively. This can be explained as follows: Saturn will give him the inertia and tirelessness needed of *Binah*, the Great Ocean, His Chit likewise is tuned to the province of Time and Eternity, is indefatigable; and finally with the physical in perfect balance of the 6: these three constitute Strength or 336. For Courage, we have 464, that is Sat and physical tuned to Jupiterian energies, that of the Ruling Father, the Material King, with all the powers of Fortune at his command, while the Affective or 2nd wheel, his mind, is in Tiphareth, crucified in its Will and fatally committed.

Likewise the Adept, who with Courage (464) crosses the Abyss, and relinquishing the sheath of the Self, then shines in the sky to brighten the eyes of men, either as an evening star (464) from which he hangs from Jupiter whilst he burns; or a morning star (441) like the Magi and the solstice falling star of Venus *en route* to adorn and anoint and gilden the Living Word.

A High system of Magick is here implied in which the talisman or object of operation is the Initiate himself. As such, the operator and operand are again in unison like the Charioteer, and so there can be no objection and the issue of the operation should by Necessity be Success. This Will be, unless the material itself be corrupt or the operation an aberration to Nature and Love. The Student should be wary of the Formulae he applies, for its success is most certain.[31]

The Word Made Flesh

On the Magus:

"He is the First and the Last. How shall He cease to Number Himself?"

WHILE THERE is *Chokmah*, there is Division. That is, the act of intellectualizing requires observation and subjective experience of the object. The task of the adept is to remove the subjective from his experience. However, the introductory notes on apophenia and other disorders are inconsequential to the Student in *Chokmah*. For the consciousness that is established in *Chokmah* knows no separation between itself and the object. He exists in the Present, He is that which moves

31 There being no transmission medium to present an obstacle.... Incidentally, this is an example of the futility of 'warnings'; and a blatant appropriation of their ultimate use: to attract, that is entice, the brave and the daring. It's difficult to imagine how the brute can do himself any harm. If the 'wheels' are imagined constructs, then how is he who hasn't mastered Mind meant to possess them? Furthermore, turning one's attention or chakras or bodies to this 'sphere' or that 'sphere' is nonsensical enough to keep the unimaginative away. A simple test and repeated experiment will verify Results.

while motionless. In this Present, there is no Time—time being the province of BINAH—for cognition to take place. Furthermore separation between subject and object is necessary for perception or the subject's experience of the object.

More pertinent still to the Officer in this Grade, is the lack of separation between Himself and any Object he unites with. In this sense, to number a thing is to number himself, for he combines Himself and communes with the Object (that is, he brings that portion of his microcosm to the fore). Because he is That, he hath no Place for the Understanding or the Knowledge —which are the Palaces which the Keys of the *Qabalah* open. Indeed, because the Understanding is Darkness, where there is Light there is evidence of his opposition or Ignorance, For Truth like Light travels invisibly through Space[32] and it is only when it is confronted with some obstacle to its passage that it Shines. For this shining is like all other Fire and it is the very Truth or Law that is consumed.

The one who enters *Binah* has been made Universal. Before Understanding dawned, was the ray of every star pouring into his Being, for he is the Daughter and a Window. And as Nemo he was crowned sovereign of all that Burns underground. He has closed the circle, he is Father and Son, creator and creation, He is First and Last (1 and 400), he is East and West, (EW=1 + 400); he is Alpha (1) and Omega (400).

The movement from 401 to 441 critical to the Initiate in *Chokmah*, denotes the addition of an M, the symbol of self-sacrifice.[33] Only then is this the saying Of All Truth (OAT - the

32 The sun is bright but the space around it is dark and IT is only when it hits a planet or an asteroid or some other rock that presents an obstacle to its passage that the World around it is enflamed with Light: so is it with Samadhi and all the other Ecstasies.)

33 As seen from beneath the Veil of the Abyss, for this self-sacrifice entails no sacrifice at all, IT being His Will.

reversal or traversal of the TAO). All this pertains to *Chokmah* which follows *Binah*, the Understanding. Note, that "Palace of Understanding" = 882 = which is 441 + 441[34], which implies that the movement from the 3rd to the 2nd sphere requires reduction of one half to arrive at unity of the 441 (accomplished through BABALON)—a sort of ceasing of the reflection. What remains must then be further reduced (by KAOS) to 21 (441 = 21 x 21), by the destruction of the lower wheel. In the past, this was thought to imply death, and *Kether* was said to be unattainable by the living.[35]

The task of the officer in *Chokmah* is to perfect the operation of his Word through his Wisdom which is born of the Understanding[36]. And this Understanding is the circumference of the circle that is Knowledge, the Serpent which swallows its tail and has no Center until the Circle contracts itself to a Point. (See notes on the geometric interpretation of Number.) He employs the *Qabalah* then, to ensure his Operation is aligned with the Law and the Universe, knowing that it would prove futile otherwise. In this Way, he fulfills the Law and his task, and acts as the Hand of the Creator, naturally and necessarily for He is ineffective otherwise.

---

34 Note that 441 is also The Law + Thelema = 220 + 221 and that MT in the Old Key is Mem Tau = 440 and and the addition of the aleph (A) implies a passage of 440 into 441 which resolves into 21. ($441=21^2$) *Liber B vel Magi* in particular, provides instruction on effecting this operation; Liber 418 maps the entire initiatory experience.
Also: The Name Babalon = Breasts of Babalon = 441 a number neccessary to the birth of a Magus. [The Name Babalon = 106 + 115 + 156 = 221 + 156 = THELEMA + BABALON, pre-418; but post-418, we have N non-final as per 2nd Aire where N continueth, so that Babalon = 220, and now, "The Name (221) Babalon(220)" = 221 (Thelema) + 220 (the Law) = 441], [Breasts of Babalon = 106 + 175 + 90 + 176 (L balanced) = 441]. See the Living Key chapter in this book for more on this and similar matters.

35 It is certain that the dead have no use for Kether or anything else, so that it would be odd that Nature would take such explicit pains to reserve anything for them.

36 Recall that these are the technical titles of the Sephira: Daath (the false sphere) is Knowledge; Binah is the Understanding; Chokmah, the Wisdom; and Kether, the Crown.

Gematria

Demonstration (Gematria)

IN THIS section, we show some preliminary methods and results of the application of the *Gematria* for the New Aeon *Qabalah* and the English Key specifically. A cursory examination of some of the more prominent or eye-catching phrases or Formulae contained in Liber AL vel Legis and other Class A documents is presented.

A perusal of the lexicon (provided in an appendix to this book) will show that the old formulae are preserved under this new system of ordering and value, and in most cases, further elucidated as we should expect. We can use by way of an example, the two formulae linked to the supernals of the Tree of Life (BABALON and KAOS) which in the past were symmetrical and coincident (*His fourfold word to balance Her sevenfold word*) both equalling to 156 (156 = 12 × 13 the Union Perfect)[6]:

(K A O S) סועכ[1]	=156 =	נעלאבאב(B A B A L O N)
60 + 6 + 70 + 20	= 156 =	2 + 1 + 2 + 1 + 30 + 70 + 50

Applying the new key, we find that the symmetry and the equality of the formulae for these two Sephira not only hold, but that their numerical key is preserved:

6 See Liber 418, and Sephir Sephiroth: The letter A is taken for an Ayin here, and the O as Vau: an approximation necessary in the old Aeon, and no longer needed in the new Key as is for BABALON =156= KAOS in the New KEY as is now shown.

KAOS	= 156 =	BABALON
30 + 4 + 80 + 42	= 156 =	6 + 4 + 6 + 4 + 50 + 80 + 6

Now we ask, if the English Key confirms the old operation, what further elucidations might the English Key reveal? Note: If we take the value of O long, then we have:[7]

KAOS	= 276 =	BABALON
30 + 4 + 200 + 42	= 276 =	6 + 4 + 6 + 4 + 50 + 200 + 6

> Observe that 276 = Σ23 indicating 276 as the glyph which expresses the summation of all the ideas contained in the set {1,...,23}; 23 traditionally corresponding to the glyph of nascent life.[8] Supposing we wish to confirm the nature of this development. Working in the old key, we note that the addition of 120 to the old formulae (156) yields the new Aeon value (276). The student will remark that 120 denotes the god ON[9] who sits beyond the gate BABALON. In fact, the name Babalon etymologically signifies "The Gate to the God ON," [10] Babylon, being the City of Fifty Gates, and ON being the Key to unlocking the Vault that is 120.[11] The glyph 276 or (156 + 120) therefore, indicates the success and issue of the original formula, containing as it does, all that is needed for its successful fruition—namely, the summation of all ideas preceding it (the entirety of the Knowledge to be found in the Old Law (the key of 22 glyphs and the next) so that the old Key is fulfilled in the new.)

7 Note that we also have 'Babalon' = 4+ 6 + 4 + 6 + 50 + 80 + 70 = 220 = 'the Law'. And that The Gates of Understanding = 1156 (scale of 156) = The Wisdom of the New Aeon

8 See "The Meaning of the Primes" included in the Sephir Sephiroth, Weiser

9 Besides being expressly stated in Liber 418, Qabalistically, He is ען (Ayin-Nun) which is 70+50 in the old key.

10 BAB is gate; AL is a title of god; ON is a godname for the Sun.

11 In the 12th Aire. N.B. 120 = Σ15

Furthermore if Babalon is etymologically equivalent to the Gate (Babal) ON, then let us play with its values for N, the Gate as we have already done for O. We observe that BABAL ON = 156 with N final, and 220 otherwise so that Love and the Law are both implied. Further technicalities are elucidated: This N takes on two possible values: 6 or 70 depending on which side of the gate One is ON. And that Gate that is N, is the Gate that the Key ON opens, which opened from one side is 156 (150 + N_f) and from the other 220 (150 + N) which are both BABALON.

If we direct our attention to *Liber al Vel Legis*, we see that the Book is in its design and construction, a perfect example of *Gematria* along a number of dimensions extending to a form of closed geometry. These equalities and concordances revealed by the English Key are even more astonishing in light of the fact that this writing predates the discovery of the key by over a century. The title page alone is rich with such indications. A cursory glance yields a number of contiguities as we are able to demonstrate now.

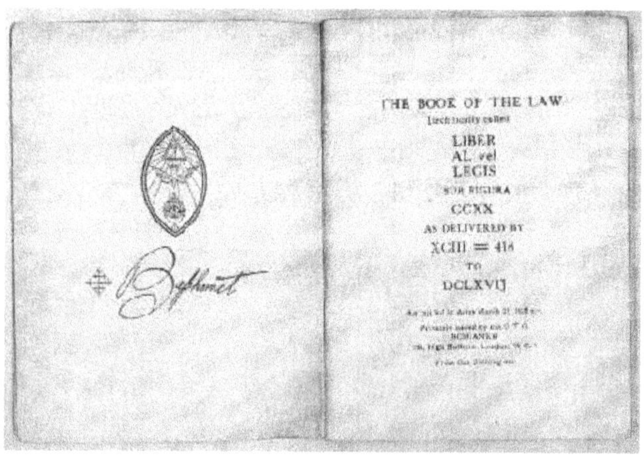

THE BOOK OF THE LAW
LIBER
AL vel
LEGIS
CCXX
AS DELIVERED BY
XCIII = 418
TO
DCLXVI

Figure 2 - Liber vel Legis - Cover Page, (c) Ordo Templi Orientis, 1926, 1938, 2008.

The book's technical title is Liber *AL vel Legis, sub figura CCXX* or *The Book of the Law*. It contains 220 verses, which fact was given as the reason for its numeration as CCXX in Roman Numerals. We are now able to verify that "The Law" has a key of 220 in the English *Qabalah* though the Authors at the Time could not have known this.[12]. Qabalistically then, "The Book of the Law" can be transliterated as "The Book of 220" which coincides with its technical name: Liber CCXX[13].

In the next line, we learn that the Book was "delivered"[14] by 418 to DCLXVI. We learn that the author of the Book calls Himself AIWAZ and provides the Key of this Name as 418. We see that the English Key confirms this as AIWAZ = 4 + 4 + 400 + 4 + 6 = 418.

Also note, that the book is declared as "given by 418 to DCLXVI" which is 666 in Roman numerals, and that this coincides with the birth name of the scribe, though he was not at the time in possession of the Key and sought in vain to confirm this attribution, transliterating to Greek and Hebrew.[15] Finally, the scribe's Name under the ordinance of that Order (*Perdurabo)*, equates not only with his birth name, but also with that of the God presiding over the Book.[16]

Besides the *prima facie* values, we have geometries that we can develop along the different dimensional values of the Letters. As we have seen in the sections on "The Living Key", we have

---

12 The Law = (98 + 7 + 1) + (50 + 4 + 60) = 220

13 Lat: Book 220

14 In this case, dictated.

15 However, the English Key verifies this equality, for Edward Alexander Crowley (the legal birth name of the scribe) = 666 in the English Key; while Aleister Crowley translates to 440 + 220 that is Knowledge + The Law. Edward Alexander Crowley = **666**= $\sum 36$

16 Perdurabo = Crowley = Horus = 440 ("The Law" into Chokmah i.e. 220 x 2), a number of perfection already experientially dear to Thelemites: and here they have their confirmation.

concordant values for all these formulae along the various planes, N/N_f, S/S_f, O/Ō, w/W, etc.

AIWASS or AIWAZ as the name is variably spelled is given as the Author of this book. By Table I (with w=60), we find that AIWAZ sums to 78 and AIWASS to 156[17] in the new key, providing us with a further clue as to the interpretations and the scale of geometries we wish to apply. As AIWAZ, He is 78 or that current into *Kether* or the first sphere of emanation. When manifest as AIWASS, He is 78 × 2 or 156 which is the number for KAOS and BABALON and is the same current into the second sphere of manifestation, the Intelligible Word, *Chokmah*. Observe also that this transition from the closed Z termination of the first variant of the name, into the prolonged double S in the second and the accompanying phonetic changes (the sound of steam escaping) acts as a further hint of the nature of this Change.

Finally, as already noted, AIWAZ with W activated is 418, the glyph for the Great Work accomplished coinciding with the enumeration of the same name in the Greek key[18].

AIWAZ who numbers himself 418, calls the scribe *Ankh Af na Khonsu* which is 602 which is again the key of the birth name of the scribe by *Gematria*[19]. With these two simple words, He reveals the entirety of the Key in its Active and Static Forms, leaving no Mystery nor Doubt, but Certainty Alone.[20]

All this as regards the title page only. Upon opening the book,

---

17 Hence Perdurabo's unconscious Love for this Number, inciting him to unite the Supernal Formulae to it by force of Creation (the Aleph reconstituted into Ayin to yield 156 in KAOS).
18 αιϝασσ=1+10+1+6+200+200=418 (alpha, iota, digamma, iota, sigma,sigma - the same holds true for the Coptic; In Hebrew, איוָאס = 1+10+6+1+60 = 78 = AIwAZ = 4+4+60+4+6
19 See the section, *The Living Key*.
20 See Section on Active and Passive Glyphs in this Book for a full examination of these two names and their active and passive states.

the concordances grow. We leave these to the next section where we discuss the technical terms encountered along with their enumeration and formulae.

Liber Al vel Legis, received by Perdurabo in Cairo, Egypt in the year 1904, contains three chapters, each written in one hour in three successive days beginning at noon, on April 8, April 9, and April 10.

The first chapter introduces NU who appears to be speaking and is described as the "*Lady of the Starry Heaven*" or the "*Queen of Space*".[21] We are introduced: "*I am Nuit, and my word is six and fifty. Divide, add, multiply and understand.*" Liber Al I, 24-25. It is the Goddess herself that provides the injunction.

For NU is 56 in the old Key. Her word is "six and fifty" not "56"; that is, it is spelt out, not enumerated. Note:

> "Six and fifty" = 42 + 4 + 9 (six, with S final) 4 + 6 + 8 (and) 10 + 4 + 10 + 98 + 6 (fifty) = 55 + 18 + 112 = 201 = Thelema (L imbalanced).
>
> [six = 24 + 4 + 9 = 37] + [Fifty = 10 + 4 + 2 + 98 + 70 = 184 with T final= 221 = "Thelema" (with L balanced);
>
> while [six = 24 + 4 + 9 = 37] + [FiFty = 10 + 4 + 10 + 89 + 70 = 183, with T non-final] = 220 = "The Law"
>
> So that her Word is alternately "Thelema" (in two variant cases, pre- and post-418) and "The Law" (220) in another.

And so we Understand that this simple statement contains within it increasingly detailed facts and assertions to comprise a full and complete exegesis on the Goddess.

In the second chapter, it is Nu's complement, HADIT that now

21 Liber vel Legis, I, 27

speaks. He is eternal energy, the Infinite Motion of Things. He is the "*flame that burns in every heart of man, and in the core of every star.*"[22] These statements confirm and further elucidate upon the discoveries we've just made. For note: HADIT =**112** with T final and 112 = 56 × 2, the old glyph for Nu upon *Chokmah*; i.e. Mazloth – a star in Her body); while with T non-final, he is 121 which 11^2, confirming his subsequent statements: "*I am The Empress & the Hierophant. Thus eleven, as my bride is eleven.*"[23]

Finally, in the third chapter, we hear from Ra-Hoor-Khuit, the "Hawk-headed Lord of Silence & of Strength"[24] and "a god of War and of Vengeance"[25]. He is the active form of Heru-Ra-Ha. *Gematria* defines his Nature definitively:

> The two halves of the One God HERU RA HA:
>
> RA HOOR = **11 × 13 × 3** : The Magical Force (11) acting upon Love (13) acting upon Binah (3), while:
>
> HOOR PAAR KRAAT = **11 × 13 × 4**, The Magical Force (11) acting upon Love (13) acting upon Chesed (4)
>
> RA HOOR KHUIT = **759** = 666 + 93
>
> *Ra* = The Sun, *Hoor* = The Horizon, *Khu* = Light
>
> RA HOOR KHU = 13 + 416 + 237 = **666** = $\sum 36$, affirming him as an essentially Solar Diety. **13** = Ra (The Sun) = YH the Father and the Mother of the old glyph, and also AHBH (אהבה, Love)[26] and AChD (אחד , Unity) of the same. **416** denotes the God's elemental Form (104 × 4) or the Messiah[27]

22 Ibid, II, 6

23 See pages 276-279 for a full treatment of these verses.

24 Ibid, III, 70

25 Ibid, III, 3

26 Note that, אהבה = 5 + 2 + 5 + 1 = 13 = אחד = 4 + 8 + 1 Ø, and that AHBH which in the new Key is 22: the entirety of the old Law, which the Book of the Law now places in proper relation as under Will, i.e. under Thelema (Will is English for the Greek ΘΕΛΗΜΑ).

27 Note that Ra-Hoor-Khuit is called "The Visible Object of Worship"; MESSIAH = 40 + 1 + 24 + 24 +4 + 4 + 7 = 104.

into the 4th sphere (Power) which further breaks down to Love acting Materially (13 × 8 × 4) through Mercury (The Word). **237** is Khu: He is the very Self of RA-HOOR and all that this entails as explained above.

PAAR KRAAT = **156 =** KAOS = BABALON = KAOS, the Victorious Queen in the old Key.

HOOR PAAR KRAAT = **572** = O Nuit! = The Prophet and his Bride [Hoor (416) + PAAR KRAAT (156)]

ANKH AF NA KHONSU = 111+ 6 + 74 + 531= 722

= RA HOOR KHUIT + *56 (NU)*

These details are interesting because they predate the discovery of the key by over a century, and suggest that the Author had Knowledge the Scribe did not possess, and is the first indication of the evidence to be found within its pages of the *supra*-conscious origin of the Key and the Intelligent Design of these Historic Events.

Logically speaking, these facts are an impossibility. Even in possession of the key, the intricacy of this construction and the control over events past and future (including the naming of said individuals at time of birth), besides the apparent intricacy of the construction and the perfections inherent in the symmetries and geometries—all indicate powers of intelligence beyond the realm of human abilities. Such perfection, as in the formation of crystals and the snow flake for instance, arises from the unadulterated influence of natural forces and not from Man's conscious design.

Analysis of Liber Al Vel Legis

A QUICK summary of the more technical terminology to be found in Liber *AL vel Legis* is here presented. The reader can confirm these values by referring to Table I[28]. The Student is left to his or her Wisdom to interpret the significance of these correspondences. Indication is provided only where the difficulty of the subject requires further comment. Formulae are presented in upper case letters.

We remind the student of the significance of certain numbers, already experientially known, and explained as best as might be possible in the old Key. Among such numbers, which we find confirmed in this analysis, we note: 56, 78, 93, 111, 156, 220, 333, 388, 418, 440, 441, 666, 718, 777, 883, 888 and the scales thereof for which we have external Evidence.

Ø – denotes Hebrew Key
Tf – denotes t final used
Sf – denotes s final used
Nf – denotes n final used
κ – denotes hard c
⅃ – denotes L upright
ω – denotes initial w

28 NOTE: Magical formulae always employ final values at the termination of the word, the god name formulae never do.

The Law = **220** (hence number of the BOOK CCXX)

The Law = (98 + 7 + 1) + (50 + 4 + 60) = 220

HORUS= **440** = (┘) Crowley = Knowledge = Winged Globe = Secret Word = Kundalini = Great Work

HORUS_f and HORUS. These are 458 and 440 respectively. We expect the current of Horus to persist through this Aeon. Taking the formula for this current then, with a non-final (non-terminating) S we have 440, a further glyph of these currents and a general formula for many operations under this new scheme :

As 40 into 11 it is the magickal force (11) of the glyph M (M = 40), whose properties are also general attributions of the God: e.g. They typical image of the God is that of a naked child, surrounded by an egg of blue, and pressing the index finger to his lips. The egg of blue is the womb, which is the motherhood of M, this womb is the sea of Binah, which is M, and finger to the lips denotes the silence of M[29].

As 220 into 2, it is the intelligible manifestation of The Law (220) in the sphere of the Living Word (2, Chokmah).

As 44 into 10, it is Authority (4 into 11, the magickal force of Jupiter, and the elements) over the 10th sphere or Material Plane (*Malkuth*).

AIWAZ = 4 + 4 + 60 + 4 + 6 = **78**

(that is, *Aiwaz* manifest in Kether versus *Aiwass* the same force manifest into Chokmah) This is the number given by Him for His name. It had not been confirmed until now.

N.B 78 = $\sum 12$ the summation of all numbers from 1 to 12, and their synthesis.

29 See "The Letter M".

AIWASS (*SSf*) = 4 + 4 + 60 + 42 + 42 = **156**

(Aiwaz manifest into Chokmah = 78 × 2 = 156. Note the curious transition from the Z to the double s and the accompanying phonetic changes. A mystery is here concealed as to the distinction between these two manifestations.)

S is the serpent that climbs the Tree of Life, while Z is the Lightning that flashes through the sephiroth.

AIWAZ *(W)* = 4 + 4 + 400 + 4 + 6 = **418**

(Aiwaz with W activated gives us the formulaic number for this Being, as declared by Himself in *Liber Al vel Legis.*)

HOOR = 7 + 200 + 200 + 9 = **416** = Winged Secret Flame, The Sacred Mysteries, Place of Silence

The elemental Form of Horus (Note his Two Eyes) explained below.

RA HOOR KHU = 13 + 416 + 237 = **666** = $\Sigma 36$, affirming him as an essentially Solar Diety.

Ra = The Sun

Hoor = The Horizon

Khu = Means Light, and symbolized to the Ancient Egyptians the concept of the Self (The impersonal Life force that manifests in the Soul)[30]

RA-HOOR-KHU or 13 + 416 + 237 is now 666, the word into Tiphareth, versus 444 of the old system (the word into Chesed), essentially reaffirming this force as Solar. See mystical numbers of the heavenly bodies.

Ra-Hoor or The Sun on the Horizon

30 For religionists, Khu can be interpreted as the Soul and the phrase "*The Khabs is in the Khu, not the Khu in the Khabs*" – Liber vel Legis I, 8 and can be translated as "Heaven is in the Soul; not the Soul in Heaven".

Ra-Hoor-Khu or The Light of the Sun on the Horizon

13 = Ra (The Sun) = YH the Father and the Mother of the old glyph, and also AHBH (אהבה, Love)[31] and AChD (אחד , Unity) of the same.

416 denotes the God's elemental Form (104 × 4) or the Messiah[32] into the 4th sphere (Power) which further breaks down to Love acting Materially (13 × 8 × 4) through Mercury (The Word).

Combining this with Ra we have 13 + 13 × 32 = 13 × 33 or 13 × 11 × 3 for RA HOOR: The Magical Force (11) acting upon Love (13) acting upon Binah (3). Note the idea of Power and how this magickal force is applied to Binah in one case (the active and not in the passive form) in light of the 12th Aire: *"There is no power that may endure save only the power that descendeth in this my chariot from Babylon".*[33]

Note that RA HOOR = 13 × 11 × **3** while HOOR PAAR KRAAT = 13 × 11 × **4** and that RA HOOR and HOOR PAAR KRAAT are the active and passive formulae of the same God HORUS and together make 1001.

237 is Khu: He is the very Self of RA-HOOR and all that this entails as explained above.

237 = 79 × 3; 79 a prime oddly omitted from the traditional literature[34], and this current acting upon *Binah* once again, so it is again that Power that descends along *Cheth* (which is 418 spelt fully *Cheth* + *Yod* + *Tau* = 8 + 10+ 400 in the old key) the Chariot of BABALON and the path uniting *Binah* to *Geburah*, the 5th sphere.

When combined into the Unity of the God's name, these add up to 666 which is the summation (and so contains the idea)

31 Note that, אהבה = 5 + 2 + 5 + 1 = 13 = אחד = 4 + 8 + 1 Ø, and that AHBH which in the new Key is 22: the entirety of the old Law, which the Book of the Law now places in proper relation as under Will, i.e. under Thelema (Will is English for the Greek ΘΕΛΗΜΑ).

32 Note that Ra-Hoor-Khuit is called "The Visible Object of Worship"; MESSIAH = 40 + 1 + 24 + 24 +4 + 4 + 7 = 104.

33 Babylon is a corruption of BABALON, the Formula by which one transcends and releases the Energies of Binah.

34 See the Sephir Sephiroth.

of all the glyphs from 1 to 36. It is the most mystical of the numbers for the Sun, and reaffirms this as essentially a Solar diety. It is the triple *Aleph* or the Living Word into the 6th sphere, Tiphareth, the Human Consciousness.

RA HOOR KHUIT = **759** = 666 + 93

(93, a number dear to Thelemites, denoting the Old Aeon glyph for *Aiwass* and *Thelema*, is here added as a termination to the God Name, indicating the manifestation of the God and its FORMULAE as described above. The suffix of IT denotes manifestation.)

PAAR KRAAT = **156 =** KAOS = BABALON = KAOS, the Victorious Queen in the old Key. Reference notes on Aiwass.

HOOR PAAR KRAAT = 416 + 156 = **572** = O Nuit! = The Prophet and his Bride [Hoor (416) + PAAR KRAAT (156)] = LOTUS = One Sword = One of Heaven = Universal Heart

Here we see the elemental form of the God (HOOR) combining with the Supernal energies. Observe that:

RA HOOR = **11 × 13 × 3** : The Magical Force (11) acting upon Love (13) acting upon Binah (3), while:

HOOR PAAR KRAAT = **11 × 13 × 4**, The Magical Force (11) acting upon Love (13) acting upon Chesed (4)

And that these are two halves of the One God HERU RA HA.

Note also, The Prophet and his Bride = 572 = HOOR (416) + BABALON (156), of which The Beast and The Scarlet Woman are emissaries. HOOR PAAR KRAAT is Harpocrates in the Greek or HORUS the Child. He is the Child God of the Love Between these two Forces.

His is The Universal Heart of the Aspirant. He is denoted as the Silent and Passive form of the God HERU RA HA.

HOOR PA KRAAT = 416 + 7 + 136 = **559**

13 is left out of formulae in this title of the God

ANKH F N_f KHONSU = 111 + 2 + 6 + 531 = 650 = L.U.X.

ANKH AF NA KHONSU = 111+ 6 + 74 + 531= 722

= RA HOOR KHUIT + *56*

ANKH AF NA KHONSU (*ŏ*) = 111+ 6 + 74 + 531= 602

ANKH = **111** (The triple *Aleph* – an old glyph of the Word emanating from Creation.)

KHONSU (*ŏ*) = **401** = "He is the First and Last" : the *Aleph*(1) and the *Tau* (400); that is, he is EW on the scale, the East and the West – HE contains the entire tradition / Path with Him.

KHONSU = **531** = The Virgin and the Man = Inviolate = The glory Ineffable = Thy Secret Temple = Secret & Not[35]

HAD = **19**

A prime number, indicating the current to be found in the 2nd Aire. Traditionally, interpreted as *the* feminine glyph. See also Job in the Tradition.

NU = **270** = $3^3 \times 10$

The Supreme Goddess Unmanifest. Note this action upon the 3rd sephira raised exponentially (think: recursively) upon itself: and this acting upon Malkuth, the Kingdom, or the glyph 1 0 which as Unit and Space contains All.

IT = **93**

(A suffix to God names and formulae, indicating manifestation, i.e. that He or She is manifest: eg, Nu, Had versus Nuit, Hadit)

35 Liber vel Legis, III, 39: read: …the word secret & not (and) only in the English

HADIT =**112** = An Ibis, Chit, Ptah, Path, Beth, Magician

All these ideas pertaining to Chokmah and the Grade Therein : (112 = 56 × 2, the old glyph for Nu upon Chokmah; i.e. Mazloth – a star in Her body); the Ibis which is sacred to Thoth, the Egyptian form of Mercury which "presides" over Chokmah in his office as the Living Word; Ptah partaking of this Sephira as well as after Uranus; Chit is the *mindstuff* – the effusive river of energies called thought; Beth is the corresponding Path of the Magician, i.e. the Magus[36]

THELEMA = **221** = The Shrine

The word of the law is Thelema" might translate : The Word (Aleph) + The Law = Thelema : 1 + 220 = 221)

BES NA MAUT = **456** = Enginery of War = The Chief of All (L averse) = O Blessed Beast (L averse) = Uraeus

MAUT = **333** = Fallen and Defiled

The number of Choronzon in the old Key

MAAT = **137** = Thebes

TA NECH = **93** + 108 = 201, *Tf*

TA NECH = 102 + 108 = 210 = Σ20 = A Babe in an Egg, Titan

COPH NIA = **93 + 78** (= 93 + AIWAZ) = 171

ABRAHADABRA = 23 + HAD + 23 = **65** = Aleph = (The double word of power uniting the 6 and 5 = 65)

L.U.X. = **650** = Ankh f n Khonsu (= 65 x 10 = Abrahadabra x 10) = Night of Time = NOX (ŏ)

> L.U.X. which culiminates in the Union with HGA is the equivalent of 65 (or the two-fold word, ABRAHADABRA) into the material plane or 10th sphere (650) is the other half of N.O.X. which together are 13 x 10 x 10.

My heart =**156** = AIWASS = BABALON = KAOS

36 The Grade and Title given to the Initiate operating at this level (Chokmah, or the second sphere).

My tongue = **699** = Word of the Law = A Secret Key of this Law

Restriction = 465 = $\sum 30$ = Black Brothers = Double = Wickedness

BE-WITH-US = **418** = Let ASAR be with ISA = The Silver Star = Perfection = The Prophet (ŏ)

(418 – a Glyph for the Great Work accomplished and Abrahadabra (Ø) in the old Key. Note also in the injunction: "Let Asar be With Isa" that ASAR + ISA = 333 in the old Key and 73 in the new. This may be suggestive to NEMO.)

Seven spirits of unrighteousness = **1550** = 155 into Malkuth (155 = evil, veil)

NEMO = **311** = The Beast & His Bride = TARO = ROTA = Every way Perfect = The Self-Slain (See Ankh-af-na-Khonsu)

SEBEK = **439** = Crocodile

Crowned Child = **450** ="Amoun"

(Amoun is mate to Maut, father to Ankh-af-na-Khonsu: a revision of the YHVH formulae) He is both the father and son of their love.

Moloch, is Baal, which is Abel, or Apis the Bull and he appears as a man with the head of a bull, and later, a calf. In a sense, He is the dark or averse side of Kether, and has been alternately viewed as a God and a demon depending on the culture of the nation. He demands great sacrifice (often the first born), and the Initiate must slay the God's appearance in the final projection of this sphere.

Great work = **440** *Tf* = Beatific Vision, Consecrating, Horus, Kundalini, Single One

No-thing = **469** = Being Not = Let Being be Empty = The Chief of All

English Alphabet = **486** = Key of this Law

Cosmos = **518** = Chaos is my name = Egg of Blackness

(Cosmos is the Naming of Chaos i.e. attributing an Order to

elements in the Universe: the Egg of Blackness, which is Spirit.)

O Prophet = **521** = A Word = Saviour = ISIS, my mother = Strange Pale God = Be done with Speech = The work is ended = Annihilation = Divine Perfection

An interesting set of entries. Taken from Liber vel Legis, technically it refers to the scribe of the Book, who as a Student in Chokmah, was the Word made Flesh, which children of Men take for a Messianic force (Saviour). This prophet is extolled to abandon this bloodless Life (Strange Pale God), to be Silent[37], for the Work is ended, and the Annihilation of Himself into this Force, that is the Word (instead of opposing and so refracting it in Speech) results in the Divine Perfection – a title of Kether.

MERCURIUS = **535** = The Ruby Star = The Serpent Flame Therein = Beast of the Field

Key of the Vault = **777** = The Cup of His Gladness = Three Ordeals in One = Yea Than, Yea Theli, yea Lilith[38]

The Understanding = **701** = The Gate of the Abyss = The Four Beasts = Knowledge and Delight

City of Fifty Gates = **718** = Of All Truth = Company of Heaven

Secret Understanding = **731** = Secretest Chamber of the Palace = One Knowledge = Absolute Bliss = Sweeter than death (ϖ)

Power of Understanding = **1070** = Stabat Crux Juxta Lucem[39] = Stabat Lux Juxta Crucem[57] = Light, LIFE, LOVE, Force, Fantasy, FIRE = Wisdom and Folly

The first two entries denote the proper means of acquiring and increasing such Power as witnessed in the 10th Aire. The third lists the virtues of such a Power. The car called Millions of Years refers to the soul's path. Power of Understanding as we know by the incidence, reciprocity and identity (See BABALON and KAOS) is equivalent to Wisdom (the traditional title

37 Liber B vel Magi 2-3: "2. …the Word that is God is none other than He. / 3. How shall He end His Speech with Silence? For He is Speech."

38 The three ordeals and their passwords.

39 Two means of achieving such power. See the 6th Aire. *Lat*: Erect the Cross near the Light; and, Erect the Light near the Cross.

for Chokmah) which leads to Folly (The Fool, is a title corresponding to the Kether).

The Gates of Understanding = **1156** (scale of 156) = The Wisdom of the New Aeon

(A beautiful example of the Geometries revealed by the Key. Here we have the two Supernal Formulae, contiguous and counterbalancing themselves on the more material continuum of 10^3, Understanding or *Binah* and Wisdom or *Chokmah*, being technical terms corresponding to 2nd and 3rd spheres and here adding to 156 × 10, whose formula for transcendence and release is 156.)

The Throne of Understanding = **1288** = Watchtowers of the Universe (see Liber 418)

Winners of the Ordeal X = **1087** = The Royal and the Lofty

That Mighty Devil Choronzon = **1317** = Weird and Monstrous Speech[40] = Tremble ye O Pillars of the Universe (from 10th Aire before confrontation with this Demon)

The Stone of the Philosophers = **1366** = The Gross must pass through fire = Hold! Hold! Bear up in thy Rapture = In swoon of the Excellent Kisses!

Succumbing to the ecstasies and the Bliss destroys the Energies that are the cause of which it is the effect. Orgasm or Samadhi—these are Death. The Communion is over. Yet, it is the Reward of the Operation.

The Whirlpool and Leviathan and the Great Stone = **1371** = The dung of Choronzon = The Great Snake of Khem, the Holy One

(Note: This is one less than the Lord of the Forces of Matter. See doctrine on the Shame of Khem and 4th Aire wherein all this is enacted.)

The Lord of the Forces of Matter = **1372** = The great princes of the Evil of the World = *Olalam Imal Tutulu* (Regards Mayan, and the 2nd and 3rd Aires)

40 See 10th Aire..

Note here the (666 + 20) into Chokmah. 666 reduces to the Unity for it is the Number of a Magus, for *"He is One"*[41]. It is also three circles, taking in from above by the glyph of the numeral (see doctrine on three Wheels).

Victory over Choronzon = **1519** = Aye! Listen to the Numbers and the Words = The Athanoor called Dissolution = Unity Uttermost Showed

Aye! Listen to the Numbers and the Words: a promise to NEMO who confronts this dispersive Force. In this wise, Let Him be Sure.

The Key of the Pylon of Power = **1403** = The Chosen Priest & Apostle of Infinite Space = Warrior of Ra Hoor Khu[42] = The wisdom of Ra Hoor Khuit[22] = The Reward of Ra Hoor Khut[22]

The Stabilities of Being and of Consciousness and of Bliss = **1777** = Leaping Laughter and Delicious Langour (┘)

The Direful Judgments of Ra Hoor Khuit = **1812** = The Palace of Two Hundred and Eighty Judgments = The Wings of Maut the Vulture

Self-explanatory. Recall that Maut = 333. The Palace of Two Hundred and Eighty Judgments is encountered in the 3rd Aire after where the Seer de-feathering the Vulture takes these for the plumes of his Arrow.

Thus Is the Art and Craft of the Magus But Glamour = **2222** (Note this action : the Grand Scale of 2 and its relation to Chokmah.)

This short list[43] shows that the text of Liber vel Legis is consistent with both the English Key and the Mystical Traditions and Interpretations we have from prior researches. Meanwhile it may be of interest to compare the values of certain formulae and names in light of this new key. These revisions further

41 "One is the Magus, twain his forces..." Liber B vel Magi, 00

42 Different manifestations of the God taken verbatim from the text.

43 A comprehensive list is provided in the Lexicon as an Appendix to this book.

explicate the nature of the formulae in light of the new key and the New Aeon energies.

Furthermore, we note to the Student that it matters not which Key is employed (such are the Perfections) to reveal the Ordered Beauty and layered statements concealed in the structure of the text. However, we do proffer the argument that the best Truth is the newest Truth for this New Truth must contain the Wisdom and Knowledge preceding it, either preserving it, or destroying it in extending its realm of interpretation. The old Glyphs are in the very least, guilty of anachronism and will contain in their interpretation all the prejudices, errors and myopias of the Age in which it had its Birth and was nourished. It was not so far long ago, in the scheme of things that Science and the evidence of Our Senses, once led Humanity to believe that the Sun revolved around a flat Earth. Today, proponents of "Creationism" in the most bigoted sense of the word, still abound, teaching ignorance and suppressing Fact and Inquiry. Blind belief like Faith is unacceptable for the Student of any Science and arrests his or her development. We note that this new truth does not contradict the orthodox view but by building upon it, adds to it, impelling it to a new height and a broader vista.

Genesis of the English Key

THOSE who have entertained the possibility that the Universe might be the Bed for the Play of Forces Aware and Intelligent[1], were probably led to an investigation of the question, no matter how cursory. This investigation, had it ever truly commenced, may have been abandoned at one time or other, due to either want of progress, lack of direction, or no clear starting point. In fact, the task being so simple, one appears to be accosted by insurmountable perplexities at the onset, as seems to be the case with all simplicity until it is born within one. Had these questions not died and the investigations not ceased, they would have lead to the formulation of principles, the testing, application and iterative refinement of those principles. The integration of the traditions and knowledge preceding also play a part in this validation. New truth contains and further explicates old truth, never entirely destroying them, but preserving their convenience, in the same way, that it is sufficient for us to apply Newtonian principles and its approximations to the larger scale operations of the material world. Finally, the laws of any Science must be constructed upon empirical results. The results are sufficient as to the workability of the theory, though the theory must always fail to fully encapsulate that Reality.

In truth, it is sufficient for the Student to go out onto the street armed with a pen and paper and begin investigation of the phenomenon around him. He can read in the facts of Nature, and in the Names of things, in the street signs, in the door numbers,

1 The *observer effect* in Modern Physics and the famous *Double Slit Experiment*, seem to confirm this: Even the humble subatomic particle "behaves" differently if it "knows it is being watched". See also *Schrödinger's cat.*

and in the time on his watch, all these forces in operation. The student has only to take down names, numbers and will soon extract patterns, and pushing through such patterns will deduce correspondences, and from these, the General Laws or principles the Student may test through Experiment, until he or she finds the weave of the fabric itself. An exhausting task, it is perhaps too much for one lifetime which may be better spent enjoying oneself than counting letters and numbers, and looking for meaning in Life.

The famous line from Liber vel Legis (Liber vel Legis, II, 76), has long been suspected of containing, if not the key to the English *Qabalah*, then some other important discovery. Ever since this mysterious sequence of characters was followed by the line "What meaneth this O Prophet?" every earnest Student has applied his power to it, and in his zeal has seen gold wherever something glittered. We present it here, in its original form.

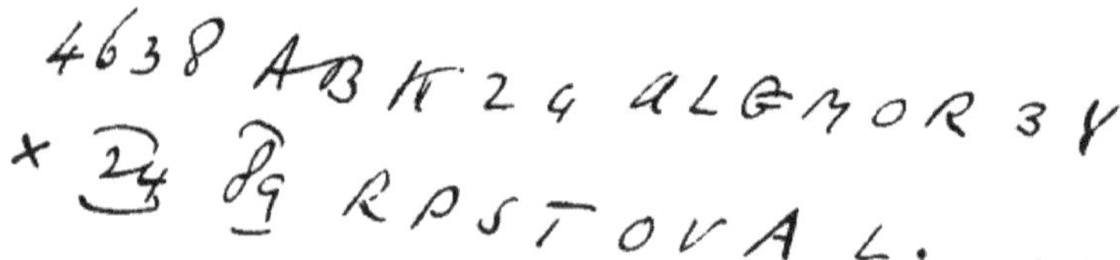

Figure 1 - Liber AL II, 76, (c) Ordo Templi Orientis, 1926, 1938, 2008. Published with permission. All rights reserved

It is important to examine the original closely. The editors in the process of typesetting have made assumptions. For instance, the eighth character has been established as the numeral "2" ever since the book was first printed. There has never been any question made of this, but it might just as easily denote the letter "z". More grieving still, some of the characters are not letters at all, though they have been printed as such. Among these we note the 12th position, [glyph], which editors give as G, and [glyph] which is given as Y.

In reality, [glyph] is the sign of the failure of the squaring of the circle mentioned: "then this circle squared in its failure is a key also." – Liber Al, 3, 47.[2]

× is not a multiplication sign as some have suggested, nor the letter X as others have; but the male half of the squaring of the circle the symbol of which is: [glyph] as shown in the text, which in its two variant forms lead to the success or failure of this squaring.

The remaining characters are symbols that the Student will recognize. Some are numbers, others are letters. The nineteenth and twentieth figures appear with arcs drawn above and below them suggesting a reversal of digits. We will have more to say on this in a moment.

Glyph Analysis: Liber al Vel Legis, II, 76

"Change not as much as the style of a letter..."[3]

"...Then this line drawn is a key: then this circle squared in its failure is a key also..."[4]

"Divide, add, multiply, and understand."[5]

As has been mentioned earlier, publishers have taken assumptions

2 The two bars fail to form the cross that centers and supports the circle.
3 Liber AL, I, 54.
4 Liber AL, III, 47.
5 Liber AL, I, 25.

in typesetting the original manuscript. The manuscript itself contains a number of injunctions to preserve the original and to not change so much as 'the style of a letter'. We suggest some interpretations for the Student's reflection, indexing the original entries :

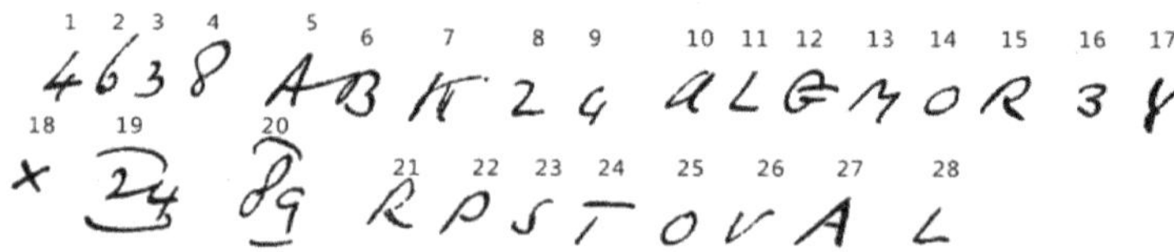

1st Position: This 4 differs from that 4 which appears at position 9 and which might also be taken for a g. This one clearly not. This 4 is crossed, and the one at position 9 is not; and these correspond respectively to the male and female forms of the 4 glyph, the A and I.

2nd Position: A curious six; it cannot be mistaken for a lowercase b.

3rd Position: A 3 but might be a scripted z.

4th Position: Curious this eight: it appears upside-down.

5th and 6th Position: These two uppercase letters are united and correspond to the fifth and sixth position. Their union denotes an operation on f. F is the father, A the Sun (son) alone it is f = 2 (from Beth) when containing the A, it is F or 10 (from A + B, 4 + 6 – already established with positions 1 and 2) and denotes a return to union (f = 2 and these two become 1 and 0 or 10=F and denote the final operation of Chokmah that reduces the Magus to Selflessness. Finally, the glyph also contains the writing "1 to 3" if one looks closely enough (e = 1, f = 2, e + f = 3,) and this glyph is in actuality 3 conjoined in 1 (1 = 3) which is the essential operative power of the letter [f is 1 -> 3 and F 3 -> 1]

7th Position: K appears to be an I with a T resting on IT (I column, T altar/Table) IT = 93 and K is the Virgin or the Arrow hitting its Target (the spiritual virgin, that is, the renewed/resurrected man or woman and not the physical virgin who is neither.) There is here concealed an entire commentary on the Aeonic shift concealed in these letters. This is discussed fully in the next pages. [6]

8th Position: The numeral 2 and the letter z

9th Position: A G, a 4 and a cj that is 3 + 1 and shows how the g unites the soft c and j phonetically, in glyph and mathematically. See the 10th position.

The 10th Position: An A that unites with the G(4) preceding it as discussed. This glyph also conceals both forms of J;

The 11th Position: The first appearance of L glyph. L imbalanced (the old Lamed) which with the G gives 50 the number of the Gates of Death; and hence the glyph of the 'failure of the squaring of the circle' that follows and the tilted M after it.

The 12th Position : Here is the glyph for the failure of the squaring of the Circle, as mentioned in Liber AL, III, 47. Compare with Liber Al III, 76. For this reason the letters on either side of it are imbalanced – the M succeeding is off tilt.

13th Position : This M is tilted and looks more like an upside W (viz position 9). Balancing the L and the mysteries of 2nd Aire and the Grade of Magus are here dealt with, primarily as concerns the passage from 401 to 441 and the mysteries of the letter M and the Hanged Man, elsewhere discussed in this book and in the Tradition.

14th Position : An O. Could be a zero. Similar to position 25.

15th Position : An R. Again similar to position 21.

16th Position : A 3 distinct from that of 3rd position which might be taken for a scripted z.

17th Position : A Y that reminds one of the Greek gamma.

18th Position : The 'x' and the male half of the squaring of the circle.

19th Position : 24 with arcs above and below suggesting a switching of digits corresponding to final and non-final states.

20th Position : 89 with the same arcs above and below suggesting a switching

6 See section " Tzaddi is not the Star"

of digits.

19th and 20th Positions : Both have these arcs above and below them. We will see how these positions correspond to the U and W which must also be switched when Active and reduces the imbalance of the old glyphs due to the Aeonic Shift or due to the passage of Osiris to Horus at the Equinox, or from Pisces to Aquarius... This requires a switch of the traditional assignments regarding Aries and the corresponding glyphs.[7]

21st Position : An R (The I component looks erect, at least more so than that of position 15)

22nd Position : A P that looks very much like a Greek ro.

23rd Position: An S

24th Position : A T, with the bar not touching the pillar.

25th Position : The Letter O again.

26th Position : The Letter V.

27th and 28th Positions : AL (Aleph Lamed) a key of this Book, terminates and seals the string of characters.

Methodology

WE understand that any new Law or Key must fulfill the old Law in a very similar way that Quantum Mechanics must contain and further explain Newtonian Physics: The truth unfolds; it is never displaced. This new Key must be a development of the systems we've known to date. It will find its birth precisely at the point where the old system breaks down.

7 See section on "Methodology" and "The Procession of the Aeons" that follow.

We begin then, by converting these symbols to their elemental set in the old Aeon Key[8]. Being in possession of no better means at this point, we are at least wise in applying old truths and confirmed ways of interpreting the glyphs. Converting, we have the following list of ordered values as illustrated in table II.

These values can be confirmed by referring to Table X which lists the old Aeon Key:

Figure	Trans-literation	Values	Figure	Trans-literation	Values
4		*4*	R	*resh*	*200*
6		*6*	3		*3*
3		*3*	X	*teth, tau*	*9, 400*
8		*8*	24 w/ arcs		*24, 42*
A	*aleph*	*1*	89 w/ arcs		*89, 98*
B	*beth*	*2*	R	*resh*	*200*
K	*kaph*	*20*	P	*peh*	*80*
Z	*zayin*	*7*	S	*samech,shin*	*60, 300*
4		*4*	T	*teth, tau*	*9, 400*
a	*aleph*	*1*	O	*vau, ayin*	*6, 70*
L	*lamed*	*30*	V	*vau*	*6*
M	*mem*	*40*	A	*aleph*	*1*
O	*vau, ayin*	*6, 70*	L	*lamed*	*30*

Table II - New Key Mapping[9]

8 We also know that there will be a direct correspondence (bijective mapping) between these two elemental sets or Keys.

9 Note that we have omitted the symbol for the squaring of the circle (the 12th position) for which there is no corresponding glyph in the old key.

We have then, an ordered set of values corresponding to glyphs provided us which we have interpreted in the Old Key. What this list of ordered values represents, we cannot be sure. However, we can hypothesize and proceed to testing. We have no reason to think that the ordering of this set has been altered or elaborated upon in anyway. Nor is it safe to presume it hasn't. In any case, let us list out the glyphs we have for the English Language alongside these values and examine this ordering for where this construction fails—for herein will lie the portals to further discovery. We present the results in table III.

Figure	Values	Figure	Values
A	*4*	N	*6, 70*
B	*6*	O	*200*
C	*3*	P	*3*
D	*8*	Q	*10*
E	*1*	R	*9, 400*
F	*2*	S	*24, 42*
G	*20*	T	*89, 98*
H	*7*	U	*200*
I	*4*	V	*80*
J	*1*	W	*60, 300*
K	*30*	X	*9, 400*
L	*50, 70*	Y	*6, 70*
M	*40*	Z	*6*

Table III - Numbering English Letters

A studied reflection upon this table by the Student will yield a number of discoveries. The table holds the precise transition mapping of the old glyphs into the new Key symbols in a yet dynamic and albeit inchoate, form. A quick glance shows that we have double values where we would expect them, single values for glyphs we wouldn't, mystery where we know it to be, and concordance of phonetics and values (O and U for instance) as well as attribution. Some further revelations are contained in these lines,[10] which we are now in a position to explore.

We call the attention of the Student once again to those glyphs in the 12th, 18th, 19th and 20th positions and to the mappings presented in the Table III of this chapter. We note the arcs above and below the 19th and 20th glyphs, which correspond to the S and T in the Roman Script alphabetting. Note that S and T appear two steps to the right in the 22nd and 23rd positions in the original text and correspond respectively to the W and X in the Roman Script alphabet systems. These arcs serve two purposes: to indicate final and non-final values for the letter by reversing the digits; secondly, they correct (via the formula ST=131) the value for W and X (initial) by reversing their positions and confirm the procession of the Aeons and the adjustment of the ROTA wheel discussed elsewhere in this book.

"צ is not the Star" - Liber Al I, 57

The 7th position in Liber Al II,76 seems to denote a K followed by a 'Z' as we've mentioned. Looking closely, this 'K' is actually composed an 'I' and a 'T' resting on it. This 'T' has fallen away from the 'Z', which combined was *Tzaddi* of the Old Key. 'J' is involved in this transition. Note that *Tzaddi = 90 = T + j = 89 + 1 = 90*, so that *Tzaddi* equals Tj where 'T' is final, and that this falling of Tzaddi the Emperor into Tfinal releases a 'J'.

10 There are too many... See for instance the Appendix for a discussion on this.

But *TZ* or *T + Z* is *95* so that the glyphs are not yet balanced:

Aeon II	→	Aeon III
Tzaddi (90)	Tz	T (89) + Z(6) = 95

Hence there must be some balancing factor here not yet perceived. Let us denote this glyph by the symbol α, and let α_{II} be its value in Aeon II and α_{III} denote the same in Aeon III. What we seek then is to satisfy the following relation:

α_{II} *T Z (Aeon II)* → α_{III} *KZ (Aeon III)* [11]

Fortunately, Liber Al tells us what this factor α is. When we have the 'I' operate upon the 'TZ', the 'T' falls away from the 'Z' to lean up against the 'I' and form a 'K' as indicated by the 7th position glyph. Now, when the 'T' falls away from the 'Z', it ceases to be a *Tzaddi* in the Old Key and becomes a *Teth = 9* so that *T + Z = 16*:

I T Z (Aeon II) → *KZ (Aeon III)*[12]

At this point, we know that α_{II} is *Yod* and that $a_{III} = a_{II} - 5$ so that, if α_{II} as *Yod = 10* then $a_{III} = 5$ and a_{III} must be the Roman Script or English *Qabalah* equivalent to the Hebrew *Yod* which we know to be transliterated to 'I' or 'J'. In positions 9 and 10, which correspond to 'I' and 'J' respectively, we can see that both forms of the letter are concealed as well as their values (1 and 5 in the case of J). We also note that Yod of Aeon II has a value of 10 and that it must be distributed into its Aeon III equivalents fully (the *I* and the *J*); and finally that this is Accomplished as follows:

11 Or the equation: $a_{II} + Tzaddi_{II} = a_{III} + T_{III} + Z_{III}$ (subscripts here denote the Aeon).
Now, $\alpha_{II} + Tzaddi_{II} = \alpha_{III} + T_{III} + Z_{III}$, *iff*
$\alpha_{II} + Tj_{II} = \alpha_{III} + T_{III} + Z_{III}$, *iff*
$\alpha_{II} + 90 = \alpha_{III} + 89 + 6$, *iff*
$\alpha_{III} = \alpha_{II} - 5$

12 Also note that position 8 is both a Z and a 2 so that: I x T x Z = Yod x Teth x Zayin = 10 x 9 x 2 = 180 = K x Z = 30 x 6 = 180. For addition we have : I + T + Z = Iod + Teth + Zayin = 26 ; K + Z = Kaph + Zayin = 27; While K + Z = 36 in Aeon III.

$$Yod\ (10) = 1\ (j) + 4(I, i) + 5\ (a_{III})$$

We note that both lower and upper cases for the '*I*' glyph are established prior and so that this α_{III} is in fact some form of 'J'.[13]

We make the 'I' (Diana's Arrow) act upon this process as indicated in the 7th position glyph and demonstrated above. This balances all the equations:

(100) | *Iod (10) + (90) Tzaddi* → a_{III} + *TZ (89 + 6), where* $a_{III} = J = 5$.

(26 + 1) | a_{III} + *Iod (10) + Teth(9) + Zayin(7)* → *Kaph(20) + Zayin(7), where* $a_{III} = j = 1$

So for Aeon II, we see that the $a_{III} = j = 1$ is released whereas in the present Aeon we have:)

(37) | *Iod + (Kaph + Zayin)* → a_{III} + *KZ (Aeon III)* where $\alpha_{III} = j = 1$ (the j released above).

In this way the system is again Balanced. We know *Tzaddi* as Emperor to be a fallacy and that the introduction of the Yod shows this destruction – the 'T' falls away from the 'Z' and unites with the I to form the 'K' – the renewed, the Daughter. This along with some other passages, fully explains the switching of *Tzaddi* as Emperor (the Aeon II He = 5 or J in Aeon III) and the disappearance of the glyph into 89[14] or T_f and the role that J has in all of this. Note also that *He* transliterated as 'H' corresponds to the 8th position glyph which is alternately a 2 or 'Z' depending on the Aeon and that the difference of these two is again 5, the Ploughshare.

13 If this is not sufficiently clear, then note that when the numeral 5 operates upon another number it invariably returns itself or a 0 or O the glyph of Yoni (1 x 5 = 5, 2 x 5 = 10, 3 x 5 = 15, 4 x 5 = 20, etc). If 5 were female then IT could engender females only (5s and 0s).

14 A number particular to the "Black Brothers" and the wrong kind of silence.

The 5th and 6th positions A-B are linked suggesting that they be considered as a single glyph, corresponding to the F (capitalized). The 5th and 6th positions are evaluated at 4 and 6 respectively, so that taken together the F is 10 (4 + 6). This, as we witness later, is in fact, the first of a sequence of operations that determine the process and the resultant of these composite glyphs.

Finally examining position 9 again, or 4 , we see a glyph that simultaneously resembles a 4, a *g*, and a *cj*. It also resembles an almost perfect J when turned 120° to the left:

4 cj J

A G, a 4 and a cj that is 3 + 1 and shows how the g unites the soft c and j phonetically, in glyph, sonics and mathematics while the number 4 and the letter G (union) a hint to unite the four glyphs on either side of it: To the left we have AEON II symbols which we've translated to ABKZ as above; to the right of it: AEON III glyphs (A L G M). The mysteries of the letter G involve the squaring of the circle as per Liber Al, and are connected with the Key through these lines and the mysteries in the original ms. contained in III, 47. Students should note that the original ms. contains a line drawn through the text uniting the B through to the J, showing the Word is established in the 4 corners. For if we take these four letters in sequence we find all the composite glyphs that we require later on to complete the system into the Aethyrs and the Trees of Life and the World, and also the precise means by which they are composed and developed:

(AB) (BI) (IT) (KZ) (4 or cj,g) 4a (aL) (LG) (GM)

And the fact that these are four is included once again in the 'chance shape of the letters' (primarily this 4 glyph in the 9th position which looks simultaneously like a 4, a g, and a cj.

AB is F and BI is Ph, both 10; IT is 93, KZ is CH or 37.

4a is J or 5, aL is 31 or Sh; LG is L averse ; GM is w which is M upside down.

AB is F =10 : The Father unites the Word(B) with A, while Ph =10 unites the Word with I. The Pregnant Goddess is the I (I = 4 = A) the Arrow conjoined with the Word, etc.

Appendices

A Note on Astrology

THE PRINCIPLES of astrology and its notions appear anachronistic if not antiquated. Not only is the Universe not geocentric; it is not heliocentric. Any representational model of the Universe with the Earth at its center, or even the Sun, is likely to affront the scientific and philosophic sensibilities of an honest man. Nonetheless, its practical applications still hold, especially in matters cosmological and impersonal. For though it is a crude model and disregards all but the coarsest of Effects, it might at least be accurate within those confines its science was originally bound by. Unfortunately the lofty considerations contained in these researches are often employed (and thus rendered ineffective) in matters of a personal and private nature. Thus we hear of Humanity applying to Astrology in matters of Divination for such mundane questions as, which career path to choose, or whether or not to invest in the commodities market. The influences of the planetary bodies, their gravitational pulls and the shadow they cast over Us, are too broad and pervasive an effect, for it to have any Personal or personally directed effect, especially when the Sky is cut so broadly as it is in the Zodiac; especially as the Sky (and the Bodies ascendent and descendent bejewelling her Body) covers all on the Planet equally.

If the perceptual universe is a Field of relativity as modern Physics holds, then one can take any point in Space and fix it as the origin of a System of coordinates, or as a fixed point from which to calculate displacements, velocities and the angles of entry of other bodies in the Field. In Astrology, one takes the Sphere of Earth or Malka as the fixed point about which all else revolves.

If one takes the Earth as the center of the system, then the Sun (and other bodies) appears to trace an elliptical orbit about the dome of the sky over the course of each year called the ecliptic. This imaginary line or ecliptic is what is termed the Zodiac belt. In fact, the orbital paths of the planets rarely deviate more than 8 degrees of this imaginary line.[15]

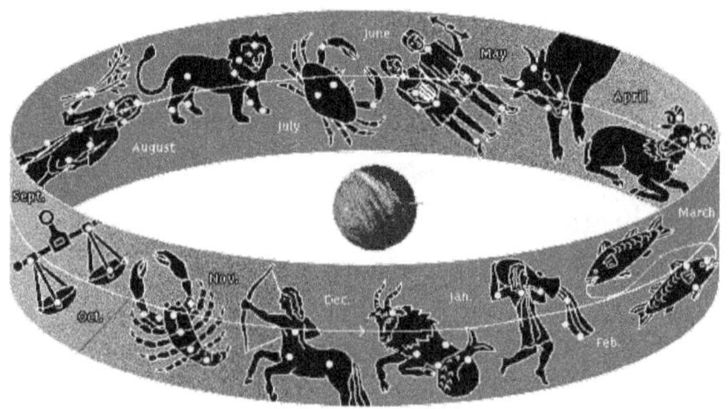

If we place the Earth at the center of this belt, then the skies and all the Bodies within Her, can be said to 'revolve' around the planet. This in any case, are the conditions as they appear to us here, from our vantage on the surface of the Planet.

15 In the same way that gravitational fields create the rings of Saturn and flatten all in its Wake to a revolving Disk, the Same happens with the Sun, its gravitational field and all the bodies in the Solar System.

This belt is now divided equally into twelve segments, so that in this System, the Sky is flattened to a Disc (from a sphere supposedly) and divided into 12 equal segments or Houses. This division leaves 30 degrees for each House. The number of segments, like those of the Clock, appear arbitrary at first or convenient at best, as do their attributions. They are presented here in summary form.

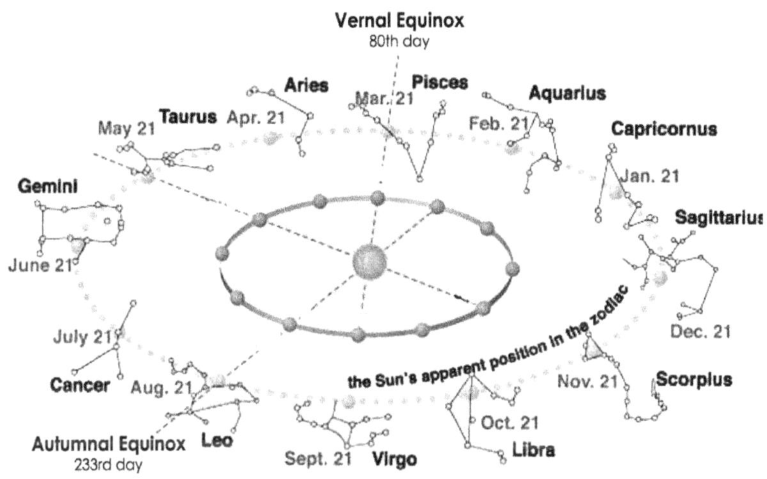

By placing the Earth at the center of this disc, the skies can be said to 'revolve' around the planet. In this way, the separate bodies of the heavens (the sun, the moon, the planets, comets and stars), will be each within a particular House at any point in time.

The collective positions or map of the locations of the stellar and planetary bodies are said to exercise an influence over the Earth. We will not argue for or against this whim. But within this system it is one thing if Venus is in Taurus (harmonious) and another if it is in Scorpio. It is also a different case altogether if Venus is in Taurus while Mars is in the House as well. There is a further discrepancy as to the angle Venus in its House at that time, makes with the Earth.

The theory then is that the individual positions of all the bodies combine together to collectively determine the influence field that wafts over the planet and is thus in itself, significant as to ultimately affect the general conditions of the Malka plane.

The names of the twelve Houses and their glyphs are as follows:

Astrological Houses

Glyph	Sign	English Title	Position	Date Set
♈	Aries	The Ram	0-30	March 21-April 20
♉	Taurus	The Bull	30 - 60	April 21-May 20
♊	Gemini	The Twins	60 - 90	May 21-June 20
♋	Cancer	The Crab	90 - 120	June 21-July 22
♌	Leo	The Lion	120 - 150	July 23-August 22
♍	Virgo	The Virgin	150 - 180	August 23-September 22
♎	Libra	The Scales	180 - 210	September 23-October 22
♏	Scorpio	The Scorpion	210 - 240	October 23-November 21
♐	Sagittarius	The Archer/Centaur	240 - 270	November 22-December 21
♑	Capricorn	The Sea-goat	270 - 300	December 22-January 19
♒	Aquarius	The Water-Carrier	300 - 330	January 20-February 19
♓	Pisces	The Fish	330 – 360	February 20-March 20

Also, each House has a ruling planet or God and these are more significant that is, constricting or salient as an influence, than any other consideration. Besides these 'Rulerships' there are also elemental and planetary attributions in varying phases, as well as other subtleties we present shortly.

Planetary Rulerships

	Sign	Ruling Planet/God	Elemental Attribution	Yin / Yang
♈	Aries	Mars	Cardinal Fire	+
♉	Taurus	Venus	Fixed Earth	-
♊	Gemini	Mercury	Mutable Air	+
♋	Cancer	Moon	Cardinal Water	-
♌	Leo	Sun	Fixed Fire	+
♍	Virgo	Mercury	Mutable Earth	-
♎	Libra	Venus	Cardinal Air	+
♏	Scorpio	Pluto	Fixed Water	-
♐	Sagittarius	Jupiter	Mutable Fire	+
♑	Capricorn	Saturn	Cardinal Earth	-
♒	Aquarius	Uranus	Fixed Air	+
♓	Pisces	Neptune	Mutable Water	-

In addition to the planetary rulerships, there are also Houses in which a planet can be exalted, in detriment or in "Fall". Planets are said to be in their fall in certain signs, implying a waning of their force; and exalted in others, implying a waxing of their force. In general, planets will be in detriment in those signs opposite to the signs they rule. The table on the following page indicates which planets are exalted, in detriment or in fall in the various signs.

To summarize: One body affects another either harmoniously or disharmoniously, that is, either mitigating or increasing the effect of the first via:

(1) their general and natural sympathies (concordances) and,

(2) their position relative to each other.

The study of the theory of The Harmony of the Spheres which lies in a sense, at the base of the system, is therefore Necessary.

Planetary Rulerships

Glyph	Sign	Ruler	Exalted	Detriment	Fall
♈	Aries[1]	Mars	Sun	Venus	Saturn
♉	Taurus	Venus	Moon	Mars	
♊	Gemini	Mercury		Jupiter	
♋	Cancer	Moon	Jupiter	Saturn	Mars
♌	Leo	Sun		Saturn	
♍	Virgo	Mercury		Jupiter	
♎	Libra	Venus	Saturn	Mars	Sun
♏	Scorpio	Mars (Pluto)		Venus	Moon
♐	Sagittarius	Jupiter		Mercury	
♑	Capricorn	Saturn	Mars	Moon	Jupiter
♒	Aquarius[1]	Saturn (Uranus)		Sun	
♓	Pisces	Jupiter (Neptune)	Venus	Mercury	

We present summary tables of these two factors, (1) *concordance* and (2) *position*. Students familiar with the Astrology may forego these tables.

Concordances

Each house is said to group properties particular to it, and each House has its Motto and interpretation:

	SIGN	MOTTO	ENGLISH	TITLE	GENERAL INTERPRETATIONS
♈	Aries	*Vita*	Life	House of Self	Physical appearance, traits and characteristics. Ego. Aggression, leadership, enterprise, warfare, government, anger, impulses, inspiration, vengeance.
♉	Taurus	*Lucrum*	Wealth	House of Value	Money, property, acquisitions. Cultivation and growth. Self-Worth. Stability/stagnation, beauty, pleasure, material things, love, debauchery, prosperity, maintenance of status quo, stubbornness.
♊	Gemini	*Fratres*	Brothers	House of Communications	Higher education and childhood environment. Communication. Siblings. Cleverness, trickery, commerce, analysis, reason, intellect, dispute, changeability.
♋	Cancer	*Genitor*	Parent	House of Home and Family	Ancestry, heritage, roots. Early foundation and environment. Maternal archetypes. Caretaker of the household. Cyclic end of matters. Intense emotion, rapid movement, changeability, oracles and divination, adaptability, hidden things.
♌	Leo	*Nati*	Children	House of Pleasure	Recreational and leisure activities. Games and gambling. Creative self-expression. Royalty, nobility, stability/stagnation, inspiration, passion, leadership.
♍	Virgo	*Valetudo*	Health	House of Health	Routine tasks and duties. Skills or training acquired. Health and overall well-being. Service performed for others. Preservation.
♎	Libra	*Uxor*	Spouse	House of Partnerships	Close relationships. Marriage and business partners. Agreements and treaties. Diplomacy. Open (known) enemies. Attraction. Beauty, pleasure, intellect, communication, aesthetic senses, love.
♏	Scorpio	*Mors*	Death	House of Reincarnation	Cycles of Deaths And Rebirth. Sexual relationships. Occult, psychic and taboo matters. Regeneration. Self-transformation. Warfare, aggression, intense emotion, hidden things
♐	Sagittarius	*Iter*	Journeys	House of Philosophy	Culture. Long distance travels and journeys. Religion. Law and ethics. Knowledge. Experience through expansion. Learning, changeability, inspiration, religion.
♑	Capricorn	*Regnum*	Kingdom	House of Social Status	Ambitions. Motivations. Career. Status in society. Government. Authority. Father or father figure. Breadwinner of the household. Leadership, restriction, limitation, rapid movement.
♒	Aquarius	*Benefacta*	Friendship	House of Friendships	Groups, clubs and societies. Higher associations. Benefits and fortunes from career. Hopes. Wishes.
♓	Pisces	*Carcer*	Prison	House of Self-Undoing	Mysticism. Places of seclusion, self-imposed imprisonments. Things not apparent to self, yet clearly seen by others. Elusive, clandestine, secretive or unbeknownst matters. Retreat, reflection and self-sacrifice. Unconscious/subconscious. Unknown enemies.

Positions

We summarize the different aspects positions may have upon two bodies in the following table. Note that a position (conjunction, sextile) can be favourable or unfavourable depending on the planets involved, their ruling gods and whether or not these planets are harmonious or opposite in character. (*See polarities, Yin/Yang, Detriments, etc.*)

CONJUNCTION (0° ± 7°) Intensification **(major, favorable)**	A conjunction occurs when two planets are from 0 to 7 degrees of each other. In this case their energies mix with each other to an equal degree and either (1) reinforce each other, giving emphasis to the planet's expression, or (2) interfere with each other, cancelling each planet's expression.
SEMI-SEXTILE (30° ± 3°) Support **(minor, favorable)**	This aspect is of mixed quality. The planets involved will be in inharmonious signs. The planets may support each other materially, but because the harmonies indicate the need for attention to both contrasting energies so that each may operate effectively.
SEMI-SQUARE (45° ± 3°) Friction **(minor, unfavorable)**	The semi-square is similar to a square, but weaker in its effects.
SEXTILE (60° ± 5°) Opportunity **(major, favorable)**	The planets involved are of the same in polarity, quality, and functions harmoniously.
QUINTILE (72° ± 5°) Creativity **(minor, favorable)**	Here any contrasting elements won't be in direct opposition; likewise any concordant elements will not have a direct supporting effect, but buttresses the operation.
SQUARE (90° ± 7°) Challenge, Obstacle **(major, unfavorable)**	In this aspect, the energies clash, each trying to gain ascendency over the other regardless if they be harmonious or not (for they remain two separate things and at best create a third which is the union of the two and an another thing altogether, separate from the original object of the operation.
TRINE (120° ± 7°) Harmony **(major, favorable)**	Angles here again indicate no direct opposition, but a buttressing support.
SESQUI-QUADRATE (135° ± 3°) Agitation **(minor, unfavorable)**	This aspect indicates minor obstacles that overcome easily.
QUINCUNX (150° ± 3°): Adaptation **(minor, unfavorable)**	Close to being in direct opposition, it is difficult to harmonize the energies of two bodies at this angle. There is a call for atavistic Change.

On the Procession of the Aeons

--Students not familiar with the basic principles of Astrology should refer to the "Notes on Astrology" chapter in this book.

OBSERVE that by means of the Zodiac belt, the perceptual universe has been reduced from 3 dimensions to 2 dimensions, and that this two-dimensional space has been further reduced to twelve discrete units. The Zodiac is in fact then, no more than an ecliptic system of coordinates; and Astrology employs a projectional map of the universe onto the two-dimensional using this ecliptic system of coordinates.

The Hindu zodiac meanwhile, uses a sidereal coordinate system which takes into account fixed stars and other immobile bodies. As early as Mesopotamia, Humanity was already aware that these fixed bodies were not fixed as such, but were moving very slowly: approximately 1° every 72 years. At this rate, the whole Sky (or Universe to Mesopotamian Man) traces a complete revolution and comes full circle, ends the cycle and begins anew, every,

$$72 \text{ x } 1° \text{ x } 360° = 25\,920 \text{ years.}$$

By consequence, every 25 920 / 12 = 2160 years, the sphere of fixed Bodies enters into a new astrological House as it traces its path through the cycle. For this reason, we are said to enter into a new Aeon every 2000 years or so, as we have done most recently in March 1904, in entering the Age of Aquarius or the Aeon of Horus, as it is called by some. In this way, every 2160 years or so, a great paradigm shift occurs in the Universe, where a 'new God sits at the Equinox', and a new Sign presides over the operations of the Planet; and so the World undergoes violent contortion under the sudden cultural, spiritual, political, material (etc.) Change to accommodate the shifting of the Guards.

The Procession of the AEONS

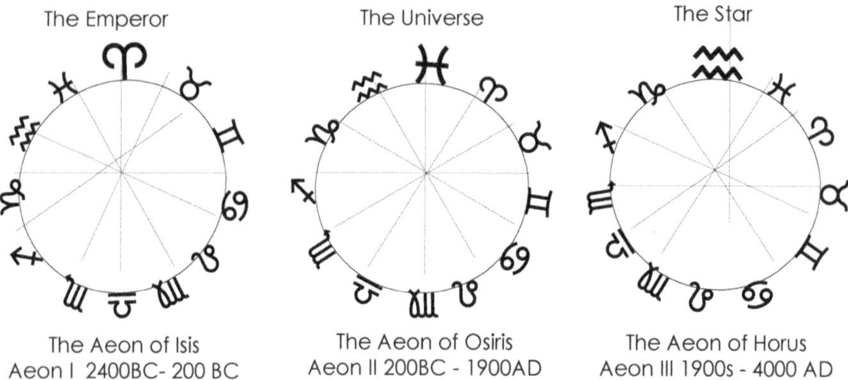

Observe that if we fold the ellipse of the zodiac belt into a helix about Pisces, we find it touches precisely at the spot where Aries and Aquarius meet.

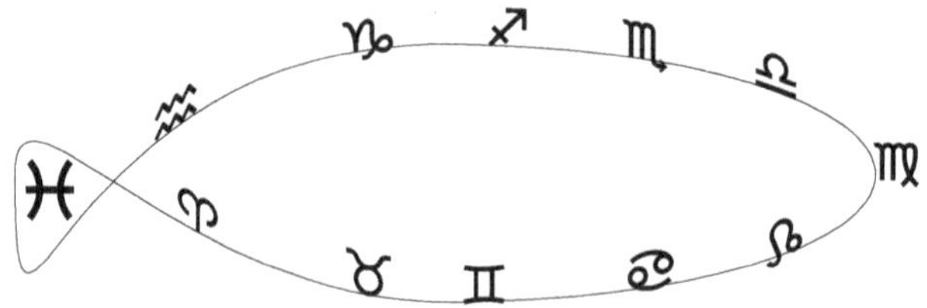

Thus, in this Age of Aquarius, we see the Fires of Aires, the House in which Mars (L) rules and the Sun (A)[1] is exalted, burning and

1 Hence the title of the document announcing the inception of the Aeon as Liber AL (*liber* is Latin for book). L upright adopts a Martian quality, pre-418.

shining into the fixed Air of Aquarius, and not Libra as one would expect. Yet others have suggested that, it is not the Seat at the Equinox that revolves but the Houses themselves, so that in this, the Age of Aquarius, the Aeon of Horus (Mars + Sol) takes on the rulerships and other diverse properties of the House of Aries (not only the TARO card, as will be discussed.) This would imply essentially exchanging one House for the other. We see Error in this, but understand that beneath the Veil where the ROTA wheel operates, there is no need for distinction between what is image as reflection and what is image as projection, for Union of Object and Subject is the Goal, and the distinction (or the question) was illusory to begin with.

We see that subtleties present themselves in the New Aeon system. Some of these confirm the latest of scientific discovery (especially as relates to physics, relativity and observer effects) and empirical advances; while yet others appear to block progress along specific lines.

A note on the Key Scale of the old system, Aeonic and Post-418 attributions.

We note that the keys of the ROTA as well as any old glyph set are designed for pre-418 and Osirian Aeon consciousness and effects. As such, they are anachronistic and ineffective in those cases where they are mal-aligned to the realities of the present. Thus the ATU 16 'House of God' is attributed to *Pé*, or Mars. In the English Key, this is clearly L averse and the accompanying imbalance that precipitates the Fall (as illustrated in the card's design). Yet these conditions cease to be in post-418; and in the Supernals, there is no L averse.

Now, it is clear that the ROTA wheel bears its effects through the Elements, so that above the Veil these effects cease to disturb the Initiate. Also, the Initiate will note that He will have burned the Book of Thoth in the 8th Aethyr, for in this Book is contained all the Wisdom of the Aeon *Past,* and Hadit burning in the Initiate's Heart, breathes his Fire into the Page of History, so that his Bride may be Free of History and born Virginal once again.

However, as technical matters are concerned, the ROTA wheel itself spins beneath the Veil and throws out Fortune and Image from its centre in accordance to The Law. We can not expect this Wheel to remain unaltered, to not have shifted somewhere in its axis, to not have slowed down or accelerated.

Note, the line in Liber AL vel Legis (a Class A document):

> "*All these old letters of my Book are aright, but Tzaddi is not the Star.*" – Liber Al I, 57.

In the past, this has been taken to mean that *Tzaddi* was incorrectly attributed to ATU XVII – The Star. We call attention to the mention of 'these old letters' in the text, reminding the Student of what has been said about the Book of Thoth and the Aeon Past.

Now if *Tzaddi* is not the Star, then some other letter must be; and *Tzaddi* must be replaced by that which it replaces to maintain the integrity of the system. For reasons of symmetry, Aries was switched with Aquarius signalling the dawn of the 3rd Aeon, the Aeon of Horus as some have called it. Now, *Hé* the Daughter is The Star (Aquarius) which one would generally attribute (via alliteration) to H, and *Tzaddi* the Emperor (Aries) to Z. However we know the *Cheth* (Ch) glyph to have transformed itself into the H (so that the C is implied); and that this glyph corresponds to the Chariot, which is traditionally attributed to Cancer, the

Crab. We will see shortly how *Tzaddi* did not resolve into the Z (which corresponds more directly to the *Zayin* of the old key), but instead the R is now the Emperor and of the House of Aries.

According to this system then, we have two states so far:

Pre-Aeon	**Post-Aeon**
Tzaddi – The Star – ♒ – 🜁	Tzaddi – The Emperor – ♈ – △
Hé – The Emperor – ♈ – △	Hé – The Star – ♒ – 🜁

This is the solution proposed by 418-666-1111 as is noted frequently in his documentation.

However, the line is: "*All* these old letters of my Book are aright, *Tzaddi* is not the Star." It does not say that *Hé* is not the Emperor, or that *Hé* is the Star. In fact, quite the opposite, for it states explicitly that "*all* these 'old' letters of my Book are aright", so a deeper mystery is here implied. Since we are not so much concerned with these "old" letters as we are with the new, we call the Student's attention to the fact that *Tzaddi* once 90 in value, is non-existent in the new system, and has been displaced to 89, that of T final, a number particular to the Black Brothers.

Some are of the Opinion, that the attribution of the TARO card alone does not suffice, but that it is the Sky itself that revolves and so leads the Seat or Equinox to the House which remains fixed. In this way, Aries has switched positions with Aquarius on the pivot of Pisces, because the Sky has revolved, so that in this corner of the Sky (Aquarius), it is now Mars that Rules and the Sun which is exalted, while in Aries, Saturn is exalted. This arrangement appears at first to coincide with the declaration of Liber 220 and its codex as AL (Sun + Mars) whose

Union composes the Body of Ra Hoor Khuit, and the apparent 'demotion' of The Emperor Card or ATU IV in the old ROTA, which is now relegated to the Saturnian, where the fiery nature of the card is rendered null by the Waters of *Binah*. However, the Aeon itself may be more properly viewed as Saturnian in its action for this very reason—a point which serves to illustrate the distinction between rulerships and exaltations. The Aeon though apparently Martial in its Rulership (the God and the Planet are two different Ideas however concordant they be), certainly is not exalting Harmony: as is the case of the formulae of the old Aeon. The Aeon is more properly Saturnian in its influence, as all are attracted to *Binah* and to the Crossing of the Abyss and to the accomplishment of 418. Aquarius the Water-Bearer, bears the waters of *Binah* to Humanity. This small realization may frame and serve to explain the reason for the Class A texts, the *Qabalah* itself, and the establishment of the Aethyrs materially in Nature.

There may be other considerations for this switch as well. Note Liber Al, II, 15-16:

> *15. "For I am perfect, being Not; and my number is nine by the fools; but with the just I am eight, and one in eight: Which is vital, for I am none indeed. The Empress and the King are not of me; for there is a further secret."*
> *16. "I am The Empress & the Hierophant. Thus eleven, as my bride is eleven."*

We apply to *Chokmah* to gain a fuller sense of the meaning in these two lines:

Note that for the old Key, we have the following:

> Empress ≡ Daleth ≡ 4; Emperor ≡ He ≡ 5; Hierophant ≡ Vau ≡ 6
> Also note that The Empress is ATU 3, the 4th card; The Emperor ATU 4, the 5th card; The Hierophant ATU 5, the 6th card on the ROTA wheel.

For the new Key, we have the following:

Empress ≡ D ≡ 8; Emperor ≡ R ≡ 9; Hierophant ≡ V ≡ 80

Note also that certain terms are capitalized (e.g. "Not"). The English Key gives the following for these technical terms:

- 'Not' = 248 = 31 x 8
- King = 124 = 31 x 4
- Empress + Hierophant = 31 x 13
    - Empress = 120 (with s final) & Hierophant = 283
- 'eight' = 121=11^2 = Hadit
- perfect = 144 = 12^2
- 'eleven' = 223. Π

The meaning of these lines now becomes clear:

Line 15

For I am perfect, being Not — He is 31 into 8 (i.e. The word into Mercury — "31 is a secret key of this Law." N.B. 31 = *Aleph* + *Lamed* or AL and hence the title of the Book, Liber AL; or SH in the new key, equivalent to *Shin* in the Hebrew Key).

and my number is nine by the fools; — Nine is R, the Emperor, or the King. (N.B. 'fools' is not capitalized - that is, does not refer to The Fool of Atu 0)

but with the just I am eight -- He is Hadit (eight = 121 = Hadit). Also : Empress + Hierophant = ATU 3 + ATU 5 = 8 in the TARO and 8 + 80 in the English Key (8 into 11).

and one in eight -- He is one with Hadit.

Which is vital, for I am none indeed: That is He unites perfectly with Hadit, and is absorbed in his Infinity (the 8 is the symbol of infinity, but upright); he does not stand apart, that is, He is not 1 + 8 = 9, as already stated and here emphasized: (which is 'vital') he is not 9, that is he is not R, the Emperor (King) as declared clearly in the next line.

The Empress and the King are not of me; for there is a further secret. — He is not the King (31 into 4); He is perfect being Not (31 into 8). Again the emphasis: He is not 9 : Empress + King (Emperor) = *Daleth* + *He* = 9. He is not to be found in the Union of the Empress and the King, but in that of the Empress and the Hierophant, as we see in the next line.

Line 16

"I am the Empress & the Hierophant and so eleven": -- Empress + Hierophant = ATU 3 + ATU 5 = 8 (*'to the just I am eight'*) as we have noted. But also Empress = D and Hierophant = V in the English Key, so that we have 8 + 80 = 88 and the result of this division is 11. (8 into 11).

Also Hadit = 121 = 11 x 11 and so He is eleven as his bride (see below).

In yet another way, Empress + Hierophant = 120 + 283 = 403 = 31 x 13 which is AL x LA in the old key. (A full revolution on the 31, the secret key of this Law); while Empress + King = 120 + 124 = 244 = 2 x 122 (1 more than Hadit) = 4 x 61.

Finally, Empress = *Daleth* and Hierophant = *Vau* in the Old Key so that we have Empress + Hierophant = 10 and 8 + 80 = 88 *iff* 8(1 + 10)=8(11) *iff* 1 + 10 = 11. As this 8 is not merely an 8, but 'one in eight', and 'none indeed' for it disappears as its union is perfect.

"as my bride is eleven": --He is eight and she is eleven, so that we have 8 and 11 acting upon each other. And we know 8 x 11 = 8 + 80 = Empress + Hierophant. There is a further mystery here: Observer that Empress with both Ss final is 138 which is the enumeration to the words 'my bride' that precede it, so that 'my bride' = 138 = Empres$_f$s$_f$ affirming the identity between his Bride and The Empress. Note finally, that 'Hadit' and 'eight' = 121 which is 11 x 11.

We can pursue this analyses indefinitely. What we have in these lines is a perfect discrete continuum of infinity progressively revealing the Truth, Beauty and Necessity of these arrangements the more we Hunt this Truth.

Notes

The operation of any Glyph is Perfect in and of itself. This is so, despite that beneath the Veil of the Abyss its qualities have been altered, the angles of entry have been deflected and sometimes its nature transformed in the Passage. The case is made even more onerous if it is the pure Glyph one seeks while beneath the Veil of the Abyss, for at such Time, He is blind to the Perfections. And then afterwards, standing upon the Waters above the Abyss, He ceases to be concerned with that field in which the glyphs operate beneath the Veil. Such is the rule. As it is written, "Confound her understanding with darkness."

Nonetheless, these points must be kept in mind when it comes to the tables of syncreticism presented.

	AEON II		AEON III	NOTES
☉	Resh	A	A	A is the Star particular to the System.
☿	Beth	N,Y	B	N and Y are two phases of Mercury, and these (N final, Y consonant and B) are all 6. But B the Breasts of Babalon which is Mercury as the Word emanating from Chokmah is all that remains without refraction. (BREASTS (175) + OF (90) + BABALON (176, with L balanced) = 441.
♀	Daleth	V,O	D	Venus is now more intimately, Babalon or Diana as Huntress.
♂	Pe	L	F,P	(M.·.T.·.) L's are necessarily balanced. (L averse is no more. 50 the number of the gates of Death is dropped from the system: All N's final as per the 2nd Aire.
♃	Kaph	I	Z	Because Saggitarius the arrow is the House of Jupiter (The I emerges from its House, is manifest and becomes Sagittarius necessary to the Body of Babalon as Huntress.
♄	Tau	X	X	The Ordeal X is undergone (all X's are activated and Saturnian from Aries. (The R remains in Aries), i.e. X is 300 and 'Shin' or the 5 spoked Wheel of Spirit is operational.
♅		W	J	These pertain to the 10th and the 2nd Aires.
♆		U	U, F	The Cup was always there, but not Seen by those who who made the Aeon II a quest for the Grail.
⊗		T	P(as Gaia),Y	The Son sacrificed on the Table/Altar is now become the the Mother, pregnant with the Daughter that later awakens the "eld of the Father".
☽	Gimel	O	O	The Moon has waned. That false light is behind one's Shadow. (All O's cresecented)
♈	Tzaddi	R,x	R	See notes on ordeal x. The R remains the Ram, the animal noble and fierce in the lofty heights is docile like the lamb once fettered. This is the Emperor and the Principle of Government in action and properly describes the cycle of the phallus or the brute male force.
♉	Vau	W	V	The V is now doubled – VV, the Horns (the Head must be Lowered for the Horns to be of effect) are now upraised and the eyes are on the Horizon.
♊	Zayin	G	G	Union, Birth, Growth - these fundamentals have not changed except in Value.
♋	Cheth	Ch	H	What was once a compound glyph is now established.
♌	Teth	F.Q	Q	Q is mature and is replaced by F in the schema.
♍	Yod	K	K	
♎	Lamed	L av	L	The L is no longer averse; otherwise, the Initiate would have perished in the Abyss.

	AEON II	AEON III	NOTES
♏	Nun S	N	At first the S (the Son) sinks into the Piscean realm of Death and Rebirth. Then He does not sink. (See Sf and note 23.)
♐	Samekh D	I	The Vision of the Arrow vis Liber 418. These require the plumes of MAUT, then become MAAT.
♑	Ayin Tf	T	Tf is the Altar and is attributed to Capricorn the Goat, the first of animals to give their Blood to the Sacrificial Altar. It is also a number of the Black Brothers (see Liber 418) and so constitutes a promise.
♒	He M	C	These mysteries pertain to the grade of Magister Templi and the numbers 441, 156, 233, 333, 388, 883, 888 and are discussed briefly in Liber B vel Magi—specifically as regards the letter M and the Silence required to transition from 401 to 441. Note that 401 is the old key for Cursing and 441 for Truth. Now 441 = 401 + 40 so that M brings about Truth and an end to the Curse of the Magus. Observe that 401 + M = 441 is a summary of the operation. The mechanics entail uniting the wheels with Kether. We note that $401 = 20^2 + 1$ whereas $441 = (20+1)^2$ so that the action of 1 is taken into the reverberation. a. Finally, note that 20=G which is Union and pertains to those mysteries of Squaring the Circle or materializing the Will.
♓	Qoph Sf	S	The undulatory power of the Snake and the Son that walks on Water and does Not Sink: in this place the S remains.
△	Shin Z, Nf	W	Also Z the Lightning Flash now manifests not as Fire that Burns, but Electricity that Beams and passes from Fire to Light, and so Thought and information (for Light contains Image which is information).
▽	Mem C,P	M	It is improper to deal here with this austere subject. The 2nd Aethyr completes this triune initiation concealed in the Shin. (Yeah Than, Yeah Theli, Yeah Lilith). See note 3 above: a. N, the Gate of Death and Y the Tree of Life also take on revised attributions/concordances upon successful completion of 418. These are discussed in detail elsewhere in this book.
🜁	Aleph f	E	f=2 is transitory and lurks only because of the Q which it propels. Once the Q is planted and the vine not drowned in the Flood***, then F appears and the E is perceived. ***See notes on Z and especially H and the Chariot and Cancer the Crab, the one who survives the Flood.
🜃	Tau B,Y	Y	The Word is Falsehood the moment it departs the 1. That is, its very reception implies falsehood for the word is unintelligible, inasmuch as it is a Man, and a Magus, inscrutable in his mystery (see 2nd Aethyr and the whirling sword that is thrown off from him), and in that it is the Voice of Silence.

Much like the Tree of Life was meant to be a representational model of our immediate Cosmos and their influences, gravitational or otherwise, so the system of the Aethyrs will prove to be similar in its construction though this has yet to be revealed. Now on the Tree of Life, one begins in Malkuth which is Earth, the planet. As he expands his consciousness, the Student encounters the first planetoid object to touch its circumferential boundary. This would be the Moon, or Yesod, the sephira directly above Malkuth. He continues in this way until the entire solar system is contained in his consciousness.

Now we know the planets to be not fixed like pendants, but in constant motion. This orbital motion of the planets trace boundary lines around the earth and in some cases intersect. The number of aethyrs or regions produced are not arithmetic in proportion but depend on the paths of the orbit. In this way, two planets can trace orbitals that carve 1 or 2 or 3 aethyrs, while three planets can trace orbitals that carve out as much as 7 regions.

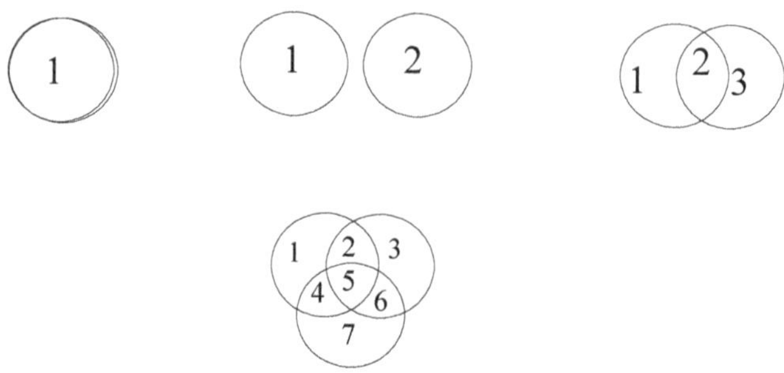

It is in this manner that the 10 celestial bodies can produce 30 Aethyrs; and it is by this means that an adequate representational model via geometric structures containing the aethyrs can be devised to replace the Trees of the Aeon past.

Correspondence

between LLLLL & GFLO

Astrological attributions:

G : I have no qualms with what you have revealed & my intent is progressive. To me it is self-evident. I question the specific attributes of each letter. I know this varies from one to the next, but I am not a skilled Qabalist. An astrological correspondence for each glyph would be much appreciated. By the way I noticed that Chŏrŏnzŏn = 333 if you count the Ch as 2 with N final. Also 333 = Scorn. Perdition. Self-knŏwledge. Sleeplessness. G, IC, IA

June 15, 2010 6:35 PM

E. : Hello G, Thank you for your note and for your calculations on the "red-eyed" Choronzon - that particular formula had escaped me. As for the astrological symbols, some form of skrying or projection is needed to confirm these attributions. This is why we've omitted them from the first edition. However, here are some preliminary results of our research. Let us know if you are able to confirm:

4 elements + 12 houses + 10 spheres = 26 glyphs of the Roman Alphabet

4 elements: Air, Earth, Fire, Water

12 houses: Aquarius, Pisces, Aries, Taurus, Gemini, Cancer, Leo, Virgo, Libra, Scorpio, Sagittarius, Capricorn

10 spheres corresponding to Sol, Mercury, Venus, Earth, Mars, Jupiter, Uranus, Neptune.

We have so far (though something not quite right here) :

A the Star, is that Star particular to our System: Sol, the 1st (or 6 in the old system)

B the Book, is the vessel of the Word, which is Hermes or Mercury, the 2nd (reflected in the 8th - HOD)

C the Womb and Sky, is Aquarius, the Water-Carrier, which is the Womb or the Sky which rains upon the Earth.

D the Bow, is Venus the 3rd (reflected in the 7th: Netzach), which is Love and the Victory (Netzach) of the propelling, penetrating force of Cupid's Bow.

E the Triple Flame, is that triple Sword (*aleph*) which is AIR.

F Force, is Mars, the Fifth which is Ph.

G the Union, is Gemini ruled by Mercury as boy Cupid and contains the projectile Arrow of Sagittarius into the sky womb of Aquarius

H the Throne, is Jupiter which is dominion over the 4.

I the Arrow/Lingam/Column, is Sagittarius, the projectile of the Archer (Cupid/Mercury)

J the Horn of Plenty, is Uranus (one of the Fathers Lost)

K the Virgin, is Virgo the Virgin wading in Water (the element ruling over this house)

L the Foot/Balance, is Libra the scales over which Venus presides

M the wave or valley, is Water - its Element form.

N the Gate, is Scorpio, another house over which Water presides.

O the Moon, is Luna in both her phases.

P the Pregnant Goddess, is Earth (the 4th Sphere-Gaia)

Q the Spermatazoon, is Leo, which is constituted by Fire, and whose symbol has the shape of the spermatazoon.

R the Birth, the exhausted Phallus, is Cancer the Crab, which comes out at night (and is ruled by Moon) and is the only creature to move sideways.

S the Serpent or the Son, is Pisces, a fish that walks on the Water.

T the Altar or Table, is Capricorn the Goat, the first of sacrificial animals: the first altars being the mountain tops where these lofty creatures enjoy gracing.

U the Cup is Neptune, the outermost which

V the Horns of Power, is Taurus, which cavorts in the Earth and is ruled by Venus

W is Fire, which is Light that gives Sight

X the Cross and Wheel is Saturn, Time

Y the Tree of the World, is Malka the Elemental Earth in her redeemed and abased forms (Y consonant, Y vowel)

Z the Lightning Flash, is the last and so the first: Aries, the Ram that breaks down the Doors to the Palaces within the Spheres.

I had a vision once of a circular garden atop a Hill. The Garden was empty, with a central fountain and a single vacant bench. At the entrance to the garden stood an arched gate. The arches were formed by two animals butting horns. The first ram and the second a goat. The ram's horns traced a three and the goat's a 7, so that together they traced 37 and this Garden was Kether. Now it strikes me that 30, Hard C or K then would be associated to the Ram, and 7 or H to the Goat.

Best,

June 18, 2010 2:20 PM

G : Hello, The research you shared with me is much appreciated. I will investigate the best I can. I have more questions about the attributions you supplied. Where does Pluto fit in this arrangement? With Mars possibly? & the 5th element of Spirit? & what about Liber XXVII? The 27 trigrams actually number 0-26 & fit nicely upon the 12 angles, 8 points & 6 faces of the *Cube*.(AL II:7) Zero would of course occupy the Space within or without(both?). Certainly there is a corresponding trigram for each letter. Maybe this is a key for a reconstructed model of the Tree of Life. Furthermore, Liber 440 implies that there is another alternative English Key yet to be discovered. HEMESH:23: *"This book is the companion of Liber Al, and there is also a key hidden herein, though the two be quite dissimilar. There are the barbarous words and there are the names of the demons: for a new Goetia, a new sorcery, shall be beheld within this treatise. I write not who shall discover this, save the scribe shall not himself care to. Indeed, an entire Goetic manual lies concealed in these words."* I understand that empirical confirmation is lacking & maybe my suggestions are hasty at this point. To me these seem to be logical suggestions. I have a great respect for your objectiveness. What is your take on all of this so far? G, IC, IA

June 22, 2010 7:50 PM

E. : Hello G, Thank you for your insights and comments. You mention a "reconstructed model of the Tree of Life". However, the Tree of Life is at best a crude approximation of the Path, which we should probably abandon for the construction of the *Aethyrs*. There appears to be no direct experience of any phenomenon, initiatory or otherwise for the *sephiroth* below the Abyss - there is only the piercing of the veils. *Tiphareth* colours the sky, and one feels its joy, but it is already behind us the moment we enter it. In the past, evolution required that Humanity rest in this Place. In reality, there was no other destination but this one, until One was Born sufficiently solar and fiery to cross the Waters that overhang *Tiphareth* which we call the Abyss. In this way, the Tree of Life is a convenient fiction. The lower *sephiroth* do not exist except in their planetary attributes and no longer correspond to any place, door, window, or initiatory experience – these having been subsumed into the collective consciousness – that is, we have evolved. (This is so, except for *Tiphareth* which remains a necessary way station and must remain open unto the lowest or 10th in the Old System, as has been mentioned.) Empirical evidence suggest that the *Aethyrs* of the Enochian system (which describe the full initiatory process - at least those parts that can be described intelligibly) map out the Initiation, with their Curses and Rewards, their Trials and their Officers for the Aeon fully and completely. This being said -- there are 30 glyphs which we can easily map to the English Alphabet by adding the four phonemes we know to actually be formulae:

TH - The CROSS (T) as a weapon (H is a Castle, a Throne denoting military and political authority).

ST - The SON is on the CROSS

QU - the EAGLE is in the CUP

PH - The Mother (P is the Pregnant Goddess) Enthroned (H, the Throne).

Note that the glyph for the Mother enthroned matches the sounds of F - the father glyph.

*There is also "IT" - the Miracle of the MASS - which is not really a phoneme but a practical suffix denoting manifestation: e.g. the difference between HAD and HADIT or NU and NUIT, RA HOOR KHU and RA HOOR KHUIT.

So, we can manage a mapping, without much of a problem. However, there is no evidence to support such a practice and I feel that we'd be "constructing" a system, which is Art when we seek Science. In the case of the *Aethyrs*, we know this to be a definite error: The *Aethyrs* themselves are comprised of many elements, sometimes Gods, sometimes Demons, always an Angel of the *Aethyr* except for the 10th, where we are abandoned to our own shadow. Each *aethyr* is a "place" propped up by a myriad number of Forces, too complex and numerous to be described by a single Glyph be it alphabetical or numerical. We can take the outermost *aethyr* for an example (the 30th – or the first one encountered) named TEX which is 414 in the old Key: the "surrounding of the 4" as the numerical glyph suggests: T is *Teth*, the serpent = 9; E is He, Window which is 5; and X the Cross, which was taken for *Tau* which is 400. Together they sum to 414, which is viewed mystically (in the Judeo-Christian tradition / key) as: the Virgin Mother (E, he, the soul) giving up her Son (T, *teth*, the serpent, the material will) to Crucifixion (X –*Tau* – the Balance of the 4 elements or power over the material). Note that the new system is more dynamic, and enters into process states: First of all: X which was once the Cross of old, is now a Wheel or in other words: an energy center. It is dynamic, it moves and is not planted on the earth like a cross (which was a Tree in the first of all systems). E is the triple light, triple flame - we have its source and need not approximate it through the Virgin Mother H. T is no longer the Altar (of Sacrifice), but the Table (for the Banquet). Whereas we had only one value for TEX denoted 414 in the old key, we now have 4 values for TEX, denoting:

She who passes through the 4 Watchtowers: 89 + 1 + 9 = 99 = Awake, FIAT, Heaven

He who passes through the 4 Watchtowers: 89 + 1 + 300 = 390 = Golden Egg, Naught, Only, Space Beyond, Evening Star, Eightfold, Wonders, Wand createth

Or,

He who does not pass through the 4 Watchtowers: 98 + 1 + 9 = 108 = Hell, Dog, falsifier

She who does not pass through the 4 Watchtowers 98 + 1 + 300 = 399 = Dissolved, Mysteries Averse, Slime of Khem, Unright

All this is instructive, but lamentably the subject of another topic altogether... What strikes me most is the eloquence of the old system: we had balanced increments in the glyphs: 1, 2, 3, 4, 5, 6, 7, 8, 9, 10, 20, 30, 40, 50, 60, 70, 80, 90, 100, 200, 300, 400; while this is not the case with the new: 1, 2, 3, 4, 6, 7, 8, 9, 10, 20, 30, 40, 50, 60, 70, 80, 89, 98, 200, 300, 400 (Here the 90 is displaced once to 89 and the 100 is displaced twice to 98...)

You also mention Pluto, which we now acknowledge to be extraneous to the System. (Pluto was downgraded from its status as a planet the moment we acquired precise mathematical knowledge of its (non-) orbital path.)

As for the Trigrams, we've never looked into these specifically, but it should be a straightforward matter. The Liber Trigrammaton is classified Class A for a reason: It describes perfectly the path of Initiation. As the Liber Trigrammaton already orders the glyphs by their "degree" of materialization / manifestation / initiation, the job becomes a simple one: Ordering the Glyphs in an incrementing series with respect to their numerical values (e.g.: e, f and p as these equal 1,2 and 3) is essentially equivalent to moving through increasing degrees of materialization (or manifestation). So, the matter is a simple one. The attributions of the Roman Glyphs to the trigrams are deemed Class A. I will share them in a separate post.

June 24, 2010 2:39 PM

G : I appreciate the detailed explanation of why & how the Tree of Life is a crude representation of the Universe made obsolete by the more clear revelation of the 30 *Aethyrs*. I understand. Anxiously & curiously I await the Roman Glyph correspondences of the Trigrams. I've noticed that in the Enochian System each *Aethyr* is represented by a Trinity of Glyphs. What are the Roman Glyph(s) for the Spirit Wheel? Maybe the North & South Nodes of the Moon would be the short &

long O respectively. I suspected that Pluto would be left out & makes perfect sense. When you wrote out the numerical sequence of the Roman Glyphs as: 1, 2, 3, 4, 6, 7, 8, 9, 10, 20, 30, 40, 50, 60, 70, 80, 90, 100, 200, 300, 400. Why didn't you write them out as: 1, 2, 3, 4, 6, 7, 8, 9, 10, 20, 24, 30, 40, 42, 50, 60, 70, 80, 89, 98, 200, 300, 400? This seems to be is a more precise arrangement. Why did you leave out the S & S final values (24 & 42), but included all the other continuous & final values? Have you noticed that the 5 is also missing? In the Greek *Qabalah* the 6 only seemed to be missing because it was an outdated letter that resembles the F, Digamma. I wonder what this means for the English Key.

The central number is 30, the number of *Aethyrs* with 11 values on each side which reminds me of the Winged Globe, Hadit. (You have to excuse my sometimes overactive imagination) There seems to be 23 different single-letter values which reminds me of the comment you made about Σ23 = 276 = BABALON, "the glyph of nascent life" page 66-67 of The *English Qabalah ..."(the key of 22 glyphs and the next) so that the old key is fulfilled in the new.)*" Because there are 23 single-letter values it does not seem to fit very easily with the 27 Trigrams according to consecutive numerical order. The displacement of 90 & 100 for 89 & 98 & the insertion of 24 & 42 seems to be connected to the mystery of ST = 131 which is 31 in the Greek Key, the letter Stigma. (Book 4, page 163 Chapter 5) Obviously there's something about S & T which is the reason for the seemingly disrupted eloquence, hypothetically speaking of course. Thank you G, IC, IA

June 29, 2010 10:15 AM

E. : Thank you for your latest... A couple of points: - We put up the trigram correspondence the very same day in a separate post. Let us know your thoughts... - What do you mean by "spirit wheel"? What device is this? - The S does not Sink to the Ground. It crawls or is planted firmly. If it was omitted from that Assessment, it was because of an Imperfection on our Part. Your numerical sequencing is thus more complete. But I Will not write, nor speak of this Thing that pluralizes each other Thing Any More.) - Yes, F is one of the lost Father glyphs, now restituted, concealed in the Ph glyph: that Fortress that guards the Pregnant Goddess.

June 29, 2010 10:58 AM

G : Excuse me I didn't know where to find your post... but now I have it. I have many points of interest... If it be thy Will to discuss them. The Spirit Wheel I speak of is 31 bis., the Hebrew letter SHIN (Fire/Spirit) or the 5th element, symbolized as a circle with 8 spokes which I am sure you are familiar with. I will need some time to study more in depth the attributions deemed as Class A & the astrological correspondences you supplied me, but so far I have this question: Does it matter that the Trigrams may inherently have astrological correspondences of their own that does not actually fit the correspondences that you have attributed? For example: the last 8 basic Trigrams (Fu-hsi/Ba-gua) are planetary (Liber 777), but L,N,O,V,T,U,X & W according to your attributions represent ♎, ♏, ☾, ♉, ♑, ♆, ♄ & ▲ respectively. There are 12 Trigrams before the last 8 that certainly appears to be the Zodiac & the first 7 must be elemental/outer planets. Is there an explanation for this? Thank you G, IC, IA

June 29, 2010 7:22 PM

E. : Hello G, Please see comments to your helpful insights below. First, I think it important to note that these attempts at a syncreticism as one sees in Liber 777 are qualitative listings of attributions, qualities or characteristics of that heading, but may be misleading in that they were never meant to affirm equality. To take the simplest example, the notion of 1 belongs equally to *Kether* and to *Aleph*. However, to say that *Aleph* is *Kether* is to equate two separate notions. *Aleph* is a letter; *Kether* a *sephira*. They are never one and the same thing. Likewise, if *Aleph* is the first letter, whose enumeration is 1, this might correspond to A the first letter in the alphabetic sequence or to E, whose value in English *Gematria* denotes 1. Also, E is the triple flame - a title of *Aleph*. However, this does not mean that *Aleph* is E or that E is *Aleph*; but that the Idea that once engendered *Aleph* now manifests in E. Hence, the historical interest in the *Aleph* and the old keys, but which correspond to a past Aeon. (Note that this Aeon is both historical and personal). The Heavens, the Sky, This and That, even the Star of the Soul that is fixed: but they are fixed on That Wheel that revolves with the Aeons. *Aleph* remains a letter or glyph in the Hebrew system, while E is a letter of the Roman Script. It can be said that the older glyphs (Hebrew, Greek, etc) contain knowledge and formulae of "historical interest": It provides a roadmap of its evolution through the Aeons. However, all these notions of *Shin* and of balancing the elements are somewhat anachronistic. Liber Trigrammaton is not an attempt to integrate the trigrams to the Old System, but the Work of revitalizing them and constituting them into the Aeon.

"The Spirit Wheel" you mention which is "31 bis" in the tables or the Hebrew letter SHIN (Fire/Spirit) or the 5th element, symbolized as a circle with 8 spokes, or the glyph "Sh",(300) which is now 31, which is again equivalent to AL, in the Old Key. All this has to do with the practical application of Knowledge to effect Change on the Micro- or Macrocosm. The Wheel, in this case, is a symbol; it does not exist in and of itself. To use it, charge it, fix it, project it, or pass through it, is first to create it, and so is the province of that Practical Art that effects Change. The same holds for the alphabet attributions and what concerns Liber Trigrammaton: To say that V corresponds to Taurus and so is Venutian and not Martian (or Saturnian for that case) is nonsensical until viewed in the proper perspective. (We are talking about a letter after all.) All this is a convenient truth at best; jargon at worst. RaHoorKhuit, the Sun on the Horizon, God of War of Vengeance--is He solar? Martian? Or both? Is he not exactly like Us? And so is he not Love? And so he is Venutian, too. Certainly He is the Word in Action - which makes him Mercurial. But the Sun is a Star (a collection of burning gases); Mars, Venus, Mercury are Planets, and in this case, Roman gods and goddesses. These are Beings or Ideas distinct and apart from RHK. It is critical never to depart too far from common sense. All this, is fairly close to Madness as it is in the Eye of the World which must be taken into the Balance. First, these correspondences do not denote equality Ascendency over the 4 for example, is denoted in the 5 (or the 5th element, as you say) which is also the sign of Man, the Pentagram. But to say that the Star is the Wheel or that the Wheel is the Circle, is to take things higher as mentioned. Secondly, though these correspondences are fixed in order for the Aeon, they Change with Time. Thirdly, the tables of correspondences in Liber 777 are class D, while the attributions provided are Class A.

July 6, 2010 9:06 AM

The Trigrams

July 12, 2010 3:20 PM

E. : Note that M (the 4 into 10) is the pivot point between S and S final: the Self-Sacrifice differentiates between S-The Son and S-The Serpent: which you can read to mean what you Will. Similarly, the passage from T to T final is mediated first, by the L-glyph (The Balance - post-418), the Active Gate (N), the Y vowel that takes the 2 and unites into 1, and the V that does the same, but more proximally. I apologize for the previous errors, and thank you very kindly for pointing them out.

July 12, 2010 7:14 PM

G : What particularly draws my attention to the Trigrams is their form or appearance according to the Position of the Point. That there are 12 (Zodiac) with a Single Point & there are 8 (inner planets) with None. There are 4 (the elements) that are Coupled & 2 Divided (Uranus & Neptune) & 1 Triune (Spirit) which makes for XXVII in All. This symmetry gives the perception of 5 elements, 10 planets & 12 constellations. Among the 12 that are Single Pointed, there are 3 distinct sets of 4 that visually appear to be 3 phases (Cardinal, Fixed & Mutable) transitioned by the 4 elements or Bigrams (the Chinese name of this Tetragrammaton escapes me). & even more of an equation is the fact that each One represents a numeral counted in base 3 using the numbers 0 - the Point/Tao, 1 - the Line/Yang & 2 - the Broken Line/Yin. (note: AL I:24 "six and fifty" 6/50 = 0.12) The bottom position of the Trigram has the value of 1; the middle, 3 & the top, 9. At least, this has been the result of my research which maybe you can confirm or negate. Each one counted accordingly to the rules given above gives this random sequence: 0, 1, 2, 3, 6, 9, 18, 4, 5, 7, 8, 10, 11, 19, 20, 12, 15, 21, 24, 13, 14, 16, 22, 17, 23, 25 & 26 Now the set of 8 (the corners of the *Cube*) & 12 (the angles of the *Cube*), thus numbered, both add up to 156 & the 7 (the faces & Space within/without of the *Cube*) adds up to 39, a reflection of 93. 9 & 3 when multiplied gives 27, the *Cube* or Hadit.

July 13, 2010 5:51 PM

E. : The Perfections are such that They are manifest from no Matter which Ray One takes to the source. First of all, evidence appears to confirm your methodology which (for this reason) I'm sure will produce a number of exciting revelations. Multiplication by 0, 1, 2 alternatively is the equivalent to distilling the operation as it manifests into the Supernal Spheres. In fact, Liber Trigrammaton describes perfectly, the resolution of the 9=2 equation: that is, it describes in entirety the development of the Babe of the Abyss into a conscious element of the 2nd sphere (*Chokmah*). For This reason you were asked if you were 9=2, and hence the injunction to "look and see". At such a Place, the Man is conscious of three Wheels that constitute his Being[1]. (The Supernals, the Christian Trinity, Mind-Body-Soul, Beast-Man-God etc and all other triune / trigram constructions: are descriptions of these—especially Liber Trigrammaton, the Document on IT.). The Current blows and turns the Wheels this quickly or that slowly according to their Alignment. (Angle to the Current). These Wheels are Chakras, they are the Supernal *Sephiroth*, use whichever Name you Will that humanity has given this phenomenon in the course of history. They constitute the ultimate composition of Man and the physiological body of the Man in 2, who is 1 (9=2). Perdurabo himself divides the 6 by 50. This may be of interest for the very reasons you describe. However, "six and fifty"** means six + fifty, or as Crowley might have said, NU brings Death (50) to the 6 (the Son) which is the birthing of the Babe of the Abyss within the Four WatchTowers in the desert set at the foot of the Sea of

1 Liber AL in its 3 chapters can be seen as a complete discourse upon these three wheels and the ultimate solution to their alignment on all planes, intellectual, moral, political, physiological and behavioral. Note the deities associated to each wheel: Nuit, Hadit, Ra-Hoor-Khuit.

Binah[2]: the result of which produces the process of distilling whatever current into Being through the three Wheels (0,1,2) in an attempt to reduce all to 000 (from the 400-401-441-883-888-000). Assuming the trigrams describe such a state, your method holds. O is the action into the *Ain Soph Aur*. 1 into *Kether* and the 2 into *Chokmah*. He seeking to solve 9=2 operates at this level instinctually. Perdurabo knew this but didn't have the mapping of the English letters, despite having written them out so plainly in Book 220. Nonetheless, having walked those Aires, he was able to describe them perfectly, though he was blinded to the glyph attributions. Just so all this might be even more wondrous and miraculous. It makes one think all this is a ruse, until one sees that the perfection of the Key extends beyond the book and into material reality as they are manifest through time. It seems you are destined to find some form of resolution / concordance between the two systems. Your Knowledge and Play of these are Beyond where my Will points. Wherever this Path leads, you are walking alone (as far as I can tell), and so a shining light for the rest of us. Your arrangement does produce 156 for the Houses and 156 for the Planets; and the remainder (which is the Initiate in this Place) is indeed 39, which into 4 (the Material) is again 156 (=39x4).

July 14, 2010 2:01 PM

**Note: Her word is "six and fifty" not her name. Six and fifty is 220 which is 'The Law'.

G : I did not mention that AL I:24 is followed by AL I:25 "Divide (= 0.12), add (= 56), multiply (= 300)" I assure you that I am not alone nor is this my personal discovery, but those who have knowledge of this have gone astray & their assumptions are unreliable. I have drawn my own conclusions.

I have always thought that the Trigrams dictated their own correspondences & from that here is what I have configured. For convenience I will mention each Trigram from its base 3 value ranging from 0 - 26 in 3 different groups:

The Five Elements = 30: 0 (E) = Spirit, 1 (f) = Fire, 2 (C,P) = Water, 9 (Z, Nf) = Air, 18 (B, Yc) = Earth.

The Ten Planets = 165: 3 (I) = Uranus, 6 (A) = Neptune, 13 (L) = Saturn, 14 (N) = Mercury, 16 (O) = The Sun, 22 (V) = Jupiter, 17 (T) = Venus, 23 (U) =

2 Note that this association of Nun with Death, and the view that NU brings 'death' is essentially an error of the old patriarchal view or Aeon. It is more properly attributed to Gate as it is in the English language and as suggested by its shape in the Roman Script. She oversees the death and her emissary Nephthys may do the killing, but she presides over the generative and birthing stages as well. So to call it Death (versus Birth) is an error of shortsightedness. The proper symbol however, would harmonize these two.

The Moon, 25 (X) = Mars, 26 (W) = The Earth.

The Twelve Signs = 156: 4 (H) = Aries, 5 (D) = Libra, 7 (R,x) = Cancer, 8 (F,Q) = Capricorn, 10 (K) = Leo, 11 (G) = Aquarius, 19 (S) = Scorpio, 20 (M) = Taurus, 12 (Sf) = Sagittarius, 15 (L averse) = Gemini, 21 (w) = Pisces 24 (Tf) = Virgo.

My method of analyzing the Trigrams are almost completely mechanical. If the above Zodiac attributions are found to be in error this is the key of my premise: The 4 Bigrams or Tetragrammaton (described from top to bottom line): double Yang is Fire, double Yin is Earth, Yang-Yin is Air & Yin-Yang is Water. The Position of the Point: The top is Cardinal, the middle is Fixed & the bottom is Mutable. I've noticed (among other things) that the 14th Trigram numbered as 19 in base 3 is attributed S - The Serpent which is HAD (7 + 4 + 8 = 19); AL II:22. Interesting that it is also in alignment with Scorpio, which is the Solar equivalent of the Chinese Serpent in their Lunar Calendar. The Trigram attributed to Libra bears the resemblance of the Scales. There are other interesting correspondences but I have not yet thoroughly looked them over. I present them for the Analysis of you & your companions. I appreciate the Grace of your Presence...

July 15, 2010 3:03 PM

G : I am assuming that more than likely Ŏ is assigned to the 23rd Trigram along with V or where does it fit?

July 16, 2010 5:49 PM

E. : Yes, it is the feminine to the masculine V. As regards your previous post: How interesting your attributions are! They appear to be all averse! The problem here (or the subtlety) is that the equality is not bi-directional and specific only to value. W = 400 implies that W has the value of 400, but not that 400 has the value of W. 400 can be the value of many formulae (all equivalent to W finally), while the glyph W has only one value. Furthermore W is a letter, 400 is a number; they are both glyphs, but as we can see by their shapes they are distinctly not the same glyph - so that equality sign here must be qualified. In fact, a new notation should be developed that suggests a mapping and not an equality - this would solve this particular difficulty once and for all. There are two distinct analyses one can pursue:

(1) one may look at the glyph and determine which elemental, planetary, outer-system division qualify its manifestation.

(2) one may look at the element, the planet, the outer-system division of the

12 zodiac houses and determine which glyph qualifies that phasing.

Take the third sphere for instance: Going in : BINAH, Queen Mother, the Root of Water and all that is Reflective. Going out: BINAH, Saturn - a dry old man. Do we classify the third sphere as Saturnian? Or do we classify it as Water? In this case, are you mapping the trigrams to the elemental-sphere-zodiac system? Or are you mapping the elemental-sphere-zodiac system to the trigrams? It depends on the intended application. This is my Understanding of That which you seek to Establish: As you assert, there are 4 elements and 1 fifth that sets them in Motion; there are 12 outer system divisions (the zodiac belt) and 8 planets, one Sun, and the Moon which is neither but distinct in Herself. (There are many other planetary moons, but too distant to affect physical matter on the planet as the Moon does, e.g. the tides, the gravitational pull of liquid in the brain, a woman's menstrual cycle, a man's lunacy...) Together they make 27, or as 0-26 by your numbering. You have three tiers, which are multiplicative orders of base 3: 1,3,9. At each tier you permute three values: the dot, the solid line, the broken line. These you number 0,1,2. Three dots would be the lowest valued trigram: 0. Three solid lines would have the highest value, $1 x 2 + 3 x 2 + 9 x 2 = 26$. You've permuted the range. The only thing left to do is to determine what to map that range to. I know Nothing of these matters of dots and broken lines. I look however, and the Vision is clear, austere, crystalline, immutable. This is what I see. This is what I Know. In this Place,

O

O

O

is correctly attributed.

O

O

———

is FIRE (not Air).

O

O

— —

is AIR (not EARTH)

— —

O

O

is correctly attributed.

— —

O

O

is Earth (not FIRE)

In this way, you have E SPIRIT; f EARTH; Cs, P WATER; Z,Nf FIRE; and B,Yc AIR which Works. Correct the attributions and you will find the System that revolves All into One. (Do you see yet that Liber Trigrammaton describes the *Aethyrs* in reverse Order, that is, from W the Outermost into E, the first? Three lines, become three circles, three circles, three spinning wheels.) In love,

July 16, 2010 10:56 PM

G : I greatly appreciate the correction. You have opened my eyes. I have rethought my attributions with a different approach. This should be a more perfect fit. The Five Elements = 30: 0 (E,J) -> Spirit, 1 (f) -> Earth, 2 (Cs,P) -> Water, 9 (Z, Nf) -> Fire, 18 (B, Yc) -> Air. The Ten Planets = 165: 3 (I) -> Jupiter, 6 (A) -> The Sun, 13 (L) -> Venus, 14 (N,Y) -> Mars, 16 (O) -> The Moon, 22 (V,Ŏ) -> Mercury, 17 (T) -> The Earth, 23 (U) -> Neptune, 25 (X) -> Saturn, 26 (W) -> Uranus. The Twelve Signs = 156: 4 (H) -> Sagittarius, 5 (D) -> Taurus, 7 (R,x) -> Cancer, 8 (F,Q) -> Leo, 10 (K) -> Virgo, 11 (G) -> Gemini, 19 (S) -> Scorpio, 20 (M) -> Aquarius, 12 (Sf) -> Pisces, 15 (L averse) -> Libra, 21 (w) -> Aries, 24 (Tf) -> Capricorn. Sigma 26 = 351 Thank you

July 17, 2010 9:49 AM

G : I am thinking of switching these attributions. 5 (D) -> Taurus, (or Libra?) 15 (L averse) -> Libra, (or Taurus?) I am inclined to think this a better fit. Thank you.

July 17, 2010 10:21 AM

E. : Close but something still isn't right. V and O are definitely not Mercurial. I Wonder why you make this attribution. Is there a Reason? Some other problems: B and D have been switched in your system. (But oddly, I recall something about this. I don't recall if this was a veil, aeonic or initiatory.) In any case: Why do you not make D Saggitarius? w Taurus? H, Aries? As for the Spheres: L is not Venus in this Place. N cannot be Mars. Mars for V,O (the natural choice) is Old Aeon, and Nihilism. Old value for Pe, Foot, War, which is 80. L is Mars, despite my oedipal blindness to it. Look: AL = SUN+MARS= Horus = RHK,HPK = MARS+SUN = LA Believing this Love Venetian is what leads to Trouble. N,Y are the two phases of Mercury - mitigated for there is something else here, that wanes and fades in this light. It is Apollo disappearing. V,O is Venus ascendent, Venus falling. Test them. Charge them talismanicly, skry or project. Take a subject - yourself perhaps the wisest choice - or an Enemy - and fix a sequence of trigrams designed formulaicly. Observe the results. If it doesn't work, something's wrong. I see all manner of potential in this System.

July 19, 2010 10:36 PM

THE CUBE OF SPACE & the 30 Aethyrs

G : Your corrections are infinitely beyond any reason I ever thought I had. But one last correction... 4 (H) -> Cancer, 7 (R,x) -> Aries, H is not only the Castle Fortress & Throne, but the Chariot & the 4 Pillars & Elements surrounding it. It is appropriately assigned to the Crab that has a hardened protective covering & Armored Charioteer of the Castle, the House of the Moon. ABRAHADABRA! R,x is the Emperor implying the impotence of material authority, Anarchy or the fallen government in its proper place. This also forms a perfect symmetry of the 12 Trigrams. Place them on the Wheel of the Zodiac & see how they appear to be opposite. The attributions cannot be any more Perfect for if this is possible It lies Beyond Me. This *Qabalah* of Trigrammaton takes the form of a 3 dimensional transparent Cube in Space which appears to be not only of Art, but Science for it seems to mathematically express Relativity within a Glyph. This is what I meant in my mistake by a "reconstruction" of a "Tree of Life", but in this place it is a Hiero-Glyph of the 30 Aethyrs. Properly mapped out, each edge is the sum of the 2 sides that meet at that edge & each corner is the sum of the 3 sides that meet at that corner. This is what I want you to see. - is a connection n is a corner (8) (n) represents an edge:

(12) 17-(11)-14-(12)-13-(10)-16-(15)-17, this is the face of 9 (top)

26-(20)-23-(21)-22-(19)-25-(24)-26, this is the face of 18 (bottom)

13-(10)-16-(7)-25-(19)-22-(4)-13, this is the face of 1 (front)

26-(20)-23-(5)-14-(11)-17-(8)-26, this is the face of 2 (back)

22-(4)-13-(12)-14-(5)-23-(21)-22, this is the face of 3 (right)

17-(15)-16-(7)-25-(24)-26-(8)-17, this is the face of 6 (left)

There is much more work to be done as you can see. My appreciation is beyond any word of thanksgiving. Love is the law, love under will.

G :...& Zero is the Space within this *Cube*. The opposite sides of the *Cube* when added are multiples of 3. They are 3, its Square(9) & *Cube*(27). These are my directional coordinates for the *Cube* of Space which you can confirm or not: 0(E,J)-> is the N-S/E-W Horizontal Axis of the Center. & the 6 Faces: 1(f)-> is Above on the Face of the Vertical Axis 2(Cs,P)-> is Below on the Face of the Vertical Axis This Central Axis is a Triune of Spirit, Father & Mother. 3(I)-> is the Face of the North 6(A)-> is the Face of the South 9(Z,Nf)-> is the Face of the West 18(B,Yc)-> is the Face of the East If I may quote LIBER 418, the first couple of sentences of TEX, the 30th *Aethyr*, "I AM IN A VAST CRYSTAL CUBE in the form of the Great God Harpocrates. This cube is surrounded by a sphere." (AL II:7) It is curious to me that in AL this particular mention appears in the 2nd Chapter, 7th verse, 2 & 7 which is 27 together. So far it seems to me that the *Cube* represents dimensions of psycho-physical reality & the sphere surrounding it are the Rings of the 30 *Aethyrs* & it is puzzling to me how 30 would fit into 27. These are the Antigrams or Opposite Trigrams: To determine an Antigram simply change each line of the Trigram to its opposite. The Tao has no opposite so it would remain unchanged. The opposite of Yin is Yang & vice versa. Notice how they are located on the opposite ends of the *Cube* & that they include ST = 131, O/U = 200, A/I = 4 & Z,Nf/BYc = 6 as Antigrams. Now these pairs are apart of a much larger set of 729 Hexagrams which, of course, includes the 64 Hexagrams or the *I Ching*. Not only are they representations of pictographs, but numbers derived from the Ternary base 3 numeral system of counting. As you know the first or bottom position is counted as 1 & each successive level upwards is multiplied in value by 3 so that the sequence up to 6 levels yields 1, 3, 9, 27, 81, 243 & these are in turn multiplied by the 0, 1 or 2 that are placed at that position. Therefore the number range 0 through 728 (or even more with 7, 8 & 9 positions) can be represented by the combination of these Trigrams in the form of a Hexagram. For example: 666 can be represented as 24/18. The Trigram valued at 24 has the value of 648 when placed above another & this added to the number 18 Trigram gives 666, a combination unique to that number. In this system any number can be reduced to 2 or 3 (or even more if necessary) symbols which seems to work well with the *English Qabalah.* Likewise letters can be converted into Ternary values, AL for example would give 360 or 175 if expressed in the form of a Hexagram (13/6 or 6/13) depending on which letter is considered the top or bottom. Because the Trigrams are read from the bottom as the first going up this, it seems to me, corresponds with reading left to right so that the A is at the bottom & L on top. The Hexagram 3/12 which can be written out as 010110, representing the 0, 1 or 2 in its respective position, is the number 93 & when this is overturned, reversed or consecutively reordered from the bottom & placed from the top we have 011010 or 4/3, the number 111. This system opens up another dimension altogether for relativity, interpretation & its possibilities. Indeed every number is infinite. A brief & by all means simple demonstration, if you will: The Hexagram 14/0 is Spirit & Mercury which could imply the Spirit of Mercury & has the value of 378. According to the unwritten Lexicon of the *English Qabalah* 378 (Σ27) = Hermes, the messenger. Hephaestus.

I am inclined to point out what appears to be a strictly limited & certain way of going about simple arithmetic using the system of the Trigrams. For instance, there is no such number as a 13 in this system that is the sum of 8 & 5 as we have in the familiar decimal system of counting. I am not certain yet exactly what this signifies. The way that addition works in this way is based upon an availability/vacancy or possibility of a union between 1 of 3 corresponding positions when placed side by side. The bottom line of one Trigram must be added to the bottom line of another & so on all the way to the top until a new Trigram is revealed. There are only 4 possible operations of addition that can be solved with the same 3 numbers 0, 1 & 2 & these are 0+0, 0+1, 0+2 & 1+1 for the answer must be 0, 1 or 2 (because there is only the Tao, Yang & Yin to place at any given position). A 1+2 is impossible & would require a representation of 3 broken lines which we don't have. There are 20 (12 lines & 8 corners or points) combinations obtained by simple addition (of the 6 Faces) that take part in the formation of the *Cube* & there are 36 unmanifested & in all there are 56 unique pairs that can be added together based upon the unique "physics" of the Trigrams. The last 8 Trigrams are not only triplicities, but their triplicity is squared or they are actually the sum of 3 unique pairs of astrological signs combined with one of the elements or either the Sun or Jupiter each....

August 7, 2010 7:58 PM

G : For now I have settled on the coordinates for the *Cube* of Space that I am comfortable with & these are: The Sun above & Jupiter below. 2(Cs,P)-> West & Water 9(Z,Nf)-> South & Fire 1(f)-> East & Air not Earth 18(B,Y)-> North & Earth not Air According to Book 418 these are the correctly assigned elements to each station. I had to switch the elements attributed to 1 & 18. The structure of the *Cube* made me realize something was wrong. I am of the opinion that: B, Y - The Book of Knowledge is made from the Tree of Life or the Tree of this World which grows out of the element of Earth & She is a Woman. Was it not Eve who gave the fruit to Adam & he did eat? (My interpretation of the Bible is Gnostic) This Book & the Pages thereof are also the Breasts of Our Lady. It is here that the Pentacle or "the Coin redeemeth". The verse of this Trigram reads: "Also a Woman arose, and veiled the Upper Heaven with her body of stars." f - The lost Father is of the element of Air which is the Breath or force of the Word whose weapon is the Sword. I first thought it was strange & curious that you would attribute this to Earth, but had no reason to change it. Maybe you could explain why you have attributed them as such if you find this to be in error. Also *Cube* of Space = 474 (2x237, Khu) = Soul. Mother Earth. Tree of Life. Merkaaba = 98 = T, the Table

August 8, 2010 3:10 PM

G : Please let me know your thoughts on all of this. If I am not mistaken, I believe that the Sun should be placed below. In relation to any horizon a star or the Sun cannot appear to rise or set if it is not below it & Hell is to be found in the lower regions at the center. The lower region or the bottom face of the Merkaaba of the Old Aeon represented the self & was the position of *Tiphareth* on the Tree of Life which you have explained to me has not changed according to the location of the *Aethyrs*. The number 6 for the Trigram of A attributed to the Sun seems to implicate this. If this still holds up in this New Aeon reconstruction of the *Cube* of Space (= Tree of Life) then it would also imply quite profoundly that "Every man & every woman is a star" AL I:3 I have reconfigured my *Cube* of Space to fit these dimensions. Thank you.

G : All of this is at the spur of the moment. It has come to my attention upon contemplation that the *Cube* of Space has 3 more than 27 components which makes 30 in all for the *Aethyrs* each to have their own place. These are my attributions for the 30 *Aethyrs* that encircle the *Cube* of Space & I am interested in what you think about them:

The Inner Dimensions:	The Faces:	The Edges:	The Corners:
LIL -> 0, the Center	LIT -> 1	ICH -> 4	TOR -> 13
ARN -> 1 & 2, the East-West Axis	MAZ -> 2	LOE -> 5	NIA -> 14
ZOM -> 3 & 6, the Above-Below Axis	DEO -> 3	ZIM -> 7	UTI -> 16
PAZ -> 9 & 18, the North-South Axis	ZID -> 6	UTA -> 8	DES -> 22
	ZIP -> 9	OXO -> 10	ZAA -> 17
	ZAX -> 18	LEA -> 11	BAG -> 23
		TAN -> 19	RII -> 25
		ZEN -> 20	TEX -> 26
		POP -> 12	
		KHR -> 15	
		ASP -> 21	
		LIN -> 24	

The *Old Merkaaba* was missing individual attributions to the 8 corners & this *Cube* is missing 3 for the triple axis of the center.

If any of this is plausible, which I suspect is, this should give the descriptive correspondences needed to navigate & solve this Chinese Puzzle Box.

August 21, 2010 1:52 PM

G : In my eyesight the Edges & Corners don't seem to be correctly attributed. A few of them are, but the rest would have to be reordered. At least this is what I see at the moment. I am still looking them over. I am in doubt because I cannot understand why would they not be in perfect order in relation to the *Cube*.

Thank you.

August 22, 2010 7:52 AM

G : This is my attempt at a correct placement of the *Aethyrs* along the Trigrammatic dimensions of the *Cube* that I think would fit best. The ones that I believe fell correctly in place according to the numerical order of the 30 *Aethyrs* are marked "(the same)" except for the Space & the Faces which are all the same & with I can see no problem.

The Space:	The Faces:	The Edges:	The Corners:
LIL -> 0, the Center	LIT -> 1	LOE -> 4	TOR -> 13 (the same)
ARN -> 1 & 2, the East-West Axis	MAZ -> 2	KHR -> 5	DES -> 14
ZOM -> 3 & 6, the Above-Below Axis	DEO -> 3	ZIM -> 7 (the same)	ZAA -> 16
PAZ -> 9 & 18, the North-South Axis	ZID -> 6	LEA -> 8	NIA -> 22
	ZIP -> 9	OXO -> 10 (the same)	RII -> 17
	ZAX -> 18	UTA -> 11	UTI -> 23
		ZEN -> 19	BAG -> 25
		IKH -> 20	TEX -> 26 (the same)
		POP -> 12 (the same)	
		TAN -> 15 (the same)	
		ASP -> 21 (the same)	
		LIN -> 24 (the same)	

?

Thank you.

August 23, 2010 9:44 AM

G : {In my comment above, TAN -> 15 is marked "(the same)", but this is an error.}

I cannot imagine the attributions we have worked out being in error no more than 1 or 2 out of place, which I seriously doubt (having no other inkling), still this would not satisfy or compensate for the 14 *Aethyrs* that appear to be out of order according to my attributions thus far. I have dismissed this possibility as an influence of confusion. My conclusion, at this point, is that the 20 *Aethyrs* below the Great Abyss, immediately following, were meant to be in disarray or disordered & the 9 *Aethyrs* above this Great Abyss, the 10th *Aethyr*, to be in perfect alignment for obvious reasons, I suppose.

As for these:

ARN -> 1 & 2, the East-West Axis

ZOM -> 3 & 6, the Above-Below Axis

PAZ -> 9 & 18, the North-South Axis

My attributions here cannot be taken literally. I only mean the Space in between these opposite Faces & not a combination thereof which serves only to conveniently pin point a location. I believe that each axis should be represented by a Single Isolated Point whereby there is no symbolical distinction other than its position as Upper, Middle or Lower. It is impossible to have such representation as I have listed within That Space where there is Nothing Before All of these which would explain the "missing" attributions. Thus to be more precise:

ARN -> • (Upper), the East/West Axis

ZOM -> • (Middle), the Above/Below Axis

PAZ -> • (Lower), the North/South Axis

"Here is Nothing under its three forms. It is not, yet informeth all things"

Thank you,

August 29, 2010 11:41 AM

G : ... All of this implicates to me that the traditional ordering of the 30 *Aethyrs* are relatively incorrect. This further implicates, as we may already know, that these below the Abyss need not always be traveled in order & that their order is relative to the traveler, although these may have their own order of manifestation...

August 29, 2010 9:07 PM

I have Reason to believe that the Trigram of Aries should be of the 11th *Aethyr* & the Trigram of Aquarius must be of the 13th *Aethyr*...

September 2, 2010 8:45 AM

G : ... Please excuse the many comments, I am trying to keep you up to date as it comes, if you are following along.

I have made Trigram 10 to be of UTA & Trigram 11, OXO. This seems more appropriate.

Thank you,

September 2, 2010 11:31 AM

G : Unless you have any objections, I would consider my attributions of the *Aethyrs* complete & ready for your examination. I believe that I have reached the limits of my own Understanding in this matter.

The Space:	The Faces:	The Edges:	The Corners:
LIL -> 0, the Center (the same)	LIT -> 1 (the same)	LOE -> 4	TOR -> 13 (the same)
ARN ->BETWEEN 1 & 2, the East-West Axis	MAZ -> 2 (the same)	KHR -> 5	DES -> 14
ZOM ->BETWEEN 3 & 6, the Above-Below Axis	DEO -> 3 (the same)	IKH -> 7	ZAA -> 16
PAZ ->BETWEEN 9 & 18, the North-South Axis	ZID -> 6 (the same)	LEA -> 8	NIA -> 22
	ZIP -> 9 (the same)	UTA -> 10	RII -> 17
	ZAX -> 18 (the same)	OXO -> 11	UTI -> 23
		ZEN -> 19 (the same)	BAG -> 25
		ZIM -> 20	TEX -> 26 (the same)
		POP -> 12	
		TAN -> 15	
		ASP -> 21 (the same)	
		LIN -> 24 (the same)	

???

September 3, 2010 12:35 PM

E. : Thank you for your comments, your invaluable research, and the pdf we received. We are preparing tables of correspondences and your *Cube* will prove of inestimable interest I am sure. Once the tables are complete, we should be able to attribute them to the *Cube* with greater facility. I will keep you posted on the project and its progress and please continue to update us on your research. You may wish to prepare a little treatise on the *Cube* and its applications as well, for discerning Students for eventual publication.

September 3, 2010 1:52 PM

G : I believe that I have reached the limits of assigning the *Aethyrs* upon the *Cube*. For now they seem to be perfect in my Sight, for now. I wouldn't know where to begin in writing a brief treatise on the subject; this I must carefully contemplate, but you need not to wait. I am simply glad that all of this is getting out & coming together.

As you know, there are 12 & 8 Trigrams that sum to 156 each when divided as corners & edges, stars & planets. These same 12 & 8 or 20 can also be divided as odd & even numbers, a set of 10 each that have the sum of 156.

I have figured the correct order of reading the Trigrams according to their ternary representation in using Arabic numerals (similar to binary) when changing them to letters or numbers. This is also mathematically implicated by the multiplied structure of each level. The first level is the ones place; the middle, tens & the top, hundreds & in a Hexagram the fourth would be the thousands place & so on when changing each line into a number. Of course, 0 is for the Tao, 1 is Yang & 2 is Yin. Thus we have for Trigram 1 the representation of 001 or 1 & for Trigram 6, 020 or simply the number 20. Left to right is top to bottom whether it is a number or a letter (which are numbers), I believe they should be treated the same. For instance, AL would indicate that the Trigram of the Sun be placed above that of Mars giving us the value of 175, however, with LA we get 360, the degrees of a Circle which is Not.

There is an interesting synchronicity in expressing the Trigrams or replacing their lines & dots with Arabic numerals. Trigram 4 (Cancer) is an 11 (011) which corresponds with the Elevenfold Word ABRAHADABRA of Atu VII. (Interesting also how the legends of the Holy Graal often hearken back to the age of Castles, seeing that H, the Castle, is attributed to the Cup-bearing Charioteer.) It is also the 11th *Aethyr* in the order that I have attributed. Trigram 14 (Mercury) is 112 & this is the value of *Beth* & other related ideas. It is not for these reasons alone that I believe the *Aethyrs* should be renumbered according to their Trigrammatic order. I would like a second opinion.

September 6, 2010 1:10 PM

G : I have reassigned 19 to POP, the 19th *Aire* & 12 to the 18th *Aire* called ZEN. This is more intimately agreeable.

I would like to make a suggestion regarding the letter attributions of the 2nd, 3rd & 4rth Aires, I believe these should be PH, ST & QU respectively. After coming to this conclusion I've noticed that if you place the values of each phoneme in a 3 x 3 grid from top to bottom in this order:

010

131

210

... you get an interesting picture of the *Son on the Cross* that extends Above & Below, to which the 3rd *Aire* has been assigned. If you add these 3 we get 351 (Sigma 0-26), the *Gematria* value of the 7 letters that form the 6 sides (f, C/P, I, A, Z/N, B/Y) & the center (E) of the *Cube* &, of course, it is the sum of the 27 Trigrams engendered by these & all of this is contained within the Triple Axis of the Space. There are other qualities that can be observed that I have not mentioned. I wonder what you see in all this.

September 14, 2010 9:13 AM

E. : The matter I found disagreeable was centered about the Y: the Y being a Fork, and terminating in 6 on the Left, and 70 on the Right. The 6 Understand, is the Son in the old aeon, the self-sacrificing solar diety, while the 70 is the Eye, and the glyph of the Goat, or the Horned and Hooved One, or the devil in the old aeon religions centered about the 6. This has little to do with the old aeon keys, but more with a growing distinction in my mind between what I am calling the active and the passive. Recall, that one generally has the Choice of whether to remain in the 6th sphere or proceed. There is no other Point of Rest.

As you know, the book discusses (briefly) a doctrine of active and passive glyphs, centered on experiential/phenomenological evidence of differing values certain letters can take depending on their position or their state. These letters are L, which can be balanced or imbalanced, the O which can be full or crescented, the Y which can be taken on the left or right (consonant or vowel), the C which can be hard or soft....

I believe this has to do with a Choice or a state the Student finds himself in. It occurs to me for instance, that for the A.'.M.'.T.'. the L is always balanced - this being an essential task of the M .'. T .'. and the door through which She passes from the 3rd sphere into the 2nd - hence the 5 footprints of the Camel - which can be of three types depending on the Man. (VVVVVV, LLLLLL, JJJJJJ --Note that all these are equivalent, but that the V is the L balanced on the point). This means that beneath that veil the formulae KAOS=BABALON is employed as 276 (depending on whether he makes the 0 full or crescented- the moon, the reflective consciousness - does he divide it into a crescent, resolve the arch into two points, or complete the circle?) But passing the 1st Veil (of lunar consciousness - Paroketh as they called it) KAOS=BABALON=156 and remains so, until he is on *Beth*. Here KAOS remains at 156 but BABALON is now 176 which is 156 + the union (G) (his view of the Queen has undergone Change).

The issue becomes whether to present the totality of the key to the world, including the balanced L of which the world has no experience until it has passed into the 3rd sphere fully at which point in time, He needs no instruction from the stars but is of the body of stars itself. As they say, He is the First and Last, how shall He cease to Number himself?

These are matters that I am still currently contemplating/investigating.

As you know, we mean to produce a second edition of the book. We are interested in including your research (I'll discuss this with you in greater details when the time comes) and do continue to send along anything you feel might be pertinent.

September 27, 2011 2:21 PM

**(In this way, it may appear 'reasonable' to switch the usual syncretic attributions for C and K. For if C is the Cup and Aquarius and so Queens, while K the Virgin is Scorpio and so the Hermit: how is that we find the Queens waning and not the Hermit? Also the old line in Liber Al: "Tzaddi is not the Emperor - that is, while Z must still be Aries in Nature, the glyph of its manifestation on the ROTA is not "The Emperor" or ATU IV. If one takes this as a fact, integrity and symmetries inherent in the system imply further readjustments of the ROTA key to accommodate this change. For instance, very basically: if Tzaddi is not the Emperor, then some other glyph must be, and so this requires switching out a second glyph. If it switches out with the first we are done; otherwise the system cascades. Perhaps at the end of the Aeon, all we will have of the C is its part in the Ch glyph: i.e. She is enthroned alway.)

November 22, 2011 12:46 PM

The Squaring of the Circle & Miscellany

G : Some possible errors that I have noticed in your Numerical Lexicon of The *English Qabalah*: Decay = 49 not 50 Noise = 179 or 299 not 419 Crocodile = 292(ŏŏ,kk)/412(ŏ,kk)/532 not 439 Great Work = 422(Tf)/431/771(W) not 440 The Great Work = 877 not 777 Concubine = 491 not 518 Annihilation = 521 not 525 NOX = 570/279(x)/450(ŏ) LUX = 550/570/259/279 not 650 LUXFIRE = 574(F)/566(f) not 666 SEBEK (page 79) = 62 not 439 or Crocodile(412) Edward Alexander Crowley = 602(Nf)/642/666/706(LL) & when activated 1006(W) or 1297(X,W) On page 64 I could not figure out how you arrived at 1111, maybe you could explain this & the other calculations above. Thank you & I hope with you all is well.

July 28, 2010 10:24 AM

G : N.O.X. is not 550 (page 190) nor is it 650 (page 78) but you can arrive at 506 if you count the N as final & 386(ŏ,Nf) is another possible value. Also N.O.X. = 95(Nf,ŏ,x). It seems that in these errors (also with L.U.X.) the X has been counted as 400 which would make 550 & 650 possible when it is my understanding that X = 300. Thank you.

July 28, 2010 11:46 AM

E. : You are operating under Old Aeon (Pre 418) dynamics. X is the old Aeon Tau, so 400, not Shin, 300. The Cross is not the Spirit (300), it is the Material (400). Also, you fail to see the point of LUX NOX, which are formulae. They have three letters, so three phases, and thus three numbers in separate Places. The phases are L-Laverse, O horned - O full, x inert - X active. In this way for instance at the tail end of LUX, with formulae finalized: 50+200+400=650. Similarly for LUXFIRE which is the movement from 303 to 666. LuxFire = 70+200+9+10+4+9+1 = 303 to LaverseUXfIRE=50+200+400+2+4+9+1=666 And likewise for The Great Work which has too many phases of too unspecific generality to be of interest here. Yet to show you: The=106 Great =132 Work=539 =777. All formulae operate this way - and we now have all the transitional glyphs. There are bound to be clerical errors and we are grateful for pointing any of these out to us. Best,

July 28, 2010 2:08 PM

G : What I don't completely comprehend about the section of METHODOLOGY within the chapter of DISCOVERY on page 25 is: How L got its values of 50 & 70? What are the equations for the circle squared in its failure & its success? 4638 ABKZ 4 aL "O=" MR3YX + (24) (89) RPSTOVAL What is the significance or affect of the AL at the end of this string of numbers & letters & symbols? How did O (=200) get its other value of 80? Why is R listed in Table III as having the values 9 & 400? Does this mean that R has double values? I did not realize until now how W received its value of (60 &) 300 . This was left out in Table II & III on page 26 & 27 respectively, but page 173 of the LEX I KON seems to confirm what I assumed to be true on page 53 that W = 400 which I now can see clearly to be incorrect. Thank you for setting me on the Right Path.

July 28, 2010 8:42 PM

E. : Hello G, Thank you for calling my attention to certain faults with the current edition of the book. It is not a simple matter to compile a lexicon. In any case, a new, more extensive work is being prepared. I believe some of your original research should be included. We can discuss that at a later time. Also, a revised edition with many of those errors you mention already corrected was released in the Spring of this year. I wonder what version of the book you have... As for your questions: I believe you are asking for rational responses to explain the existence of facts. I have no explanation for why gravity exists, or why there are 8 planets (discounting Pluto). Likewise, any explanation I can have for why there are 26 letters will be a fiction, so I can not satisfactorily explain how any letter gets its values. The fact that a letter has a value, the fact that *Gematria* works, the fact that *Qabalah* is, and the *Aethyrs* are fixed, defies all rational presumption and any reasonable explanation to begin with. As such, attempting to explain these things in the marketplace is to incite stoning. These things are. There is no "Because". However, I will try and provide responses to your questions wherever possible. I will begin with the simpler ones first.

--How L got its values of 50 & 70? How did O (=200) get its other value of 80?

L's values change formulaicly - pre and post the 2nd *Aethyr*. O refers to different phases Post and Pre the 10th *Aethyr*. I have no rational explanation for this. However, the evidence is "evident".

--Why is R listed in Table III as having the values 9 & 400? Does this mean that R has double values?

R is linked to X in the Key and certain Places as you know. However, r should not have been ascribed the value of X, only x.

--What are the equations for the circle squared in its failure & its success?

The equation is in fact the entire passage from Liber AL:

4638 ABKZ 4 aL "O=" MR3YX + (24) (89) RPSTOVAL[3]

This apparently nonsensical sequence of glyphs is the most astounding Scientific Discovery we are likely to have for another Aeon. It contains the totality of Truth in the simplest Form imaginable. It holds the entirety of the Key, and all Keys preceding it. (As you know it is a simple surjective mapping of this sequence to the Roman Script glyphs that maps the Key). It contains also the Whole Path and the formulaic pivots in the *Aethyrs* when you take the glyphs in their appropriate manifestations. The Pivots

3 *LHS* = 4 6 3 8 ABKZ 4 aL "O="
RHS = MR3YX + (24) (89) RPSTOVAL
Note LHS = RHS as we will show later: *4638 ABKZ 4 aL "O="* = 4818 = 2 *2399 (a prime) = *MR3YX + (24) (89) RPSTOVAL*

are S, T, L, O, C, W, X In this way, your question on equality is a complex one, for they will hold on all Planes. For instance, immediately after the O (the circle) is formulated we have: MR3YX = 131 when Y is vowel = ST – the first step – after this All is Open. Afterwards, MR3YX is 67 when Y is consonant which is equal to the first terms of the sequence on the other side of the equation: 4638 ABKZ (taken individually: 4+6+3+8+4+6+30+6) And that similarly, if we take the character preceding and succeeding in the sequence, (The Envelope), we have: "O= MR3YX +" = 220 with Y vowel and = 156 with Y consonant. (Two formulae we know well). (the '+' glyph here taken for Cross, that is lower x) Also making O full, and X active (400) should yield the formula / value for the Scarlet Woman. (667).

(These differing values are for vowel/consonant – however their "Force" is refracted when passing through the Supernals – a different terminology should be used here. Thus formulaicly, it is 220 before, and 156 after, though Y in the Word may not have changed its syllabic status. Materially, however, the rule will hold: but again refracted according to the Position of that Eye. In this Way, for the purposes of disseminating the Key, it is perhaps best not to mention the distinction but only offer both possibilities, allowing each to decide for One-self. Thus the hard categorization of vowel and consonant is perhaps not desirable.)

The circle squared in its failure & its success is a mystery connected with G glyph – and applies to your dividing the sequence in half with that Glyph you denote by "O=". A further hint: This G glyph is composed of a C and two horizontal bars (like an equality / equation), that enter, cross themselves, and are embraced (or swallowed you might say) by the C glyph behind it becoming the O. The point is that the cross props up the circle and in this way the circle squared becomes the Wheel, i.e. Motion is stirred in the MT and the Pyramid dissolves. *3 Wheels make the Body of the Child. 3 Wheels, 5 wounds, 7 points of light.* Your question about the circle squared is thus a loaded one. This deals with That practical operation that guides and propels Evolution. Then you show the string, dividing it into halves through an equality sign that is there and NOT there. Yet here are the Perfections, for like Schrodinger showed, if it is Possible, it IS, and so the Truth must hold equally in both possible worlds, for, Seeing as the Sequence is Truth, the equality you seek thus Operates at All levels or Planes, and from All Angles of the Tablet. Converting to Number to provide an example:

4638 ABKZ + aL "O =" we convert to 4638 4 6 30 6 + 4 70 80 (She is not full- the bars stand Without her Womb) and the Bar which I or 4.

So on one side of the "Equation" we have 4638 + 4 + 6 + 30 + 6 + 4 + 70 + 80 + 4 = 4842 = MR3YX + (24) (89) RPSTOVAL

MR3YX + (24) (89) RPSTOVAL we convert to 131 (the ST is formulated) + 4116 (hence S and T final, (x) (y) implies multiplication) + 477 (and now the O is full).

NOTE:

MR3YX = 40 + 9 + 3 + 70 + 9 = 131 & MR3YX = 40 + 9 + 3 + 6 + 300 = 358 * MR3YX = 40 + 9 + 3 + 6 + 9 = 67

(24) (89) = 2136 & (42)(98) = 4116

RPSTOVAL = 9 + 3 + 113 + 200 + 80 + 4 + 50 = 459 & RPSTOVAL = 9 + 3 + 113 + 80 + 80 + 4 + 70 = 339

On the other side Union is accomplished and O is full: O = 200

"O =" MR3YX + (24) (89) RPSTOVAL = 200 + 67 + 4116 + 459 = 4842.

Hence, the equation is fulfilled. And yet there are others. I have seen the equation hold at 4818 as well I believe with the O taking in the bar being interpreted as a process of G. (' +', '=' and '()' are the only three true mathematical operands in this equation). As regards it success and failure. A further hint is concealed in the word "circle" in the line "then this circle squared in its failure is a key also' (Liber AL 3, 47): success lies in hardening the C: with c soft we have circle = 70; with hard c: 97. Note that in a different phase, (O full) we have the LHS = 4918, while "O=" MR3YX + (24) (89) RPSTOVAL = 4920 (which is 70 x 70 + Union "G" which conceals the Operation (note the G is the C accepting the bar, the sword in the cup, etc) or the first glyph "O =" in its initial operatory stage. The LHS lacks an 'f'. Where has it gone? It is concealed in 4638 ABKZ (4, 6, 30, 6; 4636) All this has been for the "0=" glyph at the stage that the "0=" glyph has become O (in either phase) but before so, it is a C (in both phases) and afterward a G. So, you can work out the equations for C hard passing to C soft as well. Similarly, you will get the varying equalities (and / or Reflections) depending on which side of that pivot *Aethyr* you are ON. Brevity and want of Interest precludes Us from further commentary on these Matters. The phrase "*its failure & its success*" also has the stench of a formula. Regards,

August 7, 2010 2:35 PM

G : I didn't mean for my questions to become overly complex, but thanks a lot for the effort. I just wanted you to point out to me the simplicity of it all & this would have been enough. By simplicity I mean the way you lined up the alphabet alongside the enigmatic string of symbols. L you have explained as much as you could in this place, but there is an AL terminating this string without any letter lining up with them after the letter Z in the 27th & 28th position which is left blank on page 26. I currently have the 2008 edition; I was not aware of any other until now. If you cannot go into this I will move on. On page 60 you have plainly written out that when W is Activated: "AIWAZ is 4 + 4 + 400 + 4 + 6 = 418 (HAD x 22)" "AIWASS is 4 + 4 + 400 + 4 + 42 + 42 = 496 (=Σ31)" Yet in your *Gematria* comment you have plainly written out that when X is Activated: L.U.X. is 50 + 200 + 400 = 650 & that "X is the old Aeon Tau, so 400, not Shin, 300. The Cross is not the Spirit (300), it is the Material (400). " So why does the activated W in AIWASS is counted as 400? Thanks to your comment I am now able to plainly see that W has the value of Samekh & Shin upon examination of the placement of the S in Table II on page 26 where it appears without this notification in parentheses. Yet in one place W is 400 & in another X is 400. Actually the most consistent clerical error to be found throughout your book, especially if you check the LEX I KON, is that W always = 400 when activated. So that I am perfectly clear on this, if W is 400 for the sake of formulae when & how is it? Because it does not line up quite in that way. If I must go on without an explanation then I would have to assume that AIWAZ = 318 & not 418 which I find somewhat unacceptable. Thank you for your Understanding.

August 7, 2010 4:26 PM

E. : Hello G, Sorry for the Silence and thank you once again, very kindly, for your questions and concerns which shed light on what is salient and important in these matters. The Great Work , 777 : The 106, Great 132, Work 539 (with the W in X) = 777. But here all the Ts are final - with T's non-final, and the W and X pivoted (W 400), we have: The 97 Great 123 : The Great = 220 ("The Law") Now Work: 519 (with with O crescent: 400+80+9+30) so that we have 739 or 519 and 220. When O becomes Full and w inactive, we have Work = 60+200+9+30 = 299 - which with 220 is again 519. So that at this phase, The Great Work which equals 519 is simply Work (or work and The Law). In this Way, "The Great Work" = 220 + "The Great Work" while in the 739, while the 519 = The Great Work contains in itself another 220 + work (299 = 60+200+9+30). The formula is self-referential, with 220 always left over. With O horned, it is 417 which with the 1 (AMT) becomes 418 as "The Law" with the 1 is its formula. As you Know, Aiwaz is without question 418 and the first step in The Great Work is without question the tuning of the three wheels to the 7th sphere - Victory & Love (777). You'll see IT manifest again and again. That His Arms should fall, that W should be 300 and X 400, is my own War. (X is \/ sitting atop /\) Note the process: \/ --> \../ --> /\ --> /\ --> \./\./ --> \/\/ : the Double 'U' , that is the Two Cups.) and that IT is NOT Sight (W) that gives Birth to the Universe (X), but the Materialization of the *Cube* (X) that makes Manifest the Universe (W) is again War. In the Great Work, all Aeons are passed and revolved into 1. (CON'T BELOW)

August 16, 2010 11:35 AM

E. : (CON'T from ABOVE) I know of others who are interested in your Work on the *Cube*. I watch with Wonder. As you can see, the Key is in flux, which I believe describes the dynamic / relativistic Nature of The Law (220) as well as the reactive Nature of the Play of Forces. Others are doubtful that this is Not so at All, but only a middle Step and that your *Cube* is the materialization of the Key. Where they see a *Cube*, I see a Prism that refracts the Light into Three Rays. Note, what was written earlier about operating under Osirian configurations and old Aeon Keys: how Sight (W) engenders or leads to the X - an essentially pessimistic view and the Lie of Religion. The Law affirms the Joy and Rapture of the Hosts: that the X opens into the W. Yet from Here, the W sits before the X. In Time, the 3rd sphere, BINH, the Conquering Goddess, the ringed/crowned planet and Old Man Saturn : One is Immortal and then Dies. One must die to be immortal. Yet the Immortality of the Babe precedes the Death of the M T - a Contradiction whether looked at from Above or from Below, yet Harmonized on the Horizon where the two meet. Illogical though our perceptions or cognitions may be, there are literal facts and evidence corroborated by others. All this talk of death and immortality for instance, and W and X, and BINH and Saturn may ring pleasantly, may even ring True - but what does it mean? What do we know? Physically the B A will not age, and cannot suffer decay or disease. He may remain there eleven years and burn in Hell, until he is molten and purified. After eleven No One is extracted One Way or another. Upon moving forward, He, the Queen takes on the cloak of Old Man Time, and those eleven years descend upon the M T like a Veil in a moment. Even this No Man (NEMO) that moves forward : He/She is a contradiction, one hand like a song that touches, and the other a cataract to Hell, one side of him fire the other side of her Ice, All of Darkness and All of Light and the Whole of the Universe married in one Spark, which he Contains before becoming A M T and equilibrating the 3 Wheels and becoming One to again Become Nothing, because he is Everything, before becoming One, which is another Nothing - another Nothing because it Contains all the Worlds preceding it which we've established to be a series of Nothings. Nothing upon nothing upon nothing, each of them sparks and worlds. Each human (man and woman) a Star. Each Star: a World and a System. I am Glad that you find AIWAZ 318 unacceptable. Your words (if you listen to yourself) Signal that you Know IT. That then is a Stone that you should have no Question of, regardless of what Fools might Say. Star & System. Are you able to send over graphical representations the cube (2 dimensional would do fine)? thanks, in Love

August 16, 2010 11:40 AM

G : What is M T & A M T? Abbreviations for what? & the BA I am assuming is the Egyptian name of the astral self or something of that nature. I am willing to send what I can, but you must relate to me how or in what way you want it sent & the information I would need to send it. My suggestion would be a file by email or I could give you detailed instructions of how my *Cube* is drawn, much less of a puzzle than my last instructions, if you prefer. My time is becoming less & less by the minute. I will respond at my earliest convenience. Thank you

August 17, 2010 11:51 AM

E. : BA - Babe of the Abyss (between the 4th and the 3rd spheres) MT - in the 3rd sphere (the 440) AMT - in the 2nd sphere (the 441) W = Double U = 2 x U = 2 x 200

Book 5

Class A-B Document

Delivered by LLLLL, Feb 7, 2011

000. Triple is the Fire.

00. Three-tongued is the Word.

0. Thou Knowest Not what is To Come.

1. Thou carest Not for What is, Was, shall be.

2. It worketh in Thee, through Thee. It Divideth Thee, for Love's sake so that mine Fire hath what to Burn.

3. I am the Hawk-Headed Lord of Silence. He who flieth through the Waters and swimmeth in the Air.

4. Where I am, is neither Vision nor Voice. For the music that confoundeth thine Ear, and the Brilliance that dazzleth the Eye.

5. Thou who art all Sight and Fire, who art like the Dew on the Flame, art Blind and Dumb to the apes of mine little brother Thoth, for thine Eye is trained on the wonder Asit on the Horizon.

6. My wings I've sewn of the veils of modest women, from the garlands of Queens and the heel of Babalon. The Ash that is your Soul prepared for the day of MAAT, is taken up in the Gust of mine flight.

7. Heed not! Hail not! Hark not! Stop not!

8. I am the serpent coiled about the heart of Babalon and the mitre of the Horn on Baphomet's head.

9. And I am their child, and the Father of that Child, and the Father of that light in the Child's Eye.

10. The Children of Men cannot fathom thy Tongue.

11. The Word is Secret & Not. If Thou canst Not see IT, It is because Thou Art within IT.

12. It cometh first in Six, then in 5, finally in Four.

13. When it is Three it is One and it reverberateth Not.

14. There is a Reward O Man! A Garden Golden, a ram's horns and a Lamb's head arched in Love over the Door.

15. This Door I've made Open for the Promise and the Sake and the Word that liveth Eternal.

16. Make easy the Way for my Chosen Ones. There is War. There is the Island.

17. When I am come to Earth, I am a black stone. Thou shalt know Me by my name, fivefold like the Star that is made of Her Body. Know me and do me Worship, for I am the Child who leapeth from the Womb of Nuit, thrice-armed and Innocent.

18. This Promise is my Covenant, Stone and Heart, the Vault of mine Soul, for the littlest drop thou pourest out to Me, for even the dew on the Flower, if IT be done in my Name, then Thou shalt Know me for a Season and a Season even if Thou knowest Not.

19. And if in the Cities, in the Night, amongst the multitude, thou Speakest my name even if in Secret, then the Banquet shall be Thine and the nuptial Bed laid out though thou shakest at sound of the Flute thereof.

20. Trust not. Yield not. Test me. In the Perfections I delight. Because is Not where I am.

21. I am the Word that turneth within thee like a Wheel.

22. There is Division where I am Not.

{23.

0. Behold! I leap bare-armed from the Egg of Blue.

00. And my laughter is the quaking of Earth.

000. All is Play! All is Joy! Love & war. To me! To me!}

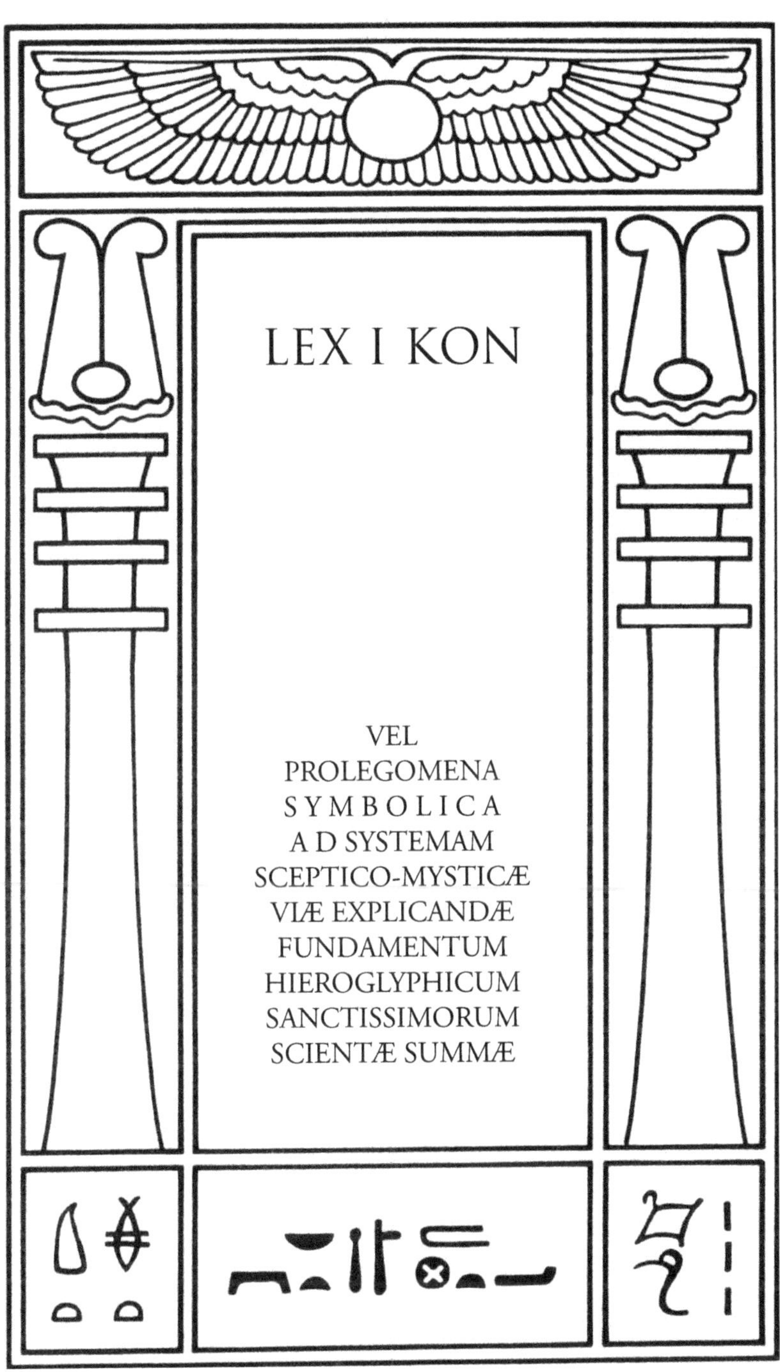
LEX I KON
VEL
PROLEGOMENA
SYMBOLICA
A D SYSTEMAM
SCEPTICO-MYSTICÆ
VIÆ EXPLICANDÆ
FUNDAMENTUM
HIEROGLYPHICUM
SANCTISSIMORUM
SCIENTÆ SUMMÆ

LEXICON

This numerical lexicon presents a list of English expressions in order of increasing numerical value. Words with possible final or initial values have been included. Formulae are presented in all their operational variants (final values, L's averse and upright). The Lexicon provides an exhaustive list of English formulae and phrases taken from Class A Documents from various Traditions.

Every effort was made to verify the accuracy of the entries. In matters of critical importance, the Student should verify the summations, paying special attention to matters discussed under the section "The Living Key".

We present the numerical dictionary below. Some annotations follow:

Nf – denotes N final value used.
Sf – denotes S final value used.
Tf – denotes T final value used.
k - denotes hard c
ŏ - denotes soft o
W - denotes activated W (W initial)
n! – denotes the factorial of *n*
∑n – we use to denote the summation of the integers from 1 to n.
∏ - denotes a prime number

	1			
		e,E		
		J		
Π 2!	**2**			
		f		
Π Σ2	**3**			
		C		
		P		
	4		2^2	
		A		
		I		
		Pé		
Σ3 3!	**6**		*2×3*	
		Af		
		B		
		N		*Nf*
		Z		
Π	**7**			
		Be		
		H		
		Pa		
	8		$2\times4 = 2^3$	
		A.·.A.·.		
		Ape		
		Bee		
		D		
		Hé		
	9		3^2	
		r,R		
		x		
Σ4	**10**		*2×5*	
		Face		
		Pen		*Nf*
		Q		
Π	**11**			
		APEP		
		Ha		
	12		*2×6 = 3×4*	
		Peace		
Π	**13**			
		Deep		
		Dei		
		Die		
		PAN		*Nf*
		PAZ *(the cry of the 4th Aethyr)*		
		RA		
		Zen		*Nf*
		ZIP *(the cry of the 9th Aethyr)*		
	14		*2×7*	
		Ear		
		ZAA *(the cry of the 27th Aethyr)*		
Σ5	**15**		*3×5*	
		Aha!		
		Bed		
		Fade		
		Far		
	16		$2\times8 = 4^2 = 2^4$	
		Eden		*Nf*
		Fear		
		Fire		
Π	**17**			
		Air		
		Apex		
		Babe		
		Bean		*Nf*
		Chief		
		Pain		*Nf*
		Rice		

RII *(the cry of the 29th Aethyr)*

18 *2×9 = 3×6*

Bad
Deed
Din *Nf*
Faced
Here
Peach
Red
ZID *(the cry of the 8th Aethyr)*

Π **19**

ARN *(the cry of the 2nd Aethyr)* *Nf*
Bar
Fair
HAD
ZAX *(the cry of the 10th Aethyr)*

20 *2×10 = 4×5*

Add
Bare
Bear
Circe
Deepen *Nf*
Facere
Fierce
G
Head
PAAR
Zain *Nf*

Σ6 **21** *3×7*

Dead
Hera
Pierce
Rhea

22 *2×11*

A Deed
Acacia
AHIH

Π **23**

Abide
Arab
Exceed
Herb
Rain *Nf*
Rich

4! **24** *2×12 = 3×8 = 4×6*

Appear
Chain *Nf*
Fixed
Ga
Hair
IAIDA
Jihad

25 *5^2*

Cedar
Pride

26 *2×13*

See

27 *3×9 = 3^3*

Bird

Σ7 **28** *2×14 = 4×7*

Beard
Bread
Bride
Hard

Π **29**

Headed
Heard
Pierced
Sea

30 *2×15 = 3×10 = 5×6*

BAG *(the cry of the 28th Aethyr)*
Big
K

Π **31**

ASP *(the cry of the 21st Aethyr)*
Precipice
Seb

32 *2×16 = 4×8 = 2^5*

Arched
Gaia
ISA

33 *3×11*

Archer
Cease
Gedi

34 *2×17*

Hidden *Nf*
Ka
Radix
Sin *Nf*

35 *5×7*

Ash
Barren *Nf*
Rabbin *Nf*
Seer
Space
Spice

Σ8 **36** *2×18 = 3×12 = 4×9 = 6^2*

Aegean *Nf*
Seere

Π **37**

Fish
Grace
Green *Nf*
Six

38 *2×19*

Aspen *Nf*
Gizeh
Harder!
High
Keen *Nf*
Rise

39 *3×13*

Preparer
Shape
Speech

40 *2×20 = 4×10 = 5×8*

Can *Nf, k*
Kin *Nf*
M
Shed
Spade

Π **41**

ASAR
Egg
IKH *(the cry of the 11th Aethyr)*
Resh
Shin *Nf*
Spare
Spear

42 *2×21 = 3×14 = 6×7*

Ache *k*
Arise!
Grade
Jasper
Raise
S_f *Sf*

Π **43**

Ark
Beseech
Fresh

44 *2×22 = 4×11*

Am
Cain *Nf, k*
Chesed
Kaph

Σ9 **45** *3×15 = 5×9*

Caesar
His Face
Praise
Sphere

46 *2×23*

I Ache *k*
KHR *(the cry of the 20th Aethyr)*
RHK

Π **47**

Abased
Desire
Men *Nf*
Sharp

48 *2×24 = 3×16 = 4×12 =6×8*

Aim
Arisen *Nf*
Garden *Nf*
I Am
Kaaba

49 *7^2*

BES *Sf*
Crab *k*
Spider

50 *2×25 = 5×10*

L
Man *Nf*
MAZ *(the cry of the 6th Aethyr)*
Scarab
ZIM*(the cry of the 13th Aethyr)*
Decay *k, y*

51 *3×17*

Amen! *Nf*
Dark
DES (the cry of the 26th Aethyr)
Harsh
Hemp

52 *2×26 = 4×13*

Mad

Π **53**

APIS *Sf*
Ram

54 *2×27 = 3×18 = 6×9*

A Man *Nf*
AL
Pieces *Sf*
Sign *Nf*

Σ10 **55** *5×11*

Desired
LEA *(the cry of the 16th Aethyr)*
Lie
Sapphire

56 *2×28 = 4×14 = 7×8*

ADAM
Ares *Sf*
Ceres *Sf*
Ibis *Sf*
ISIS
Jahim
Seek

57 *3×19*

A Ram
AMRI
Beds *Sf*
Life

58 *2×29*

Carapace *k*
Damn *Nf*
Fires *Sf*
Fleece
Pale

Π **59**

Frigga
Iris *Sf*

Pisces
Sake
Shaddai

60 *2×30 = 3×20 = 4×15 =5×12 = 6×10*

Aires *Sf*
Amber
Aries *Sf*
BAL (*the sword)*
Beggar
w

Π **61**

Are Abased
ABEL
Apple
Bael
Help
KHEPH-RA
Made He
Place

62 *2×31*

Dagger
Dream
HADES *Sf*
Heads *Sf*
Jew
Mixed
SEBEK
Speak
Zazas *Sf*

63 *3×21 = 7×9*

Deal
Deli
Few
Half

64 *2×32 = 4×16 = 8^2 =4^3 = 2^6*

Axle
Rides *Sf*
Skin *Nf*

65 *5×13*

ABRAHADABRA
Aleph
Arabs *Sf*
Field
Hail!
Palace
Spica *k*

Σ11 **66** *2×33 = 3×22 = 6×11*

Breezes *Sf*
Disk
Laid
Sea-Green *Nf*

Π **67**

Ages *Sf*
Assiah
Blaze
Pearl
Web
Wife

68 *2×34 = 4×17*

Alpha
Chapel
Hazel

69 *3×23*

Blade
Dew
Image

70 *2×35 = 5×14 = 7×10*

Back *k*
Brahma
Chamber
Decarabia *k*
Learn *Nf*
Liber
Redeemer

Spark
Y

Π **71**

72 *2×36 = 3×24 = 4×18 =6×12 = 8×9*

Alder
Child
Eye
Healer
Magpie

Π **73**

Leader
Libra
War
Wide

74 *2×37*

Apparel
Defiled
His Speech
Isis *Sf*
Scribe *k*
Shark
Wear

75 *3×25 = 5×15*

Aye!
Giel
He is Speech

76 *2×38 = 4×19*

Dagim
Eagle
Flag
Sacred *k*
Shame

77 *7×11*

Elixir
Fence
Fine
His Grade
PAN
Pisces *Sf*
Scarab *k*
Self
Spaces *Sf*
Spices *Sf*
YH

Σ12 **78** *2×39 = 3×26 = 6×13*

AIWAZ
Khem
NIA *(the cry of the 24th Aethyr)*

Π **79**

Agiel
End
Isle
Kamea
Lidded
Majic *k*
Seal
Sides *Sf*
Sleep

80 *2×40 = 4×20 = 5×16 =8×10*

Agares *Sf*
Bay
O *ŏ*
Piscis *Sf*
Ships *Sf*
V
Zasas *Sf*

81 *3×27 = 9^2 = 3^4*

Bane
Beware!
Mem
NECH
Regimen *Nf*
Sacrifice *k*

82 *2×41*

Day
Eve
Glad

Π **83**

Girl
Mark
NEFER
Please
Prey
Spears *Sf*

84 *2×42 = 3×28 = 4×21 =6×14 = 7×12*

Ayin *Nf*
Find
Flesh
Grades *Sf*
Hebrew
Large
Maker
Near
Off *ŏ*

85 *5×17*

Bedchamber
Bend
Kael
Like
Magician *Nf*
Palace *L*

86 *2×43*

ADNI
Cries *Sf, k*
Dance
Faery
Fiery
Freya
Ghebers *Sf*
Hagiel
Leash
ON *Nf, ŏ*
Parabrahm
Pasiel
POP (*The Cry of the 19th Aethyr*) *ŏ*

87 *3×29*

DANAE
Drawn *Nf*
Five
GRAAL
Spheres *Sf*

88 *2×44 = 4×22 = 8×11*

Ass *SSf*
Bind
Chance
Children *Nf*
Ended
Even *Nf*
He is Mad
KALI
Maim
Saw
Vice

Π **89**

Be Glad
Hand
Khabs *Sf*
Ox *ŏ*
T *Tf*
Wise

90 *2×45 = 3×30 = 5×18 =6×15 = 9×10*

Are Sacred *k*
DIANA
Prana
Prince
Zayin *Nf*

Σ13 **91** *7×13*

Aeon *Nf, ŏ*

Binah
Elm
Ever
Freyr
Glacier
Marriage
Pass *SSf*
Reward

92 *2×46 = 4×23*

Aldebaran *Nf*
Girdle
Indeed
Jackal
Ready
ZON *(the cry of the 3rd Aethyr)* *Nf, ŏ*

93 *3×31*

Beams *Sf*
COPH *ŏ*
Deva
Feet *Tf*
Fever
Girders *Sf*
IT *Tf*
Melee
Vir

94 *2×47*

Eat *Tf*
Friend
Hexagram
Swan *Nf*

95 *5×19*

Arms *Sf*
Fit *Tf*
Hod *ŏ*
Indra
Lime
Mars *Sf*
Meal
Prop *ŏ*
Ram's *Sf*

96 *2×48 = 3×32 = 4×24 =6×16 = 8×12*

I Am Arisen *Nf*
Indian *Nf*
Madim
Pit *Tf*

Π **97**

Circle *k*
Flame
Lamp
Lies *Sf*
Palm
Pang
Rod *ŏ*
Vepar
Viper

98 *2×49 = 7×14*

AGNI
Deceive
Graphiel
Imal
Mask
Say

99 *3×33 = 9×11*

Awake
Bat *Tf*
FIAT *Tf*
Heaven *Nf*

100 *2×50 = 4×25 = 5×20 = 10^2*

Armies *Sf*
Beat *Tf*
Grey
HERMES *Sf*
Lamb
Madimi

Qoph ŏ
Raven *Nf*

Π **101**

A Lamp
Being
Difference
Hammer
Hawk
Key
Kiblah
Lamen *Nf*
Magick
Nigh
Skies *Sf*

102 *2×51 = 3×34 = 6×17*

Art[1] *Tf*
Fog ŏ
Malice
Sigil

Π **103**

Chit *Tf*
Ixion *Nf*, ŏ
Lamed
Lapis *Sf*
Places *Sf*
Radiance
Ring
River
Send

104 *2×52 = 4×26 = 8×13*

All
Hybrid
Ill
Jews *Sf*
LIL *(the cry of the 1st Aethyr)*
Messiah
Shemesh

Σ14 **105** *3×35 = 5×21 = 7×15*

Adept *Tf*
ALHIM
Chandra
Change
Divide
Flamed
Give
I Am Life
Marbas *Sf*
Nike
Parasa-Rama
Qabalah *L*
Ten *Nf*

106 *2×53*

Fall
Fill
Ghagiel
Lares *Sf*
Samekh
Sand

Π **107**

Cakes *Sf, k*
Desirable
Farmer's *Sf*
Fields *Sf*
Palaces *Sf*
Pall
Thee

108 *2×54 = 3×36 = 4×27 =6×18 = 9×12*

Censer
Disks *Sf*
Dog ŏ
Hell
NECH *k*
Scream *k*
TAN (*the cry of the 17th Aethyr)* *Nf*

	Falsifier		F
	Tin		Nf
Π **109**			
	Leraikha		
	Lesser		
	Pearls		Sf
	Save		
	Scale		k
	Tree		
110		*2×55 = 5×22 = 10×11*	
	Cereals		Sf
	Gemmêd		
	Hanged		
	Heart		Tf
	Marble		
	Primal		
111		*3×37*	
	ANKH		
	ART		
	Given		Nf
	Hill		
	Middle		
	Qedemel		
	Shdi Al Chi		
	Tied		
112		*2×56 = 4×28 = 7×16 =8×14*	
	Beth		
	Danger		
	HADIT		Tf
	Path		
	Presence		
	PTAH		
	Ringed		
	Rite		
	Seven		Nf
	Sparks		Sf
	Tear		
Π **113**			
	Ateph		
	Divided		
	Eater		
	Emerald		
	Fallen		Nf
	Fifth		
	Hiding		
	Melee		L
	Naked		
	Pleiades		Sf
	Teach		
	Warm		
114		*2×57 = 3×38 = 6×19*	
	AMN		
	Amy		
	Blessêd		
	Crane		k
	Eyes		Sf
	Giver		
	Grave		
	LAW		
	SET		Tf
	Soph		ŏ
115		*5×23*	
	ALLAH		
	Amen		
	Banish		
	Bath		
	Belial		
	faith		
	GBVR		
	Gimel		
	Gleam		
	Hearing		
	Mane		
	Name		

Riding
Serve
Shrine

116 *2×58 = 4×29*

Abaddon *Nf, ŏ*
Cheth
I, HADIT *Tf*
Severe
There
Three

117 *3×39 = 9×13*

A Fifth
Cancer *k*
Depth
Halphas *Sf*
Sat *Tf*
Sit *Tf*
Sphinx

118 *2×59*

Aretz
Death
Eagles *Sf*
Kiss *SSf*
Seat *Tf*
Yama

119 *7×17*

Averse
Earth
Pallid
PHTAH
Shiva
Slime

Σ15, 5! **120** *2×60 = 3×40 = 4×30 =5×24 = 6×20 = 8×15 = 10×12*

AIWASS
COPH *k, ŏ*
Pillar
Sense
Thebai
Black *k*

121 *11^2*

Daath
Drink
Eight *Tf*
Emery
Father
HADIT

122 *2×61*

Carry *k*
Feather
Fight *Tf*
Fly
Girt *Tf*
Headdress *SSf*
Islam
Mind
Theban *Nf*
Thrice

123 *3×41*

Faith *F*
Army
Gate
Great *Tf*
Inspired
MARY
Mercy
SAMAEL
SET
Triad
Virgin *Nf*

124 *2×62 = 4×31*

Abramelin *Nf*
Balam *L*
Birth

Days *Sf*
Essence
Heathen *Nf*
Hymen *Nf*
Inspirer
King
Milk
Sky
Tzedeq
Vim

125 $5 \times 25 = 5^3$

Ayel
Bathin *Nf*
Berith
Breath
Camel *k*
Certain *Nf*
Deifieth
Girls *Sf*
Kisses *Sf*
Line
Marks *Sf*
Nile
Rays *Sf*

126 $2 \times 63 = 3 \times 42 = 6 \times 21 = 7 \times 18 = 9 \times 14$

Arise! Arise! Arise!
Beareth
Breathe
Copper *k, ŏ*
Eat Rich
Hither
Therein *Nf*
Vis *Sf*
Years *Sf*

Π **127**

Agate
Bends *Sf*
Palaces *Sf, L*
PASHT *Tf*
Play
Rich Headdress *Sf*

128 $2 \times 64 = 4 \times 32 = 8 \times 16 = 2^7$

Abideth
HADITH
Himself
Lance
Magick *k*
Nail
Plane
Shaddai El Chai
Sink
Spell
Tzaddi

129 3×43

Right *Tf*
Snake

130 $2 \times 65 = 5 \times 26 = 10 \times 13$

An Ibis *Sf*
Chains *Sf*
Chit *Tf, k*
Erect *Tf, k*
Flashes *Sf*
Ganesha
Hail! Hail
Hawk-Headed
Hismael
I Am HERMES
The Fire *F*

Π **131**

Cybele
Damned
Doric *k, ŏ*
Hands *Sf*
Meet *Tf*

	New		
	ST		
132		*2×66 = 3×44 = 4×33 =6×22 = 11×12*	
	ARARITA		
	Desert		*Tf*
	He is He, He is He, He is He		
	Hereafter		
	Lady		
	Land		
	Pincers		*Sf*
	Princes		*Sf*
	Tiger		
	Yahel		
133		*7×19*	
	A Snake		
	Kimaris		*Sf*
	Qadosh		*ŏ*
	Red Gleam		
	Reserved		
	Spirit		*Tf*
	Take		
	Yield		
134		*2×67*	
	Breathed		
	Craft		*Tf, k*
	Damiana		
	Eyelid		
	Girdles		*Sf*
	Kill		
	Medicina		
	My Hair		
135		*3×45 = 5×27 = 9×15*	
	Arising		
	Bright		*Tf*
	Demon		*ŏ, Nf*
	Evil		
	Live		
	Malkah		
	Masses		*Sf*
	Myrrh		
	Perfect		*Tf, k*
	Psyche		*k*
	Shall		
	Step		*ST*
	Veil		
Σ16 **136**		*2×68 = 4×34 = 8×17*	
	Beryl		
	East		*ST, Tf*
	KRAAT		*Tf*
	Rekht		*Tf*
	SATAN		*Nf*
	Thigh		
Π **137**			
	Black Bean		*Nf, k*
	MAAT		*Tf*
138		*2×69 = 3×46 = 6×23*	
	Away		
	Blind		
	Eighteen		*Nf*
	Empress		*SSf*
	Fangs		*Sf*
	My Bride		
	Past		*ST, Tf*
	Pyramid		
	Secrecy		*k*
Π **139**			
	Climbed		*k*
	Flames		*Sf*
	Gather		
	Gemini		
	Linden		*Nf*
	Sickle		*k*
	Sitri		
	Spectre		

	Staff		ST
	Taken		Nf
140		2×70 = 4×35 = 5×28 =7×20 = 10×14	
	Iceland		
	Ineffable		
141		3×47	
	HEKATE		
	Lever		
	Rest		ST,Tf
	The Seer		
142		2×71	
	Beast		ST,Tf
	Greater		
	IADNAMAD		
	Left		Tf
	Limbs		Sf
	Sixth		
143		11×13	
	APOPHIS		Sf, ŏ
	Circle is Red		k
	Devil		
	Exempt		Tf
	Hawk's		Sf
	Increase		k
	LIT *(The Cry of the 5th Aethyr)*		Tf
	Mate		
	OMPEHDA		ŏ
	Pagans		Sf
	Time		
	Vesica		k
144		2×72 = 3×48 = 4×36 =6×24 = 8×18 = 9×16 = 12^2	
	Bliss		SSf
	Ecclesia		kk
	Jasmine		
	Knees		Sf
	Sight		Tf
	Star		ST
	Veilêd		
145		5×29	
	Angel		
	Assyrian		Nf
	Great Deep		
	Hawk's Head		
	Lift		Tf
	Nine		
	Philadelphia		
	Reveal		
	Rivers		Sf
146		2×73	
	AMRIT		Tf
	Basilisk		
	First		ST,Tf
	Hybrids		Sf
	Kether		
	Mati		
	Tejas		Sf
	Them		
	Weave		
147		3×49 = 7×21	
	Adramelek		
	Fates		Sf
	Feasted		ST
	I Am Heaven		Nf
	The Spear		
	Tips		Sf
148		2×74 = 4×37	
	Aires Fall		
	Cteis		Sf
	Hardly		
	I Am Hermes		Sf
	Krishna		
	Phallic		k
	Priest		ST,Tf

Qesheth
Sciences *Sf*

Π **149**

Beatific *k*
Blanched
Captain *Nf, k*
Dagger Drawn *Nf*
Fire *Qadosh* *ŏ*
Passing
Poplar *ŏ*
Ram's Eye
Rock *k, ŏ*
Sabbath
The Ark

150 *2×75 = 3×50 = 5×30 =6×25 = 10×15*

Crayfish *k*
Dogs *Sf, ŏ*
Hell's *Sf*
Hermit *Tf*
Indicible
Malphas *Sf*

Π **151**

Aspect *Tf, k*
Breast *ST, Tf*
Expected *k*
Fine Apparel
Peacock *k, ŏ*
Trees *Sf*
Viridis *Sf*

152 *2×76 = 4×38 = 8×19*

Atman *Nf*
Cities *Sf*
Damned & Dead!
KRAATH
Leaping
Magical *k*
Merti
Mitre
Penance
Sekhet *Tf*
Sieves *Sf*

Σ17 **153** *3×51 = 9×17*

End His Speech
Hills *Sf*
Hissing
Men's *Sf*
Penned
Rashith
Silence

154 *2×77 = 7×22 = 11×14*

Basket *Tf*
Eremite
Gardens *Sf*
Inner
Ivy
Paths *Sf*
Revealed
Sabians *Sf*
Secret *Tf, k*
Shachath
Sol *ŏ*

155 *5×31*

ASI and ASAR
Decans *Sf, k*
Jewels *Sf*
Revealer
Thebes *Sf*
Vine

156 *2×78 = 3×52 = 4×39 =6×26 = 12×13*

Adepts *Sf*
AIWASS *SSf*
BABALON *Nf, ŏ*
Healing
KAOS *Sf, ŏ*

Micael *k*
PAAR KRAAT *Tf*
Tail
Task
The Man *Nf*

Π **157**

Beetle
His Captain *Nf*
It Dies *Sf*
Means *Sf*
Names *Sf*
Shrines *Sf*

158 *2×79*

Balance *L*
Deities *Sf*
Demeter
Frenzy
Glass *SSf*
His Mercy
Mirth
Slayer
Yod *ŏ*

159 *3×53*

Eleven *Nf, L*
He is Great *Tf*
Lakshmi
PA KRAATH
Poppy *ŏ*
Slave
Table
The Ram
Wayfarer

160 *2×80 = 4×40 = 5×32 =8×20 = 10×16*

Ananda
Bahimiron *Nf, ŏ*
Banner
Banyan *Nf*
Island
Lithe
Might *Tf*
Sakti
Sandal
Signs *Sf*
Space Marks *Sf*
Theli

161 *7×23*

Await *Tf*
Every
Frogs *Sf, ŏ, F*
Great Sea
Hearts *Sf*
Never
Promise *ŏ*

162 *2×81 = 3×54 = 6×27 =9×18*

Bastard *ST*
Delivered
Gnarled
Pillars *Sf*

Π **163**

Beleth
CHAOS *Sf, k, ŏ*
Dagdagiron *Nf, ŏ*
Lifted

164 *2×82 = 4×41*

Abyss *SSf*
Alphabet *Tf*
Feathers *Sf*
Shabbathai
Yhvh

165 *3×55 = 5×33 = 11×15*

Altar
Cast *ST, k*
Fertile
Gates *Sf*

	Self-Slain		*Nf*
	Triads		*Sf*
	Triple		
	166	*2×83*	
	Ameshet		*Tf*
	Engine		
	Gamigina		
	Kings		*Sf*
	Mandrake		
	Nakhiel		
	Redeemeth		
	Sceptre		*k*
	Spirits		
	Tiriel		
Π	**167**		
	Breaths		*Sf*
	Divine		
	Salt		*Tf*
	Smite		
	168	*2×84 = 3×56 = 4×42 =6×28 = 7×24 = 8×21 = 12×14*	
	Answer		
	Archangel		
	Breathes		*Sf*
	Daleth		
	Making		
	Silver		
	Small		
	Speaketh		
	The Dagger		
	Twin		*Nf*
	169	*13²*	
	Embassy		
	Filth		*F*
	Maidens		*Sf*
	Next		*Tf*
	Single		
	Sister		*ST*
	The Half		
	Thick		*k*
	Visible		
	170	*2×85 = 5×34 = 10×17*	
	Cypress		*SSf*
	Delicacy		*k*
	Highest		*ST, Tf*
	Light		*Tf*
	Remains		*Sf*
	Spells		*Sf*
	White		
Σ18	**171**	*3×57 = 9×19*	
	COPH NIA		*ŏ*
	Discipline		
	Elect		*Tf, k*
	Energy		
	Exalted		
	Gone		*ŏ*
	Rain-Maker		
	172	*2×86 = 4×43*	
	Animal		
	Jewelled		
	Seemeth		
	Twain		*Nf*
	Type		
	Watch		
Π	**173**		
	Chant		*Tf*
	Ending		
	Gamaliel		
	Incense		
	OIT (*the twelvefold table*)		*Tf, ŏ*
	174	*2×87 = 3×58 = 6×29*	
	Lily		
	Shalt		*Tf*
	Shells		*Sf*
	175	*5×35 = 7×25*	

Bhavani
City
Life & Death
Marsyas
Pity
Strike *ST*
Sweet *Tf*

176 *2×88 = 4×44 = 8×22 =11×16*

Calls *Sf, k*
Cross *SSf, ŏ*
Diviner
English
Fifty
Hot *Tf, ŏ*
Kissing
Prophecy *ŏ*
Seven
The Redeemer

177 *3×59*

APEP Deifieth ASAR
Eighties *Sf*
It Beams
The Khabs
Veils *Sf*

178 *2×89*

Bacchanal *k*
Begone! *ŏ*
Rich Jewels *Sf*
Sinner
Sweat *Tf*
Terrible
Wrath

Π **179**

Dancing
Delight *Tf*
Dweller
Fiery Feet *Tf*
Itself
Light
Within *Nf*

180 *2×90 = 3×60 = 4×45 =5×36 = 6×30 = 9×20 = 10×18 =12×15*

Emblems *Sf*
Maketh
Miracles *Sf, k*
Praying
Pyramids *Sf*
The Scribe *k*
Thine
Vessel
Weather

Π **181**

Ahrimanes *Sf*
Christ *ST, Tf, k*
Shachath *k*

182 *2×91 = 7×26 = 13×14*

Artificial
Center
Enemy
Nemesis *Sf*
Talk
The Eagle
VTI (*The Cry of the 25th Aethyr*)

183 *3×61*

Midst *ST, Tf*
Mightier
Steel *ST*
Stélé *ST*
Ta-Nech
Yesod *ŏ*

184 *2×92 = 4×46 = 8×23*

Athena
Bartzabel
Beasts *ST, Sf*

Many
Marvel
Spirits *Sf*

185 *5×37*

Avenger
Knave
Last *ST, Tf*
Master *ST*
The Seal
Times *Sf*

186 *2×93 = 3×62 = 6×31*

Claws *Sf, k*
Least *ST, Tf*
Lighten *Nf*
Man-Child
Sacred Heart *Tf, k*
Stars *ST, Sf*
Zenith

187 *11×17*

Angels *Sf*
Beneath
Giant *Tf*
Jacinth
Myself
Than He
Wretched

188 *2×94 = 4×47*

Lingam
Radiant *Tf*

189 *3×63 = 7×27 = 9×21*

Aethyr
Enterer
Pythean *Nf*
Ygdrasil

Σ19 **190** *2×95 = 5×38 = 10×19*

Flaming
Magick Dagger *k*
Neither
Night! *Tf*
Nymph
Owl *ŏ*

Π **191**

A Basilisk Egg
Primeval
The Magician *Nf*
Tyrian *Nf*

192 *2×96 = 3×64 = 4×48 =6×32 = 8×24 = 12×16*

Character *kk*
Grant *Tf*
Listen *ST, Nf*
Prophet *Tf, ŏ*
Stable *ST*
Themis *Sf*

Π **193**

Breasts *ST, Sf*
Death-Shriek
Marsyas *Sf*
Temple

194 *2×97*

Anarchy *k*
Athenian *Nf*
Bindeth
Intifada
Niddering
Song *ŏ*
Sweeter

195 *3×65 = 5×39 = 13×15*

Christian *ST, Nf, k*
His Might *Tf*
Soft *Tf, ŏ*
The Wise

196 *2×98 = 4×49 = 7×28 =14^2*

Extended
Templi

Π **197**

	Belts	*Sf*
	Prophesy	*ŏ*
	Serpent	*Tf*
198	*2×99 = 3×66 = 6×33 =9×22 = 11×18*	
	Artemis	*Sf*
	Astral	*ST*
	COPH NIA*—See 171, and notes on the Letter C, particulary as it deals with the Active Properties of this letter in Special Considerations Section.	*k, ŏ*
	My Children	*Nf*
	PERTINAX	
	Petals	*Sf*
	Shalehbiron	*Nf, ŏ*
Π **199**		
	Afflicted	*k*
	Avatar	
	Beetles	*Sf*
	Blessing	
	Lynx	
	Nazareth	
	Night!	
	Particle	*k*
	Shining	
200	*2×100 = 4×50 = 5×40 =8×25 = 10×20*	
	Balances	*Sf, L*
	Eighty	
	O	
	Three Grades	*Sf*
	U	
201	*3×67*	
	Brilliance	
	Hermits	*Sf*
	MAKHASHANAH	
	Navies	*Sf*
	See & Strike	*ST*
	Slaves	*Sf*
	*Thelema *—L averse, See 221.*	
202	*2×101*	
	Alchemy	*k*
	Sandals	*Sf*
	Tall	
	Tripod	*ŏ*
	Vibrate	
203	*7×29*	
	Cross	*SSf, k, ŏ*
	Ha-Gilgalim	
	The Circle	*k*
	Up!	
204	*2×102 = 3×68 = 4×51 =6×34 = 12×17*	
	Skew-Wise	
	Syphilis	*Sf*
	Teth	
205	*5×41*	
	Beast & His Bride	*ST*
	Blasphemy	
	Hand & the Pen	*Nf*
	Heavens	*Sf*
	Navel	
	Satyr	
	Secrets	*Sf, k*
	Teeth	
	The Bat	*Tf*
	Trample	
	Tremble	
	Va-Da'ath	
206	*2×103*	
	Bahlasti!	*ST*
	Darkness	*SSf*
	POP (*The Cry of the 19th Aethyr*)	
	Ravens	*Sf*
207	*3×69 = 9×23*	
	Across	*SSf, k, ŏ*
	Altars	*Sf*

Eyeless *SSf*
Garlands *Sf*
Ho!
Lastadza *ST*
Oh!
Scarlet *Tf, k*
The Key

208 *2×104 = 4×52 = 8×26 =13×16*

Do
IAO
Minerva
OAI
Reptiles *Sf*
Sweet Chian *Nf*
The Empress

209 *11×19*

DEO (*The Cry of the 7th Aethyr)*
Ginseng
Give All
Magister *ST*
Prithivi
Pylon *Nf, ŏ*
Think

Σ20 **210** *2×105 = 3×70 = 5×42 =6×35 = 7×30 = 10×21 = 14×15*

A Babe in An Egg
Abyssinia
Archangels *Sf*
Giveth
Infernal
Lalita
Open *Nf*
Princely
Rue
TA-NECH *k*
The Jews *Sf*
Titan *Nf*

Π **211**

Deal Hardly
Every Man *Nf*
Hope
HUA
Shameless *SSf*
Soften *Nf, ŏ*
Vomica *ŏ*

212 *2×106 = 4×53*

Duce
Empty
Iod
Nara-Singh
Nectar *k*
ZON *(the cry of the 3rd Aethyr)* *Nf*

213 *3×71*

Aur
Chefu
Pure
Stand *ST*

214 *2×107*

Absinthe
Clearly *k*
Doric Girl *k, ŏ*
Ganymede
John *Nf*
Lesser Adept *Tf*
Lying
Ocean *Nf*
Privileges *Sf*
Spangles *Sf*

215 *5×43*

Hod
Olive *ŏ*
Orb
Urn *Nf*
Vast *ST, Tf*

Witches *Sf*

216 *2×108 = 3×72 = 4×54 =6×36 = 8×27 = 9×24 = 12×18 =6³*

Buer
Carrying *k*
Levanah
Netzach *k*
Plant *Tf*
Robe
Upper
Vesta *ST*
Zero
Zion *Nf*

217 *7×31*

Father's Eye
Few & Secret *Tf, k*
Fylfat *Tf*
HERU
Planet *Tf*
Serpent Apep
Smyrna

218 *2×109*

Basilisk Eye
King's Chamber
Obeah
Odin *Nf*
Queen *Nf*

219 *3×73*

Abode
An Angel
Assembly
Far-Off
Iron *Nf*
Light Shed
Penates *Sf*
Rejoice
The Ateph
The Divided
The Pleiades *Sf*

220 *2×110 = 4×55 = 5×44 =10×22 = 11×20*

Azure
BABALON*—N non-final. See Section Special Considerations and entry 156 *ŏ*
Balances *Sf*
EVE and ADAM
Existence *ST*
Go
Knight *Tf*
My Heart *Tf*
Ruah
The LAW
Wealth

221 *13×17*

Born *Nf*
Burn *Nf*
Ego
Lights *Sf*
Meaneth
Road
Tarshishim
The Shrine
Thelema *L*

222 *2×111 = 3×74 = 6×37*

Adore
Apron *Nf*
Athens *Sf*
Babylon *Nf, ŏ*
Blessed God *ŏ*
Galangal
Horn *Nf*
New Aeon *Nf, ŏ*
Roar
Spelling

The Three Vessels *Sf*

Π **223**

Force *F*

Ixion *Nf*

Starry *ST*

Thy Kaaba

Vesica Piscis *Sf, k*

224 *2×112 = 4×56 = 7×32 =8×28 = 14×16*

Navy

The Sign

Watchers *Sf*

225 *3×75 = 5×45 = 9×25 =* 15^2

Burin *Nf*

Cacique

High Beneath

Kashenyaiah

My Name

Spilling

Strive *ST*

The Wheel

226 *2×113*

Dynamic *k*

I Am the Eye

Large Limbs *Sf*

Mankind

Oriax

Π **227**

A Lamp Therein *Nf*

Irritate

Masters *ST,Sf*

Order

The Father

Yielding

228 *2×114 = 3×76 = 4×57 =6×38 = 12×19*

A Secret Place *k*

God Living

Π **229**

Druid

Forbid

Mine Eyes *Sf*

Onyx *ŏ*

The Cat *Tf, k*

The Gate

Veiling

Virgins *Sf*

230 *2×115 = 5×46 = 10×23*

Aeons Amen *Nf, ŏ*

Always *Sf*

Delights *Sf*

Enslave

Judge

Son *Nf*

Sun *Nf*

The Heathen *Nf*

The King

Σ21 **231** *3×77 = 7×33 = 11×21*

Adorer

My Father

Shu

Tempt *Tf*

Tiphareth

232 *2×116 = 4×58 = 8×29*

Forehead

Forge

Grey Land

Here and Hereafter

233 1×233, 13th Fibonacci number

Abide With Me

Against *ST,Tf*

Buddha

CUP *k*

Ecstasy *ST*
Eternal
Guide
King's Bedchamber
LILITH *L*
Preserveth
Priestess *ST,SSf*
Refuge
Satiate
Thy Carapace *k*
What Axle

234 *2×117 = 3×78 = 6×39 =9×26 = 13×18*

An Island
Oak
Pharaoh
Pigeon *Nf*
Push
Rose
Sore

235 *5×47*

Chymical *kk*
Metals *Sf*
Strange *ST*
The Snake
Yea Theli

236 *2×118 = 4×59*

Amaranth
Caverns *Sf, k*
Established *ST*
Ordered
Vigilance

237 *3×79*

cube *k*
Drug
Gladness *SSf*
Khu
Refuse
Rosa

238 *2×119 = 7×34 = 14×17*

A Pigeon *Nf*
Babe in the Egg
Gored
Prince-Priest *ST,Tf*

Π **239**

And Means *Sf*
Black Earth *k*
Cor *k*
Mighty
Revealing
The Red Gleam
War-Engine
Wrong *ŏ*

240 *2×120 = 3×80 = 4×60 =5×48 = 6×40 = 8×30 = 10×24 = 12×20= 15×16*

Coin *Nf, k*
Core *k*
Kore
Libitina
Mu
Rush
Supper

Π **241**

& Its Red Flame
Ancient *Tf*
Avatars *Sf*
Chosen *Nf*
HERU-RA-HA
Nights *Sf*
Sappho
The Perfect *Tf, k*
The Veil
Things *Sf*
Twined
Versicles *Sf, k*

242 $2\times121 = 11\times22$

Midnight — *Tf*
Saints — *Sf*

243 $3\times81 = 9\times27 = 3^5$

A War-Engine
Cruce — *k*
Invisible
Nightshade
Person — *Nf*
Prophets — *Sf, ŏ*
Saxon — *Nf*
The Black Bean — *Nf, k*

244 $2\times122 = 4\times61$

AUM
Bruise
Forbidden — *Nf*
MAU
Reason — *Nf*
The Pyramid

245 $5\times49 = 7\times35$

Corn — *Nf, k*
Elephant — *Tf, L*
Enginery
O Caesar
This Path

246 $2\times123 = 3\times82 = 6\times41$

Attis — *Sf*
Evening
Length

247 13×19

Calvary — *k*
Cord — *k*
Dragon — *Nf*
Geburah
Greater Adept — *Tf*
Majesty — *ST*
Meanest — *ST, Tf*

248 $2\times124 = 4\times62 = 8\times31$

Availeth
Createth — *k*
Crux — *k*
Serpents — *Sf*
Sufferer
The Beast — *ST, Tf*

249 3×83

& the Circle is Red — *k*
Ipos — *Sf*
Ninth
Pentagram
The Circle is Red — *k*
The Wheels
Travail
Zeus — *Sf*

250 $2\times125 = 5\times50 = 10\times25$

Excrement — *Tf, k*
Gigantic — *k*
Matter
Meru
Metallic
Nameless — *SSf*
O Man — *Nf*
Ruach — *k*
Shattered
Terrible Child
Vengeance
Weakness — *SSf*
Withdraw!

Π **251**

Deus — *Sf*
Existeth — *ST*
From
Leo
LOE (*The Cry of the 12th Aethyr*)
Midnight

The Angel
The Great Deep

252 *2×126 = 3×84 = 4×63 =6×42 = 7×36 = 9×28 = 12×21 =14×18*

Eros *Sf*
Folly *ŏ*
Manifest *ST,Tf*
Style *ST*
Tarpesheth
The Basilisk
The First *ST,Tf*
Thyself
Zodiac *k*

Σ22 **253** *11×23*

Infinite
Qadosh
Raum
Seven Spaces *Sf*

254 *2×127*

Ascendency
Epheus *Sf*
Gorse
Hippogriff
Lament *Tf*
Lao
Leviathan *Nf*
Luce
Oil
The Aires Fall

255 *3×85 = 5×51 = 15×17*

Aloe
At An End
AUM HA
Fear Not *Tf, ŏ*
Guardian *Nf*
Seven Sides *Sf*
The Ram's Eye
The Sabbath
Yantra

256 *2×128 = 4×64 = 8×32 =* $16^2 = 4^4 = 2^8$

Blessed Beast *ST,Tf*
CHAOS *Sf*
Perfume
Squared
The Hermit *Tf*
Triangle
Victim *k*
Winners *Sf*

Π **257**

Battle
Blue
Exempt Adept *Tf*
Foras *Sf*
Forces *Sf*
Human *Nf*
Impure
Letter
Life and Death
Opal
Paimon *Nf*
Pentacle *k*
Sugar
Swastika *ST*

258 *2×129 = 3×86 = 6×43*

Alexandrite
Mantis *Sf*
Old
People
Robes *Sf*

259 *7×37*

Casting *ST, k*
Cleaving *k*
Fear Invisible
Firmament *Tf*

	Minister	ST
	Qliphoth	ŏ
	Season	Nf
260	2×130 = 4×65 = 5×52 =10×26 = 13×20	
	Ecstasy	ST, k
	Hyperbolic	k, ŏ
	Lambent	Tf
	Lion	Nf
	Pantacle	k
	Rule	
	Space and Time	
	The Christ	ST,Tf
261	3×87 = 9×29	
	Abodes	Sf
	Crucified	k
	Crucifix	k
	Flux	
	Great Grey Sea	
	Latchet	
	Woe	
262	2×131	
	Carrion	Nf, k
	Cerebus	Sf
	Cockatrice	k, ŏ
	Death-Star	ST
	Domain	Nf
	Eloah	
	Existences	ST,Sf
	The Adepts	Sf
Π **263**		
	As Ye Will	
	Cup-Bearer	k
	Emperor	
	Enchanter	
	Hair of Her Head	
	Haures	Sf
	Ompehda!	
	Roads	Sf
264	2×132 = 3×88 = 4×66 =6×44 = 8×33 = 11×24 = 12×22	
	A Great Miss	SSf
	A Lion	Nf
	Curse	k
	I Am the Heart	Tf
	Pestilence	ST
	Python	Nf, ŏ
	Score	k
	Secret Key	k
	Severities	Sf
	Straight	ST,Tf
	Typhon	Nf, ŏ
265	5×53	
	Abominable	ŏ
	Ducal	
	Flora	
	Hold!	
	Nemyss	SSf
	Priapus	Sf
266	2×133 = 7×38 = 14×19	
	Because	k
	Bow	
	Dark Orb	
	Gethsemane	
	Own	Nf
	Pregnant	Tf
	Purple	
	System	ST
	The Signs	Sf
267	3×89	
	How	
	Kindness	SSf
	Lord	
	Magick Staff	ST, k
	Mantras	Sf

O Pearl
Plants *Sf*
Recorder *k*
Selfishness *SSf*
The Great Sea

268 *2×134 = 4×67*

Build
Fearful
His Cup *k*
I Am Existence *ST*
Imago
Jesus *Sf*
Myrtle
Nakedness *SSf*
Planets *Sf*
Soma
Three Sieves *Sf*
Thy Feet *Tf*
Veilêd Sky

Π **269**

Apocalypse *k, ŏ*
Apostle *ST, ŏ*
Black Sabbath *k*
Lucifer
Ruler
The Magick Dagger

270 *2×135 = 3×90 = 5×54 =6×45 = 9×30 = 10×27 = 15×18*

AUMGN *Nf*
Cubic *kk*
Failure
Gods *Sf*
Kokab
Nu!
Petty

Π **271**

Cleaveth *k*
Come! *k*
Dissolve *ŏ*
High Priestess *ST,SSf*
Holier
Inverted
Joy
Knights *Sf*
Leavings *Sf*
Mirror
One!
Sacrament *Tf, k*

272 *2×136 = 4×68 = 8×34 =16×17*

Aquila
Behold!
Cursed *k*
Eyeless Hawk
Fantasy
Help & Hope
Ordeal
Wise Ta-Nech

273 *3×91 = 7×39 = 13×21*

Bandmaster *ST*
Litanies *Sf*
Orchids *Sf*
Power
Star&Snake *ST*

274 *2×137*

Amalekites *Sf*
Availest *ST,Tf*
Direful
Down *Nf*
Excellent *Tf*
Goal
Laodicea
Mako
Parliament *Tf*
Tempest *ST,Tf*

275 *5×55 = 11×25*

Adimiron	*Nf*
Blackness	*SSf, k*
Cups	*Sf, k*
Guides	*Sf*
Leopard	
Mystic	*ST, k*
Secret Rite	*k*
Sole	

Σ23 **276** *2×138 = 3×92 = 4×69 =6×46 = 12×23*

A Strange Fish	*ST*
BABALON*	*Nf*
KAOS*—See notes on the "fullness" of O and entry 156.	*Sf*
Line Drawn	
Nun	*Nf*
Raise the Spell	
Roses	*Sf*
Strings	*ST,Sf*
Ten Palaces	*Sf*
The Highest	*ST*
Tremble Ye	

Π **277**

Globe	
Infinite Chain	*Nf*
Lobster	*ST, ŏ*
Obey	
Odyssey	*ŏ*
Servant	*Tf*
Shichiriron	*Nf*
Svastika	*ST*
Whore	
Word	

278 *2×139*

Become	*k*
Camio	*k*
Ephesus	*Sf*
Gold	
Magistry	*ST*
My Claws	*k*
Negative	
Pulse	
Secret Name	*k*
Supreme	
Yod	

279 *3×93 = 9×31*

Dissolved	*ŏ*
Done	
Drugs	*Sf*
Guebres	*Sf*
Kurm	
My Sister	*ST*
NUX	
O Chi Balae	
The Incense	
Thy All	
Training	
Urn	

280 *2×140 = 4×70 = 5×56 =7×40 = 8×35 = 10×28 = 14×20*

Bahimiron	*Nf*
Clingeth	*k*
NEPHTHYS	
Spare Not	*Tf, ŏ*

Π **281**

A Word	
Aeacus	*Sf, k*
Cattle	*k*
Luke	
Powder	

282 *2×141 = 3×94 = 6×47*

A Secret Name	*k*
Arrow	
Dreadful	

	Folk	
	Sheol	
	Zagreus	*Sf*
Π **283**		
	Crucem	*k*
	Dagdagiron	*Nf*
	Demiurge	
	Deona	
	Dispersion	*Nf*
	Heavenly	
	My Incense	
	Opened	
	Osiris	*Sf*
	There is A Veil	
284	*2×142 = 4×71*	
	Body	
	Destiny	*ST*
	Great Cities	*Sf*
	It is Revealed	
	Loki	
	Mexico	*k*
	Sow	
	Travels	*Sf*
	Vau	
285	*3×95 = 5×57 = 15×19*	
	Coeli	*k*
	Disguise	
	Globéd	
	Golden	*Nf*
	Ruby	
	The Red Powder	*ŏ*
286	*2×143 = 11×26 = 13×22*	
	Anaphaxeton	*Nf, ŏ*
	Be Done	
	Borne	
	Brilliant	*Tf*
	Cajole	*k*
	For He is Speech	
	Thirty	
287	*7×41*	
	AMENNTI	
	At Last	*ST, Tf*
	Attained	
	Blush	
	Furcas	*Sf, k*
	Giant Glacier	
	Kohl	
	Nefertiti	
	Severity	
	Star-Lit	*ST, Tf*
	THE CHRIST	*ST, Tf, k*
	Thy Presence	
288	*2×144 = 3×96 = 4×72 =6×48 = 8×36 = 9×32 = 12×24 =16×18*	
	Circus	*Sf, k*
	Horsemen	*Nf*
	Infinite Space	
	Magus	
	My Wings	
	Sightless	*SSf*
	Star&Star	*ST*
	Under	
	Voice	
	Wickedness	*SSf, k*
	Yea Lilith	
289	*17^2*	
	And He is Exalted	
	Dove	
	Furnace	
	Hindu	
	I Behold Pan	*Nf*
	Lurk!	
	Profane	
290	*2×145 = 5×58 = 10×29*	

Abstinence *ST*
ADONAI
AMMON *Nf*
Cow *k*
IACCHUS *Sf, k*
Nasatanada
Nubian *Nf*
Squares *Sf*
The Many
Thine Heart *Tf*
THOTH *ŏ*
Thy Name
Twelve
Valkyries *Sf*

291 *3×97*

Above
Chokmah
Gone
Mors *Sf*
Show
Sweet Cakes *Sf, k*
The Avenger
The Last *ST,Tf*
The Master *ST*
Thistle *ST*
Urania

292 *2×146 = 4×73*

A-Cold *k*
Bacchus *Sf, k*
Fastness *ST,SSf*
I Bear His Cup *k*
Pleasure
Put *Tf*
Rotten *Nf, ŏ*
The Stars *ST,Sf*
Void

Π **293**

Almighty
Coiled *k*
Forms *Sf*
Knewest *ST,Tf*
OIT *(the 12-fold table)* *Tf*
Superficies *Sf*
Thy Death

294 *2×147 = 3×98 = 6×49 =7×42 = 14×21*

Betrayeth
crystal *ST, k*
Lucem
New Chaos *Sf, k, ŏ*
Oracle *k*
Phoenix
Sweet Heart *Tf*
Thine Eyes *Sf*
Thyatira
Yoga

295 *5×59*

Horned
Ruddy
Six and Fifty
Warrior

296 *2×148 = 4×74 = 8×37*

Black Cross *SSf, k, ŏ*
Hot *Tf*
Hour *ŏ*
Primum
Soldier
Ten Palaces *Sf, L*
The Magick Dagger *k*
Vast Sacrifice *ST, k*

297 *3×99 = 9×33 = 11×27*

Blasteth *ST*
Ringed With Fire
Sixfold

298 *2×149*

	Amaimon		Nf
	Dung		
	Green Serpent		Tf
	Mysteries		ST,Sf
	Perfumes		Sf
	The Prophet		Tf, ŏ
	Thy Mercy		
	Victims		Sf, k
299		13×23	
	As One		
	Azure-Lidded		
	Boat		Tf
	Brightness		SSf
	Few and Secret		Tf, k
	Fires of Life		
	Gods&Men		Nf
	Letters		Sf
	Lucis		Sf
	Red Powder		
	Tzbavth		
	Wise TA-NECH		k
	Work		
Σ24 **300**		2×150 = 3×100 = 4×75 =5×60 = 6×50 = 10×30 = 12×25 =15×20	
	Aleph is Madness		SSf
	Art and Craft		Tf
	Peoples		Sf
	Showed		
301		7×43	
	Cholem		
	Christians		ST,Sf, k
	Cone		k
	Delos		Sf
	Emptiness		SSf
	Juggler		
	Little		
	Ministers		ST,Sf
	Mobile		
	Nogah		
	Speak Not		Tf, ŏ
	Sword		
302		2×151	
	Atu		
	Elohim		
	For Ever		
	Full		
	Great Light		Tf
	Gums		Sf
	Prophet of Had!		ŏ
	Rules		Sf
	TAO		
	Tau		
	Tawny		
	UTI (*The Cry of the 14th Aethyr)*		
303		3×101	
	Cast Away		ST, k
	Elements		Sf
	Hundred		
	Purple & Green		Nf
	Rosy		
	Shadow		
	Yesod		
304		2×152 = 4×76 = 8×38 =16×19	
	Helios		Sf
	Holies		Sf
	Orange		
	Penguin		Nf
305		5×61	
	A Sword		
	Crown		Nf, k
	Hurt		Tf
	The Afflicted		k
	Thy Kisses Abide		
	Tube		

306 $2\times153 = 3\times102 = 6\times51 = 9\times34 = 17\times18$

Accurséd! *kk*
Bull
Distant *ST, Tf*
Indigo
Magus *Sf*
My Spangles
Omnipresence *ŏ*

Π **307**

Beginnings *Sf*
Censor
Enswathes *Sf*
Magnificent *Tf*
Moses *Sf*
Osprey
Surya
Tor
Women *Nf*
Worship

308 $2\times154 = 4\times77 = 7\times44 = 11\times28 = 14\times22$

Rel Moai
Thy Spirit *Tf*
Yea Lilith *L*

309 3×103

Alchemists *ST, Sf, k*
Bondage
Earth and Hell
Lords *Sf*
Oath
Planetary
Sparrow
The Cross *SSf, k, ŏ*

310 $2\times155 = 5\times62 = 10\times31$

Ineffable Light *Tf*
Low
Sworded
Toad
Woman *Nf*

Π **311**

NEMO
ROTA
TARO
The Beast & His Bride *ST*
The Hand & the Pen *Nf*
Topaz

312 $2\times156 = 3\times104 = 4\times78 = 6\times52 = 8\times39 = 12\times26 = 13\times24$

Entwined
Evoke
Flow
Juxta
Prophet *Tf*
Rejoicing
Silver Star *ST*

Π **313**

Closed *k*
Crimson *Nf, k*
Damned in Hell
Divorced
Force and Fire
Goat *Tf*
Gross *SSf*
Joys *Sf*
Next Step *ST*
Ninety
Ones *Sf*
Pluck *k*
Saecula *k*
Torn *Nf*
Turn *Nf*
Virgo

314 2×157

Laurel

Lazuli
Longing *ŏ*
Naked Brilliance
Ordeals *Sf*
Parrot *Tf*
Peridot *Tf*
Porta
Starlight *ST,Tf*
Thor
Thy Staff *ST*

315 *3×105 = 5×63 = 7×45 =9×35 = 15×21*

Gryphon *Nf*
I Who Am
Other
Pang of Fire
Powers *Sf*
Upper Heaven *Nf*
Who I Am

316 *2×158 = 4×79*

A Silver Star *ST*
Chariot *Tf*
Forth
Hrumachis *Sf*
I Will Spear Thee
Jupiter

Π **317**

A Goat *Tf*
Aeons *Sf*
Below
Brows *Sf*
Drunk
Eligos *Sf*
Hibiscus *Sf, k*
Hyperbolic Life *k, ŏ*
Janus *Sf*
Laural
Leopard's *Sf*
My Altars *Sf*
Torch

318 *2×159 = 3×106 = 6×53*

Labyrinth
Nettle
Patior
Vision *Nf*
Whole

319 *11×29*

A Mighty Eagle
Bones *Sf*
Intimate
Kut! *Tf*
Pergamos *Sf*
Persephone
Words *Sf*
Worshipped

320 *2×160 = 4×80 = 5×64 =8×40 = 10×32 = 16×20*

Aught *Tf*
Bar of Heaven *Nf*
Lower
No Man *Nf*
Plagues *Sf*
Shut *Tf*
The Lesser Adept *Tf*
Worshipper

321 *3×107*

Ariton *Nf*
Expansion *Nf*
Goddess *SSf*
Lone
Move
Mystery *ST*

322 *2×161 = 7×46 = 14×23*

Capricorn *Nf, kk*
Infinity
Mundi

323 *17×19*

	ALGMOR	
	Chief of All	
	Elements	*Sf, L*
	Half-Formed	
	Night-Sky	
	O Marble Pan	*Nf*
	Pure Heart	*Tf*
	Return	*Nf*

324 *2×162 = 3×108 = 4×81 =6×54 = 9×36 = 12×27 = 18²*

	Arrows	*Sf*
	Indus	*Sf*
	Khephra the Beetle	
	Luna	
	Rapture	
	Surpass	*SSf*

Σ25 **325** *5×65 = 13×25*

	Alone	
	Hathor	
	Hellebore	
	Homini	
	Mockers	*Sf*
	Ruins	*Sf*
	Sepulchre	*k*
	Undesired	
	Ye Lament	*Tf*

326 *2×163*

	Amdusias	*Sf*
	Further	
	Goeth	
	Khut	*Tf*
	Last Lever	*ST*
	Number	
	Oriens	*Sf*
	Scarlet Heart	*Tf, k*
	Terror	
	The Existence	*ST*
	Upwards	*Sf*

327 *3×109*

	Art and Craft	*Tf, k*
	Assyrian Eagles	*Sf*
	Burns	*Sf*
	Deceive the Virgin	*Nf*
	Eight Belts	*Sf*
	Holy	
	I, APEP the Serpent	
	Quartz	
	World	

328 *2×164 = 4×82 = 8×41*

	Adonis	*Sf*
	Goddesses	*Sf*
	Horns	*Sf*
	Hyssop	
	Servants	*Sf*

329 *7×47*

	Anguish	
	Covered	*k*
	Homeward	
	Mystical	*ST, k*
	Penelope	

330 *2×165 = 3×110 = 5×66 =6×55 = 10×33 = 11×30 = 15×22*

	Ages of Sleep	
	Flower	*F*
	Blessed Are the Eyes	
	Brother	
	Division	*Nf*
	Enlightened	
	Gemmêd Azure	
	KHUIT	*Tf*
	Now	
	Pomegranate	*ŏ*
	Sitteth	

	The Watchers		*Sf*
Π 331			
	Doves		*Sf*
	End of Man		*Nf*
	First & Last		*ST*
	Hanuman		*Nf*
	His Name is Silence		
	Love		
	Napula		
	Selflessness		*SSf*
	Sorceress		*SSf*
	Yohimba		
332		*2×166 = 4×83*	
	Flaming Wand		
	Holier Place		
	I Am Destiny		*ST*
	Just		*ST,Tf*
	Suffering		
	Twilight		*Tf*
333		*3×111 = 9×37*	
	A Pylon		*Nf*
	Be Near Us		*Sf*
	Bifrons		*Sf*
	Fallen and Defiled		
	Great Goddess		*SSf, ♉*
	Half-Formed Face		
	MAUT		*Tf*
	Royal		
	Second		*k*
	Secret Light		*Tf, k*
334		*2×167*	
	Among		
	Aphrodite		
	Diamond		
	Flaming Star		*ST*
	I Call It Eight		*Tf*
	Mitylene		
	Precipice of Being		
	Rushing		
	Shining Veil		
	The God		
335		*5×67*	
	Intimate Fire		
	Ten Kings		*Sf*
	Value		
	Virus		*Sf*
	Yophiel		
336		*2×168 = 3×112 = 4×84 =6×56 = 7×48 = 8×42 = 12×28 = 14×24= 16×21*	
	Blue-Lidded		
	Charioteer		
	Elixir of Life		
	Fertility		
	God FIAT		
	Inverted Palace		
	Naberius		*Sf*
	Oracles		*Sf, k*
	Plumes		*Sf*
	SAMAEL & LILITH		
	Shi-Loh-Am		
	Sons		*Sf*
	Strength		*ST*
	The SON		*Nf*
	The SUN		*Nf*
	Verbum		
	Wisdom		
Π 337			
	Disport		*Tf*
	Genius		*Sf*
	I Ache for Thee		
	In the Middle is Red		
	Misericordia		*k*
	Ships of War		
	Three Lights		*Sf*

Volac
Warriors — *Sf*

338 *2×169 = 13×26*

Eternal Change
Expiration — *Nf*
HORUS — *Sf, ŏ*
Host — *ST, Tf*
Ibis-Headed One
Pillar of Fire
Spear of Mars — *Sf*

339 *3×113*

Dust — *ST, Tf*
Giant Time
I Am the Master — *ST*
The Cup — *k*
The Sephiroth — *ŏ*
Thick Darkness — *k*
Thy Body — *ŏ*
To Me

340 *2×170 = 4×85 = 5×68 =10×34 = 17×20*

Being Not — *Tf, ŏ*
English Alphabet — *Tf*
Hercules — *Sf, k*
I Am A-Cold — *k*
Ill-Ordered
Justice — *ST*
Lover
Mohammed
Rise Up & Awake!
Synthesis — *Sf*

341 *11×31*

Choronzon — *Nf, ŏŏŏ*
None
Saturn — *Nf*
Store — *ST*
Works — *Sf*

342 *2×171 = 3×114 = 6×57 =9×38 = 18×19*

Abrogate
Action — *Nf, k*
Quest — *ST, Tf*
Sorath
Success — *SSf, k*
Tenderness — *SSf*

343 $7\times49 = 7^3$

Crocell — *k*
Factor — *k*
Forest — *ST, Tf*
Hrumachis — *Sf, k*
Lightning
Swords — *Sf*
The Archangels — *Sf, k*
The Khu

344 *2×172 = 4×86 = 8×43*

Astor — *ST*
Lightening
Seventy
Shamrock — *k*
Stabilities — *ST, Sf*
Stainless — *ST, SSf*
The Prince-Priest — *ST, Tf*
Tomb
Undefiled
Yoni

345 *3×115 = 5×69 = 15×23*

Fall Not — *Tf, ŏ*
Goshawk
I Lift Myself
In One
Passover
Penetrant — *Tf*
Shadows — *Sf*
The Black Earth — *k*
Thrush

346 *2×173*

Aquamarine
Beloved
Great Waters *Sf*
The Magick Staff *ST*
Valefor

Π **347**

Abiegnus *Sf*
Anaphaneton *Nf, ŏ*
Bennu
Daughter
Dispersion
God Phtah
Guardeth
Pallid God

348 *2×174 = 3×116 = 4×87 =6×58 = 12×29*

Bulls *Sf*
Geranium
Green Dragon *Nf*
Honey
Wonder

Π **349**

Ansuel
Bahlasti! Ompehda! *ST, ŏ*
Flame and Light *Tf*
Glory
The Invisible
Toel
Vowed

350 *2×175 = 5×70 = 7×50 =10×35 = 14×25*

Alloces *Sf*
All-Wandering
Asmoday
Baphomet *Tf*
Botis *Sf*
But Exceed! Exceed!
Kill Me! Kill Me!
Kings of Æ
Misericordia Dei *k*
Rushing Fire
Trump
Tzaphiriron *Nf*
Upper Eyelid

Σ26 **351** *3×117 = 9×39 = 13×27*

Acquiring *k*
Amethyst *ST, Tf*
Creator *k*
Eternity
Ineffable hope
Slayer in the Deep

352 *2×176 = 4×88 = 8×44 =11×32 = 16×22*

A Green Dragon *Nf*
Creation *Nf, k*
Creature *k*
Damascus *Sf, k*
Fill and Will
The Severities
Toil

Π **353**

Bull-Men *Nf*
Circle Squared *k*
He is Drunk
Nile-God
Rainbow
Ruling
Sephiroth
The Dragon
The Greater Adept *Tf*
Trinity

354 *2×177 = 3×118 = 6×59*

Day and Night *Tf*
Houses *Sf, ŏ*
Method

	Perfection	*Nf, k*
	Vayu	
	Wolf's	*Sf*
355	*5×71*	
	Beyond	
	Dragon's Head	
	Mother	
	Strangely	*ST*
	The Pentagram	
356	*2×178 = 4×89*	
	Forties	*Sf*
	Inverted Palace	*L*
	Minos	*Sf*
	Phallus	*Sf*
	Samael & Lilith	*L*
	Secret Temple	*k*
	Unwedded	
	Vassago	
357	*3×119 = 7×51 = 17×21*	
	Arcanum	*k*
	Certainty	
	Changeful	
	Exorcist	*ST, Tf*
	Low Men	*Nf*
	Obelisks	*Sf*
	Others	*Sf*
358	*2×179*	
	By Thine Art	*Tf*
	Fulfill	
	Ghost	*ST, Tf*
	Muslim	
	Unbind	
Π **359**		
	Bowels	*Sf*
	Doric God	*k, ŏ*
	Harlot	*Tf*
	Holding	
	Mercury	*k*
	Not	*Tf*
	Nut	*Tf*
	O Wayfarer	
	The Seven Spaces	*Sf*
	Virginity	
360	*2×180 = 3×120 = 4×90 =5×72 = 6×60 = 8×45 = 9×40 = 10×36 =12×30 = 15×24 = 18×20*	
	A Phallus	*Sf*
	Hutamah	
	Know	
	Means and Means	
	Moly	
	Secret Serpent	*Tf, k*
	Seven Spirits	*Sf*
361	19^2	
	Death of ASAR	
	Demons	*Sf*
	Guardians	*Sf*
	Original	
	Supernal	
	Sweet Wines	*Sf*
	Thagiriron	*Nf*
	The Demon	*Nf*
	Triumph	
362	*2×181*	
	Building	
	Caligula	*k*
	Kithairon	*Nf*
	Lao Tan	*Nf*
	O Pillars	*Sf*
	Peace in the Highest	*ST, Tf*
	The Triangle	
	The Victim	*k*
	Thelemites	*Sf, L*
363	*3×121 = 11×33*	

Ivory
Laboring
Leopard's Skin *Nf*
Mighty King
NUIT! *Tf*
The Swastika *ST*

364 $2\times182 = 4\times91 = 7\times52 = 13\times28 = 14\times26$

Buddhist *ST,Tf*
Coming *k*
Flowers *Sf*
I Ache for Thee *k*
Moznaim
Nastiness *ST,SSf*
Speech of the Babe
The People

365 5×73

Agelong
Ritual
Seasons *Sf*
The Qliphoth *ŏ*
Unfit *Tf*

366 $2\times183 = 3\times122 = 6\times61$

Betulah
Hunt *Tf*
Its Name Be Death
Known *Nf*
Lifted Up
Lion's *Sf*
Point *Tf*
Upanishads *Sf*
Uplifted

Π **367**

All-Wandering Air
AMMON RA
Chariots *Sf*
Concealed *k*
Fulfilled
Hominis *Sf*
Leonis *Sf*
Stability *ST*
The Crucifix *k*
Viceroy

368 $2\times184 = 4\times92 = 8\times46 = 16\times23$

Face of the Man *Nf*
Isis Rejoicing
Lilium *L*
Nashimiron *Nf*
Numbers *Sf*
Opening
The Death-Star *ST*
Tower
Toy
Tree of Life
Zelator

369 $3\times123 = 9\times41$

Barbatos *Sf*
Cult *Tf, k*
Husbandman *Nf*
Ipsissimus *Sf*
Note
Talkative
The Hair of Her Head
Worlds *Sf*

370 $2\times185 = 5\times74 = 10\times37$

Clover *k*
Everlasting *ST*
Knower
O Light *Tf*
Redemption *Nf*
Stork *ST*
Vulcan *Nf, k*

371 7×53

Bitterness *SSf*
Duant *Tf*

His Wisdom
Most — ST, Tf
Must — ST, Tf
No Difference
To War

372 — *2×186 = 3×124 = 4×93 =6×62 = 12×31*

Almond
Brothers — Sf
Kingdom

Π **373**

Atone
Champions — Sf
Circumference — k
Giver of Life
I Am Alone
Ithuriel
Loves — Sf
Quarters — Sf
Result — Tf
Suyasel
Unite

374 — *2×187 = 11×34 = 17×22*

Bennu Bird
Burnt — Tf
Castor — ST, k
Fire from Thee
Sacred Mysteries — ST, Sf, k
Soft Light — Tf, ŏ
The Planets — Sf
The Veilêd Sky

375 — *3×125 = 5×75 = 15×25*

Laughing
My Nemyss — SSf
Peace in the Midst — ST, Tf
Swordsman — Nf
The Apocalypse — k, ŏ
The Black Sabbath — k

376 — *2×188 = 4×94 = 8×47*

Diamonds — Sf
Egg of Spirit — Tf
HERU-PA-KRAATH
Infinite Mercy
Initiating
Ovals — Sf
The Space Beyond — ŏ
Threefold

377 — *13×29*

Let ASAR Be With APEP
Pure Will
Sunray
The Name Babalon — Nf, ŏ
The One
The Sacrament — Tf, k

Σ27 **378** — *2×189 = 3×126 = 6×63 =7×54 = 9×42 = 14×27 = 18×21*

Jasmine & Rose,
Scripture — k
Unfading
Wheel of Life

Π **379**

Beauty
Burning
Forty
Knees of Him
NUITH
Star & the Snake — ST

380 — *2×190 = 4×95 = 5×76 =10×38 = 19×20*

Hosts — ST, Sf
Lying Spectre — k
Lying Spirits
Modest — ST, Tf
Narcissus — Sf
Pastos — ST, Sf
Prince Beast Priest — ST, Tf

Storm *ST*
Tzelmoth *ŏ*
Weapons *Sf*

381 *3×127*

Calypso *k*
Isis-Hathor
Joineth
Lust *ST,Tf*
Mighty Wind
Money

382 *2×191*

Lovers *Sf*
Mighty Devil
Nature
Nuns *Sf*
O Cobbler *k, ŏ*

Π **383**

An Oath
Fixed MERCURY *k*
Hermanubis *Sf*
The Infinite Chain *Nf*
The Word

384 *2×192 = 3×128 = 4×96 =6×64 = 8×48 = 12×32 = 16×24*

Adorant *Tf*
Astrum *ST*
Mighty Angel
North
Pointed
Purity

385 *5×77 = 7×55 = 11×35*

A Word and A Deed
Abyss of Sapphire
Centaur
End of All
Fortify
Invoke
Lightnings *Sf*
Pure Water
Throne
Vishnu

386 *2×193*

Abhorent *Tf*
Desolate
ISA the Sufferer
The Victims *k*
Three Gods *Sf*

387 *3×129 = 9×43*

Legions *Sf*
Two-Headed

388 *2×194 = 4×97*

Beware! Hold! Raise
Circle in the Middle *k*
End of Thee
Forth-Speaker
Holy Place
The Arrow

Π **389**

A Single Robe
Another
Centauri
Daughters *Sf*
His Method
Laughter
The Veil Has Fallen *Nf*
Universe

390 *2×195 = 3×130 = 5×78 =6×65 = 10×39 = 13×30 = 15×26*

Eightfold
Evening Star *ST*
Golden Egg
Naught *Tf*
Only
Space Beyond

Symbol
Wand Createth *k*
Wonders *Sf*

391 *17×23*

Conjure *k, ŏ*
Garden of Spices *Sf*
Hermaphrodite
His Phallus *Sf*
Musicians *Sf*
Silenus *Sf*
Tuat *Tf*
Venom

392 *2×196 = 4×98 = 7×56 =8×49 = 14×28*

Athanor
Hearts of Men *Nf*
O Prophet! *Tf, ŏ*
Virtue

393 *3×131*

Bride of Chaos *Sf, k, ŏ*
Eye of Shiva
Holiest *ST, Tf*
Intellect *Tf, k*
Jehannum
Maruts *Sf*
Practicus *Sf, k*
Sanguine
The Giant Glacier
Throned
Thunder
Venus *Sf*
Working

394 *2×197*

Accompanied *kk*
Creatures *Sf, k*
Hierophant *Tf*
Openly
Toils *Sf*

395 *5×79*

Equilibrated
Spice and Gold
Star-Lit Heaven *ST, Nf*

396 *2×198 = 3×132 = 4×99 =6×66 = 9×44 = 11×36 = 12×33 =18×22*

Christus *ST,Sf*
Enswathes Thee
Secret Refuge *k*
Snows *Sf*

Π **397**

Gladiator
His Building
Infinite Bliss *SSf*
Mothers *Sf*
Shaarimoth
Twenty

398 *2×199*

Chaos is my Name *k, ŏ*
Closed Palace 418 *k, L*
Fire of His Angel
Imperfection *Nf, k*
Let ASAR Be With ISA
Little Flame
Lying Spirits *Sf*
Pole-Star *ST*
Sat-Chit-Ananda

399 *3×133 = 7×57 = 19×21*

Dissolved
Fire and Sword
I Am Eternity
Lapis Lazuli
Mysteries Averse *ST*
Slime of Khem
Unright *Tf*

400 *2×200 = 4×100 = 5×80 =8×50 = 10×40 = 16×25 = 20^2*

	A Great Curse		k
	All Ordeals		
	Conquer!		k, ŏ
	Defunct		Tf, k
	Harmony		
	My Fair One		
	Selflessness is Self		
	Tarot		Tf
	VVVVV		
	W		W
Π	**401**		
	Children of Men		Nf
	Heavenly Kiss		SSf
	We		W
	402	*2×201 = 3×134 = 6×67*	
	Commander		k
	His Stability		ST
	ISIS Shall Await ASAR		
	Secret & Not		Tf, k, ŏ
	Stone		ST
	The Vast Sacrifice		ST, k
	Thirty-Three		
	Tunic		k
	Wicked On Earth		k, ŏ
	Window		
	403	*13×31*	
	Every Way Perfect		Tf
	Fortress		SSf
	ISIS and OSIRIS		
	Kiblah for Ever		
	Our Law		ŏ
	Supernals		Sf
	404	*2×202 = 4×101*	
	Accurst		ST, Tf, kk
	Cactus		Sf, kk
	Christianity *—C soft here, see Special Considerations and entry 431		ST
	Complement		Tf, k, ŏ
	Jesus Christ*—C soft here, see Special Considerations and entry 431		ST, Tf
	Mallow		
	Thaumiel		
	The Green Serpent		Tf
	405	*3×135 = 5×81 = 9×45 =15×27*	
	Mazloth		
	The Fires of Life		
	The Red Powder		
	The Work		
	War and Vengeance		
Σ28	**406**	*2×203 = 7×58 = 14×29*	
	Application		Nf, k
	It is Written		Nf
	Seven Delights		Sf
	The Peoples		Sf
	407	*11×37*	
	Dance of Shiva		
	Doric Boy		k, ŏ
	HARPOCRATES		Sf, k
	His Kingdom		
	Inhabitants		Sf
	Rituals		Sf
	Throat		Tf
	Thy Nakedness		
	Web		W
	Wife		W
	408	*2×204 = 3×136 = 4×102 =6×68 = 8×51 = 12×34 = 17×24*	
	Current		Tf, k
	Excellent Kisses		Sf
	Falutli!		
	Geomancy		
	Great is the Beast		ST, Tf
	Grinding-Up		

Sunset *Tf*

Π **409**

A Ram's Horns *Sf*
Beware Therefore!
Blind One
Mentu
Most High *ST*
Olympas *Sf*
OXO (The Cry of the 15th Aethyr)

410 *2×205 = 5×82 = 10×41*

Breathed the Light *Tf*
Child HORUS *Sf, ŏ*
Curse Them *k*
Food
Fortresses *Sf*
Sparrowhawk
Time is Not *Tf, ŏ*
Towers *Sf*
Toys *Sf*

411 *3×137*

Four
KHONSU *ŏ*
Lengthening
Oyster *ST*
Stable Abode *ST*
Tahuti
The Crown *Nf, k*
There Shall Be An End

412 *2×206 = 4×103*

A Shining Pylon *Nf, ŏ*
Circle of Emerald *k*
Gehinnom
Holy *Qabalah*
My Great Light *Tf*
No Beast *ST*
The Magus *Sf*
Truth

413 *7×59*

First and Last *ST, Tf*
Generation *Nf*
Minute
Morning
Organisms *Sf*
Teonim
This and That *Tf*
War *W*
Wide *W*

414 *2×207 = 3×138 = 6×69 =9×46 = 18×23*

Bare and Rejoicing
Empress and the King
Holy GRAAL
Image of An Image
Kingdoms *Sf*
Loves Sake
New CHAOS *Sf, k*
Proof
Wear *W*

415 *5×83*

All is Dispersion *Nf*
His Weapons *Sf*
Hood
I Write Not *Tf, ŏ*
Temple At Thebai
The Oath
The Sparrow
Twelve Rays *Sf*
Unveiler
Veiled One
Work is Ended

416 *2×208 = 4×104 = 8×52 =13×32 = 16×26*

Chalcedony
Cosmos *Sf, k, ŏ*
Dagger of Penance

Holiness *SSf*
HOOR
Hour
Place of Silence
The Owl

417 *3×139*

Company *k*
Door
Infinite Abyss *SSf*
My Worship
O Serpent Apep
On His Forehead *ŏ*
Points *Sf*
The TARO
Their Gods & Their Men *Nf, ŏ*
Whole Heaven *Nf*
Wolf's Bane

418 *2×209 = 11×38 = 19×22*

Barren Words *Sf*
Be-With-Us *Sf*
Corinth *k*
Crystal-Gazing *ST, k*
Let ASAR Be With ISA *L*
First Ordeal *ST*
Hoofed
Invisibility
The PROPHET *Tf*
THE SILVER STAR *ST*

Π **419**

Destroy *ST*
Noise *ŏ*
Orion *Nf*
Reconcilers *Sf, k*
Send Forth
Serpent of APEP
The Damned in Hell
The Goat *Tf*

420 *2×210 = 3×140 = 4×105 =5×84 = 6×70 = 7×60 = 10×42 = 12×35= 14×30 = 15×28 = 20×21*

Adytum
Great Voice
His Throne
Lofty
My Servants
Proud
The Naked Brilliance

Π **421**

Darkness is Made Light *Tf*
Day of MAAT *Tf*
Deo Duce
Flamed Forth
Gryphon's *Sf*
Speak Not *Tf*
The Other
Titahion *Nf*

422 *2×211*

Head of the Swan *Nf*
Innocence
My Prophet *Tf*
O Babylon *Nf, ŏ*
Prophet of Had! *ŏ*
Until

423 *3×141 = 9×47*

All Words *Sf*
Anchorite *k*
Because and His Kin! *Nf, k*
Christus *ST,Sf, k*
Dark Brothers *Sf*
Tzabaoth
Vault *Tf*
Vault *Tf*
Winged Secret Flame *k*
Ye Mockers *Sf, k*

424 *2×212 = 4×106 = 8×53*

End of Time
Loving
Our Bed
The Vision *Nf*
Violet *Tf*

425 *5×85 = 17×25*

Fire of Madness *SSf*
Golden Eagle
Radiant God
Rhinoceros *Sf, ŏ*
Virgin and the Man *Nf*

426 *2×213 = 3×142 = 6×71*

Aurora
Great White King
Inspiration *Nf*
The Bar of Heaven *Nf*
Thorns *Sf*

427 *7×61*

Father of All
Hiding of Hadit *Tf*
Pall of Death
Stolas *ST,Sf*
Sworded Sphinx
Thrones *Sf*

428 *2×214 = 4×107*

Centuries *Sf*
Good
O God
Orientis *Sf*

429 *3×143 = 11×39 = 13×33*

Destroyer *ST*
Half Known *Nf*
Head of the Hawk
HOOR-RA
It Burns *Sf*
Judgment *Tf*
Malkuth
RA HOOR
Rejoice With Me
Ruby Star *ST*
Serpent Flame Therein *Nf*
The Chief of All
The Elements *Sf, L*
Winged With Flame
Wise *W*

430 *2×215 = 5×86 = 10×43*

Bewitchments *Sf*
Half-Concealed *k*
Holy Ring
Judgement *Tf*
Philosophers *Sf, ŏ*
Strong *ST*
Wedge *W*

Π **431**

Christianity *ST, k*
Jesus Christ *ST,Tf, k*
Kabeshunt *Tf*
Thanksgiving
The Priest Answered *ST*
Water of Life

432 *2×216 = 3×144 = 4×108 =6×72 = 8×54 = 9×48 = 12×36 = 16×27= 18×24*

Holy *Qabalah* *L*
Horizon *Nf*
House
Infinite Within *Nf*
Passionate
Primeval Things *Sf*

Π **433**

Argument *Tf*
Globéd Priest *ST,Tf*
Heart of Hadit *Tf*
Name Thereof

None Indeed
Potest ST,Tf
Slaves Shall Serve
Sweet Are my Kisses Sf
Thy Robes Sf
Virtus Sf

434 *2×217 = 7×62 = 14×31*

Ancient Marvel
Birth of Hell
Circle in the Middle is Red k
Eight and the Three
Horror
Longing
Small Dark Orb
Statue ST
Together

Σ29 **435** *3×145 = 5×87 = 15×29*

Bringer-Forth
Eye in the Midst ST,Tf
Five Bulls Sf
Frontiers Sf
Gargantuan Nf
Man of Earth
Thunders Sf
Weak W

436 *2×218 = 4×109*

Book
My Number
Sevenfold
The Gemmêd Azure
Their Brows Sf
Thy Name is Death

437 *19×23*

Hierophantic k
Poison Nf
Source

438 *2×219 = 3×146 = 6×73*

Arouse
BES-NA-MAUT Tf
Great Bull
The Holier Place
Thy Cup-Bearer k
Whips W

Π **439**

Crocodile kk, ŏ
Gladiators Sf
Infinite Stars ST,Sf
Sebek my Lord
Substance ST

440 *2×220 = 4×110 = 5×88 =8×55 = 10×44 = 11×40 = 20×22*

Beatific Vision Nf
Consecrating kk, ŏ
Delightful
Empty God
Go! Go!
Great Work Tf
HORUS
Knowledge
Kundalini
My Son is He
Neapolitan Nf
Perdurabo
Purpose
Secret Word k
Single One
THAT and THIS Sf
The Flaming Star ST
Thick Leavings Sf, k
Wingêd Globe
Zazas, Zazas, Nasatanada Zazas

441 *3×147 = 7×63 = 9×49 =21²*

A Morning Star ST, ŏ
Lapis Lazuli & Jasper

Lonely
My Love
One Light *Tf*
Sixfold Star *ST*
The Name BABALON *ŏ*

442 *2×221 = 13×34 = 17×26*

Argentum
Exalted One
Lowest *ST,Tf*
The Elixir of Life
Unity
Universal
Vim Patior

Π **443**

Her Soft Feet
Meal & Honey
Neptune
Orison *Nf*
Pure Black Marble *k*
Stature *ST*
Sweet-Smelling

444 *2×222 = 3×148 = 4×111 =6×74 = 12×37*

Birth of Death
Comedy of Pan *Nf, k, ŏ*
Crucifixion *Nf*
Eye is Seventy
Not Extended *ŏ*
Obeah and the *Wanga* *ŏ*
Sequor
Stones *ST,Sf*

445 *5×89*

God & the Adorer *ŏ*
Hierophant's *Sf*
In the Beginning
Malediction *Nf, k*
Opus *Sf*
Right and the Averse
Sole Light *Tf*
The Giant Time
Vitriol

446 *2×223*

Give Me Thy Kisses *Sf*
Moon *Nf*
My Fertility
Poseidon *Nf*
Prostate *ST*
The English Alphabet *Tf*
The Lover
Thy Joy
Wicked *W*

447 *3×149*

By His Wisdom
End of Their Desire
Exposure
Opium
Taotzem
Unveils *Sf*

448 *2×224 = 4×112 = 7×64 =8×56 = 14×32 = 16×28*

Evil Ones *Sf*
God the Blessed
Lance of Death
Swallow
The Secret Light *k*
The Word ABRAHADABRA

Π **449**

All Penetrant *Tf*
End the End the End
Hermes the Invisible *Sf*
The Forest *ST*

450 *2×225 = 3×150 = 5×90 =6×75 = 9×50 = 10×45 = 15×30 =18×25*

AMOUN *Nf*
Crowned Child *k*
Kings for Ever

Memento
Neophyte
Sempiterno
Tear Down

451 *11×41*

Lovely
Monster *ST*
Princes of Evil
River of AMRIT *Tf*
Second Death *k*

452 *2×226 = 4×113*

Bath of Myrrh
Fool
Osiris Myself
Sacrifice of Maidens *Sf, k*
Spouse
The Beloved
The Great Waters *Sf*
The Prophet and His Bride! *ŏ*
Under Will

453 *3×151*

Chosen Priest *ST, Tf*
Great Goddess *SSf*
Loathing
Radiant Triangle
The God Phtah
Warm *W*

454 *2×227*

A Golden Hawk
Lower Eyelid
Mansions *Sf*
Number Himself
Snowdrop *ŏ*

455 *5×91 = 7×65 = 13×35*

Cup of Circe *k*
My Secret Centre *k*
Shining Triangle
The Glory

456 *2×228 = 3×152 = 4×114 =6×76 = 8×57 = 12×38 = 19×24*

Abyss of Years *Sf*
BES-NA-MAUT *Sf, Tf*
Night-Blue
O Blessêd Beast, *ST*
Second Triad *k*
Turtle
Uraeus *Sf*
Vice of Kings *Sf*

Π **457**

Alpha Centauri
Law is for All
One in Seven *Nf*
Scourge
Strong in War *ST, ŏ*
Taphthartharath

458 *2×229*

A Single Ruby
Great Terror
Horus *Sf*
New World

459 *3×153 = 9×51 = 17×27*

Arise, O Serpent Apep
God Shu
Trumpeter
Wheel *W*

460 *2×230 = 4×115 = 5×92 =10×46 = 20×23*

Citlaltepetl
Cube in the Circle
Drink to Me
Flood
Iniquity
Perfections *Sf, k*
The Brothers

Π **461**

	Bellowing	
	Feather of MAAT	Tf
	Fields of Light	Tf
	Floor	
	Orobas	Sf
	Star and the Snake	ST
	The Mother	
462	2×231 = 3×154 = 6×77 =7×66 = 11×42 = 14×33 = 21×22	
	Armour	
	Day of Wrath	
	Elephant God	
	Precious	Sf
	The Forties	Sf
	Unstable	ST
Π **463**		
	Begone! Ye Mockers	k, ŏŏ
	Elevenfold	
	THAT is God	
	That Veil is Black	
	The Exorcist	ST
	The Low Men	Nf
	Thy Voice	
	Vestments	ST,Sf
464	2×232 = 4×116 = 8×58 =16×29	
	An Evening Star	ST
	Blood	
	Courage	k
	Enthroned	
	Guardian Angel	
	My Number is 11	
	Terminus	Sf
	Traitors	Sf
Σ30 **465**	3×155 = 5×93 = 15×31	
	Angel of Death	
	Double	
	So Chosen	Nf
	Solitude	ŏ
466	2×233	
	By the *Iod* and the *Pe*	ŏ
	Cup Preserveth	k
	Directions	Sf, k
	Knoweth	
	My Secret Temple	k
	One in Eight	Tf
	The Secret Serpent	Tf, k
Π **467**		
	Beatific Vision	Nf, k
	City of DIANA	
	Cry of the Man	Nf, k
	Eve and the Serpent	Tf
	Grace of God	
	Spirit Alone	
	The Infinite Bliss	
468	2×234 = 3×156 = 4×117 =6×78 = 9×52 = 12×39 = 13×36 =18×26	
	Eternity and Space	
	I Lift Thee Up	
	R P S T O V A L	
469	7×67	
	Arise! Move! and Appear!	
	BAHLASTI! OMPEHDA!	ST
	Be He Damned for A Dog!	ŏ
	Dog- Faced Demons	ŏ
	Labour	
	Let Being Be Empty	
	My Bowels	Sf
	Nothing	
	Olive Oil	ŏ
	Pyromancy	
470	2×235 = 5×94 = 10×47	
	Bosom	
	Coin Redeemeth	k
	Goods	Sf

	One Particle	k
	Opened Mine Eye	
	Scorpio	k
471	*3×157*	
	Aormuzdi	
	Every Woman	Nf
	Five Pointed	
	Great and Terrible Seal	
	Hands of the Man	Nf
	Juno	
472	*2×236 = 4×118 = 8×59*	
	Ardours	Sf
	Cohesion	Nf, k
	Here Abideth Terror	
	Obligation	Nf, ŏ
	The Known	Nf
473	*11×43*	
	A Nothing	
	All Worlds	Sf
	Aquarius	Sf
	Children of Earth	
	Liquor	
	Mahasatipatthana	
	The All-Wandering Air	
	Unimaginable	
	Weird Winged God	
	Wicked	W, k
474	*2×237 = 3×158 = 6×79*	
	Fish-Hook	
	He Knoweth	
	Houses	Sf
	I Am the Worshipper	
	My Silence is Mightier	
	Shells of Abaddon	Nf, ŏ
	Soul	
	Speak Truth	
	The Tree of Life	
	The *Zelator*	
475	*5×95 = 19×25*	
	Sevenfold Speech	
	The Worlds	Sf
	Tzalalimiron	Nf
	Wine	W
476	*2×238 = 4×119 = 7×68 =14×34 = 17×28*	
	& Therein Am I As A Babe in An Egg	
	I and the Earth Are One	ŏ
	Noon	Nf
	Pregnant Goddess	SSf, ŏ
	Refuse Not	Tf, ŏ
	Scorpion	Nf, k
	Sixty-One	
	The Knower	
477	*3×159 = 9×53*	
	Penned Indus	Sf
	Rise O my Snake	
478	*2×239*	
	A White Goat	Tf
	Attainment	Tf
	Books	Sf
	Divination	Nf
	Fortify It!	Tf
	Light is One	
	Wishes	W, Sf
Π **479**		
	Prince & Apostle	ST
	Submitted	
	The Giver of Life,	
	Trample Down	Nf
	Whirled	W
480	*2×240 = 3×160 = 4×120 =5×96 = 6×80 = 8×60 = 10×48 = 12×40= 15×32 = 16×30 = 20×24*	
	Fire & Blood	

Judgments *Sf*
Look
Lucifuge
Plough
Starry Blue *ST*
Strength & Sight *ST,Tf*
The Sacred Mysteries *ST,Sf, k*
Union *Nf*

481 *13×37*

Brilliant Stars *ST,Sf*
Encloseth *k*
Eye of the Hawk
Judgements *Sf*
King Against King! *ST*

482 *2×241*

Elephant God *L*
Emblems of Death
Sigil of the Eye
The Egg of Spirit *Tf*
Wand *W*
Wind *W*

483 *3×161 = 7×69 = 21×23*

Elevenfold *L*
Mercy Let Be Off!

484 *2×242 = 4×121 = 11×44 =22²*

A Further Secret *Tf, k*
Aught in Sacrifice *k*
Bound
Father of All Life
Peradventure
Perfect, Being Not *Tf, k, ŏ*
The Wheel of Life
Walk *W*

485 *5×97*

Hound
Lord of Fire
Shells of the Dead
The Qliphoth
The Star & the Snake *ST*
Unique

486 *2×243 = 3×162 = 6×81 =9×54 = 18×27*

Prince-Priest the Beast *ST,Tf*
There is Success *SSf, k*
Weave *W*

Π **487**

Every Number
Foolish
Gone Forth *ŏ*
Goose's *Sf*
Volatile

488 *2×244 = 4×122 = 8×61*

Great Angel HUA
Khabs in the Khu
Nameless Goal
Nations *Sf*
The Eternal Rock *k, ŏ*
The Lovers *Sf*

489 *3×163*

Glory Ineffable
Lonely Am I
My Lord Hadit *Tf*
Out *Tf*
Pillar of Salt *Tf*
Silence & Strength *ST*

490 *2×245 = 5×98 = 7×70 =10×49 = 14×35*

Dog Cerebus *Sf*
Loom
Shrouds *Sf*
Swoon *Nf*

Π **491**

Axle of the Wheel
Flaming Sword
Foot *Tf*

He Hath Drawn the Black Bean *Nf*
Holy Alphabet *Tf*
Initiator
Sweeter Than Death
Victory *k*

492 *2×246 = 3×164 = 4×123 =6×82 = 12×41*

Black Brothers *Sf, k*
Initiation *Nf*
Knowest *ST,Tf*
Restriction *ST, Nf, k*
Scourged *k*
Scream of the Eagle *k*
Sorceress Shall Be Desired

493 *17×29*

Bright Glory
Delusion *Nf*
Knower, and Me
Rhadamanthus *Sf*
Sulphur
Wit *W, Tf*

494 *2×247 = 13×38 = 19×26*

Be Done With Speech
Conquering *k, ŏ*
Double-Headed
Equinox
Fools *Sf*
Shew-Stone *ST*
The Wretched & the Weak
Violent *Tf*
Wing *W*

495 *3×165 = 5×99 = 9×55 =11×45 = 15×33*

A Flaming Sword
Bal is the Sword
King's Daughter
Lady Nuit *Tf*
My Image in the East *ST,Tf*
O Warrior
Ultimate

Σ31 **496** *2×248 = 4×124 = 8×62 =16×31*

Accursed Are They *kk*
Falsehood
The Evening Star *ST*
The Space Beyond
The Wand Createth *k*

497 *7×71*

Necromancy *k*
Palace of the King
Thy Light is in Me

498 *2×249 = 3×166 = 6×83*

Dionysus *Sf, ŏ*
Enough
IAO and OAI
Murmur
No God
OTO
Sacrifice Cattle After A Child
The Athanor
The Hearts of Men *Nf*
Wanga *W*

Π **499**

Image of God
Incarnation *Nf, k*
Nay Are None
The Bride of Chaos *Sf, k, ŏ*
The Eye of Shiva
The Pylon
Unveiling
Upon Them! *ŏ*
Wayfarer *W*

500 *2×250 = 4×125 = 5×100 =10×50 = 20×25*

Ape of Thoth *ŏ*
Change is stability *ST*

Egg of Blue
Flutters *Sf*
Moloch
The Hierophant *Tf*
Tzelmoth
Ways of the Ka!
What *W, Tf*

501 *3×167*

Just I Am Eight *ST, Tf*
Mantras and Spells *Sf*
Secret of His Being *k*
The Star-Lit Heaven *ST, Nf*
Trumpeters *Sf*
Understand *ST*
Well *W*
Wheels *W, Sf*

502 *2×251*

Chamber of the King
Death of A Sinner
Eternal Rock *k*
Ho! Warrior
Sorrow
Wit *W*
Writ *W, Tf*

Π **503**

Cast Down *ST, k*
Doubt *Tf*
Eight Quarters *Sf*
Thee and Thy Staff *ST*
Wingêd *W*

504 *2×252 = 3×168 = 4×126 =6×84 = 7×72 = 8×63 = 9×56 = 12×42 =14×36 = 18×28 = 21×24*

Eternal One
Heart and the Serpent *Tf*
Love Chant *Tf*
The Fire of His Angel
The Pole-Star *ST*

505 *5×101*

Eye of my Father
Formula

506 *2×253 = 11×46 = 22×23*

Be Upon Them! *ŏ*
Blessing & Worship
Choose Ye
Dweller of Nile!
Rosy Cross *SSf, k, ŏ*
TAN is the Balances *Sf, L*
The TUAT
Transport *Tf*
Voice of Fire

507 *3×169 = 13×39*

Apollo
Beds of Purple
Cauldron *Nf, k*
Others Are Secret *Tf, k*
Sagittarius *Sf*
Tall crown *Nf, k*

508 *2×254 = 4×127*

Devourer
Eunuch *k*
Eye in the Triangle
Nameless Goal *L*
Outer
Punishment *Tf*
The Practicus *kk*
The Stone *ST*
The Wicked On Earth *k, ŏ*
Virgin Goddess *SSf*

Π **509**

Key of It All

510 *2×255 = 3×170 = 5×102 =6×85 = 10×51 = 15×34 = 17×30*

Dolores *Sf*

	Future	
	Life Which Abideth in Light	*Tf*
	Mighty One	
	Poisoned	
	Pyramid of Light	*Tf*
	Spider's Web of Silver	
	Tincture	*k*
	Woods	*Sf*
511	*7×73*	
	All Rituals	*Sf*
	Inviolate	
	Tetragrammaton	*Nf, ŏ*
512	*2×256 = 4×128 = 8×64 =16×32 = 8^3 = 2^9*	
	Columns	*Sf, k, ŏ*
	Delicious	*Sf*
	Logos	*Sf*
	O PROPHET!	*Tf*
	Pomegranate in Hell	*ŏ*
	Seek A Spouse	
	The Seven Delights	*Sf*
	Uttereth	
	Water	*W*
	Water the Rose	
	Write	*W*
513	*3×171 = 9×57 = 19×27*	
	His Attainment	*Tf*
	Nubian Slave	
	The Rituals	*Sf*
	Under the Earth	
	Vigour	
	Word of Sin	*Nf*
514	*2×257*	
	Cube in the Circle	*kk*
	Pit Called Because	*kk*
515	*5×103*	
	Beast of the Field	*ST*
	Iacchus Invisible	*k*
	Lord the Beast	*ST, Tf*
	Multiply	
	The Blind One	
	The Most High	*ST*
	There is No Difference	
516	*2×258 = 3×172 = 4×129 =6×86 = 12×43*	
	A Secret Glory	*k*
	Abomination	*Nf, ŏ*
	All Truth	
	Khabs is in the Khu	
	Serpent Woman	*Nf*
	Souls	*Sf*
	Waters of Death	
	Write, & Find Ecstasy	*ST, k*
517	*11×47*	
	His Name Concealed	*k*
	I Am Nothing	
	My Throat	*Tf*
	Palace of the King	*L*
	Wines	*W, Sf*
518	*2×259 = 7×74 = 14×37*	
	Chaos is my Name	*k*
	Concubine	*kk, ŏ*
	Egg of Blackness	*SSf, k*
	The Crocodile	*kk, ŏ*
	Wrath	*W*
519	*3×173*	
	Blanched Eyeless Beetles	*Sf*
	Exclusively	*k*
	Her Holy Cteis	*Sf, k*
	Light of my Bride	
	Queen of Space	
	Unicorn	*Nf, k*
520	*2×260 = 4×130 = 5×104 =8×65 = 10×52 = 13×40 = 20×26*	
	Crowned Beast	*ST, Tf, k*
	Dance Together	

	Enginery of War	
	No More	
	Play of the Magician	*Nf*
	The Empress and the King	
	Weather	*W*
	Wisdom is the Man	*Nf*
Π **521**		
	Chaos and Night and Pan	*Nf, k, ŏ*
	Divine Perfection	*Nf, k*
	Enlightenment	*Tf*
	ISIS my Mother	
	Saviour	
	Strange Pale God	*ST*
	The Work is Ended	
	Tyrian Purple	
522	*2×261 = 3×174 = 6×87 =9×58 = 18×29*	
	Conquest	*S T, T f, k, ŏ*
	Regulus	*Sf*
Π **523**		
	Boat of Ra	
	Glamour	
	Our Law	
	Skin of Breasts	*ST,Sf*
	Thanatos	*Sf*
	The Infinite Abyss	*SSf*
	There is One God	*ŏ*
	To my Name	
524	*2×262 = 4×131*	
	Children of Light	*Tf*
	Crablouse	*k*
	Forneus	*Sf*
	Outer Fire	
	The First Ordeal	*ST*
	Triumphant	*Tf*
	Wands	*W, Sf*
	Winds	*W, Sf*
525	*3×175 = 5×105 = 7×75 =15×35 = 21×25*	
	Annihilation	*Nf*
	Destroyeth	*ST*
	Good Flame	
	Hathoor	
	Innermost	*ST,Tf*
	Mistletoe	*ST*
	Ruins of Eden	*Nf*
	Uranus	*Sf*
	Whoredom	
526	*2×263*	
	Column	*Nf, k*
	Deal Hardly With Them	
	Scarlet Woman	*Nf, k*
	Serpent of Death	
	The Adytum	
	Weighing	*W*
527	*17×31*	
	Eternity calls	*Sf, k*
	False Moon	*Nf*
	God of Lies	*Sf*
	Hounds	*Sf*
	Stainless Abode	*ST*
	That of Death	
	The Darkness is Made Light	*Tf*
	Waves	*W, Sf*
Σ32 **528**	*2×264 = 3×176 = 4×132 =6×88 = 8×66 = 11×48 = 12×44 = 16×33= 22×24*	
	Court	*Tf, k*
	Equilibrium	
	Glasya-Labolas	*Sf*
	Silver and Gold	
	The Great Work	*Tf*
	There is No Law	
	Twain His Forces	*Sf*
529	*23²*	
	Ahathoor	

	Heart of IAO	
	Manhood	
	South	
	The Dark Brothers	*Sf*
	The Winged Secret Flame	*k*
530	*2×265 = 5×106 = 10×53*	
	Child Horus	*Sf*
	Clouds	*Sf, k*
	Rich Fresh Blood	
	Sword and the Spear	
	The Second Death	
531	*3×177 = 9×59*	
	Crystal Cube	*ST, kk*
	Khonsu	
	Snakestone	*ST*
	The Virgin and the Man	*Nf*
	Thy Secret Temple	*k*
532	*2×266 = 4×133 = 7×76 =14×38 = 19×28*	
	Crucified One	*k*
	End and the Beginning	
	Every Heart of Man	*Nf*
	System & System	*ST*
	The Great White King	
	Trigrammaton	*Nf*
	West	*ST, W, Tf*
533	*13×41*	
	Antinomies	*Sf*
	Clamour	*k*
	Emanations	*Sf*
	Masses of Flaming Hair	
	Pale Or Purple	
	The Hiding of HADIT	*Tf*
	The Pall of Death	
	The Sworded Sphinx	
534	*2×267 = 3×178 = 6×89*	
	Bright, Evening Star	*ST*
	Great Pyramids of Gizeh	
	Great Stone	*ST*
	There is Naught	*Tf*
535	*5×107*	
	Blue & Gold	
	Compassion	*Nf, k*
	He God is One	
	MERCURIUS	*Sf, k*
	Stars Concealed	*ST, k*
	The Ruby Star	*ST*
	The Second Triad	
	The Serpent Flame Therein	*Nf*
	The Wise	
536	*2×268 = 4×134 = 8×67*	
	Made He the Worlds	*Sf*
	Mystery of Pan	*ST, Nf*
	Prophets Shall Prophecy	*ŏŏ*
	Severe the Ordeals	*Sf*
	The Evil Ones	
	The Holy Ring	
	Wings	*W, Sf*
537	*3×179*	
	Priest & Apostle	*ST*
	Sparrow God	
	The Water of Life	
	Their Gods & Their Men	*Nf*
538	*2×269*	
	Blooms	*Sf*
	The Holy *Qabalah*	*L*
	The Infinite Within	*Nf*
	The Primeval Things	*Sf*
539	*7×77 = 11×49*	
	The Globéd Priest	*ST, Tf*
	The Heart of HADIT	*Tf*
	The Name Thereof	
	The Slaves Shall Serve	
	Waist	*ST, W, Tf*

540 *2×270 = 3×180 = 4×135 =5×108 = 6×90 = 9×60 = 10×54 = 12×45= 15×36 = 18×30 = 20×27*

Loveliness *SSf*
The Ancient Marvel
The Birth of Hell
The Eight and the Three
Virgin of All Men *Nf*

Π **541**

Book Ten *Nf*
Leaping Laughter
No-One
Our Lady
Shoulders *Sf*
Spirit of Prophesy *ŏ*
The Eye in the Midst *ST, Tf*
The Man of Earth
Torsion *Nf*
Unstable Isle *ST*

542 *2×271*

Hierophant's Name
Nay for Myself
White Brothers *Sf*

543 *3×181*

Curse of His Grade *k*
Drunkenness *SSf*
Emancipations *Sf*
New Truth
The Rose-cross *SSf, k, ŏ*
Thy Toy

544 *2×272 = 4×136 = 8×68 =16×34 = 17×32*

Covenant *Tf, k*
Cursed Cursed *kk*
Lighten Thine Eyes *Sf*
Night of Time
The Vice of Kings
Vishu-Hari-Krishna-Rama
Will *WL*

545 *5×109*

Little Flowers *Sf, ŏ*
Love-Philtres *Sf*
Mighty Are the Stars *ST, Sf*
Mouth
My Fields and my Gardens *Sf*

546 *2×273 = 3×182 = 6×91 =7×78 = 13×42 = 14×39 = 21×26*

Holy Assembly
Lion-Roar
Summus *Sf*
The Wingêd Globe

Π **547**

Destroy Himself *ST*
Subtlety
The Sixfold Star *ST*

548 *2×274 = 4×137*

Face of the Sun *Nf*
Goodly
Motion *Nf*
O Scribe and Prophet *Tf, k, ŏ*
The Exalted One

549 *3×183 = 9×61*

Now Rejoice!

550 *2×275 = 5×110 = 10×55 =11×50 = 22×25*

Chain Armour
Grade of Magus *Sf*
Key of this Law
Mine is the Sword
NOX *X, ŏ*
Resinous *Sf*
The Birth of Death
The Comedy of Pan *Nf, k, ŏ*
The Eye is Seventy
The *Obeah* and the *Wanga* *ŏ*
Twelvefold

Wear to Me Jewels!

551 *19×29*

KRONOS *Sf*
Mind of the Father
O my Chosen! *Nf*
PLUTO
The Right and the Averse
The Sole Light *Tf*

552 *2×276 = 3×184 = 4×138 =6×92 = 8×69 = 12×46 = 23×24*

All Power Given
Claws of the Eagle *k*
Clerk-House *k*
Distant Drug *ST*
Face of Mohammed
Golden Cross *SSf, k, ŏ*
Incubus *Sf, k*
Majic Liquor *k*
Sacrifice Cattle After A Child *kk*
There Shall Ye Find Them
Troops *Sf*
Universal Heart *Tf*
World Elephant *Tf*

553 *7×79*

A Worm *W*
Languor
Mercy of God
O Nile-God
Paths of the Tree
Taurus *Sf*

554 *2×277*

Circle of the Sabbath *k*
Father and Creator *k*
Grade of a Magus *Sf*
Parthenogenesis *Sf*
Waters *W, Sf*

555 *3×185 = 5×111 = 15×37*

Born in A Stable *ST*
Secret, O Prophet! *Tf, k, ŏ*
The End the End the End
Unassuaged

556 *2×278 = 4×139*

Disruption *Nf*

Π **557**

Bind Nothing!
Companion *Nf, k*
The Princes of Evil
The Second Death *k*

558 *2×279 = 3×186 = 6×93 =9×62 = 18×31*

Concealment *Tf, k*
Drawn By Doves *Sf*
The Fool

559 *13×43*

Hoor-Pa-Kraat *Tf*
Shadow of a Man *Nf*
The Chosen Priest *ST, Tf*
The Radiant Triangle

560 *2×280 = 4×140 = 5×112 =7×80 = 8×70 = 10×56 = 14×40 = 16×35= 20×28*

Mother and the Babe
Ronove
Wealth *W*
Wheel of the Spirit *Tf*
Young

Σ33 **561** *3×187 = 11×51 = 17×33*

Bull of Apis *Sf*
Mother Darkness *SSf*
My Fleece is White and Warm
Overcome *k*
The Shining Triangle

562 *2×281*

Auramoth
Fire and Blood
Folly Against Self *ST, ŏ*

	Order & Value	
	Strength and Sight	ST, Tf
	The Second Triad	k
	Wings of the Eagle	
Π 563		
	O Nuit	Tf
	The Law is for All	
	the Three-Fold Regimen	Nf
564	2×282 = 3×188 = 4×141 =6×94 = 12×47	
	Almighty One	
	Manifestation	ST, Nf
	Mighty Sepulchre	k
	Purification	Nf, k
	The Great Terror	
	Trouble	
	Whirling	W
	Worship Impure	
565	5×113	
	Beautiful	
	Parts of the Earth	
	Plant the Rose	
	Splendour	
	The God Shu	
	The Wheel	
566	2×283	
	Eyes of Jesus	Sf
	I Have Opened Mine Eye	
	The Perfections	Sf, k
	Withholdest	ST, Tf
567	3×189 = 7×81 = 9×63 =21×27	
	Chariots of Fire	
	Corn of Ceres	Sf, k
	Hollow	
	Light, Love, Life	
	Sons of Men	Nf
	The Christian Church	ST
568	2×284 = 4×142 = 8×71	
	Great Book	
	Lion Mau	
Π 569		
	Nemyss of Secrecy	k
	Smooth	
	To Come	k
570	2×285 = 3×190 = 5×114 =6×95 = 10×57 = 15×38 = 19×30	
	Comfort	Tf, k
	Grey Land my God	
	The Traitors	Sf
Π 571		
	Contending	k
	Heart of the Star	ST
	The Angel of Death	
572	2×286 = 4×143 = 11×52 =13×44 = 22×26	
	Courtesan	Nf, k
	Heliotrop	
	HOOR-PAAR-KRAAT	Tf
	Interpenetrateth	
	O NUIT!	
	One of Heaven	Nf
	One Sword	
	The Children of PTAH	
	The Cup Preserveth	k
	This Child is Also Abel	
	World Elephant	Tf, L
573	3×191	
	Key of the Abyss	SSf
	Smite the Peoples	Sf
	The Beatific Vision	Nf, k
	The City of DIANA	
	The Perfect and the Perfect	Tf, kk
	The Pillars Are the Cross	SSf, k, ŏ
	What Axle	W
574	2×287 = 7×82 = 14×41	

	Blade of the Serpent	Tf
	Damned for A Dog	
	Fall of Because	k
	My Blood	
575	5×115 = 23×25	
	Kings of the Earth	
	Lamentation	Nf
	The Snake is Entwined	
	Times of Darkness	SSf
	Varruna-Avatar	
576	2×288 = 3×192 = 4×144 =6×96 = 8×72 = 9×64 = 12×48 = 16×36= 18×32 = 24^2	
	Four Gates	Sf
	Path of the Adepts	Sf
	The Coin Redeemeth	k
Π **577**		
	Accursed One	kk
	Ages Beyond the Ages	Sf
	Birth of Form	
	Hindoo Kali	
	O my Lord	
	Swords & With Spears	Sf
578	2×289 = 17×34	
	Abominable Ones	Sf, ♉
	Dogs of Reason	Nf, ♉
	No-Thing-Tree	
	Nuteru	
	Of the Gods	Sf
	Yod He Vau He	
579	3×193	
	Golden Sun	Nf
	Infinite Number	
	Love is the Law	
	Obey my Prophet!	Tf, ♉
	War-Engine	W
	Wrong	W, ♉
	Xenopilus	Sf
	Yellow Priest	ST, Tf
580	2×290 = 4×145 = 5×116 =10×58 = 20×29	
	Government	Tf
	Mongol	
	Night-Blue Sky	
	Psychopomp	k
	Secret Door	k
	The Cup Preserveth He	k
	Twelve Squares	Sf
	Under the Stars	ST, Sf
	Wounds	Sf
581	7×83	
	Abyss of the Great Deep	
	Phallus of ASAR	
	Strong Knights	ST, Sf, ♉
	Whirling Air	W
582	2×291 = 3×194 = 6×97	
	Scorpions	Sf, k
	The Scorpion	Nf, k
583	11×53	
	Absolute	
	Consoled	k
	Queen of Heaven	Nf
	Sign of the Beetle	
	Whirlpool	
584	2×292 = 4×146 = 8×73	
	As Brothers Fight Ye!	
	Bend Upon Them	♉
	Consoler	k
	Fire and Light in Their Eyes	Sf
	Fountain	Nf
	O Purity!	
	The Light is One	
585	3×195 = 5×117 = 9×65 =13×45 = 15×39	
	Death for the Dogs	Sf, ♉

My Armies and my Navies *Sf*

586 *2×293*

Blade of the Pylon *Nf, ŏ*

Blossoms *Sf*

Nought *Tf*

The Starry Blue *ST*

Π **587**

Come Forth *k*

Dagger Destroyeth *ST*

LUX in *Luce*

Serpent of Delight *Tf*

Shadow of An Ape

The Eye of the Hawk

588 *2×294 = 3×196 = 4×147 =6×98 = 7×84 = 12×49 = 14×42 =21×28*

Aeon of my Father *ŏ*

Force of COPH NIA *ŏ*

Priest of the Princes, *ST,Sf*

The Emblems of Death

The Sigil of the Eye

589 *19×31*

Angel of the East *ST, Tf*

Comforter *k*

Count *Tf, k*

Strive With His Might *ST, Tf*

The Wheels

Tongue

590 *2×295 = 5×118 = 10×59*

Lotus *Sf*

Splendour & Pride

The Father of All Life

Weakness *W, SSf*

Withdraw! *W*

591 *3×197*

Apophis and Typhon *Nf, ŏ*

Cow of Heaven *Nf, k*

One Knowledge *ŏ*

Palace of the Queen *Nf*

Resurrection *Nf, k*

592 *2×296 = 4×148 = 8×74 =16×37*

Devouring

Great Flood

Joy of Earth *Sf*

The Prince-Priest the Beast *ST, Tf*

Wine of the Sabbath

Π **593**

Hierophantic Task *k*

Rivers of Pestilence *ST*

594 *2×297 = 3×198 = 6×99 =9×66 = 11×54 = 18×33 = 22×27*

Desolator

Fresh Fever from the Skies *Sf*

The Christian Church *ST, k*

The Great Angel HUA

Σ34 **595** *5×119 = 7×85 = 17×35*

Desolation *Nf*

Four Beasts *ST,Sf*

Gate of the Abyss *SSf*

Known & I Never

Lovely Star *ST*

Radiance of Thoth *ŏ*

Secret House *k*

Sevenfold Table

The Glory Ineffable

Understanding *ST*

596 *2×298 = 4×149*

Girdles of Gold

I and the Earth Are One

Pregnant Goddess *SSf*

Secrecy of the Hermit *Tf, k*

Silence of Things *Sf*

Sky of NU

Winners *W, Sf*

597 *3×199*

	Father of All Light	*Tf*
	The Axle of the Wheel	
	The Flaming Sword	
	The Holy Alphabet	*Tf*
	The Victory	*k*
598	*2×299 = 13×46 = 23×26*	
	Holy One	
	Scepter of the King	*k*
	The Rose and Cross	*SSf, ŏ*
	The Scream of the Eagle	*k*
	The Sorceress Shall Be Desired	
Π **599**		
	Delusions	*Sf*
	Manyhood	
	Mount	*Tf*
	O Wayfarer	*W*
	The Knower, and Me	
600	*2×300 = 3×200 = 4×150 =5×120 = 6×100 = 8×75 = 10×60 =12×50 = 15×40 = 20×30 = 24×25*	
	His Splendour	
	In His Victory	*k*
	The Shew-Stone	*ST*
	Throne of Ra!	
	Wine of Iacchus	*Sf*
	Wonderful	
Π **601**		
	Abyss of Joy	
	Black Eunuch	*k*
	Enlightened One	
	Kisses of the Stars	*ST,Sf*
	Prometheus	*Sf*
	The King's Daughter	
	Woe	*W*
602	*2×301 = 7×86 = 14×43*	
	Empress & the Hierophant	*Tf*
	First Voice Speaketh	*ST*
	Horses of the Sea	
	Liber Trigrammaton	*Nf*
	Sword of Heaven	*Nf*
603	*3×201 = 9×67*	
	Lord the Sun	*Nf*
	Mighty is the Sun	*Nf*
	Tooth	
604	*2×302 = 4×151*	
	Devoureth	
	For Ever for Ever	
	Holy Word	
605	*5×121 = 11×55*	
	Girt With A Sword	
	Primeumaton	*Nf*
	The Image of God	
	Tips of my Feathers	*Sf*
	Writing	*W*
606	*2×303 = 3×202 = 6×101*	
	A Spark Shut Up	
	Child of Suffering	
	Conversation	*Nf, k, ŏ*
	Cor Leonis	*Sf, k*
	The Ape of THOTH	*ŏ*
	The Ways of the Ka!	
	Whirlings	*W, Sf*
	Wolf Betrayeth	
Π **607**		
	A Tooth	
	Bread of the Sacrament	*Tf, k*
	Gone Forth	
	Name of Thy Name	
	One is Thy Spirit	*Tf*
	Splendrous	*Sf*
	The Mantras and Spells	*Sf*
	The Secret of His Being	*k*
	Thy House	
	Ultimate Sparks	*Sf*

Understandeth ST
War and of Vengeance
Who W

608 2×304 = 4×152 = 8×76 =16×38 = 19×32
Accursêd for Ever kk
The Death of A Sinner
Wrath of God

609 3×203 = 7×87 = 21×29
Centre of the Wheel
Conqueror k, ŏ
Lift Up Thyself!
Magister VVVVV ST
O Mentu
Unto Me

610 2×305 = 5×122 = 10×61
Sleep of *Shiloam*
The Eternal One

611 13×47
Frenzy of Form
Palace of the Queen Nf, L
Thousand

612 2×306 = 3×204 = 4×153 =6×102 = 9×68 = 12×51 = 17×36 =18×34
A Tawny Bull
Be Girt With A Sword
Lord of Time
O Sweet God
O Truth!
The Clamour
The Dweller of Nile!
The Voice of Fire

Π **613**
Breath is Iniquity
Eater of Dung
Mourning
Pain of Division Nf
Porta Lucis Sf

614 2×307
Champions of Life
Minister of Silence ST
System and System ST
The Eye in the Triangle

615 3×205 = 5×123 = 15×41
Five Pointed Star ST
Force of COPH NIA k, ŏ
Locusta ST, k
Sign of the Enterer
The Key of It All

616 2×308 = 4×154 = 7×88 =8×77 = 11×56 = 14×44 = 22×28
Double-Wanded
Precious Water
Sunflower
The Just I Am Eight, ST
The Life Which Abideth in Light Tf
The Mighty One
Written W, Nf

Π **617**
Beloved One
Concourse k, ŏ
Genitor-Genitrix
God in an Horse
Hammer of Thor
Immortality
Overworld
Secret Ardours k
Sleep of *Shi-Loh-Am*
Whore W
Word W

618 2×309 = 3×206 = 6×103
Ancient Tower
Chosen Ones Sf
Death-Shriek of the Sphinx
Hermit Lover Earth

	Holy *Chokmah*		
	Individuum		
	Mugwort		*Tf*
Π	**619**		
	Knowledge & Delight		*Tf*
	The Heart and the Serpent		
	The Word of Sin		*Nf*
	Voice of PAZ is Ended		
	620	*2×310 = 4×155 = 5×124 =10×62 = 20×31*	
	Philosophus		*Sf, ŏ*
	The Cube in the Circle		*kk*
	The Pit Called Because		*kk*
	621	*3×207 = 9×69 = 23×27*	
	Cry of Woman		*Nf, k*
	Seal the Book		
	Thought		*Tf*
	622	*2×311*	
	Abominations		*Sf, ŏ*
	It Blooms		
	Mountain		*Nf*
	Seven is Lone and Far		
	The Khabs is in the Khu		
	The Waters of Death		
	Unquenchable		
	Ye Twin Warriors		
	623	*7×89*	
	Evocation		*Nf, k*
	Lord of the Garden		*Nf*
	My Number is Eleven		*Nf, L*
	The Palace of the King		*L*
	White Black and Gold		
	624	*2×312 = 3×208 = 4×156 =6×104 = 8×78 = 12×52 = 13×48 =16×39 = 24×26*	
	Be Thou HADIT		*Tf*
	Lord of Thebes		*Sf*
	Nothingness		*SSf*
	Thou Art He		
	To Number		
	625	*$5×125 = 25^2 = 5^4$*	
	Pyramid of Ruby		
	Pulse of His Heart		*Tf*
	Snows Are Eternal		
	The Blanched Eyeless Beetles		*Sf*
	The First and the Last		*ST, Tf*
	The Light of my Bride		
	The Pyramid of Light		
	The Queen of Space		
	626	*2×313*	
	Great Equinox		
	Heart Strings of Men		*ST, Nf*
	One Person Am I		
	The Crowned Beast		*ST, Tf, k*
	The Play of the Magician		*Nf*
	627	*3×209 = 11×57 = 19×33*	
	Fornication		*Nf, k*
	Wine of Iacchus		*Sf, k*
	628	*2×314 = 4×157*	
	Invisible Throne		
	Knowledge & Delight		
	Little World		
	Mystery of Change		*ST*
	Stooping		*ST*
	Wickedness		*W, SSf, k*
	629	*17×37*	
	All Words and Signs		
	King Thy Brother		
	Lady of the Aethyr		
	The Egg of Spirit A Black Egg		
	The Skin of Breasts		*ST, Sf*
Σ35	**630**	*2×315 = 3×210 = 5×126 =6×105 = 7×90 = 9×70 = 10×63 = 14×45= 15×42 = 18×35 = 21×30*	
	A Flaming Book		
	Children of the Light		*Tf*

Flesh and Blood
The Children of Light *Tf*
The Outer Fire
Waverings *W, Sf*

Π **631**

Andromalius *Sf*
Flame that Burns *Sf*
Star of Ruby *ST*
Tongues *Sf*

632 *2×316 = 4×158 = 8×79*

The Serpent of Death

633 *3×211*

I Am A Black and Terrible God
The Ancient Whore
The False Moon *Nf*
The God of Lies *Sf*

634 *2×317*

Child & that Strangely *ST*
Mary Inviolate
Peace in the Lowest *ST, Tf*
Sun the Rose
Tortoise

635 *5×127*

Frontiers of Eden *Nf*
The Heart of Iao
Warrior *W*

636 *2×318 = 3×212 = 4×159 =6×106 = 12×53*

Beth is Falsehood
Gates of Amennti
Life that Abideth in Light *Tf*
The Child Horus *Sf*
The Sword and the Spear
Unknown *Nf*

637 *7×91 = 13×49*

Most High God *ST*
The Cry of the Man *k*

638 *2×319 = 11×58 = 22×29*

Concealed One *k*
Crowned Lion *Nf, k*
Head of A Crocodile *kk, ŏ*
Master of Form *ST*
My Throne and Place
The Crucified One *k*
The End and the Beginning
Vulture

639 *3×213 = 9×71*

Adorations *Sf*
Five and the Six Are Divorced
Him Whose Name is Silence
Lady of the Night!
Sons of Earth
Work *W*

640 *2×320 = 4×160 = 5×128 =8×80 = 10×64 = 16×40 = 20×32*

Devil of the Aethyr
Divide, Add, Multiply
Lonely Thing
Stability of Him *ST, L*
The Bright, Evening Star *ST*
The Great Stone *ST*

Π **641**

Everlasting One *ST*
The Blue & Gold
The Hands of the Man
Unicellular

642 *2×321 = 3×214 = 6×107*

ASI Fulfilled of ASAR
Aum! Let It Fill Me!
Otherworld
The Prophets Shall Prophecy *ŏŏ*
There is No-God
Vine that Clingeth *k*

Π **643**

Lord Initiating

Supreme Ritual
There is One God
644 *2×322 = 4×161 = 7×92 =14×46 = 23×28*
Stele of Revealing *ST,L*
O Snake of Emerald
Oil of Abramelin
645 *3×215 = 5×129 = 15×43*
Mitre and the Winged Wand
646 *2×323 = 17×38 = 19×34*
Shameless in Deed As in Word
Womb *W*
Π **647**
Covered With A Rich Headdress *SSf, k*
Eyes of Flame and Light *Tf*
House of Ra
Tom O'bedlam
Unprofitable
Women *W, Nf*
Worship *W*
648 *2×324 = 3×216 = 4×162 =6×108 = 8×81 = 9×72 = 12×54 = 18×36= 24×27*
Half of the Word
Joy of Life & Death!
The White Brothers *Sf*
There is No God Where I Am *ŏ*
Whose Life is One
649 *11×59*
Anhalonium
Ten Divine Ones *Sf*
Worm *W*
Your Light *Tf*
650 *2×325 = 5×130 = 10×65 =13×50 = 25×26*
Joy&Beauty
LUX *X*
Spelling is Defunct *Tf, k*
The Night of Time
Woman *W, Nf*
651 *3×217 = 7×93 = 21×31*
I Blaze Upon Thee
My Shoulders *Sf*
Slaves of Because *k*
652 *2×326 = 4×163*
Ill-Ordered House *ŏ*
Pan Pan Io Pan Io Pan *Nf*
The Holy Assembly
Wolf *W*
Π **653**
Cynocephalus *Sf*
Pluck the Rose *k*
654 *2×327 = 3×218 = 6×109*
Black Cross of Themis *Sf, k, ŏ*
Delightful Ocean *Nf*
Lust & Power *ST*
The Eyes of Jesus
Wine of Iacchus *Sf, kk*
655 *5×131*
Bitterness of Death
Corrupteth *k*
Masters of the Pyramid *ST*
Omnipotent *Tf, ŏ*
The Corn of Ceres *k*
We Are Upon Thee
Who I Am *W*
656 *2×328 = 4×164 = 8×82 =16×41*
Heaven of Urania
His Thought *Tf*
Many & the Known *Nf*
The Grade of Magus *Sf*
657 *3×219 = 9×73*
Armies of the Lord
Plumes of Maat *Tf*
Sixth Interior Sense
658 *2×329 = 7×94 = 14×47*

Breath of Love
Enchanter Shall Rule
Latchet of His Sandal
Night of Forces *Sf*
The Claws of the Eagle *k*
The Distant Drug *ST*
The Face of Mohammed
To Know
Whole *W*
Without *Tf*

Π **659**

Desolation
Four-Square
The Mercy of God
The Paths of the Tree
Words *W, Sf*
Worshipped *W*

660 *2×330 = 3×220 = 4×165 =5×132 = 6×110 = 10×66 = 11×60 =12×55 = 15×44 = 20×33 = 22×30*

Destruction *ST, Nf*
The Circle of the Sabbath *k*
The Grade of a Magus *Sf*
Worship Then the Khabs
Worshipper *W*

Π **661**

Abstruction *ST, Nf*
He is the First and the Last *ST, Tf*
Heart of the Rose
Three Days and Three Nights *Sf*

662 *2×331*

Black to the Blind *k*
Secret Serpent Coiled *kk*
Upon the Cross *SSf, k, őő*

663 *3×221 = 13×51 = 17×39*

City of the Pyramids *Sf*
Father of Justice *ST*
Outcast *ST, Tf, k*
Permutation *Nf*

665 *5×133 = 7×95 = 19×35*

Fear Not, O Prophet, *őő*
Infinite Circle of Emerald *k*
Little Flowers *Sf*
Ninth Hour
Pillar of Lightning
Seasons Thereof
Sigil of the Demon *Nf*

Σ36 **666** *2×333 = 3×222 = 6×111 =9×74 = 18×37*

Gimel is Glamour
I Am Life, and the Giver of Life,
LUXFIRE
Plumes of MAAT
RA-HOOR-KHU
The Mother and the Babe
The Pillars Are the Cross *SSf*
Thy Foot *Tf*

667 *23×29*

Choose Ye Well!
Eightfold Word
Five Wounds *Sf*
World *W*

668 *2×334 = 4×167*

Christus in Cruce *ST*
O Scribe and Prophet *Tf, k*
Pillars of Hercules *k*
Servants of Babalon *Nf, ő*
The Order & Value
Uplifted from Him

669 *3×223*

Great and Terrible Word
His Child & that Strangely *ST*

670 *2×335 = 5×134 = 10×67*

Cast Thou *ST, k*
Lord Thy God

Manifestations ST,Sf
The Mighty Sepulchre k
The Obeah and the Wanga
Wisdom and Folly ŏ

671 *11×61*

Fourfold
Might of Thy Breath,
The God & the Adorer
The Parts of the Earth,

672 *2×336 = 3×224 = 4×168 =6×112 = 7×96 = 8×84 = 12×56 = 14×48= 16×42 = 21×32 = 24×28*

Cubic Stone ST, kk

Π **673**

Beautiful God ŏ
Ineffable Emanations Sf
Prophet of NU! ŏ
Ravens of Dispersion Nf
Subtlety Therein! Nf
The Sons of Men Nf
Violent Light Tf
Whirling Air and Rushing Fire
Winged Light W, Tf
With the Wand Createth He k

674 *2×337*

Queen of Night Tf
The Great Book
The Lion MAU

675 *3×225 = 5×135 = 9×75 =15×45 = 25×27*

Four Great Princes Sf
I Forbid Argument
Sacrament of the Graal k
The Nemyss of Secrecy k
Unto Thee
Word for Myself

676 *2×338 = 4×169 = 13×52 =26²*

Danger & Trouble

The Priest of the Princes ST
Tourmaline
Wisdom W

Π **677**

The Heart of the Star ST
Warriors W, Sf

678 *2×339 = 3×226 = 6×113*

Eight and One in Eight Tf
Flood of Fire
He Shall Deceive the Very Elect Tf, k
The Child of the Prophet Tf, ŏ
To Me! to Me!
Worship Then the Khabs Sf

679 *7×97*

Abyss of Glory
Circumference of All k
The Key of the Abyss SSf
Tribulation Nf

680 *2×340 = 4×170 = 5×136 =8×85 = 10×68 = 17×40 = 20×34*

OXO *(The cry of 15th Aethyr)* X,ŏ
The Blade of the Serpent Tf
The Fall of Because k
Vultures Sf

681 *3×227*

Cometh Hurt Tf, k
Eagle-Snake-Scorpion Nf, k
Heaven of Jupiter
The Kings of the Earth
Works W, Sf

682 *2×341 = 11×62 = 22×31*

Angels of the Heavens Sf
Chains of Choronzon Nf, k, ŏŏŏ
Everlasting House ST, ŏ
Persecutions Sf, k
Word ABRAHADABRA W

Π **683**

& Not Other
A Veiling of this Shrine
O Filth! Filth! Filth!
The Birth of Form
The Hindoo Kali

684 *2×342 = 3×228 = 4×171 =6×114 = 9×76 = 12×57 = 18×38 =19×36*

Existence of Existences *ST,Sf*
Incorruptible *k*
Is None Other
Number of the Man *Nf*

685 *5×137*

Holy Ghost *ST,Tf*
O City of God *ŏ*
Sacred Unto Me *k*

686 *2×343 = 7×98 = 14×49*

Master of the Temple *ST*
Son of Night! *Tf*
The Night-Blue Sky
Trees of Eternity

687 *3×229*

Let ASAR Be the Adorant *Tf*
Ruddy Clouds *k, ŏ*
Wine of the Sacrament *Tf*

688 *2×344 = 4×172 = 8×86 =16×43*

Bed of Juno
Lust & Worship *ST*
Most High God Amen *ST, Nf*
Wonder *W*

690 *2×345 = 3×230 = 5×138 =6×115 = 10×69 = 15×46 = 23×30*

A Rich Man from the West *ST,Tf*
Eye of HOOR
Fountains *Sf*
Modest Woman *ST, Nf*

Π **691**

Crowned Goat *Tf, k*
Forces of Matter

692 *2×346 = 4×173*

Child of the Prophet *Tf*
God Terminus *Sf*
Metallorum

693 *3×231 = 7×99 = 9×77 =11×63 = 21×33*

One Hundred and Six
The Dagger Destroyeth *ST*
The Serpent of Delight *Tf*

694 *2×347*

Magician and the Exorcist *ST,Tf*
Milk of Thy Breasts *ST,Sf*
Wolf's *W, Sf*

695 *5×139*

Darkness of Her Womb
O Lord God
Shameless and Wanton *Nf*
Sphinx of the Gods *Sf*

696 *2×348 = 3×232 = 4×174 =6×116 = 8×87 = 12×58 = 24×29*

A Light Before Thine Eyes *Sf*
Flaming Rosy Cross *SSf, k, ŏ*
Let ASAR Be the Adorant
The Scarlet Woman *k*

697 *17×41*

Creatures of Earth *k*
Strong in War *ST, W,ŏ*
Supernal Wisdom

698 *2×349*

Aeon of Saturn *Nf, ŏ*
Glory to Him
The Great Flood
The Wine of the Sabbath

699 *3×233*

Hawk-Headed Mystical Lord! *ST*
Multitude
My Tongue

	Obey my Prophet!		Tf
	Symbol of Thee		
	The Face of Isis-Hathor		
	Word of the Law		
	700	2×350 = 4×175 = 5×140 =7×100 = 10×70 = 14×50 = 20×35 =25×28	
	Bird of Juno		
	Gates of Eternity		
	Song to IAO		ŏ
	The Shells of Abaddon		Nf
Π	**701**		
	The Ages Beyond the Ages		Sf, Sf
	The Four Beasts		ST,Sf
	The Gate of the Abyss		SSf
	The Lovely Star		ST
	The Sevenfold Table		
	The Understanding		ST
	702	2×351 = 3×234 = 6×117 =9×78 = 13×54 = 18×39 = 26×27	
	Conjuration		Nf, k, ŏ
	Day of Be-With-Us		Sf
	Pain of the Goat		Tf
	The Secrecy of the Hermit		Tf, k
	The Sky of NU		
	Trinity of Triads		
Σ37	**703**	19×37	
	Conventicles		Sf, kk
	Rod of Destiny		ST
	The Father of All Light		Tf
	The Owl and the Bat		Tf
	Ways of the Khu!		
	704	2×352 = 4×176 = 8×88 =11×64 = 16×44 = 22×32	
	Sappho and Calypso		k
	The Holy One		
	705	3×235 = 5×141 = 15×47	
	My Secret House		k
	Star of Mercury		ST, k
	706	2×353	
	All-Touching		
	Gnarled Oak of God!		ŏ
	The Throne of Ra!		
	Weak One		W
	Whose Name is One		
	707	7×101	
	But I Go Dancing		
	Cup of His Gladness		SSf, k
	Householder		
	I Adore Thee in Song		ŏ
	The Body of the Snake		ŏ
	Scarlet Concubine		kkk, ŏ
	'Stablished in the Void		ST
	The Enlightened One		
	The Kisses of the Stars		ST,Sf
	708	2×354 = 3×236 = 4×177 =6×118 = 12×59	
	An End to Life and Death		
	The Empress & the Hierophant		Tf
	The First Voice Speaketh		ST
	Wotan		W, Nf
Π	**709**		
	Holy Nuns		Sf
	Mystery of His Breast		ST,Tf
	O Self Beyond Self		
	Star-Splendour		ST
	Twelvefold Table		
	Worlds		W, Sf
	710	2×355 = 5×142 = 10×71	
	Damn Them Who Pity!		
	Keen and the Proud		
	Masters of the Temple		ST
	My Word is Six and Fifty		
	Return Return		Nf
	The Holy Word		
	711	3×237 = 9×79	
	One is the Magus		Sf

One Knowledge
To War *W*

712 *2×356 = 4×178 = 8×89*

Emphatically my Chosen *Nf, k*
Holy Throne
Lonely One
The Child of Suffering
The Wolf Betrayeth *W*
Your Refuge

713 *23×31*

Blessed Be Thy Name for Ever
Blood-Thirst *ST, Tf*
Frogs Upon the Earth *ŏŏ*
Joyous *Sf*
Not in One
Secret Key of this Law *k*
Universal Peacock *k*
Wine and Strange Drugs *ST*
Wings of MAUT *Tf*

714 *2×357 = 3×238 = 6×119 =7×102 = 14×51 = 17×42 = 21×34*

Ankh F N Khonsu
Day of Judgement *Tf*
Wine of the Sacrament *Tf, k*

715 *5×143 = 11×65 = 13×55*

His Name Writ Openly
Radiance of THOTH
Shameless and Wanton *Nf, L*
Style of A Letter *ST*
World of Stars *ST, Sf*

716 *2×358 = 4×179*

Flaming Orange Apron *Nf*
Virtue of Mind

717 *3×239*

Light of the Sun *Nf*
Spade of the Husbandman *Nf*
The Empress & the Hierophant
The Palace of the Queen *Nf, L*

718 *2×359*

City of Fifty Gates *Sf*
Company of Heaven *Nf, k*
Little Door
Of All Truth
Righteousness *SSf*
The Face of the Sun
The Rose and Cross *SSf*
Wheel of Life *W*

Π **719**

Eremite of Nuit *Tf*
In Homini Salus *Sf*
Mystery of the Wedge *ST*
Sit and Conjure *k*
The Flame that Burns
The Pain of Division *Nf*

6! **720** *2×360 = 3×240 = 4×180 =5×144 = 6×120 = 8×90 = 9×80 = 10×72= 12×60 = 15×48 = 16×45 = 18×40 =20×36 = 24×30*

Hold Up Thyself!
Solomon *Nf*
Thy Mouth
Weapons *W, Sf*

721 *7×103*

Body of the Snake
Flame Upon the Altar *ŏ*
The Five Pointed Star *ST*
The Force of COPH NIA *k, ŏ*
The Sign of the Enterer

722 *2×361 = 19×38*

ANKH-AF-NA-KHONSU
Christus in Cruce *ST, kk*
The Bread of the Sacrament *k*

723 *3×241*

The Beloved One
The Hammer of Thor

The Sleep of *Shi-Loh-Am*
The Word

724 *2×362 = 4×181*

Continuity *k, ŏ*
The Death-Shriek of the Sphinx
The Holy Chokmah

725 *5×145 = 25×29*

Elohim Tzabaoth
Fools of Men *Nf*
Glorious *Sf*
Place Where Was No God
Power of the Star 418 *ST*
The Voice of PAZ is Ended
Who Are of Us *Sf*
Winged Assyrian Bull Men *Nf*

726 *2×363 = 3×242 = 6×121 =11×66 = 22×33*

Four Powers *Sf*
Hawk-Headed Mystical Lord! *ST, k*
His Loving Kindness *SSf*
Not Two
The Philosophus *Sf, ŏ*
Two-And-Thirty
Uttereth Clearly *k*

Π **727**

Absolute Bliss *SSf*
Host of Angels *ST,Sf*

728 *2×364 = 4×182 = 7×104 =8×91 = 13×56 = 14×52 = 26×28*

Mountains *Sf*
My Chosen Ones *Sf*
The Lord of Silence
The Mountain *Nf*

729 *3×243 = 9×81 = 27^2 =9^3 = 3^6*

The Lord of the Garden *Nf*
There is Death for the Dogs *Sf, ŏ*

730 *2×365 = 5×146 = 10×73*

Hell Unquenchable
King Among the Kings *Sf*
The Lord of Thebes *Sf*
The Stélé of Revealing *ST*
The Word that is Seven *Nf*
Uplifted in Thine Heart *Tf*
Wand Createth *k*
Wonders *W, Sf*
Work, & Be our Bed

731 *17×43*

I Beseech Thee O my Lord
The Snows Are Eternal

732 *2×366 = 3×244 = 4×183 =6×122 = 12×61*

Cor Scorpionis *Sf, kk, ŏ*
Law of the Strong *ST, ŏ*

Π **733**

Blade of the Phallus *Sf*
Ministers of the Beast *ST,Tf*
Our Passionate Peace *ŏ*
Whose Spirit is One
Working *W*

734 *2×367*

Aormuzdi and Ahrimanes *Sf*
No Blood
The Word Eternity

735 *3×245 = 5×147 = 7×105 =15×49 = 21×35*

Naked Mountain *Nf*
O Warrior *W*
The Lady of the Aethyr

736 *2×368 = 4×184 = 8×92 =16×46 = 23×32*

By Wise TA-NECH I Weave my Spell
The Wand Createth *Wk*

737 *11×67*

His Conjuration *Nf, k, ŏ*
Unutterable

738 *2×369 = 3×246 = 6×123 =9×82 = 18×41*

Sun of Midnight *Tf*

The Pomegranate in Hell

Thunderbolt *Tf*

We Who Were Dust *ST, Tf*

Π **739**

Infinite Stars Thereof *ST*

One is Thy Beginning!

740 *2×370 = 4×185 = 5×148 =10×74 = 20×37*

Angel that Guardeth Me

Beauty of His Essence

Choose Ye An Island!

Goat-Hoofed

Reveal It to the Wise

Unite By Thine Art

Virgin of Eternity

Whole of the Law

Word that is God

Σ38 **741** *3×247 = 13×57 = 19×39*

Child of Eve and the Serpent *Tf*

Proud and Mighty

The Frontiers of Eden *Nf*

742 *2×371 = 7×106 = 14×53*

All Their Words Are Skew-Wise

HOOR-KHUT *Tf*

Love and Anguish

Master of the Pentagram *ST*

The Life that Abideth in Light *Tf*

Unfading Flowers *Sf*

Window *W*

Π **743**

Uraeus Crown *Nf, k*

744 *2×372 = 3×248 = 4×186 =6×124 = 8×93 = 12×62 = 24×31*

All Pleasure and Purple,

Lust of Light *ST, Tf, Tf, k*

Serpent of Wisdom

The Concealed One *k*

The Crowned Lion *Nf, k*

The Master of Form *ST*

745 *5×149*

Brotherhood

Gate of the God ON *Nf, ŏ*

House of my Father *ŏ*

The Five and the Six Are Divorced

The Work

War and Vengeance *W*

746 *2×373*

The Devil of the Aethyr

Turquoise

Uroboros *Sf, ŏ*

Vast Crystal Cube *ST, kk*

With Swords & With Spears *Sf*

747 *3×249 = 9×83*

A Thunderbolt *Tf*

Aeon of Wonders *Sf, ŏ*

Bastard of the Svastika *ST*

Cajole the Mother *k*

Core of Every Star *ST, k*

Countenance *k*

748 *2×374 = 4×187 = 11×68 =17×44 = 22×34*

Full Moon *Nf*

Imago Hominis Deus *Sf, ŏ*

Sons of God

The Vine that Clingeth *k*

749 *7×107*

An Invisible House

Deepen Not A Superficies *Sf*

Master of the Triangle *ST*

The Lord Initiating

The Supreme Ritual

With the Cup Preserveth He *k*

Work of the Wand

750 *2×375 = 3×250 = 5×150 =6×125 = 10×75 = 15×50 = 25×30*

A Star and A Snake and A Sword *ST*

Π **751**

Laboring of His Breast *ST,Tf*

Rapture of the Earth

Sugar of the Stars *ST,Sf*

The Mitre and the Winged Wand

Ultimate Triangle

752 *2×376 = 4×188 = 8×94 =16×47*

The Shameless in Deed As in Word

753 *3×251*

Absolute Light *Tf*

Eye in the Midst Thereof *ST*

Lust of Light *ST,Tf*

Put On the Wings *Sf, ŏ*

The Little Flowers

The Magus is Love

With the Coin Redeemeth He *k*

754 *2×377 = 13×58 = 26×29*

Hand of A Man that is Hanged

The Half of the Word

The Joy of Life & Death!

755 *5×151*

HOOR-KHUIT

RA- HOOR-KHUT *Tf*

Seven Breaths of God

The Five Wounds

Work is Ended *W*

756 *2×378 = 3×252 = 4×189 =6×126 = 7×108 = 9×84 = 12×63 =14×54 = 18×42 = 21×36 = 27×28*

Curse of Thoth *k, ŏ*

Terror of God

Π **757**

The Slaves of Because *k*

Three Ordeals in One

Whole Heaven *W, Nf*

Wolf's Bane *W*

758 *2×379*

Blood in my Heart *Tf*

Father of All Love

Harder! Hold Up Thyself!

Saeculorum *k*

Secret Understanding *ST, k*

Secretest Chamber of the Palace *ST, k, L*

759 *3×253 = 11×69 = 23×33*

Count Well *k*

RA-HOOR-KHU-IT *Tf*

The Cynocephalus *Sf*

760 *2×380 = 4×190 = 5×152 =8×95 = 10×76 = 19×40 = 20×38*

Elevenfold Word *L*

Knowledge of Death

Poison of Life

The Delightful Ocean *Nf*

The Wine of Iacchus *Sf, kk*

Π **761**

Above You

Star of Twelve Rays *ST,Sf*

The Masters of the Pyramid *ST*

The Resurrection *k*

762 *2×381 = 3×254 = 6×127*

Build the Holy Place

Table in the Vault *Tf*

The Heaven of Urania

The Many & the Known *Nf*

Victory & Joy *k*

We Are One; We Are None

763 *7×109*

By Wise TA-NECH I Weave My Spell *k*

Goat of the Spirit *Tf*
The Armies of the Lord
The Plumes of MAAT *Tf*
Winged Secret Flame *W, k*

764 *2×382 = 4×191*

Night of Nuit *Tf*
Osprey Among the Rice
The Enchanter Shall Rule
Whirled Forth in my Breath
Willow *W*

765 *3×255 = 5×153 = 9×85 =15×51 = 17×45*

& Nought Remains *Sf*
Double-Headed One
Light of Purity

766 *2×383*

Dew of the Universe
Scourge and Balances *Sf, k, L*
Supreme and Terrible God,

767 *13×59*

Great God HARPO-CRATES *Sf, k*
The Heart of the Rose
The Word Secret & Not *ŏ*

768 *2×384 = 3×256 = 4×192 =6×128 = 8×96 = 12×64 = 16×48 =24×32*

A Foolish Word
Blind Worm of Slime
Every Number is Infinite
There is No God Where I Am
The Secret Serpent Coiled *k,k*

Π **769**

Ever to Me! to Me!
Foolish Folk
Sorrow is Not *Tf, ŏ*
Terror of Things *Sf*
The City of the Pyramids *Sf*
The Father of Justice *ST*
The Outcast *ST, k*
Winged With Flame *W*

770 *2×385 = 5×154 = 7×110 =10×77 = 11×70 = 14×55 = 22×35*

Chance of Union *Nf*
Mighty and Terrible One
Millions-Of-Years *Sf*
Navel of NUIT *Tf*
Whose Light is One

771 *3×257*

Hell's Own Worm
The Ninth Hour
The Seasons Thereof
Water of Life *W*

772 *2×386 = 4×193*

Ill-Ordered House
Monstrous *ST,Sf, ŏ*
The Lord of the Aeon *Nf, ŏ*
The Plumes of MAAT
The Shameless in Deed As in Word *L*
Until It Pierce my Depth

Π **773**

Lust of the Flesh *ST*
The Eightfold Word
Trample Down the Heathen *Nf*

774 *2×387 = 3×258 = 6×129 =9×86 = 18×43*

The Servants of BABALON *Nf, ŏ*

775 *5×155 = 25×31*

Numbers & the Words *Sf*
The Great and Terrible Word
Wisdom Says: Be Strong! *ST, ŏ*

776 *2×388 = 4×194 = 8×97*

Brightness of the Heavens *Sf*
Brilliance of the Lord
Cursed Cursed Be the Earth *kk*
Lord of Beginnings *Sf*

Verbum Fit Verbum

777 *3×259 = 7×111 = 21×37*

The Cup of His Gladness *k*
The Might of Thy Breath
Thick Leavings of Red Wine *k*
Three Ordeals in One *L*
Uttermost *ST, Tf*
Very Light of God Himself *ŏ*
Yea Than Yea Theli Yea Lilith

778 *2×389*

His Original Nature
Ocean of the West *ST, Tf*
The Infinite Within *Nf, W*
Treasure-House
Wanton *W, Nf*

779 *19×41*

Daughter of the King
Horror of Time
Know & Destroy *ST*
Pillars of the World!
The Ineffable Emanations *Sf*
The Winged Light *Tf, W*
Thou Availest *ST, Tf*
Worship of NU

Σ39 **780** *2×390 = 3×260 = 4×195 =5×156 = 6×130 = 10×78 = 12×65 =13×60 = 15×52 = 20×39 = 26×30*

Beloved Shall Abide With Thee
Confound *k*
Neapolitan Boy
Ten Thousand
The Queen of Night *Tf*
Winged Globe *W*

781 *11×71*

Voice of the Master *ST*

782 *2×391 = 17×46 = 23×34*

Khem the Holy One

783 *3×261 = 9×87 = 27×29*

Love Under Will
Woe Woe Woe

784 *2×392 = 4×196 = 7×112 =8×98 = 14×56 = 16×49 = 28²*

Book is Shut *Tf*
Undefiled Knowledge

785 *5×157*

Cease to Number Himself
Heart of Blood
The Circumference of All *k*
Toys of the Magician *Nf*

786 *2×393 = 3×262 = 6×131*

Breast of An Harlot *ST, Tf*
Splendrous Serpent *Tf*

Π **787**

An Aeon and An Aeon and An Aeon *Nf, ŏ*
Babe in the Lotus *Sf*
The Heaven of Jupiter
Untouched

788 *2×394 = 4×197*

The Angels of the Heavens *Sf*
The Persecutions *Sf, k*
The Word ABRAHADABRA

789 *3×263*

Darkness Over All the Earth
Knees of the Mother
The Blue-Lidded Daughter
Womanhood
Written and Concealed *k*

790 *2×395 = 5×158 = 10×79*

Bosom of Death
Consciousness *SSf, k, ŏ*
Nectar of the Gods *Sf, k*
The Day of BE-WITH-US
The Existence of Existences *ST, Sf*

The Number of the Man
The Obeah and the Wanga *W, ŏ*
791 *7×113*
Holy Guardian Angel
I Stand and Invoke Thee *ST*
The Holy Ghost *ST*
792 *2×396 = 3×264 = 4×198 =6×132 = 8×99 = 9×88 = 11×72 = 12×66= 18×44 = 22×36 = 24×33*
Foundation *Nf*
Heart of the Ritual
The Master of the Temple *ST*
The Trees of Eternity
793 *13×61*
Light of Truth
Unto the Earth
794 *2×397*
Kingdom of the Grave
Roses of Macedonia
The Bed of Juno
795 *3×265 = 5×159 = 15×53*
Cynocephalus in Leash
Fear Not for Aught *Tf, ŏ*
Great White King and His Black Slave
My Prophet is A Fool *ŏ*
796 *2×398 = 4×199*
Balances of Truth *L*
Cocoanut *Tf, k*
Consummation *Nf, k, ŏ*
Crown of Mine Heart *Tf, k*
Style Or Value *ST*
The Modest Woman *ST, Nf*
Π **797**
Bacchus and Apollo *k, k,ŏ*
Blood Royal
My Destruction *ST, Nf, k*
The Forces of Matter
Yea Than Yea Theli Yea Lilith *L*
Your Vision *Nf*
798 *2×399 = 3×266 = 6×133 =7×114 = 14×57 = 19×42 = 21×38*
The Child of the Prophet *Tf*
800 *2×400 = 4×200 = 5×160 =8×100 = 10×80 = 16×50 = 20×40 =25×32*
Ending of the Words *Sf*
The Magician and the Exorcist *ST,Tf*
The Milk of Thy Breasts *ST,Sf*
801 *3×267 = 9×89*
Heart of A Scorpion *Nf, k*
Kingdom of the Father
Might of the Lion
Secrets of Truth *k*
Sorrow is Joy
The Sphinx of the Gods *Sf*
Universal MERCURY *k*
Word is Falsehood
802 *2×401*
Everlasting House *ST*
Five Interpenetrateth the Six
Red Rain of my Lightnings *Sf*
Veil of my Mother
803 *11×73*
Changeful Moon *Nf*
HOOR in His Secret Name *k*
Land of No-Thing
Love of NU
Stélé of Revealing Itself *ST*
The Supernal Wisdom
805 *5×161 = 7×115 = 23×35*
I Love You
The Hawk-Headed Mystical Lord! *ST*
The Word of the Law
806 *2×403 = 13×62 = 26×31*

A Mask of Sorrow
The Bird of Juno

807 *3×269*

Ruddy Clouds *k*

808 *2×404 = 4×202 = 8×101*

Child of Thy Bowels *Sf*
Mighty Names of God
The Crowned Lion *k*

Π **809**

Disguise Thy Glory
O Azure-Lidded Woman *Nf*
O Light of God
The Rod of Destiny *ST*
The Ways of the Khu!
Voice from the Abyss *SSf*

810 *2×405 = 3×270 = 5×162 =6×135 = 9×90 = 10×81 = 15×54 =18×45 = 27×30*

Enslave the Soul

Π **811**

In His Conjuration *Nf, k, ŏ*
Lords of Vision *Nf*
Lust of the Mind *ST*
Substance of Light *ST,Tf*

812 *2×406 = 4×203 = 7×116 =14×58 = 28×29*

City of the Seven Hills *Sf*
House of Wrath
Sign of Initiation *Nf*
Silver Star that Ye Adore *ST*
The Blade of the Pylon *Nf*

813 *3×271*

One, One, One
The Scarlet Concubine *kkk, ŏ*
Weird Winged God *W*

814 *2×407 = 11×74 = 22×37*

End of the Hiding of Hadit *Tf*
Forty Nine Squares *Sf*
Majesty and the Beauty *ST*
Sight of my Glory
Surrounding
The Force of COPH NIA
The Four Powers

815 *5×163*

I Pluck Thee O my God *ŏ*
The Twelvefold Table
The Worlds *Sf*

816 *2×408 = 3×272 = 4×204 =6×136 = 8×102 = 12×68 = 16×51 =17×48 = 24×34*

Censor of Worship
Falutli! Falutli!
Key of the Rituals *Sf*
The Keen and the Proud
Universe is Dissolved
Vast and the Minute *ST*

817 *19×43*

Jewelled With Twelve Stars *ST,Sf*
Priestess of the Silver Star *ST*

818 *2×409*

& It Will Be to Him As Silver
Dissolution *Nf*
Lamp of the Invisible Light *Tf*
Lord of Glory
The Holy Throne
Thou Goat *Tf*
Throned in Eternity

819 *3×273 = 7×117 = 9×91 =13×63 = 21×39*

Feet of the Most High *ST*
Mighty is the Moon *Nf*
The Wings of MAUT *Tf*

Σ40 **820** *2×410 = 4×205 = 5×164 =10×82 = 20×41*

All is Not Aught *Tf*
Song to IAO
Star & Star, System & System *ST*

Π **821**

Gate of the Evening Star — *ST*
Lord of Creation — *Nf, k*
Nine By the Fools — *Sf*
The Radiance of Thoth
The Style of a Letter — *ST*

Π 823

The Light of the Sun — *Nf*

824 *2×412 = 4×206 = 8×103*

Great God Terminus — *Sf*
Great Sigil of the Arrow
The City of Fifty Gates — *Sf*
The Wheel of Life

825 *3×275 = 5×165 = 11×75 =15×55 = 25×33*

Law of the Fortress — *SSf*
Mystery of UTI — *ST*
The Mystery of the Wedge — *ST*

826 *2×413 = 7×118 = 14×59*

Argentum Astrum — *ST*
Basket of the Beyond
Four His Weapons — *Sf*
Gnarled Oak of God!

Π 827

Philosophorum — *ŏ*
Winners of the Ordeal X

828 *2×414 = 3×276 = 4×207 =6×138 = 9×92 = 12×69 = 18×46 =23×36*

Every Man and Every Woman — *Nf*
Peace of Satiate Lust — *ST, Tf*
Pillar Established in the Void — *ST*

Π 829

A Lambent Flame of Blue
He Corrupteth the Fresh Air — *k*
The Wine of the Sacrament — *k*

830 *2×415 = 5×166 = 10×83*

Athenian Courtesan — *Nf, k*
Power of the Pentagram

831 *3×277*

Kill and Torture
The Place Where Was No God

832 *2×416 = 4×208 = 8×104 =13×64 = 16×52 = 26×32*

For Ever in the Aeons Amen — *Nf*
Snake and of the Goat — *Tf*
This Glad Word

833 *7×119 = 17×49*

Ephesus, the City of DIANA
Holy of Holies — *Sf*
Kamea of the Moon — *Nf*
Not So Chosen — *Nf*
Twelve Emancipations — *Sf*
Virtuous — *Sf*

834 *2×417 = 3×278 = 6×139*

Flood of Water
Mysteries of Creation — *ST, Nf, k*

835 *5×167*

Crown of the Yod — *k, ŏ*
For Thou Art He!
O Day of Eternity

836 *2×418 = 4×209 = 11×76 =19×44 = 22×38*

Book Tarot — *Tf*
Charioteer of the West — *ST, Tf*
The King Among the Kings — *Sf*
The Lord of the Aeon — *ŏ*

837 *3×279 = 9×93 = 27×31*

Crowned With the Winds — *Sf, k*
My Bones Are Rotten — *Nf*
Palace of the King my Son — *Nf*

838 *2×419*

The Law of the Strong — *ST, ŏ*
The Star of MERCURY — *ST, k*

Π 839

Laughing Face of Eros — *Sf*
Nastiness of Her Pleasure — *ST*
The Blade of the Phallus — *Sf*

Veil of Sorrow

840 *2×420 = 3×280 = 4×210 =5×168 = 6×140 = 7×120 = 8×105 =10×84 = 12×70 = 14×60 = 15×56 =20×42 = 21×40 = 24×35 = 28×30*

Certainty, Not Faith,
O Talkative One
To the God OAI
Ways of the Ka! *W*

841 *29^2*

Key of the Vault
Therefore Strike Hard & Low *ST*

842 *2×421*

Knower & the Known *Nf*
The Holy Hill of Zion *Nf, ŏ*

843 *3×281*

Glory of the Stars *ST,Sf*
None Other Than He
Ring of the Horizon *Nf*
Servants of Love

844 *2×422 = 4×211*

Kingdom of the Abyss *SSf*
Man Upon A Great Horse *ŏ*

845 *5×169 = 13×65*

The Infinite Stars Thereof *ST*

846 *2×423 = 3×282 = 6×141 =9×94 = 18×47*

The Angel that Guardeth Me
The Virgin of Eternity
The Word that is God
Tutulu

847 *7×121 = 11×77*

Order of the Silver Star *ST*
The Child of Eve and the Serpent *Tf*
Three Great Delusions *Sf*

848 *2×424 = 4×212 = 8×106 =16×53*

I Am the Magician and the Exorcist *ST,Tf*
Lotus of Isis *Sf*
The Water of Choronzon *Nf, k, ŏŏŏ*
Thy Great NOX *Tf, X,ŏ*
Torch of Penelope

849 *3×283*

Abrogate Are All Rituals
Division Hither Homeward
Dolphin's Tooth *ŏ*
Lord of the Tempest *ST,Tf*

850 *2×425 = 5×170 = 10×85 =17×50 = 25×34*

The Serpent of Wisdom
Where I Am These Are Not *W, Tf, ŏ*
Woods *W, Sf*

851 *23×37*

Incestuous *ST,Sf*

852 *2×426 = 3×284 = 4×213 =6×142 = 12×71*

Four Hundred & Eighteen *Nf*
Water the Rose *W*

Π **853**

No Expected House *k*
Our Passionate Peace
The Bastard of the Svastika *ST*
The Core of Every Star *ST, k*
The Sun of Midnight

854 *2×427 = 7×122 = 14×61*

Floor of the Palace *L*
Mystery of Selflessness *ST,SSf*
Ovals of Thine Eyes *Sf*
The Sons of God

855 *3×285 = 5×171 = 9×95 =15×57 = 19×45*

Pillar is 'Stablished in the Void *ST*
The Master of the Triangle *ST*
The Work of the Wand
Thou Art Not *Tf, ŏ*

856 *2×428 = 4×214 = 8×107*

Holy Hill of Zion *Nf*

Lighten the Ways of the Ka!
O God O God
Precious Water
Waters of Death *W*
Write, & Find Ecstasy *ST, W, k*

Π **857**

Expansion of the Abyss *SSf*
Girders of the Soul
Palace of the King my Son *Nf, L*
Phallus of A Goat *Tf*
The Ultimate Triangle
Thy Great NOX *X,ŏ*

858 *2×429 = 3×286 = 6×143 =11×78 = 13×66 = 22×39 = 26×33*

Book of the Law
Coiled Splendour *k*
Mount Meru
Pincers of Red Hot Iron *Nf*
The Word of Power
Vision and the Voice

Π **859**

Equinox of Osiris *Sf, ŏ*
Five Thou Shalt Find
He that Hath Given Up His Name
Name of my House
The Eye in the Midst Thereof *ST*
The Lust of Light *ST,Tf*

860 *2×430 = 4×215 = 5×172 =10×86 = 20×43*

The Hand of a Man that is Hanged,
Unto the Zenith
Wisdom is the Man *W, Nf*

Σ41 **861** *3×287 = 7×123 = 21×41*

Crown of Thoth *k, ŏ*
House of the Father
The Seven Breaths of God
The Work is Ended

862 *2×431*

Crucifixion *Nf, k, X*
House of God
Palace of Understanding — compare with 882 where L is upright. *ST*
The Curse of THOTH *k, ŏ*

Π **863**

Eye and the Tooth
House of the Virgin *Nf*
Voice of the Lord

864 *2×432 = 3×288 = 4×216 =6×144 = 8×108 = 9×96 = 12×72 =16×54 = 18×48 = 24×36 = 27×32*

Help Me O Warrior Lord
O Wingêd Snake of Light *Tf*
Strive Ever to More! *ST*
The Father of All Love

865 *5×173*

Black Brotherhood *k*
House of my Father
Shrine of the Exalted One
Whoredom *W*

866 *2×433*

Scarlet Woman *Nf, k*
The Poison of Life
Uroboros *Sf*

867 *3×289 = 17×51*

Ancient Whore *W*
Thy Druid Vestments *ST,Sf*
Victorious *Sf, k*

868 *2×434 = 4×217 = 7×124 =14×62 = 28×31*

A Splendour in my Name
Dung of Choronzon *Nf, k, ŏŏŏ*
Golden Hair and Golden Skin *Nf*
Imago Hominis Deus *Sf*
Moonwort *Tf*

Palace of the King's Daughter
Shoulders of Time

869 *11×79*

The Winged Secret Flame *k*
Unity is Dissolved

870 *2×435 = 3×290 = 5×174 =6×145 = 10×87 = 15×58 = 29×30*

With the Dagger Destroyeth He *ST*

871 *13×67*

Gods&Men Are Fools *Sf*
Road to Damascus *Sf, k*
The Double-Headed One

872 *2×436 = 4×218 = 8×109*

Be Girt With A Sword Before Me Π
Kingdom of the West *ST,Tf*
Through Love

874 *2×437 = 19×46 = 23×38*

Transformations *Sf*

875 *5×175 = 7×125 = 25×35*

Come Forth, O Children, *Nf, k*
Glory to God
Lift Up Thine Heart & Rejoice
Mystery of Toil *ST*
Ranunculus *Sf, k*
Sign of the Scorpion *Nf* Π
Stooping Dragon *ST, Nf*
The Terror of Things *Sf*
We Are Upon Thee *W,ŏ*

876 *2×438 = 3×292 = 4×219 =6×146 = 12×73*

The Chance of Union *Nf*
The Mighty and Terrible One
The Navel of Nuit *Tf*

Π **877**

Glory Be to the Sphinx
The Water of Life

878 *2×439*

The Goat of the Spirit
The Ill-Ordered House
Thou Shall Reveal IT *Tf*

879 *3×293*

Apostle of Infinite Space *ST*
Outermost *ST,Tf*

880 *2×440 = 4×220 = 5×176 =8×110 = 10×88 = 11×80 = 16×55 =20×44 = 22×40*

Book of the East *ST,Tf*
Matter and Motion *Nf*
Secret Word *W, k*
The FIXED MERCURY *k, X*
The Universal Mercury

881

Harsh Wine of Delusion *Nf*
Nemo Hoc Facere Potest *ST, k, ŏ*
The Numbers & the Words *Sf*
Universal Substance *ST*

882 *2×441 = 3×294 = 6×147 =7×126 = 9×98 = 14×63 = 18×49 =21×42*

Palace of Understanding *ST, L*
The Brightness of the Heavens *Sf*
The Brilliance of the Lord
The Prophets Shall Prophecy
White Brothers *W, Sf*

883

Abstinence from Action *ST, Nf, k*
Be Goodly Therefore
Self-Luminous *Sf*
The Very Light of God Himself *ŏ*

885 *3×295 = 5×177 = 15×59*

Complement of NU *k, ŏ*
Fill and Will of Love
How Shall He End His Speech With Silence
The Daughter of the King
The Pillars of the World!

The Worship of NU

886 *2×443*

The Beloved Shall Abide With Thee

The Wingêd Globe

Π **887**

Double-Wanded One

Purple Beyond Purple

888 *2×444 = 3×296 = 4×222 =6×148 = 8×111 = 12×74 = 24×37*

By BES-NA-MAUT my Breast I Beat *ST, Tf*

Palace of the King's Daughter *L*

Sea-Green Incorruptible Scribe *kk*

The Ending of the Words

The Master Flamed Forth as a Star *ST*

The Omnipresence of my Body *ŏŏ*

889 *7×127*

Mourning of Isis *Sf*

Sorrow is NOT *Tf*

Splendour & Rapture!

Three Impure Souls *Sf*

890 *2×445 = 5×178 = 10×89*

Fountains of Fire

The Book is Shut *Tf*

The Red Rain of my Lightnings

The Undefiled Knowledge

Wear to Me Jewels! *W*

891 *3×297 = 9×99 = 11×81 =27×33*

A Temple of Initiation *Nf*

892 *2×446 = 4×223*

Chapel of Abominations *Sf, ŏ*

893 *19×47*

Mystery of Redemption *ST, Nf*

Supper of the Passover

The Babe in the Lotus *Sf*

Ye Folk of the Grey Land

894 *2×447 = 3×298 = 6×149*

Behold the Abomination *Nf, ŏ*

Memento Sequor

895 *5×179*

A Word Not Known *Nf, ŏ*

The Knees of the Mother

896 *2×448 = 4×224 = 7×128 =8×112 = 14×64 = 16×56 = 28×32*

His Name is Righteousness *SSf*

Holy Names of God

Master of the Temple of A' A' *ST*

Oracles of the Gods *Sf, k*

Thrice and Four Times Blessed

Vault of the Adepts *Sf*

897 *3×299 = 13×69 = 23×39*

Nations of the Earth

Very Light of God Himself

898 *2×449*

Certain Holy Nuns *Sf*

Lift Up your Heads *Sf*

Mysteries of Creation *ST, k*

The Heart of the Ritual

899 *29×31*

Angel of the Moon *Nf*

Dung It About *Tf*

The Light of Truth

The Overworld Calls *Sf, k*

Toils of Mystery *ST*

900 *2×450 = 3×300 = 4×225 =5×180 = 6×150 = 9×100 = 10×90 =12×75 = 15×60 = 18×50 = 20×45 =25×36 =* 30^2

Death is the Crown of All

The Kingdom of the Grave

The Lord of Creation *Nf*

Wheel of the Spirit *W, Tf*

901 *17×53*

The Cynocephalus in Leash

The Great White King and His Black Slave

902 *2×451 = 11×82 = 22×41*

Sign of the Scorpion *Nf, k*
The Balances of Truth *L*
Wings of the Eagle *W*

Σ42 **903** *3×301 = 7×129 = 21×43*

Current of Destiny *ST, k*
Day of Be-With-Us is At Hand
Holy Chosen One
The Blood Royal

904 *2×452 = 4×226 = 8×113*

Mountain of Fire
Strength, Force, Vigour, of your Arms *ST, Nf*
The Key of the Rituals
Thy Beautiful Body *ŏ*
Worship Impure *W*

905 *5×181*

Hidden and Glorious *Sf*
The Prophet of the Aeon Arising *ŏŏ*

906 *2×453 = 3×302 = 6×151*

Joy of the World
Withholdest *ST, W, Tf*

Π **907**

Come Unto Me! *k*
House of Venus *Sf, ŏ*
Lengthening of the Lingam
Magus of the TARO
O Householder
Old King Lies Prostate *ST*
The Kingdom of the Father
The Secrets of Truth *k*
The Universal MERCURY *k*
The Word is Falsehood
Thou Art the Last *ST, Tf*

908 *2×454 = 4×227*

Blood of Saints *Sf*
O my People, Rise Up & Awake!
Seven Secret Names of God *k*
The Everlasting House *ST*
The Five Interpenetrateth the Six
The Veil of my Mother
They Shall Worship Thy Name
Thy Fornications *Sf, k*
Vault of my Body *ŏ*

909 *3×303 = 9×101*

Crowned With the Triangle *k*
The Changeful Moon *Nf*

910 *2×455 = 5×182 = 7×130 =10×91 = 13×70 = 14×65 = 26×35*

Kingdom of the Son *Nf*
The Obeah and the Wanga *W*

Π **911**

Infinite Without *Tf*

912 *2×456 = 3×304 = 4×228 =6×152 = 8×114 = 12×76 = 16×57 =19×48 = 24×38*

Diamonds in Thy Crown *Nf, k*
Moonstone *ST*
World Elephant *W, Tf, L*
World of the Word

913 *11×83*

Fangs of the Hound
Sevenfold Task of Earth
Tail of the Scorpion *Nf*

914 *2×457*

Light of the Father of All
Scourge of God *k*
Soul of the Desert *Tf*
The Child of Thy Bowels *Sf*

915 *3×305 = 5×183 = 15×61*

Her Lithe Body Arched for Love *ŏ*
Look Not Beneath *ŏ*
The Gate of the God ON *ŏ*

916 $2\times458 = 4\times229$

Judgment of the Highest *ST, Tf*

Look Not On High *ŏŏ*

Triple is the Cord of Silver *k*

917 7×131

The Lords of Vision *Nf*

The Substance of Light *ST, Tf*

Word and the Fool

918 $2\times459 = 3\times306 = 6\times153 = 9\times102 = 17\times54 = 18\times51 = 27\times34$

Hearing is of the Spirit Alone

The City of the Seven Hills *Sf*

The House of Wrath

The Sign of Initiation *Nf*

The Silver Star that Ye Adore *ST*

The Wrong of the Beginning *ŏ*

Without Form

Π **919**

My Heart & my Tongue! *Tf*

Prophet of the Aeon Arising *ŏ*

The Word of the God

Warrior Lord of Thebes *Sf*

Whirlpool and Leviathan *Nf*

920 $2\times460 = 4\times230 = 5\times184 = 8\times115 = 10\times92 = 20\times46 = 23\times40$

The End of the Hiding of Hadit *Tf*

The Majesty and the Beauty *ST*

Wounds *W, Sf*

921 3×307

God Enthroned in Ra's Seat *Tf*

The Twelve Emancipations

922 2×461

Burn to Me Perfumes! *Tf*

O ANKH-AF-NA-KHONSU!

Other Understandeth *ST*

The Universe is Dissolved

The Vast and the Minute *ST*

Universe of Love

Whose Love is One

923 13×71

Blasphemy Against All Gods of Men *ST, Nf, ŏ*

Outermost Abyss *ST, SSf, ŏ*

Purple Flashes of Lightning

The Priestess of the Silver Star *ST*

Whirlpool *W*

924 $2\times462 = 3\times308 = 4\times231 = 6\times154 = 7\times132 = 11\times84 = 12\times77 = 14\times66 = 21\times44 = 22\times42 = 28\times33$

Name of Thy House

Our Lord the Beast *ST, Tf*

The Lamp of the Invisible Light *Tf*

Ultimate Sparks Intimate Fire

925 $5\times185 = 25\times37$

Let Blood Flow

The Feet of the Most High *ST*

The Head of the Crowned Lion *ŏ*

926 2×463

Let the Fine Be Tried in Intellect *Tf, k*

My Hair the Trees of Eternity

927 $3\times309 = 9\times103$

Death is the Crown of All *k*

The Gate of the Evening Star *ST*

The Lord of Creation *Nf, k*

The Royal and the Lofty *ŏ*

928 $2\times464 = 4\times232 = 8\times116 = 16\times58 = 29\times32$

Book of THOTH *ŏ*

Crown of the *Yod*

Π **929**

All and One and Naught *Tf*

Eyes of Tetragrammaton *Nf*

Four Pillars of Water

The Stélé of Revealing Itself *ST, L*

930 *2×465 = 3×310 = 5×186 =6×155 = 10×93 = 15×62 = 30×31*
A Place Where Four Roads Meet *Tf*
Maker of Illusions *Sf*
The Great Sigil of the Arrow

931 *7×133 = 19×49*
Are Mine, O Ankh-Af-Na-Khonsu! *ŏ*
Lord of the Forties *Sf*
Secret Ardours of HADIT *Tf, k*
The Glory of the Stars *ST*
The Law of the Fortress *SSf*

932 *2×466 = 4×233*
Plumes of Truth
Thou Art He O God *ŏ*
Wine of the Sabbath *W*

933 *3×311*
Little Waverings of Balance *L*
Sorrow of my Heart
The Winners of the Ordeal X

934 *2×467*
Wings of the Swallow

935 *5×187 = 11×85 = 17×55*
Smooth Point *Tf*

936 *2×468 = 3×312 = 4×234 =6×156 = 8×117 = 9×104 = 12×78 =13×72 = 18×52 = 24×39 = 26×36*
Ecclesia Abhorent a Sanguine *kk*
The Power of the Pentagram

Π **937**
Length of Thy Longing *ŏ*
Supernal Wisdom *W*
The Self-Slain Ankh-Af-Na-Khonsu *ŏ*

938 *2×469 = 7×134 = 14×67*
The Snake and of the Goat *Tf*

939 *3×313*
My Chariots and my Horsemen *Nf*
The Kamea of the Moon *Nf*

940 *2×470 = 4×235 = 5×188 =10×94 = 20×47*
Wonderful *W*

Π **941**
Book of the Aeons *Sf, ŏ*
Day of your Wrath

942 *2×471 = 3×314 = 6×157*
O my Maker, my Master, my Mate! *ST*
Stooping Starlight *ST, Tf*
The Book Tarot *Tf*

943 *23×41*
Chymical Marriage of the Alchemists *S T, Sf, kkk*
Poisonous *Sf*
Two Score Bulls *Sf*

944 *2×472 = 4×236 = 8×118 =16×59*
From Gold Forge Steel! *ST*

945 *3×315 = 5×189 = 7×135 =9×105 = 15×63 = 21×45 = 27×35*
Guardian of the Labyrinth
The Laughing Face of Eros *Sf*
The Nastiness of Her Pleasure *ST*
The Veil of Sorrow
Whirlings of the Universe

Σ43 **946** *2×473 = 11×86 = 22×43*
The Ways of the Ka!
Wolf Betrayeth *W*

Π **947**
House of Ra and Tum *ŏ*
The Flame Upon the Altar

948 *2×474 = 3×316 = 4×237 =6×158 = 12×79*
Worm of Poison *Nf*
Wrath of God *W*

949 *13×73*
Young Universe

950 *2×475 = 5×190 = 10×95 =19×50 = 25×38*

Art and Craft of the Magus *Sf, k*

951 *3×317*

Come Ye Unto Me *k*

Self-Slain Ankh-Af-Na-Khonsu

Things of Sense and Rapture

952 *2×476 = 4×238 = 7×136 =8×119 = 14×68 = 17×56 = 28×34*

Equinox of the Gods *Sf, ŏ*

Π **953**

Spears of Mighty and Terrible Angels *Sf*

Sun, Strength & Sight, Light *ST, Tf*

The Order of the Silver Star *ST*

The Three Great Delusions *Sf*

955 *5×191*

A Temple of Initiation

Sword of the Beloved

The Lord of the Tempest *ST, Tf*

The Toys of the Magician

Vigourous *Sf*

956 *2×478 = 4×239*

Car Called Millions-Of-Years *Sf, kk*

He Understandeth IT Not *ST, Tf, ŏ*

Lust of Result *ST, Tf*

The Lord of the Aeon

957 *3×319 = 11×87 = 29×33*

Thanksgiving to God!

That Mighty Devil Choronzon *Nf, k, ŏŏŏ*

Weird and Monstrous Speech *ST, ŏ*

959 *7×137*

House of Hathor

O RA-HOOR-KHUIT! *Tf*

960 *2×480 = 3×320 = 4×240 =5×192 = 6×160 = 8×120 = 10×96 =12×80 = 15×64 = 16×60 = 20×48 =24×40 = 30×32*

His Secret Name and Splendour *k*

961 *31^2*

Behold the Queen of Heaven *Nf*

How Shall He Destroy Himself? *ST*

I Will Reward You Here and Hereafter

Lord of Initiation *Nf*

The Pillar is 'Stablished in the Void *ST*

Transmutations *Sf*

962 *2×481 = 13×74 = 26×37*

Blind Ache of the Soul *k*

The Waters of Death

Ye Twin Warriors

963 *3×321 = 9×107*

I Am the God Who Giveth All

None By the Book

Royal Uræus Serpent *Tf*

The Girders of the Soul

The Palace of the King my Son *Nf, L*

The Phallus of A Goat *Tf*

White Black and Gold *W*

964 *2×482 = 4×241*

Irritate the Vessels of the Earth

Set Thy Feet in the North

The Book of the Law

The Coiled Splendour *k*

The Vision and the Voice

965 *5×193*

The Name of my House

966 *2×483 = 3×322 = 6×161 =7×138 = 14×69 = 21×46 = 23×42*

Enough of Because! *k*

Head of the Crowned Lion *Nf, k*

Π **967**

Company of the Saints *Sf, k*

The House of the Father

968 *2×484 = 4×242 = 8×121 =11×88 = 22×44*

Sweet Words for the Kings! *Sf*

The House of God

The Palace of Understanding*— Compare with 988 where the L is upright. *ST*

Word Eternity *W*

969 *3×323 = 17×57 = 19×51*

Most Holy One *ST*

O Holy Exalted One

Prince&Apostle of Infinite Space *ST*

The Eye and the Tooth

The House of the Virgin *Nf*

970 *2×485 = 5×194 = 10×97*

Plumes of Amoun *Nf*

Ra-Hoor-Khu is With Thee

Xenopilus *x, Sf*

Π **971**

Burnt Down & Shattered

The Black Brotherhood *k*

The House of my Father

The Shrine of the Exalted One

972 *2×486 = 3×324 = 4×243 =6×162 = 9×108 = 12×81 = 18×54 =27×36*

The Wisdom of the New Aeon *Nf, ŏ*

973 *7×139*

Fastness of the Most High *ST*

974 *2×487*

Ateph Crown of Thoth *k, ŏ*

The Dung of Choronzon *Nf, k, ŏŏŏ*

975 *3×325 = 5×195 = 13×75 =15×65 = 25×39*

My Ecstasy is in Yours *ST, k*

976 *2×488 = 4×244 = 8×122 =16×61*

Ateph Crown of Truth *k, ŏ*

Encloseth the Universe *k*

My Sacred Heart and Tongue *k*

Π **977**

Terrible Armies of the Most High *ST*

The Road to Damascus *Sf, k*

Thy Great NOX *X*

978 *2×489 = 3×326 = 6×163*

Gone Forth to War

Scorpions of the Sand *k*

979 *11×89*

Woman Girt With A Sword

980 *2×490 = 4×245 = 5×196 =7×140 = 10×98 = 14×70 = 20×49 =28×35*

His Weapons Fulfill the Wheel

Not the Khu in the Khabs *Sf*

Woman of the Mysteries *ST,Sf*

981 *3×327 = 9×109*

Battle of Conquest *S T, Tf, k, ŏ*

982 *2×491*

Apron of Flaming Orange

Write Unto Us *Sf*

Π **983**

By His Wisdom Made He the Worlds *Sf*

House of the Invisible

Mystery of Iniquity *ST*

The Glory Be to the Sphinx

Thou Shalt Die to All *ŏ*

984 *2×492 = 3×328 = 4×246 =6×164 = 8×123 = 12×82 = 24×41*

Hounds of Thunder *ŏ*

985 *5×197*

Light of the Sight of Time

O Wingêd Snake of Light, Hadit! *Tf*

986 *2×493 = 17×58 = 29×34*

A Light Undesired, Most Desirable *ST*

I Will Give You A War-Engine

O Splendrous Serpent! *Tf*

Shameless in Deed As in Word *W*
Tum is More Terrible Than Ra

987 *3×329 = 7×141 = 21×47*

The Harsh Wine of Delusion *Nf*
The Universal Substance *ST*

988 *2×494 = 4×247 = 13×76 =19×52 = 26×38*

Shall Be the Whole of the Law
The Palace of Understanding *ST, L*
The White Brothers *Sf*
Thou Knowest! *ST*
Unrighteousness *SSf*
Whose Life is One *W*

989 *23×43*

Thy Toy Thy Joy
Womb of Its Mother

Σ44 **990** *2×495 = 3×330 = 5×198 =6×165 = 9×110 = 10×99 = 11×90 =15×66 = 18×55 = 22×45 = 30×33*

Now Now Now
Phallus of Amoun *Nf*

Π **991**

Men and Women of the Earth
Scarlet Concubine of His Desire! *kkk, ŏ*
Source of Creation *Nf, k*
The Complement of Nu *k, ŏ*

992 *2×496 = 4×248 = 8×124 =16×62 = 31×32*

Abide With Me, Ra-Hoor-Khuit! *Tf*
Invoke Me Under my Stars! *ST*
Kut! Hut! Nut! *Tf*
Sixfold Star of Glory *ST*

993 *3×331*

Darkness of Thought *Tf*

994 *2×497 = 7×142 = 14×71*

Four Great Princes of Evil
The Palace of the King's Daughter *L*

The Sea-Green Incorruptible Scribe *kk*
Two Eyes of Horus *Sf, ŏ*

995 *5×199*

Absolute Truth
The Mourning of Isis *Sf*
We Are Upon Thee *W*

996 *2×498 = 3×332 = 4×249 =6×166 = 12×83*

The Fountains of Fire

Π **997**

Four-Fold Terror
One Uttereth Clearly *k*
Servants of the Star & the Snake *ST*
Worship Me With Fire & Blood

998 *2×499*

Tetragrammaton Tzabaoth *ŏ*
Without *W, Tf*

999 *3×333 = 9×111 = 27×37*

Seal of Righteousness *SSf*
The Supper of the Passover
Vultures of Evil

1000 *2×500 = 4×250 = 5×200 =8×125 = 10×100 = 20×50 = 25×40 =10³*

Arrow Cleaving the Rainbow *k*
Count Well Its Name *k*
Eternity to Eternity
Green Serpent, the Serpent of Delight *Tf*
Now is Asi Fulfilled of Asar
Sword, the Balances, the Crown! *Nf, k, L*
The Visible Object of Worship *k, ŏ*
Worship Then the Khabs *W*

1001 *7×143 = 11×91 = 13×77*

Be Upon Them, O Warrior *ŏ*
Nemo Hoc Facere Potest *ST, k*
No Man can do this Thing
Seal of Solomon *Nf*

1002 *2×501 = 3×334 = 6×167*

Holy Spirit in the Trinity
Initiator and Destroyer *ST*
Sightless Storm in the Night *ST,Tf*
The Holy Names of God
The Oracles of the Gods *Sf, k*
The Vault of the Adepts *Sf*
Thought of Adonai *ŏ*

1003 *17×59*

The Nations of the Earth
The Very Light of God Himself
Union With the Many

1005 *3×335 = 5×201 = 15×67*

Half Known and Half Concealed *k*

1006 *2×503*

War of the Rose and the Cross *SSf, k, ŏ*

1007 *19×53*

Oil and Blood and Kisses *Sf*

1008 *2×504 = 3×336 = 4×252 =6×168 = 7×144 = 8×126 = 9×112 =12×84 = 14×72 = 16×63 = 18×56 =21×48 = 24×42 = 28×36*

The Sign of the Scorpion *Nf, k*

Π **1009**

The Day of Be-With-Us is At Hand
The Holy Chosen One

1010 *2×505 = 5×202 = 10×101*

Goodly Armour
NU is your Refuge
Panther's Skin of Courage *k*
The Secret Ardours of Hadit *Tf*
The Strength of the Lion *ST, Nf*
Twelve Rays of the Crown *Nf, k*
Wisdom and Folly *W,ŏ*

1011 *3×337*

Book of the Recorder *k*
Crimson Rose of 49 Petals *Sf, k*
Punishment of Pleasure
Torn Upon Wheels *Sf*
Understanding the Woman *ST, Nf*

1012 *2×506 = 4×253 = 11×92 =22×46 = 23×44*

It Shall Be to You
The Joy of the World

Π **1013**

Adonai the Beloved One
Strength of the Lion *ST*
The Little World my Sister *ST*
The Magus of the TARO
The Old King Lies Prostate *ST*
The Ring of the Horizon
Whirling Air and Rushing Fire *W*
With the Wand Createth He *W, k*

1014 *2×507 = 3×338 = 6×169 =13×78 = 26×39*

Blood of the Saints *Sf*
Brothers of the Left Hand Path
Mystery of the Supernals *ST*
The Seven Secret Names of God *k*
The Vault of my Body *ŏ*

1015 *5×203 = 7×145 = 29×35*

Word for Myself *W*

1016 *2×508 = 4×254 = 8×127*

Accurséd Be It to the Aeons! *Sf, kk, ŏ*
Government of the Earth
O Glory of Priapus *Sf*
The Kingdom of the Son *Nf*

1017 *3×339 = 9×113*

The Infinite Without *Tf*

1018 *2×509*

I Am Thy Theban, O Mentu,
The World of the Word
Until the Voice Vibrate
Worship Then the Khabs *W, Sf*

Π **1019**

		Pillars of the World!	W
		The Sevenfold Task of Earth	
		Violet Blossoms	Sf
		Whose Words Are Truth	
		Word Secret & Not	W, Tf, k, ŏ
	1020	2×510 = 3×340 = 4×255 =5×204 = 6×170 = 10×102 = 12×85 =15×68 = 17×60 = 20×51 = 30×34	
		The Light of the Father of All	
Π	1021		
		Unveiler of the Mysteries	ST,Sf
	1022	2×511 = 7×146 = 14×73	
		Mystery of Incarnation	ST, Nf, k
		Rule the Many&The Known	Nf
		The Consummation	Nf, k
		The Judgment of the Highest	ST,Tf
	1023	3×341 = 11×93 = 31×33	
		The Blind Creature of the Slime	k
3	1024	2×512 = 4×256 = 8×128 =16×64 = 32^2 = 4^5 = 2^{10}	
		Victorious City	k
	1025	5×205 = 25×41	
		Mystery of Sorrow	ST
		The Whirlpool and Leviathan	Nf
	1026	2×513 = 3×342 = 6×171 =9×114 = 18×57 = 19×54 = 27×38	
		Continuity of Existence	ST, k, ŏ
		The Fall of the Great Equinox	ŏ
	1027	13×79	
		House of Venus	Sf
		The God Enthroned in Ra's Seat	Tf
	1028	2×514 = 4×257	
		My Chariot from Babylon	Nf
		No Man can do this Thing	k
		Roar of the Gored Lion	Nf
		The Goat and the Crocodile	kk, ŏ
		The Other Understandeth	ST
	1029	3×343 = 7×147 = 21×49	
		The Purple Flashes of Lightning	
	1030	2×515 = 5×206 = 10×103	
		The Name of Thy House	
		Throughout	Tf
	1032	2×516 = 3×344 = 4×258 =6×172 = 8×129 = 12×86 = 24×43	
		Loom of Justice	ST
		Unprofitable Throne	
Π	1033		
		Ye Shall be with Me in the Abodes that are beyond Decay	
		Child and the Father of Their Love	
		Force of the Mighty One	
		Minister of Hoor-Paar-Kraat	ST,Tf
	1034	2×517 = 11×94 = 22×47	
		The Book of Thoth	ŏ
		The Ordeals of my Knowledge!	ŏ
		The Word of the Law is Thelema	
Σ45	1035	3×345 = 5×207 = 9×115 =15×69 = 23×45	
		Bosom of NUIT!	Tf
		Her Lithe Body Arched for Love	
		The Eyes of TETRAGRAMMATON	Nf
	1036	2×518 = 4×259 = 7×148 =14×74 = 28×37	
		Holy Twelve-Fold Table	
		The Maker of Illusions	Sf
		Thy Dolores Note	
	1037	17×61	
		The Secret Ardours of Hadit	Tf, k
		Thou Knewest Not	ST,Tf, ŏ
	1038	2×519 = 3×346 = 6×173	
		Leader of the Armies of the Lord	
		Lofty Chosen Ones	Sf
		Lurk! Withdraw! Upon Them!	ŏ
		The Plumes of Truth	

The Wine of the Sabbath

Π **1039**

Sons of the Morning

Word of the Law W

1040 *2×520 = 4×260 = 5×208 =8×130 = 10×104 = 13×80 = 16×65 =20×52 = 26×40*

Fall of the Great Equinox

Legions of Eternal Vigilance

The Wings of the Swallow

1041 *3×347*

A God of War and of Vengeance

House of the Juggler

O Beautiful Boy

O Pillars of the Universe

Order of the Rosy Cross *SSf, k, ŏ*

The Spears of Mighty and Terrible Angels

1042 *2×521*

Book of the Mysteries *ST,Sf*

Tetragrammaton Eloah Va-Da'ath ŏ

1043 *7×149*

Outermost Abyss *ST,SSf*

The Horror of Emptiness *SSf*

The Length of Thy Longing *ŏ*

Ways of the Khu! *W*

1045 *5×209 = 11×95 = 19×55*

Four and Thirty Whirlings *Sf*

Lurk Withdraw Be Upon Them *ŏ*

The Head of the Crowned Lion

The Stooping Dragon *ST*

1046 *2×523*

The Tail of the Scorpion *Nf, k*

Thine Own Cosmos *Sf, k*

Whose Name is One *W*

1047 *3×349*

Delicious Languor

Division of the Shadows *Sf*

The Day of your Wrath

1048 *2×524 = 4×262 = 8×131*

Ordeals of my Knowledge!

Reward of Ra Hoor Khut *Tf*

The Stooping Starlight *ST, Tf*

Thou Shalt Know

Thou Wilt *Tf*

Π **1049**

Forces in Their Concourse *k, ŏ*

1050 *2×525 = 3×350 = 5×210 =6×175 = 7×150 = 10×105 = 14×75 =15×70 = 21×50 = 25×42 = 30×35*

The Gates of Understanding *ST*

Π **1051**

Creation of the World *k*

O Thou Open Eye

Two and Twenty Privileges *Sf*

1052 *2×526 = 4×263*

Thou Art He O God

1053 *3×351 = 9×117 = 13×81 =27×39*

Wine and Strange Drugs *ST, W*

Wings of MAUT *W, Tf*

1054 *2×527 = 17×62 = 31×34*

The Word of the Law is Thelema *L*

Wine of the Sacrament *W, Tf, k*

1055 *5×211*

For Me Unveils the Veilêd Sky,

Magnificent Beasts of Women *ST*

The Company of the Saints *k*

World of Stars *ST, W, Sf*

1056 *2×528 = 3×352 = 4×264 =6×176 = 8×132 = 11×96 = 12×88 =16×66 = 22×48 = 24×44 = 32×33*

Accursed Domain of the Three *kk*

1057 *7×151*

Justice of the Most High *ST*

The Self-Slain Ankh-Af-Na-Khonsu

1058 *2×529 = 23×46*

Magistry of this Opus *ST,Sf*

1059 *3×353*

LOGOS of A New God

The Sun, Strength, Sight &Light *ST,Tf*

1060 *2×530 = 4×265 = 5×212 =10×106 = 20×53*

O Desolate Soul

Π **1061**

Glory in the End and the Beginning

How Then Shall He End His Speech With Silence

O Meal and Honey and Oil

The Crown of the *Yod* *k*

1062 *2×531 = 3×354 = 6×177 =9×118 = 18×59*

Cup of Fornication *Nf, kk*

Poison of the Infinite

The Car called Millions-Of-Years *Sf, kk*

Π **1063**

Ordeal X

1064 *2×532 = 4×266 = 7×152 =8×133 = 14×76 = 19×56 = 28×38*

A Black Shining Triangle, With Apex Upwards *Sf*

Blush of His Loveliness *SSf*

By Wisdom Hath He Made the Worlds *Sf*

Khabs is the Name of my House

1065 *3×355 = 5×213 = 15×71*

Who Are of Us *W, Sf*

Winged Assyrian Bull Men *W, Nf*

1066 *2×533 = 13×82 = 26×41*

Glory of the Most High *ST*

Inhabitants of the Worlds *Sf*

Minister of the Sacrament of Pain *ST, Nf, k*

Thou Art my Lover

1067 *11×97*

House of Ra and Tum

1068 *2×534 = 3×356 = 4×267 =6×178 = 12×89*

Every Man and Every Woman is A Star *ST*

The Blind Ache of the Soul *k*

Π **1069**

Mother of Pearl and Ivory

Prophet of RA-HOOR-KHU *ŏ*

Stable Abode of the Kings of Æ *ST*

The Royal Uræus Serpent *Tf*

1070 *2×535 = 5×214 = 10×107*

A Light Before Thine Eyes, O Prophet *Tf, ŏ*

Light Life Love Force Fantasy Fire

Power of Understanding *ST*

Stabat Crux Juxta Lucem *ST*

Stabat Lux Juxta Crucem *ST*

The Word that is Seven *Nf*

Work, & Be our Bed *W*

1071 *3×357 = 7×153 = 9×119 =17×63 = 21×51*

A Curse Upon Because and His Kin! *Nf, kk, ŏ*

Exposure of Innocence

This Saying is of All Truth

1073 *29×37*

Whose Spirit is One *W*

1074 *2×537 = 3×358 = 6×179*

Battle of Conquest *ST, Tf*

The Word Eternity

1075 *5×215 = 25×43*

1076 *2×538 = 4×269*

Of KHEPHRA and of AHATHOOR

Worship Me With Swords & With Spears

1077 *3×359*

MAUT the Vulture *Tf*

There is the Dove, and There is the Serpent

Weird and Monstrous Speech *ST*

1078 *2×539 = 7×154 = 11×98 =14×77 = 22×49*

We Who Were Dust *ST, W, Tf*

1079 *13×83*

Brilliance of our Lord

The Fastness of the Most High *ST*

1080 *2×540 = 3×360 = 4×270 =5×216 = 6×180 = 8×135 = 9×120 =10×108 = 12×90 = 15×72 = 18×60 =20×54 = 24×45 = 27×40 = 30×36*

The Ateph Crown of Thoth *k, ŏ*

Whole of the Law *W*

Word that is God *W*

Σ46 **1081** *23×47*

Footstool *ST*

Nothing Shall Stand Before His Face *ST*

Woe Unto the First *ST, Tf*

1082 *2×541*

Double Wand of Power

1083 *3×361 = 19×57*

A Sweet-Smelling Perfume of Sweat

Open the Ways of the Khu!

The Terrible Armies of the Most High *ST*

1084 *2×542 = 4×271*

The Scorpions of the Sand *k*

Vir Vis Virus Virtus Viridis *Sf*

1085 *5×217 = 7×155 = 31×35*

Do What Thou Wilt *Tf*

1086 *2×543 = 3×362 = 6×181*

With Swords & With Spears *W, Sf*

Π **1087**

Power Upon the Mother *ŏ*

1088 *2×544 = 4×272 = 8×136 =16×68 = 17×64 = 32×34*

Hawk Headed Lord of Silence & Strength *ST*

Light is Come to the Darkness *SSf, k*

The Apron of Flaming Orange

1089 *3×363 = 9×121 = 11×99 =33²*

Animal Soul of Things *Sf*

Mighty Sea, Yea, Into the Mighty Sea

My Light Shed Over You

Poison of Their Selfishness *SSf*

Spell of RA-HOOR-KHUIT! *Tf*

The Mystery of Iniquity *ST*

Thou Shalt Know Me

Towers of the Universe

With the Cup Preserveth He *W, k*

Work of the Wand *W*

1090 *2×545 = 5×218 = 10×109*

God that Sitteth Alone

Π **1091**

Half of the Word of HERU-RA-HA

1092 *2×546 = 3×364 = 4×273 =6×182 = 7×156 = 12×91 = 13×84 =14×78 = 21×52 = 26×42 = 28×39*

Word of Power *W*

Π **1093**

Torsion is Iniquity

With the Coin Redeemeth He *W, k*

1094 *2×547*

I Am Extended I Am Double I Am Profane

Unique & Conqueror *k, ŏ*

1095 *3×365 = 5×219 = 15×73*

Inviolate Fountain *Nf*

Name Thereof Shall Be No More

1096 *2×548 = 4×274 = 8×137*

Circus of Nothingness *SSf, k*
That Thou Must Die *ST*
The Phallus of AMOUN *Nf*

Π **1097**

Ho! Warrior, If Thy Servant Sink
Return Return Return *Nf*
Stabat Crux Juxta Lucem *ST, k*
Stabat Lux Juxta Crucem *ST, k*
The Scarlet Concubine of His Desire! *kkk, ŏ*

1098 *2×549 = 3×366 = 6×183 =9×122 = 18×61*

Lift Thine Head! Breathe Not So Deep-- Die!
Palace of the Splendour Ineffable *L*

1099 *7×157*

Blood of the World
Master of the Secret of Things *ST,Sf, k*
The Crimson Rose of 49 Petals, *k*
The Darkness of Thought *Tf*

1100 *2×550 = 4×275 = 5×220 =10×110 = 11×100 = 20×55 = 22×50 =25×44*

The Two Eyes of Horus *Sf, ŏ*
Warrior Lord of the Sun *Nf*

1101 *3×367*

Ho! Warrior, If Thy Servant Sink?

1102 *2×551 = 19×58 = 29×38*

Glory Be to God the Blessed
We Are One; We Are None *W*

Π **1103**

The Four-Fold Terror
The One Uttereth Clearly *k*
The Servants of the Star & the Snake *ST*
Thou Shalt Die to All

1104 *2×552 = 3×368 = 4×276 =6×184 = 8×138 = 12×92 = 16×69 =23×48 = 24×46*

Hounds of Thunder
O Wingêd Snake of Light *Tf, W*
Prophet of the Lovely Star! *ST, ŏ*
Whirled Forth in my Breath *W*

1105 *5×221 = 13×85 = 17×65*

The Seal of Righteousness *SSf*

1106 *2×553 = 7×158 = 14×79*

& They Shall Fall Before You
The Green Serpent, the Serpent of Delight *Tf*
The Sword, the Balances, the Crown! *Nf, k, L*
Yield this Body and Soul

1107 *3×369 = 9×123 = 27×41*

Body of the King Dissolve
Fierce Lust of your Pride *ST*
The Word Secret & Not *ŏ*

1108 *2×554 = 4×277*

The Holy Spirit in the Trinity

Π **1109**

Their Gods & Their Men Are Fools *Sf*

1110 *2×555 = 3×370 = 5×222 =6×185 = 10×111 = 15×74 = 30×37*

Whose Light is One *W*

1111 *11×101*

Secret Fourfold Word *k*
The Order of the Rosy Cross *k, ŏ*

1112 *2×556 = 4×278 = 8×139*

Crystal of the Future *ST, k*
Palace of the Queen my Daughter
The War of the Rose and the Cross *SSf, k, ŏ*

1113 *3×371 = 7×159 = 21×53*

Eight and Ninety Rules of Art *Tf*
Instar Hominis Summus *ST,Sf*

1114 *2×557*

Continuous *Sf, k*

1115 *5×223*

Wisdom Says: Be Strong! *ST, W,ŏ*

1116 *2×558 = 3×372 = 4×279 =6×186 = 9×124 = 12×93 = 18×62 =31×36*

Lying Spectre of the Centuries *Sf, k*

The Panther's Skin of Courage *k*

Π **1117**

The Book of the Recorder *k*

The Punishment of Pleasure

The Sightless Storm in the Night *ST*

1118 *2×559 = 13×86 = 26×43*

Aleph, Vau, Yod, Ayin, Resh, Tau

Tetragrammaton Tzabaoth

1119 *3×373*

O Warrior Lord of Thebes *Sf*

The Strength of Its Glory *ST*

The Winged Light *Tf, W*

Worship of NU *W*

1120 *2×560 = 4×280 = 5×224 =7×160 = 8×140 = 10×112 = 14×80 =16×70 = 20×56 = 28×40 = 32×35*

The Blood of the Saints *Sf*

1122 *2×561 = 3×374 = 6×187 =11×102 = 17×66 = 22×51 = 33×34*

Aha! Aha! Aha! Shut Out the Sight! *Tf*

Inspired Forth-Speaker of Mentu

Proud and Mighty Among Men *Nf*

The Government of the Earth

Thought of Adonai

Victory Over Choronzon *Nf, k, ŏŏŏ*

Π **1123**

Drink of the Milk of Thy Breasts *ST,Sf*

Neither Star Nor Moon *ST*

Woe Woe Woe *W*

1125 *3×375 = 5×225 = 9×125 =15×75 = 25×45*

But Always Unto Me

Lust & Worship of the Snake *ST*

O Babylon, Lady of the Night! *ŏ*

Ten Points of the Pentagram

1126 *2×563*

Our Delight is All Over Thee

1127 *7×161 = 23×49*

The Unveiler of the Mysteries *ST,Sf*

Σ47 **1128** *2×564 = 3×376 = 4×282 =6×188 = 8×141 = 12×94 = 24×47*

Soul of God and Beast *ST*

Π **1129**

Womanhood *W*

Written and Concealed *W, k*

1130 *2×565 = 5×226 = 10×113*

The Victorious City *k*

Thou Gladiator God

1132 *2×566 = 4×283*

Palace of the Queen my Daughter *L*

1133 *11×103*

The House of Venus *Sf*

1134 *2×567 = 3×378 = 6×189 =7×162 = 9×126 = 14×81 = 18×63 =21×54 = 27×42*

Court of the Profane *k*

Vigour of the Goat *Tf*

Virtuous Words *Sf*

1135 *5×227*

And the Name of Every Season is Death

Righteousness in Beauty

1137 *3×379*

Altar of the Holiest One *ST*

Shoulders of the Bull

1138 *2×569*

Brilliance of the Lady of the Aethyr

Lord of Light and of Darkness *SSf*

Nakedness of the Holy One

O Thou Satyr God

1139 *17×67*

The Child and the Father of Their Love

The Minister of HOOR-PAAR-KRAAT *ST,Tf*

1140 *2×570 = 3×380 = 4×285 =5×228 = 6×190 = 10×114 = 12×95 =15×76 = 19×60 = 20×57 = 30×38*

Stone of the Philosophers *ST,Sf, ŏ*

1141 *7×163*

Holy, Holy, Holy is Her Name

Word is Falsehood *W*

1142 *2×571*

Naught of our Lady

The Holy Twelve-Fold Table

1143 *3×381 = 9×127*

Day of Judgement of my God *ŏ*

The Supernal Wisdom *W*

1144 *2×572 = 4×286 = 8×143 =11×104 = 13×88 = 22×52 = 26×44*

Let It Become A Thousand *k*

The Leader of the Armies of the Lord

The Lofty Chosen Ones *Sf*

1145 *5×229*

O Thou Empty God

The Word of the Law

1146 *2×573 = 3×382 = 6×191*

Come! Lift Up Thine Heart & Rejoice *k*

The Legions of Eternal Vigilance

Untouched Virginity

1147 *31×37*

The House of the Juggler

The Order of the Rosy Cross *SSf, k, ŏ*

1149 *3×383*

Anarchy of Solitude and Darkness *SSf, k, ŏ*

The Blasphemy Against All Gods of Men *ST, Nf*

The Outermost Abyss *ST,SSf*

The Ways of the Khu!

Victory Over Choronzon *Nf, kk, ŏŏŏ*

1150 *2×575 = 5×230 = 10×115 =23×50 = 25×46*

Peace Unutterable, Rest, Ecstasy; *ST, k*

1152 *2×576 = 3×384 = 4×288 =6×192 = 8×144 = 9×128 = 12×96 =16×72 = 18×64 = 24×48 = 32×36*

Glory Unto the Snake

Wrong of the Beginning *W,ŏ*

П **1153**

And this Saying is of All Truth

The Division of the Shadows *Sf*

Word of the God *W*

1154 *2×577*

Dudu Ner Af An Nuteru

The Book of Thoth

The Ordeals of my Knowledge!

The Reward of RA HOOR KHUT *Tf*

1156 *2×578 = 4×289 = 17×68 =34^2*

The Gates of the Understanding *ST*

The Wisdom of the New Aeon

Thou Jesus of Nazareth

1157 *13×89*

Key of the Pylon of Power *ŏ*

Poisoned Arrows of the Archer

The Two and Twenty Privileges *Sf*

Unimaginable Joys On Earth

1158 *2×579 = 3×386 = 6×193*

The Beatific Vision is No More

White Tunic of Purity *k*

1159 *19×61*

The Poison of Their Selfishness
The Wings of MAUT *Tf*
Victory to the Python *Nf, k, ŏ*

1160 *2×580 = 4×290 = 5×232 =8×145 = 10×116 = 20×58 = 29×40*
Lord of Silence & of Strength *ST*

1161 *3×387 = 9×129 = 27×43*
These Are Fools that Men Adore

1162 *2×581 = 7×166 = 14×83*
Tetragrammaton Eloah Va-Da'ath

Π **1163**
The Justice of the Most High *ST*
Warrior of RA HOOR KHU

1164 *2×582 = 3×388 = 4×291 =6×194 = 12×97*
The Magistry of this Opus *ST,Sf*
Thirty-Three Thunders of Increase *k*

1165 *5×233*
Day of Vengeance of HOOR-RA

1166 *2×583 = 11×106 = 22×53*
Ultimate Sparks of the Infinite Fire

1167 *3×389*
Glory Unto the Star *ST*
Winners of the Ordeal X *W*

1169 *7×167*
A Worm A Nothing A Niddering Knave
Existeth Without Form *ST*
The Wine of the Sacrament *k*
Thou Art Also the Next *Tf*

1170 *2×585 = 3×390 = 5×234 =6×195 = 9×130 = 10×117 = 13×90 =15×78 = 18×65 = 26×45 = 30×39*
The Blush of His Loveliness *SSf*

Π **1171**
Incestuous Horus *ST,Sf, ŏ*
Of the Unimaginable Naught *Tf*
The Wand of the Force of COPH NIA *k, ŏ*
This is the Formula of the Aeon *Nf, ŏ*

1172 *2×586 = 4×293*
The Glory of the Most High *ST*
The Inhabitants of the Worlds *Sf*

1173 *3×391 = 17×69 = 23×51*
Our Lady the Scarlet Woman *Nf, k*
The House of Ra and Tum
The Space Beyond your Vision *Nf, ŏ*
Thy Permutation One!

1174 *2×587*
There is No God But God

1175 *5×235 = 25×47*
Seven Vultures of Evil
Table of Forty Nine Squares *Sf*

Σ48 **1176** *2×588 = 3×392 = 4×294 =6×196 = 7×168 = 8×147 = 12×98 =14×84 = 21×56 = 24×49 = 28×42*
I Saw Satan Like Lightning Fall from Heaven *Nf*

1177 *11×107*
The Exposure of Innocence
Thou Art Overcome *k*
Throne of Lotus *Sf*

1178 *2×589 = 19×62 = 31×38*
Our Splendour & Rapture! *ŏ*

1179 *3×393 = 9×131*
Mother of Abominations *Sf, ŏ*
Prey of Dogs and Vultures *Sf, ŏ*

1180 *2×590 = 4×295 = 5×236 =10×118 = 20×59*
Faint & Faery, of the Stars, and Two *ST*
Illusion and Falsehood

Π **1181**

1182 *2×591 = 3×394 = 6×197*

Eight, Eighty, Four Hundred & Eighteen *Nf*
Throne of Understanding *ST*
Twined About the World

1184 *2×592 = 4×296 = 8×148 =16×74 = 32×37*

He Blasteth the Flowers of the Earth *ST*

1185 *3×395 = 5×237 = 15×79*

The Beatific Vision is No More *k*

1186 *2×593*

Cubical Altar of the Universe *kk*
The Word that is God
Voice of the Ever Living One

Π **1187**

Passing Through the Tuat *Tf*
Space Beyond your Vision *Nf*

1188 *2×594 = 3×396 = 4×297 =6×198 = 9×132 = 11×108 = 12×99 =18×66 = 22×54 = 27×44 = 33×36*

Light Cleaveth Unto Light *Tf, k*
See & Strike At the Worship of Nu *ST*
The Double Wand of Power

1190 *2×595 = 5×238 = 7×170 =10×119 = 14×85 = 17×70 = 34×35*

The Serpent of Wisdom *W*

Π **1193**

Be Ready to Fly Or to Smite!
Manifestation of Nuit *ST, Tf*
Meal & Honey & Thick Leavings of Red Wine

1194 *2×597 = 3×398 = 6×199*

The Light is Come to the Darkness *SSf, k*

1195 *5×239*

How Shall He Cease to Number Himself
The Animal Soul of Things *Sf*
The Mighty Sea, Yea, Into the Mighty Sea
The Spell of RA-HOOR-KHUIT! *Tf*
The Towers of the Universe
the Treasure-House of Pearls *Sf*

1196 *2×598 = 4×299 = 13×92 =23×52 = 26×46*

In Saecula Saeculorum Amen *Nf, kk*
The God that Sitteth Alone
Thou Elevenfold God 418

1197 *3×399 = 7×171 = 9×133 =19×63 = 21×57*

The Half of the Word of HERU-RA-HA
Unassuaged of Purpose
Work, & Be our Bed in Working

1198 *2×599*

Battle of the Python and the Sphinx *ŏ*
Clamour of Thy Voice *k*
The Roar of the Gored Lion
Thunderbolt of Zeus *Sf*
Woman of Abominations *Sf, ŏ*

1199 *11×109*

Litanies of Love and Anguish

1200 *2×600 = 3×400 = 4×300 =5×240 = 6×200 = 8×150 = 10×120 =12×100 = 15×80 = 16×75 = 20×60 =24×50 = 25×48 = 30×40*

The Ateph Crown of Thoth *k*
The Life Which Abideth in Light, Yea, the Life Which Abideth in Light

Π **1201**

The Inviolate Fountain *Nf*
The Name Thereof Shall Be No More

1202 *2×601*

Sun of Midnight is Ever the Son *Nf*

1203 *3×401*

Look Upon With Gladness ŏ
Lord of the Flame and the Lightning
Mountain of the Caverns *Sf*

1204 *2×602 = 4×301 = 7×172 =14×86 = 28×43*

The Palace of the Splendour Ineffable *L*

1205 *5×241*

The Blood of the World

1206 *2×603 = 3×402 = 6×201 =9×134 = 18×67*

Golden Light of Noon *Nf*
Wisdom of the New Aeon *W, Nf, ŏ*

1207 *17×71*

Eternal and Omnipotent God ŏ
Lust and Worship of the Snake *ST*

1208 *2×604 = 4×302 = 8×151*

Pillars About the Neophyte

1209 *3×403 = 13×93 = 31×39*

A Factor Infinite & Unknown *Nf*
O Houses of Eternity
Whose Individuum is One

1210 *2×605 = 5×242 = 10×121 =11×110 = 22×55*

Body of the Milk of the Stars *ST,Sf*
Life Which Abideth in Light, Yea, the Life Which Abideth in Light *Tf*
The Prophet of the Lovely Star! *ST, ŏ*
With the Dagger Destroyeth He *ST, W*

1212 *2×606 = 3×404 = 4×303 =6×202 = 12×101*

Four Gates to One Palace *L*
I Am Nuit, and my Word is Six and Fifty

Π **1213**

Dreadful Horns of the Goat *Tf*
The Body of the King Dissolve
The Fierce Lust of your Pride *ST*

1214 *2×607*

Nothing is A Secret Key of this Law *k*
Unique & Conqueror *k*

1215 *3×405 = 5×243 = 9×135 =15×81 = 27×45*

Angel of Golden Hair and Golden Skin *Nf*

1216 *2×608 = 4×304 = 8×152 =16×76 = 19×64 = 32×38*

Thou Elevenfold God 418 *L*

Π **1217**

Tribulation of Ordeal

1219 *23×53*

Most Holy Ancient One *ST*
The Eight and Ninety Rules of Art *Tf*

1222 *2×611 = 13×94 = 26×47*

But Ye Are Not So Chosen *Nf*
Hollow Tube from Heaven *Nf*

Π **1223**

Divide, Add, Multiply, and Understand *ST*
Key to the Little Door

1224 *2×612 = 3×408 = 4×306 =6×204 = 8×153 = 9×136 = 12×102 =17×72 = 18×68 = 24×51 = 34×36*

Directly and Through Love *k*

Σ49 **1225** *5×245 = 7×175 = 25×49 =*35^2

O Wingêd Snake of Light, Hadit! *Tf, W*
The Worship of NU
Unveiling Before the Children of Men! *Nf*

1226 *2×613*

Warrior Lord of the Forties *Sf*

1227 *3×409*

Success is your Proof *k*

1228 *2×614 = 4×307*

Hermit, the Lover and the Man of Earth

It Beams It Burns It Blooms *Sf*

The Inspired Forth-Speaker of Mentu;

Π **1229**

& Ye Shall Turn Not Back for Any *ŏ*

1230 *2×615 = 3×410 = 5×246 =6×205 = 10×123 = 15×82 = 30×41*

Assembly and the Law and the Enlightenment *Tf*

Curse Them! Curse Them! Curse Them! *kkk*

Π **1231**

The Lust & Worship of the Snake *ST*

1232 *2×616 = 4×308 = 7×176 =8×154 = 11×112 = 14×88 = 16×77 =22×56 = 28×44*

Ultimate Sparks of the Intimate Fire

1233 *3×411 = 9×137*

This and that in His Conjuration *Nf, k, ŏ*

1234 *2×617*

The Knowledge and Conversation *Nf, k, ŏ*

The Threefold Book of Law

Threefold Book of The Law

Visible Object of Worship *k, ŏ*

Π **1237**

Lust & Power of Lust *ST*

Raise the Spell of RA-HOOR-KHUIT! *Tf*

1238 *2×619*

Lord of the City of the Pyramids *Sf*

The Palace of the Queen my Daughter *L*

1240 *2×620 = 4×310 = 5×248 =8×155 = 10×124 = 20×62 = 31×40*

Fifty Are the Gates of Understanding *ST*

Gates of the Understanding Are Fifty *ST*

1241 *17×73*

Infernal Adorations of Oai

Woe Unto the Second

1242 *2×621 = 3×414 = 6×207 =9×138 = 18×69 = 23×54 = 27×46*

I Disport Myself in the Ruins of Eden *Nf*

1243 *11×113*

Naked Splendour of NUIT *Tf*

The Altar of the Holiest One *ST*

1244 *2×622 = 4×311*

Hard & Low& to Hell With Them, Master! *ST*

Stones of Precious Water *ST*

The Brilliance of the Lady of the Aethyr

The Nakedness of the Holy One

1245 *3×415 = 5×249 = 15×83*

Wine of Thy Fornications *Sf, k*

1246 *2×623 = 7×178 = 14×89*

The Stone of the Philosophers *ST,Sf, ŏ*

Thy Presence, O Ra-Hoor-Khuit! *Tf*

To Unbind the Bound

1247 *29×43*

Go Forth to War *W*

The Word is Falsehood

Thy Lion-Roar of Rapture

1248 *2×624 = 3×416 = 4×312 =6×208 = 8×156 = 12×104 = 13×96 =16×78 = 24×52 = 26×48 = 32×39*

Abominable Lonely Thing of Wickedness *SSf, ŏ*

1251 *3×417 = 9×139*

Take your Fill of Love!

1252 *2×626 = 4×313*

NUIT! HADIT! RA-HOOR-KHUIT! *Tf*
The Continuity of Existence *ST, k, ŏ*
World of the Word *W*

1254 *2×627 = 3×418 = 6×209 =11×114 = 19×66 = 22×57 = 33×38*

Known and the Unknown *Nf*

1255 *5×251*

Great One of the Night of Time

1257 *3×419*

Servant of the Star and of the Snake *ST*

1258 *2×629 = 17×74 = 34×37*

The Wrong of the Beginning *ŏ*
Without Form *W*

Π **1259**

Aiwass the Minister of HOOR-PAAR-KRAAT *ST,Tf*
The Word of the God
Warrior Lord of Thebes *W, Sf*
Whirlpool and Leviathan *W, Nf*

1260 *2×630 = 3×420 = 4×315 =5×252 = 6×210 = 7×180 = 9×140 =10×126 = 12×105 = 14×90 = 15×84 =18×70 = 20×63 = 21×60 = 28×45 =30×42 = 35×36*

Go On, Go On, in my Strength *ST, ŏŏ*
Gross Must Pass Through Fire *ST*

1261 *13×97*

Now is HOOR Let Down
Watch Towers of the Universe

1262 *2×631*

Who Hath Set Thee to Save Us *Sf*
Whose Love is One *W*

1263 *3×421*

Course of the Flaming Sword *k*
Day of Judgement of my God
The Key of the Pylon of Power *ŏ*
The Poisoned Arrows of the Archer

1264 *2×632 = 4×316 = 8×158 =16×79*

Fangs of the Hound Eternity
The White Tunic of Purity *k*

1266 *2×633 = 3×422 = 6×211*

Lord of the Forces of Matter
My Ecstasy, the Consciousness *ST, SSf, kk, ŏ*

1267 *7×181*

Let Excellent Virgins Evoke Rejoicing

1268 *2×634 = 4×317*

Above the Heaven and Below Earth and Hell

1270 *2×635 = 5×254 = 10×127*

The Thirty-Three Thunders of Increase *k*

1271 *31×41*

The Day of Vengeance of HOOR-RA

1273 *19×67*

Consoled & the Consoler *kk*
Voluptuous *Sf*

1274 *2×637 = 7×182 = 13×98 =14×91 = 26×49*

Wings of the Swallow *W*

1276 *2×638 = 4×319 = 11×116 =22×58 = 29×44*

Nine and Forty Manifestations *ST,Sf*

Π **1277**

Key of the Pylon of Power

1280 *2×640 = 4×320 = 5×256 =8×160 = 10×128 = 16×80 = 20×64 =32×40*

Pity and Compassion and Tenderness *SSf, k*

1281 *3×427 = 7×183 = 21×61*

Devouring Mothers of Hell

Π **1283**

Praise Unto Thy Lady Nuit *Tf*

1284 *2×642 = 3×428 = 4×321 =6×214 = 12×107*

Perfumes of your Orison *Nf, ŏ*

1285 *5×257*

The Mother of Abominations *Sf, ŏ*

Whirlings of the Universe *W*

1286 *2×643*

Holy House of Hathor

The Thunderbolt of Zeus

1287 *3×429 = 9×143 = 11×117 =13×99 = 33×39*

Child of Wisdom and Understanding *ST*

1288 *r2×644 = 4×322 = 7×184 =8×161 = 14×92 = 23×56 = 28×46*

The Throne of Understanding *ST*

Worm of Poison *W, Nf*

Π **1289**

Opening of the Grade of Ipsissimus *Sf*

Reveal Me to the Multitude

1290 *2×645 = 3×430 = 5×258 =6×215 = 10×129 = 15×86 = 30×43*

Hawk-Headed Lord of Silence & of Strength *ST*

Π **1291**

1292 *2×646 = 4×323 = 17×76 =19×68 = 34×38*

Now is the Pillar Established in the Void *ST*

The Cubical Altar of the Universe *kk*

The Voice of the Ever Living One

1293 *3×431*

Blue-Lidded Daughter of Sunset *Tf*

O my Beloved O Lord Adonai *ŏ*

Our Lady the Scarlet Woman *Nf, W, k, ŏ*

1294 *2×647*

From the Crown to the Abyss *SSf, k*

Lord of the Sword and the Sun *Nf*

1295 *5×259 = 7×185 = 35×37*

AIWASS the Minister of HOOR-PAAR-KRAAT *ST, SSf, Tf*

Π **1297**

Wisdom of RA-HOOR-KHU-IT *Tf*

1298 *2×649 = 11×118 = 22×59*

Our Splendour & Rapture!

1299 *3×433*

Eternal One in the Sign of the Enterer

Queen of Heaven is in Travail of Child *k*

The Manifestation of NUIT *ST, Tf*

The Sun of Midnight is ever the Son *Tf, Nf*

1302 *2×651 = 3×434 = 6×217 =7×186 = 14×93 = 21×62 = 31×42*

Waters of Purification *W, Nf, k*

White Horse of the Saxon *W, Nf*

Who Worshipped HERU-PA-KRAATH *W*

1304 *2×652 = 4×326 = 8×163*

The Battle of the Python and the Sphinx *ŏ*

The Clamour of Thy Voice *k*

1305 *3×435 = 5×261 = 9×145 =15×87 = 29×45*

Confound Annihilation *Nf, k*

Moan of the Torn Bull,

Π **1307**

Lightening the Girders of the Soul

1308 *2×654 = 3×436 = 4×327 =6×218 = 12×109*

The Sun of Midnight is ever the Son *Nf*

1309 *7×187 = 11×119 = 17×77*

Tear Out my Tongue

The Mountain of the Caverns *Sf*

1312 2×656 = 4×328 = 8×164 =16×82 = 32×41

Are Its Crown, Set About the Disk *k*

The Golden Light of Noon *Nf*

The Wisdom of the New Aeon *Nf, ŏ*

1313 13×101

His Name is Righteousness in Beauty

1314 2×657 = 3×438 = 6×219 =9×146 = 18×73

Genitor-Genitrix of the Universe

The Pillars About the Neophyte

The Warrior Lord of the Forties

1317 3×439

Rosa Mundi Est Lilium Coeli *ST, L*

Tremble Ye O Pillars of the Universe

1318 2×659

Hrumachis the Double-Wanded One *k*

The Chosen Priest & Apostle of Infinite Space *ST, ŏ*

Whose Permutation is One

Π **1319**

The Dreadful Horns of the Goat *Tf*

Woman Girt With A Sword *W*

1320 2×660 = 3×440 = 4×330 =5×264 = 6×220 = 8×165 = 10×132 =11×120 = 12×110 = 15×88 = 20×66 =22×60 = 24×55 = 30×44 = 33×40

Our Chariot is Drawn By Doves *Sf*

Woman of the Mysteries *ST, W, Sf*

1322 2×661

The Outcast and the Unfit *ST, Tf, k*

Write Unto Us *W, Sf*

1323 3×441 = 7×189 = 9×147 =21×63 = 27×49

Thou Withholdest Thyself *ST*

1324 2×662 = 4×331

Great Princes of the Evil of the World

1325 5×265 = 25×53

The Most Holy Ancient One *ST*

Σ51 **1326** 2×663 = 3×442 = 6×221 =13×102 = 17×78 = 26×51 = 34×39

Hold! Hold! Bear Up in Thy Rapture;

Key to the Gate of the Evening Star *ST*

Π **1327**

Eternal and Omnipotent God

1329 3×443

The Victory to the Python *k, ŏ*

Womb of Its Mother *W*

1332 2×666 = 3×444 = 4×333 =6×222 = 9×148 = 12×111 = 18×74 =36×37

Chosen Priest & Apostle of Infinite Space *ST*

Olalam Imal Tutulu *L*

1333 31×43

They Shall Rule the Many & the Known *Nf*

Thy Stature Shall Surpass the Stars *ST,Sf*

Vowed Unto Holiness *SSf*

1334 2×667 = 23×58 = 29×46

O Thou Little Grey God

The Hermit, the Lover and the Man of Earth

1335 3×445 = 5×267 = 15×89

Covenant of His Mouth *k*

Terror of God Upon Mankind *ŏ*

The Work of the Wand

1336 2×668 = 4×334 = 8×167

Grant Me the Vision and Thy Glory

The Assembly and the Law and the Enlightenment *Tf*

The Mountain of the Caverns *Sf, k*

1337 *7×191*

Child Both Crowned and Conquering *kk, ŏ*

Worship Me With Fire & Blood *W*

Yea Woe Unto the World

1338 *2×669 = 3×446 = 6×223*

Here is Nothing Under Its Three Forms *Sf*

1340 *2×670 = 4×335 = 5×268 =10×134 = 20×67*

The Visible Object of Worship *k, ŏ*

1341 *3×447 = 9×149*

Go Forth Into the World

1344 *2×672 = 3×448 = 4×336 =6×224 = 7×192 = 8×168 = 12×112 =14×96 = 16×84 = 21×64 = 24×56 =28×48 = 32×42*

In Swoon of the Excellent Kisses! *Sf*

Rosa Mundi Est Lilium Coeli *ST, k, L*

The Lord of the City of the Pyramids *Sf*

Whom Thou Knewest Not! *ST, Tf, ŏ*

1346 *2×673*

The Gates of the Understanding Are Fifty *ST*

War of the Rose and the Cross *W, SSf, k, ŏ*

1347 *3×449*

KHEPHRA the Beetle is Greater Than the Lion MAU

The Infernal Adorations of OAI

Vigourous Food

1348 *2×674 = 4×337*

Promise of our Agelong Love *ŏŏ*

1349 *19×71*

The Naked Splendour of Nuit *Tf*

The Wicked On Earth and the Damned in Hell *k, ŏ*

1350 *2×675 = 3×450 = 5×270 =6×225 = 9×150 = 10×135 = 15×90 =18×75 = 25×54 = 27×50 = 30×45*

Eternal Energy of the Concealed One *k*

Half of the Word Called HOORPAKRAAT *Tf, k*

1351 *7×193*

The Great Snake of Khem the Holy One

1353 *3×451 = 11×123 = 33×41*

Athanor Called Dissolution *Nf, k*

1356 *2×678 = 3×452 = 4×339 =6×226 = 12×113*

O Saviour of the World

1359 *3×453 = 9×151*

O Warrior Lord of Thebes *Sf, W*

Whose Words Are Truth *W*

1360 *2×680 = 4×340 = 5×272 =8×170 = 10×136 = 16×85 = 17×80 =20×68 = 34×40*

Holy Mountain Abiegnus *Sf*

Π **1361**

Behold my Light Shed Over You!

The Great One of the Night of Time

1362 *2×681 = 3×454 = 6×227*

Love is the Law, Love Under Will

1363 *29×47*

The Servant of the Star and of the Snake *ST*

1364 *2×682 = 4×341 = 11×124 =22×62 = 31×44*

Blue Am I and Gold in the Light of my Bride

1365 *3×455 = 5×273 = 7×195 =13×105 = 15×91 = 21×65 = 35×39*

Kingdom of the Holy Ghost *ST, Tf*

The Whirlpool and Leviathan *Nf*

1366 *2×683*

The Gross Must Pass Through Fire *ST*

1369 *37²*

Confound Annihilation *k*

The Course of the Flaming Sword *k*

1370 *2×685 = 5×274 = 10×137*

Lofty Chosen Ones in the Highest *ST,Tf*

The Fangs of the Hound Eternity

1372 *2×686 = 4×343 = 7×196 =14×98 = 28×49*

The Lord of the Forces of Matter

Veil of Sorrow, & the Pall of Death

1374 *2×687 = 3×458 = 6×229*

The Word of the Law is Thelema

1376 *2×688 = 4×344 = 8×172 =16×86 = 32×43*

The Wisdom of the New Aeon *ŏ*

1377 *3×459 = 9×153 = 17×81 =27×51*

Abomination of Desolation *Nf, ŏ*

Σ52 **1378** *2×689 = 13×106 = 26×53*

None Shall Stand Before You *ST*

The Queen of Heaven is in Travail of Child

1379 *7×197*

The Consoled & the Consoler *kk*

1380 *2×690 = 3×460 = 4×345 =5×276 = 6×230 = 10×138 = 12×115 =15×92 = 20×69 = 23×60 = 30×46*

The Wings of the Swallow

1382 *2×691*

The Nine and Forty Manifestations *ST,Sf*

1383 *3×461*

My Secret Centre, my Heart & my Tongue! *k*

1384 *2×692 = 4×346 = 8×173*

Oh! Thou Art Overcome *k*

1386 *2×693 = 3×462 = 6×231 =7×198 = 9×154 = 11×126 = 14×99 =18×77 = 21×66 = 22×63 = 33×42*

Yet Therein is the Mystery of Redemption *ST, Nf*

1387 *19×73*

Above You and in You

1390 *2×695 = 5×278 = 10×139*

Kisses of the Stars Rain Hard Upon Thy Body *ST, ŏŏ*

1391 *13×107*

He Maketh Poisonous the Water

1393 *7×199*

The Child of Wisdom and Understanding *ST*

1394 *2×697 = 17×82 = 34×41*

The Word of the Law is Thelema *L*

1395 *3×465 = 5×279 = 9×155 =15×93 = 31×45*

I Call It Eight, Eighty, Four Hundred & Eighteen *Nf*

1396 *2×698 = 4×349*

The Hawk-Headed Lord of Silence & of Strength *ST*

Think Not, O King, Upon that Lie *ŏŏ*

1397 *11×127*

The Incestuous HORUS *ST,Sf*

The Joy of Dissolution *Nf*

1398 *2×699 = 3×466 = 6×233*

East At the Equinox of the Gods; *ST*

Π **1399**

Angels of the Holy Sevenfold Table

The Blue-Lidded Daughter of Sunset *Tf*

1400 *2×700 = 4×350 = 5×280 =7×200 = 8×175 = 10×140 = 14×100 =20×70 = 25×56 = 28×50 = 35×40*

The Lord of the Sword and the Sun *Nf*

1401 *3×467*

1403 *23×61*

The Wisdom of RA-HOOR-KHU-IT *Tf*

1405 *5×281*

HOOR-PA-KRAAT and RA-HOOR-KHUT *Tf*

Mystery of Dionysus Zagreus *ST,Sf*

Spilling of the Blood of the Lamb

The Eternal One in the Sign of the Enterer

Wand of the Force of COPH NIA *W, k, ŏ*

1411 *17×83*

The Moan of the Torn Bull

Twenty and Two Are the Mansions *Sf*

1412 *2×706 = 4×353*

Accurséd! Accurséd Be It to the Aeons! Hell *kk, ŏ*

Vir, and *Vis*, and *Virus*, and *Virtus*, and *Viridis* *Sf*

1413 *3×471 = 9×157*

O my Beloved! O Lord Adonai!

Our Lady, the Scarlet Woman *Nf, W, k*

Thigh of the Most Holy One *ST*

1416 *2×708 = 3×472 = 4×354 =6×236 = 8×177 = 12×118 = 24×59*

Abodes of the House of my Father

Worship Me With Swords & With Spears *W*

1418 *2×709*

No Man Shall Understand this Writing *ST*

1420 *2×710 = 4×355 = 5×284 =10×142 = 20×71*

The Genitor-Genitrix of the Universe

1421 *7×203 = 29×49*

Woe Unto the First *ST, W, Tf*

1422 *2×711 = 3×474 = 6×237 =9×158 = 18×79*

Kingdoms of the East and of the West *ST,Tf*

Π **1423**

Amri Maratza Maratza Atman Deona Lastadza Maratza Maritza *ST*

Two Hundred and Eighty Judgments *Sf*

1424 *2×712 = 4×356 = 8×178 =16×89*

The Battle of the Python and the Sphinx

The Known and the Unknown

1425 *3×475 = 5×285 = 15×95 =19×75 = 25×57*

Least of the Little Children of the Light *ST,Tf*

1426 *2×713 = 23×62 = 31×46*

Thy Blood-Thirst O my God *ST*

1428 *2×714 = 3×476 = 4×357 =6×238 = 7×204 = 12×119 = 14×102 =17×84 = 21×68 = 28×51 = 34×42*

The Rose At the Crown of the Cross *SSf, kk, ŏ*

Π **1429**

The Half of the Word Called HOORPAKRAAT *Tf*

1430 *2×715 = 5×286 = 10×143 =11×130 = 13×110 = 22×65 = 26×55*

The Great Princes of the Evil of the World

Σ53 **1431** *3×477 = 9×159 = 27×53*

Writing of the Book of the Law

1432 *2×716 = 4×358 = 8×179*

The Athanor Called Dissolution
The Key to the Gate of the Evening Star *ST*

Π **1433**

Courage is your Armour *k*

1434 *2×717 = 3×478 = 6×239*

Seven Spirits of Unrigheousness *SSf*

1435 *5×287 = 7×205 = 35×41*

I Am Above You and in You
Listen to the Numbers & the Words *ST,Sf*

1438 *2×719*

Blessing Unto the Name of the Beast *ST,Tf*

1440 *2×720 = 3×480 = 4×360 =5×288 = 6×240 = 8×180 = 9×160 =10×144 = 12×120 = 15×96 = 16×90 =18×80 = 20×72 = 24×60 = 30×48 =32×45 = 36×40*

Snake that Devoureth the Spirit of Man *Nf*
Warrior Lord of the Sun *W, Nf*

1441 *11×131*

BABALON, the Mother of Abominations *Sf, ŏŏ*
The Covenant of His Mouth *k*

1443 *3×481 = 13×111 = 37×39*

Death is Forbidden, O Man, Unto Thee
The Child Both Crowned and Conquering *kk, ŏ*

Π **1447**

Thy Star-Splendour, O Nuit! *ST,Tf*

1448 *2×724 = 4×362 = 8×181*

Let Blood Flow to my Name
The Holy Mountain Abiegnus

1449 *3×483 = 7×207 = 9×161 =21×69 = 23×63*

The Victory to the Python *k*

1450 *2×725 = 5×290 = 10×145 =25×58 = 29×50*

Until the Ibis Be Revealed Unto the Crab *k*

1452 *2×726 = 3×484 = 4×363 =6×242 = 11×132 = 12×121 = 22×66 =33×44*

The War of the Rose and the Cross *SSf, k, ŏ*

1455 *3×485 = 5×291 = 15×97*

Holy Place of the Holy House

1456 *2×728 = 4×364 = 7×208 =8×182 = 13×112 = 14×104 = 16×91 =26×56 = 28×52*

The Eternal Energy of the Concealed One *k*

1457 *31×47*

O Azure-Lidded Woman, Bend Upon Them! *ŏ*
That Which Existeth Without Form *ST*

Π **1459**

Do That, and No Other Shall Say Nay

1460 *2×730 = 4×365 = 5×292 =10×146 = 20×73*

Drunkenness of the Innermost Sense *ST*
Me in Thee Which Thou Knewest Not *ST,Tf*

1466 *2×733*

Heavenly Kiss of the Beautiful God
Wings of MAUT the Vulture

1470 *2×735 = 3×490 = 5×294 =6×245 = 7×210 = 10×147 = 14×105 =15×98 = 21×70 = 30×49 = 35×42*

War Upon the Holy One *ŏ*

Π **1471**

The Kingdom of the Holy Ghost *ST*

1473 *3×491*

Glory of Thy Countenance *k*
Peace, Peace, Peace Unto Him that is Throned Therein!

1475 *5×295 = 25×59*

Delivered from the Lust of Result *ST,Tf*

1476 *2×738 = 3×492 = 4×369 =6×246 = 9×164 = 12×123 = 18×82 =36×41*

House of the Father is A Mighty Tomb

The Lofty Chosen Ones in the Highest *ST,Tf*

1478 *2×739*

The Veil of Sorrow, & the Pall of Death

1482 *2×741 = 3×494 = 6×247 =13×114 = 19×78 = 26×57 = 38×39*

Π **1483**

My Joy is to See your Joy

The Abomination of Desolation *Nf, ŏ*

1484 *2×742 = 4×371 = 7×212 =14×106 = 28×53*

Lord of the Hosts of the Mighty *ST*

O Thou Prophet of the Gods *Sf, ŏ*

Σ54 **1485** *3×495 = 5×297 = 9×165 =11×135 = 15×99 = 27×55 = 33×45*

Manifestation of Nuit is At An End *ST*

1491 *3×497 = 7×213 = 21×71*

Vision of the Universal MERCURY *k*

1494 *2×747 = 3×498 = 6×249 =9×166 = 18×83*

Genitor-Genitrix of the Universe Vessel

Then Will the Vision Be Revealed, and the Voice Heard

1496 *2×748 = 4×374 = 8×187 =11×136 = 17×88 = 22×68 = 34×44*

The Kisses of the Stars Rain Hard Upon Thy Body *ST, ŏŏ*

1497 *3×499*

My Nemyss Shrouds the Night-Blue Sky

The Creation of the World *W, k*

1498 *2×749 = 7×214 = 14×107*

The World of the Word

Wand of the Force of COPH NIA *W*

White Tunic of Purity *W, k*

Π **1499**

Viceroy of the Unknown King

1503 *3×501 = 9×167*

Warrior of RA HOOR KHU *W*

1506 *2×753 = 3×502 = 6×251*

Word of the God Enthroned in Ra's Seat *Tf*

1509 *3×503*

The Law of the Battle of Conquest *ST, Tf, k, ŏ*

1510 *2×755 = 5×302 = 10×151*

Aye! Listen to the Numbers & the Words *ST,Sf*

Kisses of the Stars Rain Hard Upon Thy Body *ST, ŏ*

Π **1511**

Attained Unto the Grade of Magus *Sf*

The Mystery of Dionysus Zagreus, *ST,Sf*

The Spilling of the Blood of the Lamb

The Wand of the Force of COPH NIA *k, ŏ*

1512 *2×756 = 3×504 = 4×378 =6×252 = 7×216 = 8×189 = 9×168 =12×126 = 14×108 = 18×84 = 21×72 =24×63 = 27×56 = 28×54 = 36×42*

A Sword in my Hand to Push Thy Order

1514 *2×757*

Great One of the Night of Time Stirreth *ST*

1515 *3×505 = 5×303 = 15×101*

Seven Courses of Thy Soul *k*

1519 *7×217 = 31×49*

The Thigh of the Most Holy One *ST*

Unity Uttermost Showed! *ST*

1522 *2×761*

I Hunt Thee Through the Universe

Twined About the World

Π **1523**

Law of the Battle of Conquest *ST,Tf, k*

1525 *5×305 = 25×61*

Unveiling of the Company of Heaven *Nf, k*

1528 *2×764 = 4×382 = 8×191*

The Kingdoms of the East and of the West *ST*

Π **1531**

The Least of the Little Children of the Light *ST,Tf*

1533 *3×511 = 7×219 = 21×73*

Surrounding of the Four

1534 *2×767 = 13×118 = 26×59*

Foursquare, Mystic, Wonderful, *ST, k*

1535 *5×307*

Ye Shall Be With Me in the Abodes that Are Beyond Decay *k*

1536 *2×768 = 3×512 = 4×384 =6×256 = 8×192 = 12×128 = 16×96 =24×64 = 32×48*

Balance of Righteousness and Truth *L*

Voice of the Lord Upon the Waters *Sf, ŏ*

1537 *29×53*

Work, & Be our Bed in Working *W*

1538 *2×769*

Woman of Abominations *W, Sf, ŏ*

Σ55 **1540** *2×770 = 4×385 = 5×308 =7×220 = 10×154 = 11×140 = 14×110 =20×77 = 22×70 = 28×55 = 35×44*

All Rituals All Ordeals All Words and Signs *Sf*

1546 *2×773*

The Snake that Devoureth the Spirit of Man *Nf*

Π **1549**

Iacchus O Iacchus O Iacchus Be Near Us *Sf, kkk*

Whose Individuum is One *W*

1558 *2×779 = 19×82 = 38×41*

This Shall Be your Only Proof

1560 *2×780 = 3×520 = 4×390 =5×312 = 6×260 = 8×195 = 10×156 =12×130 = 13×120 = 15×104 = 20×78 =24×65 = 26×60 = 30×52 = 39×40*

Grinding-Up of the Bones of Choronzon *Nf, ŏŏŏ*

Vine that Clingeth to the Bare Body of A Bacchanal *ŏ*

1561 *7×223*

BABALON, the Mother of Abominations *Sf, ŏ*

No-Thing-Tree in the Land of No-Thing

1563 *3×521*

The Child Both Crowned and Conquering *kk*

The Holy Mountain of Kithairon *Nf, ŏ*

1566 *2×783 = 3×522 = 6×261 =9×174 = 18×87 = 27×58 = 29×54*

Resinous Woods & Gums *Sf, W*

Warrior Lord of the Forties *W, Sf*

1570 *2×785 = 5×314 = 10×157*

Glory Unto Him that is Concealed *k*

Ten in the Twenty Two Directions *Sf, k*

1572 *2×786 = 3×524 = 4×393 =6×262 = 12×131*

The Wings of MAUT the Vulture

1574 *2×787*

Pure Will, Unassuaged of Purpose,
The Promise of our Agelong Love *ŏ*

1576 *2×788 = 4×394 = 8×197*

Conversation of the Holy One *k, ŏ*

1577 *19×83*

Holy Mountain of Kithairon *Nf*

1578 *2×789 = 3×526 = 6×263*

Voluptuous Night-Sky

Π **1579**

The Glory of Thy Countenance *k*

1581 *3×527 = 17×93 = 31×51*

Woe Unto the Second *W*

1582 *2×791 = 7×226 = 14×113*

The House of the Father is a Mighty Tomb

1585 *5×317*

Wine of Thy Fornications *W, Sf, k*

1587 *3×529 = 23×69*

1590 *2×795 = 3×530 = 5×318 =6×265 = 10×159 = 15×106 = 30×53*

The Lord of the Hosts of the Mighty *ST*

1591 *37×43*

The Manifestation of NUIT is At An End *ST*

1592 *2×796 = 4×398 = 8×199*

The Five Wounds and the Five Wounds

1594 *2×797*

Astor O Thou God of Mine *ST*

Π **1597**

Dung It About With Enginery of War!
Holy, Holy, Holy Art Thou!
The Vision of the Universal MERCURY *k*

Π **1601**

O Blessed One O God O Devourer *ŏ*

1602 *2×801 = 3×534 = 6×267 =9×178 = 18×89*

Who Hath Set Thee to Save Us *W, Sf*

1604 *2×802 = 4×401*

The White Tunic of Purity *k*

1605 *3×535 = 5×321 = 15×107*

The Viceroy of the Unknown King

1606 *2×803 = 11×146 = 22×73*

Glory Unto Her that Beareth the Cup *k*

Π **1607**

Goods and Store of Women and Spices *ST,Sf*

1610 *2×805 = 5×322 = 7×230 =10×161 = 14×115 = 23×70 = 35×46*

The Snake that Devoureth the Spirit of Man

1611 *3×537 = 9×179*

Word that is God is None Other Than He

1612 *2×806 = 4×403 = 13×124 =26×62 = 31×52*

The Word of the God Enthroned in Ra's Seat

Π **1613**

Fearful is the Aspect of the Mighty and Terrible One
The Cross is the Golden Light of Noon *Nf, k, ŏ*

1614 *2×807 = 3×538 = 6×269*

Glory of the Most High is No More *ST*
Vine that Clingeth to the Bare Body of A Bacchanal *kk, ŏ*

1618 *2×809*

Manyhood Bound and Loathing

1620 *2×810 = 3×540 = 4×405 =5×324 = 6×270 = 9×180 = 10×162 =12×135 = 15×108 = 18×90 = 20×81 =27×60 = 30×54 = 36×45*

The Great One of the Night of Time Stirreth *ST*

1623 *3×541*

Great Mystery of the House of God *ST*

1625 *5×325 = 13×125 = 25×65*

Thou Art the Holy Chosen One

1626 *2×813 = 3×542 = 6×271*

Veiled Or Voluptuous *Sf*

1630 *2×815 = 5×326 = 10×163*

Kisses of the Stars Rain Hard Upon Thy Body *ST*

1631 *7×233*

The Unveiling of the Company of Heaven *Nf, k*

1634 *2×817 = 19×86 = 38×43*

Be Thou Proud and Mighty Among Men! *Nf*

Π **1637**

Wisdom of RA-HOOR-KHU-IT *W, Tf*

1638 *2×819 = 3×546 = 6×273 =7×234 = 9×182 = 13×126 = 14×117 =18×91 = 21×78 = 26×63 = 39×42*

Daughter of the House of the Invisible

1639 *11×149*

Secret of the Brothers of the Rosy Cross *SSf, kk, ŏ*

1640 *2×820 = 4×410 = 5×328 =8×205 = 10×164 = 20×82 = 40×41*

O Thou Desolator of Shrines!

1641 *3×547*

Vine that Clingeth to the Bare Body of A Bacchanal *kkk, ŏ*

1645 *5×329 = 7×235 = 35×47*

Blanched Eyeless Beetles that Have Neither Wing Nor Horn *Nf*

1648 *2×824 = 4×412 = 8×206 =16×103*

Glory Unto the Rose and the Cross *SSf, k, ŏ*

1649 *17×97*

Most Secret Cult of the Ruby Star *ST, kk*

1651 *13×127*

Thou and I, O Desolate Soul

1654 *2×827*

The Warrior Lord of the Forties

1656 *2×828 = 3×552 = 4×414 =6×276 = 8×207 = 9×184 = 12×138 =18×92 = 23×72 = 24×69 = 36×46*

Π **1657**

Lord of the Double Wand of Power

1658 *2×829*

Whose Permutation is One *W*

Π **1663**

Thou Withholdest Thyself *ST*

1664 *2×832 = 4×416 = 8×208 =13×128 = 16×104 = 26×64 = 32×52*

The Wine of Thy Fornications *Sf*

The Winners of the Ordeal X *X*

1666 *2×833 = 7×238 = 14×119 =17×98 = 34×49*

Foundation of the Holy City

Π **1667**

The No-Thing-Tree in the Land of No-Thing

1668 *2×834 = 3×556 = 4×417 =6×278 = 12×139*

Continuous One of Heaven *Nf, k*

1670 *2×835 = 5×334 = 10×167*

Leaping Laughter and Delicious Languor

1673 *7×239*

Sons and Daughters of Hermes and of Aphrodite
1679 *23×73*

In the Name of the Lord of Initiation, Amen *Nf*
1682 *2×841 = 29×58*

Therefore Art Thou Called Understanding, *ST, k*
1684 *2×842 = 4×421*

The Voluptuous Night-Sky Whom Thou Knewest Not! *ST, W, Tf, ŏ*
1687 *7×241*

I Am the Surrounding of the Four
1690 *2×845 = 5×338 = 10×169 =13×130 = 26×65*

Palace of Two Hundred and Eighty Judgments *Sf*
Π 1693

The Grinding-Up of the Bones of Choronzon *Nf, k, ŏŏŏ*
Π 1697

Direful Judgments of Ra Hoor Khuit! *Tf*
1700 *2×850 = 4×425 = 5×340 =10×170 = 17×100 = 20×85 = 25×68 =34×50*

Love One Another With Burning Hearts *Sf*
1705 *5×341 = 11×155 = 31×55*

Whirlpool and Leviathan, and the Great Stone *ST*
1710 *2×855 = 3×570 = 5×342 =6×285 = 9×190 = 10×171 = 15×114 =18×95 = 19×90 = 30×57 = 38×45*

Palace of Two Hundred and Eighty Judgments *Sf, L*
Σ58 1711 *29×59*

For I Am HORUS, the Crowned and Conquering Child *kk, ŏŏ*
1717 *17×101*

The Word that is God is None Other Than He
1720 *2×860 = 4×430 = 5×344 =8×215 = 10×172 = 20×86 = 40×43*

The Glory of the Most High is No More *ST*

The Vine that Clingeth to the Bare Body of A Bacchanal *kk, ŏ*
Π 1723

Bruise Thou my Head With Thy Foot
1729 *7×247 = 13×133 = 19×91*

The Great Mystery of the House of God *ST*
1734 *2×867 = 3×578 = 6×289 =17×102 = 34×51*

Vine that Clingeth to the Bare Body of A Bacchanal *kk*
1738 *2×869 = 11×158 = 22×79*

Show Thy Star-Splendour, O Nuit! *ST,Tf*
1743 *3×581 = 7×249 = 21×83*

The Wisdom of RA-HOOR-KHU-IT *Tf*
1745 *5×349*

The Secret of the Brothers of the Rosy Cross *SSf, kk, ŏ*
1751 *17×103*

The Blanched Eyeless Beetles that Have Neither Wing Nor Horn *Nf*
1755 *3×585 = 5×351 = 9×195 =13×135 = 15×117 = 27×65 = 39×45*

The Most Secret Cult of the Ruby Star *ST, kk*
1763 *41×43*

The Lord of the Double Wand of Power;
1767 *3×589 = 19×93 = 31×57*

Confound Her Under-standing With Darkness *ST,SSf, k*
1769 *29×61*

Of Being and of Consciousness and of Bliss *SSf, k, ŏ*

1771 *7×253 = 11×161 = 23×77*

Writing of the Book of the Law *W*

1772 *2×886 = 4×443*

The Foundation of the Holy City

Π **1783**

These Are the Seven Spirits of Unrighteousness *SSf*

1784 *2×892 = 4×446 = 8×223*

Flesh of the Indian and the Buddhist, Mongol and Din *ST, Nf*

1796 *2×898 = 4×449*

The Palace of Two Hundred and Eighty Judgments *Sf*

1803 *3×601*

Stainless Abode Yea Unto the Stainless Abode *ST*

The Direful Judgments of RA HOOR KHUIT! *Tf*

1806 *2×903 = 3×602 = 6×301 =7×258 = 14×129 = 21×86 = 42×43*

Wings of MAUT the Vulture *W*

Π **1811**

The Whirlpool and Leviathan, and the Great Stone *ST*

1816 *2×908 = 4×454 = 8×227*

The Palace of Two Hundred and Eighty Judgments *Sf,L*

1820 *2×910 = 4×455 = 5×364 =7×260 = 10×182 = 13×140 = 14×130 =20×91 = 26×70 = 28×65 = 35×52*

Thy Glory O Beloved O Princely Lover

1828 *2×914 = 4×457*

From the Lord Adonai from the Lord Adonai

Π **1831**

For I Am HORUS, the Crowned and Conquering Child *kk, ŏ*

1834 *2×917 = 7×262 = 14×131*

My Father Goeth Forth to Judge the World

O Be Thou Proud and Mighty Among Men! *Nf*

1840 *2×920 = 4×460 = 5×368 =8×230 = 10×184 = 16×115 = 20×92 =23×80 = 40×46*

Strength of Its Glory *ST,Sf*

1841 *7×263*

The Seal of the Promise of our Agelong Love *ŏŏ*

1846 *2×923 = 13×142 = 26×71*

Word of the God Enthroned in Ra's Seat *W, Tf*

1855 *5×371 = 7×265 = 35×53*

Glory Unto the Rose that is NUIT *Tf*

1874 *2×937*

Thy Name is As the Breath of Love Across All Worlds *Sf, k*

1876 *2×938 = 4×469 = 7×268 =14×134 = 28×67*

The Tree of Life and Only in A Few Places Do They Coincide *k*

Voice of the Lord Upon the Waters *Sf, ŏ*

1890 *2×945 = 3×630 = 5×378 =6×315 = 7×270 = 9×210 = 10×189 =14×135 = 15×126 = 18×105 = 21×90 =27×70 = 30×63 = 35×54 = 42×45*

The Flesh of the Indian and the Buddhist, Mongol and Din *ST, Nf*

1909 *23×83*

That Men Speak Not of Thee As One But As None *ŏ*

The Stainless Abode Yea Unto the Stainless Abode *ST*

1912 *2×956 = 4×478 = 8×239*

The Wings of MAUT the Vulture

1914 *2×957 = 3×638 = 6×319 =11×174 = 22×87 = 29×66 = 33×58*

Four Holy Living Creatures for Guardians *Sf, k*

Glory to God and Thanksgiving to God

1946 *2×973 = 7×278 = 14×139*

Now Come in our Splendour & Rapture!

The Strength, Force, Vigour, of your Arms *ST,Sf*

1947 *3×649 = 11×177 = 33×59*

Grinding-Up of the Bones of Choronzon *Nf, k*

Π **1951**

For I Am HORUS, the Crowned and Conquering Child *kk*

Word that is God is None Other Than He *W*

1952 *2×976 = 4×488 = 8×244 =16×122 = 32×61*

The Word of the God Enthroned in Ra's Seat

Σ62 **1953** *3×651 = 7×279 = 9×217 =21×93 = 31×63*

Let Excellent Virgins Evoke Rejoicing, Son of Night! *Tf*

1968 *2×984 = 3×656 = 4×492 =6×328 = 8×246 = 12×164 = 16×123 =24×82 = 41×48*

There is No Law Beyond Do What Thou Wilt *Tf*

Uttermost Abyss Unto my Throne *ST*

1975 *5×395 = 25×79*

Seal of the Promise of our Agelong Love

1976 *2×988 = 4×494 = 8×247 =13×152 = 19×104 = 26×76 = 38×52*

Ill-Ordered House in the Victorious City *k*

Π **1987**

Footstool of the Holy One *ST*

Motion About A Point is Iniquity

2000 *2×1000 = 4×500 = 5×400 =8×250 = 10×200 = 16×125 = 20×100 =25×80 = 40×50*

Glory Unto the Swordsman of the Sun *Nf*

2012 *2×1006 = 4×503*

Path that Joineth the Wisdom With the Understanding *ST*

2014 *2×1007 = 19×106 = 38×53*

Blessing & Worship to the Prophet of the Lovely Star! *ST, ŏ*

From the Golden Water Shalt Thou Gather Corn *k*

Σ63 **2016** *2×1008 = 3×672 = 4×504 =6×336 = 7×288 = 8×252 = 9×224 =12×168 = 14×144 = 16×126 = 18×112 =21×96 = 24×84 = 28×72 = 32×63 =36×56 = 42×48*

Be Thou Hadit, my Secret Centre, my Heart & my Tongue! *k*

2020 *2×1010 = 4×505 = 5×404 =10×202 = 20×101*

The Four Holy Living Creatures for Guardians *Sf, k*

2021 *43×47*

By the Moon, and By Myself, and By the Angel of the Lord!

Of Love and of Power and of Worship *W*

2030 *2×1015 = 5×406 = 7×290 =10×203 = 14×145 = 29×70 = 35×58*

God Hath Laid Upon Him the Iniquity of Us All

2037 *3×679 = 7×291 = 21×97*

This is the Truth this is the Truth this is the Truth

2038 *2×1019*

2045 *5×409*

O Thou Falsifier of the Oracles of Truth! *k*

Whirlpool and Leviathan, and the Great Stone — *ST, W*

2048 *2×1024 = 4×512 = 8×256 =16×128 = 32×64 = 2^{11}*

Π **2053**

2057 *11×187 = 17×121*

The Word that is God is None Other Than He

2062 *2×1031*

Face of your God, the Beginning of Comfort — *Tf, k*

2064 *2×1032 = 3×688 = 4×516 =6×344 = 8×258 = 12×172 = 16×129 =24×86 = 43×48*

Two-And-Thirty Books of Wisdom

2065 *5×413 = 7×295 = 35×59*

Yet the Word is Falsehood and the Understanding Darkness — *ST,SSf*

2074 *2×1037 = 17×122 = 34×61*

The Uttermost Abyss Unto my Throne — *ST*

2082 *2×1041 = 3×694 = 6×347*

Do What Thou Wilt Shall Be the Whole of the Law

The Ill-Ordered House in the Victorious City — *k*

2093 *7×299 = 13×161 = 23×91*

The Footstool of the Holy One — *ST*

2095 *5×419*

Stabilities of Being and of Consciousness and of Bliss — *ST, SSf, k, ŏ*

2096 *2×1048 = 4×524 = 8×262 =16×131*

Blessing and Worship to the Prophet of the Lovely Star — *ST, ŏ*

Π **2099**

Name of the Beast, Four-Square, Mystic, Wonderful! — *ST, k*

2105 *5×421*

Look in the Beneath and Thou Shalt See A New World

2107 *7×301 = 43×49*

One Uttereth Clearly and the Other Understandeth — *ST, k*

2115 *3×705 = 5×423 = 9×235 =15×141 = 45×47*

Arouse the Coiled Splendour Within You — *k*

2118 *2×1059 = 3×706 = 6×353*

The Path that Joineth the Wisdom With the Understanding — *ST*

2121 *3×707 = 7×303 = 21×101*

For Thou Art Submitted to the Four

2140 *2×1070 = 4×535 = 5×428 =10×214 = 20×107*

Stabat Crux Juxta Lucem Stabat Lux Juxta Crucem — *ST*

2144 *2×1072 = 4×536 = 8×268 =16×134 = 32×67*

The Secrets of Truth that Are Like Unto A Star and A Snake — *ST, k*

2151 *3×717 = 9×239*

Light of the Star and of the Moon and of the Sun — *ST, Nf*

The Whirlpool and Leviathan, and the Great Stone — *ST*

2162 *2×1081 = 23×94 = 46×47*

Burn Upon Their Brows, O Splendrous Serpent! — *Tf*

2168 *2×1084 = 4×542 = 8×271*

The Face of your God, the Beginning of Comfort — *Tf, k*

2175 *3×725 = 5×435 = 15×145 =25×87 = 29×75*

The Magus is Love and Bindeth Together this and that in His Conjuration — *k, ŏ*

2181 *3×727*

King Against King! Love One Another With Burning Hearts; — *ST,Sf*

2192 *2×1096 = 4×548 = 8×274 =16×137*

Glory Unto the Cross that is the Heart of the Rose — *k, ŏ*

2194 *2×1097*

Stabat Crux Juxta Lucem Stabat Lux Juxta Crucem ST, kk

2200 *2×1100 = 4×550 = 5×440 =8×275 = 10×220 = 11×200 = 20×110 =22×100 = 25×88 = 40×55 = 44×50*

2201 *31×71*

The Stabilities of Being and of Consciousness and of Bliss ST, SSf, k, ŏ

2205 *3×735 = 5×441 = 7×315 =9×245 = 15×147 = 21×105 = 35×63 =45×49*

The Name of the Beast, Four-Square, Mystic, Wonderful! ST, k

Π **2213**

The One Uttereth Clearly and the Other Understandeth ST, k

2214 *2×1107 = 3×738 = 6×369 =9×246 = 18×123 = 27×82 = 41×54*

Thy Name is As the Breath of Love Across All Worlds Sf, k

2220 *2×1110 = 3×740 = 4×555 =5×444 = 6×370 = 10×222 = 12×185 =15×148 = 20×111 = 30×74 = 37×60*

Knowledge and Conversation of His Holy Guardian Angel k, ŏ

2222 *2×1111 = 11×202 =22×101*

Thus is the Art and Craft of the Magus But Glamour k

2240 *2×1120 = 4×560 = 5×448 =7×320 = 8×280 = 10×224 = 14×160 =16×140 = 20×112 = 28×80 = 32×70 =35×64 = 40×56*

O Nuit, Continuous One of Heaven, Nf, k

2257 *37×61*

The Light of the Star and of the Moon and of the Sun ST, Nf

Π **2267**

2288 *2×1144 = 4×572 = 8×286 =11×208 = 13×176 = 16×143 = 22×104 =26×88 = 44×52*

Illusion and Falsehood to Enslave the Soul

2305 *5×461*

O Self-Luminous Image of the Unimaginable Naught Tf

2306 *2×1153*

The Naked Brilliance of the Voluptuous Night-Sky

2326 *2×1163*

The Knowledge and Conversation of His Holy Guardian Angel k, ŏ

Π **2339**

One is Thy Beginning! One is Thy Spirit, and Thy Permutation

2354 *2×1177 = 11×214 =22×107*

A Ka Dua Tuf Ur Biu Bi A'a Chefu Dudu Ner Af An Nuteru

2360 *2×1180 = 4×590 = 5×472 =8×295 = 10×236 = 20×118 = 40×59*

Untouched Throughout the Centuries Sf

2373 *3×791 = 7×339 = 21×113*

The Path that Leadeth from the Crown Unto the Beauty k

2380 *2×1190 = 4×595 = 5×476 =7×340 = 10×238 = 14×170 = 17×140 =20×119 = 28×85 = 34×70 = 35×68*

Magus is Love and Bindeth Together this and that in His Conjuration k, ŏ

2422 *2×1211 = 7×346 = 14×173*

It is Written, Thou Shalt Not Tempt the Lord Thy God ŏ

2448 *2×1224 = 3×816 = 4×612 =6×408 = 8×306 = 9×272 = 12×204 =16×153 = 17×144 = 18×136 = 24×102 =34×72 = 36×68 = 48×51*

There is No Law Beyond Do What Thou Wilt *Tf*

2484 *2×1242 = 3×828 = 4×621 =6×414 = 9×276 = 12×207 = 18×138 =23×108 = 27×92 = 36×69 = 46×54*

Absolute Truth Absolute Light Absolute Bliss *SSf*

2566 *2×1283*

Twenty and Two Are the Mansions of the House of my Father

Π **2633**

O Thou Titan that Hast Climbed Into the Bed of Juno *ST, k*

2667 *1×2667 = 3×889 = 7×381 = 21×127*

Glory Unto the One that Is the Child and the Father of Their Love

2736 *2×1368 = 3×912 = 4×684 =6×456 = 8×342 = 9×304 = 12×228 =16×171 = 18×152 = 19×144 = 24×114 =36×76 = 38×72 = 48×57*

The Mystery of the Knowledge and Conversation of His Holy Guardian Angel *ST,k, ŏ*

2812 *1×2812 = 2×1406 = 4×703 = 19×148 =37×76 = 38×74*

O Holy Exalted One, O Self Beyond Self, O Self-Luminous Image *k*

3139 *43×73*

Shall Not Destruction Swallow Up Destruction, and Annihilation *ST,kk ŏ Nf,*

Π **3191**

The Abstruction from the Ill-Ordered House in the Victorious City *ST, kk*

The author acknowledges GFLO for his contributions, insight and his chapter entitled "The Cube of Space". The author would also like to acknowledge the OTO for the preservation of Class A Libri and take this opportunity to remind the body and the head of that austere Order of its one and sole charge and purpose: the establishment of the law of Thelema, as a manifest political state. This is to be accomplished materially in this Aeon, thereby establishing the universal rights and freedom of all women and men. The island will be a Choice for All. It is to be the model, a refuge, the Lamp.

Those wishing to contribute or participate in the Cause, may write the author via the publisher for more information at NewAeon@8thHousePublishing.com.

8TH HOUSE PUBLISHING

For more information on other fine titles and all 8th House Publishing publications, please contact us at info@8thHousePublishing.com

DISTRIBUTED IN THE USA & CANADA BY
INGRAMS
Orders: 800.937.8202
Baker & Taylor
Orders: btinfo@btol.com or 800.775.1800.

DISTRIBUTED IN THE UNITED KINGDOM BY
Blackwell Ltd.
50 Broad Street
Oxford OX1 3BQ , United Kingdom
Orders: +44 (0) 1865 333690
mail.ox@blackwell.co.uk

DISTRIBUTED IN CANADA BY
8th House Books
Orders: sales@8thHousePublishing.com

www.ingramcontent.com/pod-product-compliance
Lightning Source LLC
Chambersburg PA
CBHW030946150426
42814CB00031B/399/J

* 9 7 8 1 9 2 6 7 1 6 2 7 5 *